MW00999556

Gardening
IN THE
Humid South

Gardening
IN THE
Humid South

Edmund N. O'Rourke Jr.
Leon C. Standifer

LOUISIANA STATE UNIVERSITY PRESS
BATON ROUGE

02   03   04   05   06   07   08   09   10   11
1   2   3   4   5
Designer: Laura Roubique Gleason
Typeface: Minion, with Poetica Chancery display
Printer and binder: Thomson-Shore, Inc.

Library of Congress Cataloging-in-Publication Data

O'Rourke, E. N.
    Gardening in the humid south / Edmund N.
O'Rourke Jr. and Leon C. Standifer.
        p. cm.
    ISBN 0-8071-2681-0 (cloth : alk. paper)
        1. Gardening—Southern States. I. Standifer,
Leon C. II. Title.

SB453.2.S66 O75 2001
635'.0975—dc21

                                        2001041409

For

Claudette Price

who described the kind of book she wanted

and laughed with us as we tried to reach the goals she had set

Contents

Illustrations

Photographs

Preface

This is a regional gardening book. We don't know much about growing plants in California or in the Midwest, but we can do a country fair job with persuading plants to grow in the humid subtropics: east Texas, Louisiana, Mississippi, Alabama, and Florida.

We will describe gardening methods according to our view of the hobby. We do not expect your complete agreement; you will soon notice that we do not always agree with each other. Broadly, we look on gardening as a leisurely, contemplative activity. As cardiovascular therapy it should rank above watching television but below the value of a daily brisk walk around the block. If the garden works you to a point of exhaustion, you are probably going about it in the wrong way. We think the garden should belong to you; the reverse is not acceptable.

We need to elaborate on that. Regardless of what you grow—annuals or perennials, ornamentals or vegetables—we think you should be able to walk through the garden and admire your work almost every day. This is recreational and relaxing; it is contemplative in that you can enjoy the wonders of growing plants. It is also challenging in that you may see something abnormal and wonder what is happening. There may be the beginnings of insect damage or of a disease, or you may notice that some of the plants are wilting when the others are not. These signs should not be cause for alarm or for a massive rescue effort; they are simply part of your hobby. Little things will go wrong, and you will have time to plan on an approach for correction.

On the other hand, you may not be able to wander through the garden every day. There are many weekend gardeners who enjoy the challenge and look forward to the exercise of working in the yard for part of every Saturday. This book is for you, also. We can show you ways to improve your garden while cutting back on the total effort required. There is another group of gardeners whose yards and gardens are so large that they will be busy all day on every Saturday, regardless of how efficient they are. This book is for you. We probably know some shortcuts that are new to you. Our approach to gardening is that consistent managed care is more effective than massive efforts at damage control. You may notice that we do not advocate large-scale use of pesticides. We promote sanitation and timely treatments.

Many good gardeners live in apartments; their garden sites are the windowsills and a few pots in living rooms. Growing plants in pots follows the same principles that apply to the backyard garden, but more so. We have a chapter dedicated to those of you who are intensive indoor gardeners. We also mention some outdoor gardening tips that you will find interesting.

Armchair gardeners make up a large group: people who enjoy dreaming of a fine garden but lack the space, time, or capacity to actually have one. (At our age, we have a strong understanding of "the mind is willing but the body is worn out.") We have tried to devise the chapters as (nearly) complete units, maybe like a series of related short stories telling different tales but using the same characters. We hope you will join us in these gardening escapades.

We think of gardening as being based on the three *P*'s: patience, persistence, and perspiration. Take your time, be as consistent as possible, work a bit—and enjoy.

We have spent a lot of time, and had some big-time arguments, pondering the question of where to start in writing about gardening. There is a fundamental problem: gardening is both an art and a science. The art is best described as "how to do it," and the science is "how come you should do it that way." The art is more fun, and more important. For example, we know the art of driving a car but, in this era of computer chips and safety devices, we have no clue as to why the car runs—or why it does not run when it should.

We are devoting the first few chapters to gardening methods that we think work best in the high-rainfall, subtropical, midsouth climate. These are essential, but not revolutionary, methods for subtropical gardening: raised beds; slope for water run-off; lime; organic matter; composting; sanitation; and pest control. Then we move on to specifics: growing potted plants, shrubs, vines, and so forth.

Throughout these discussions you will notice that we bring up interesting points that we promise to explain later. The second half of the book is devoted to those "laters." We think you will be interested in knowing why clay soil is more productive and more difficult to manage than is a sandy soil. You may wonder why the plants growing in the wettest part of your garden will suffer the most from drought. We know you will wonder why our gardens suffer more from cold damage than do those farther north, and why cold protection methods are much different. We have a lot of bits and pieces we think you will like, but only after you have read our concept of the art of gardening.

Acknowledgments

We have been in the plant racket for a long time. We would give figures but do not know how to define our beginning points. Over the years we have watched bright young Ph.D. students come and go. We have downed gallons of coffee while listening to them discuss partitioning of nutrients, modeling of sequential processes, and the wonders of cladology. We have no idea what a clad is. All of this has left us with two strong impressions: (1) Many new Ph.D.s should be handled like good wine—put into a sealed barrel until they have matured; and (2) we have forgotten more about plants than many of them know.

Writing this manuscript has largely reinforced those impressions, with slight modifications: (1) Maybe they should only be sealed in labs until they mature, but somehow they should be isolated from the public and possibly from students; and (2) many of the new ones are already mature, and know quite a bit about plants, which makes a statement about how much we have forgotten.

We appreciate the information, suggestions, and jokes from our friends throughout the campus. They frequently disagreed with our ideas, and occasionally we conceded to their arguments. We are not listing their names as endorsements, but we do appreciate help from Olen Curtis and George Caldwell (soil chemistry); Bobby Joe Miller (soil genesis); Ed Dunigan (soil microbiology); James Fontenot; Tim Raiford; James Boudreaux and Regina Bracy (vegetable production); Ed Beckham (daylilies, camellias); Quentin Jenkins (rural sociology); Bob Muller (climatology); and Steve Schurtz (landscape architecture).

Some of the photographs in this book are our own but most came from friends in the Cooperative Extension Service. We are grateful for their help.

Introducing the Authors

We, Ed and Leon, are crotchety old horticulture professors who retired several years ago. More honestly, we are as old as dirt. Leon retired in 1990 and Ed followed him the next year. We retired, not from horticulture, but from the clutches of administrators who had been keeping us from doing fun things. We were allowed to keep our offices and have access to field plots for small-scale research. Because of this we have a nearly daily routine of meeting at the horticulture department for an exercise walk around campus, followed by a long coffee session with the current faculty members, and then we go to our field plots for a few hours of work. It is a pleasant routine. We sincerely appreciate the support of the present faculty. We must grudgingly add that the administrators are moderately supportive as well.

As you will see in the book, our crotchetiness is nondiscriminatory: We frequently disagree with each other—sometimes Leon does not even agree with himself. We have left these disagreements in the text, partly because they will allow you to see different approaches to a problem, but also because our personal training and experiences are different.

Leon is a brilliant Mississippi redneck; Ed's exact words are that "Leon is brilliant, for a redneck." Ed is from the "uptown" district of New Orleans; back in the olden days New Orleans was divided into uptown, downtown, crosstown, and over-the-river. Because New Orleans traditionally has had a strong nursery plant industry, Ed earned his boyhood spending money by working in commercial greenhouses. Leon made his by mowing lawns at 25 cents per lawn; he would often make as much as 50 cents a week. Ed protests that he made little more than that and Leon was richer because 50 cents went a lot further in Clinton than it would have in New Orleans.

Both of us got our first full-time jobs in the early 1940s when the army employed us to operate M-1 rifles in Europe. More precisely, Leon broke the rifles and Ed repaired them (the army called him an armorer artificer; Leon was called a poor excuse for a rifleman). As a result of this activity, we were able to attend college and graduate school under the GI Bill. Leon's undergraduate major was soils chemistry, but he soon learned that routine analysis of fertilizer and soil samples was not an exciting profession. He then went to graduate school at the University of Wisconsin, majoring in what would now be called genetic engineering. Back then, it was just plant tissue culture. Ed, with much better foresight, majored in horticulture as an undergraduate and in pomology at Cornell's graduate school ("pomology" means he worked with apples and made applejack in the laboratory).

Ed came to Louisiana State University in 1954 on a research project to develop varieties of pear, plum, apple, and fig trees that would produce well in Louisiana. Additionally, he taught courses in whatever was needed: fruit breeding, nursery management, greenhouse management, and so forth. Leon did not arrive at LSU until 1961 and was originally in the botany department, teaching whatever he knew something about: mineral nutrition, plant growth and development, principles of weed control, and so forth. For reasons that defy explanation, his research project was to develop weed control methods for cotton production. Very soon after arriving at this fine institution, Leon discovered that the horticulture department served stronger coffee and had more lively abstract discussions than any other place on campus. Furthermore, they usually had surplus fruits and veggies, which were doled out to the coffee-table regulars. Ed and Leon met at the coffee table—frequently.

In 1967 the university sent Leon to Malaysia on a two-year assignment to help develop teaching and field research methods at a small agriculture college. (Back then, Malaysia was not nearly the modern society that it now is.) Leon was supposed to teach a course in plant science and prepare research plots in some very poor soil. As you might expect, he was assigned to teach whatever was needed: rubber production, weed control methods, and beverage crop (coffee, tea, and cacao) production. Leon learned a lot more than he taught. Mohd Noor, one of his co-workers in field research, had been a county agent in the area where Chinese farmers produced vegetables for the Singapore market. Their approach to intensive land use was a revelation. Those people did more than farm 365 days a year; they squeezed the system to get 400 growing days per year. It was extremely labor intensive, but the system produced a whole heap of vegetables. After Mohd Noor had invested months of tutoring his new co-worker, Leon began to see ways in which he could improve the system. By putting a strong emphasis on sanitation, Leon and Mohd

Noor developed insect, disease, and weed control methods that reduced both the labor input and the heavy dependence on pesticides.

After two years of fun and games, Leon returned to the university and immediately requested a transfer to horticulture so that he could work on vegetable cropping systems and participate more effectively in the coffee-table discussions, though not necessarily in that order of importance. In the meantime, Ed had come to realize that the new publish-or-perish system did not look kindly on people involved with long-term fruit tree breeding programs. Ed volunteered to take over the department's floriculture program while letting the fruit breeding die a merciful death.

Maybe this will help you see why we have some minor arguments. Leon considers himself an authority on fertilizer, soil management, and weeds. Ed believes himself to be an authority on all things horticultural but is not particularly excited about discussing fertilizer, dirt, and weeds. The absolute truth is less colorful. Each of us has extensive experience in some aspects of gardening—and we know a little bit about a lot of things. We do not, and never did, know everything there is to know about gardening. You also will notice that much of our information is old; we quit following scientific literature when we retired. Not to worry: the art of gardening is even older than we are.

Being part of the university community, we have always relied on advice from friends when we encounter problems beyond our experience. In writing this book we have drawn from the ideas of others about genetics, insect control, soil management, vegetable varieties, turfgrass management, organic matter, climatology, and so forth. We appreciate their help and will take full blame for the yarns we have spun around the solid facts they gave us.

Gardening
IN THE
Humid South

Chapter 1

CHOOSING THE SITE, STARTING A GARDEN

It seems to us that popular gardening books begin by saying you should "choose a sunny spot with fertile, well-drained, loamy soil. If the organic matter level is less than 12 percent, add some compost."

Now, look in your backyard. There is no topsoil. The subsoil is almost white and has an organic matter content of about 0.5 percent, and it is packed so tightly that you can only dig it after a rain—but, being in the humid South, you can expect frequent rains. The gardening book may say that if your soil is not very good, you should add some leaf mold and some earthworms. Folks, get realistic; if you add leaf mold and earthworms to that soil, the worms will starve to death.

At the risk of sounding like another of those gardening books, we have a statement. You really can build your soil into a very good garden. It takes time, patience, and a bit of hard work. If "those" gardening books were written for people in Iowa, or somewhere else in the upper United States, we can make a stronger statement. Your garden will eventually be more productive than anything those gardeners ever dreamed of. In the humid Deep South our climate is such that you can produce crops (vegetables or ornamentals) for twelve months of the year. This means that you will be growing two, three, or maybe four crops per year instead of one or two. On a per-crop basis, Alaskan gardens are probably the most productive but, down here, your garden works harder and produces more.

We are now three paragraphs into the book and have already run into a problem. There are several ways to start a good garden; the fundamentals are standard but every gardener has his own opinion as how to use them. Listen while we wander through the possibilities.

Ed: Leon thinks "good garden" always means a vegetable garden. Leon, there is more to gardening than producing food. Ornamentals are plants that nourish the soul.

Leon: I like flowers: okra and squash flowers are beautiful. A bush of southern peas in full flower is awe inspiring. The best way to nourish the soul is with soul food: cornbread, peas, okra, and maybe some collards with low-cholesterol fatback.

Ed: Leon, pour yourself some more coffee and shut up. I want to talk about the diversity of gardening. Some extremely good gardeners grow African violets, cacti, or herbs on a windowsill; others have potted plants scattered throughout the house during the winter and move them to a small shaded yard for warm weather. In our humid climate a person can have a nice herb garden growing in a rock pile; full sun and just a little soil tucked in at places. You can't grow (real) herbs in a vegetable garden—at least you can't in the humid South. Then there are people who grow roses, daylilies, azaleas, and camellias.

Leon: We know that many of our readers enjoy gardening for purely ornamental recreation, and that some of them have only a windowsill for garden space. However, still, and notwithstanding, we want to use a vegetable garden as the illustration of how to construct a good garden. Rapidly growing vegetable plants are the most demanding, and unforgiving, concerning good fertility, irrigation, and drainage. The tomato is the plant of choice for detecting soil fertility problems. Because tomato plants are easy to grow and have small seeds, most of the fundamental work on plant nutrition was done with tomatoes. If we use a vegetable garden and work from the idea of having poor, wet, and worn-out soil in the backyard, we will be able to explain how to rebuild topsoil and raise the soil organic matter to a reasonable level—which here in the humid South is not 12 percent. The principles would apply to all kinds of gardening but some of them could not be illustrated if we were telling about pot-grown herbs on a windowsill.

Ed: Agreed, but let me emphasize that we are working on principles that will apply to almost any plant. Also, we will be talking about problems people often encounter when they hire a professional landscape contractor to build permanent beds in a matter of one or two days. Folks, it cannot be done; we will explain why. Occasionally we will refer to long-range landscaping plans; they should include provisions for changes in your interests. In the chapter on lawn grasses we will mention that the area that began as a softball/soccer field will change as the children grow up and move away.

So, let us begin. Leon will get the first chance to explain how he thinks a new garden should be started. Ed will be given equal time, and we will argue.

The advantage is that you, the reader, will be able to pick and choose among our ideas. The result should be something that best suits your situation; after all, this is your garden.

Please remember that we are using a worst-case project and that it is a vegetable garden only because Leon likes to eat what he grows. Maybe we should add that Leon likes the "take it slow, do it with ease" approach. Ed leans more toward "get with it, build the garden, and improve it while you enjoy the flowers." When (not if) you begin to tire of Leon's detailed account, not to worry. Ed will explain the shortcuts and point out the steps he thinks are not necessary.

Leon's Garden

My (by far the better) approach is to spread the garden preparation effort over about nine months: kill the weeds, weed seeds, and plant-parasitic nematodes (nearly microscopic threadlike worms) before you try to grow a crop. This discussion is directed at things you can do to have a productive, easily managed garden. This does not mean that you must do everything I suggest; remember that Ed will get the last word. Save this for a rainy night, pour yourself some coffee, and just read. But try not to decide what you will or will not try until you have read both versions.

Remember that I am working from a worst-case situation. This means that the soil is in terrible condition: poor internal drainage, low fertility, low organic matter, and serious weed problems. If you have a deep well-drained soil, and hardly any weed problems, the procedures will be identical but take much less time. If you are rebuilding an old garden site, the soil will be much better but nematode problems will probably be worse.

I am assuming that you have the ordinary garden tools: shovel, hoe, rake, and a garden hose. You may decide to rent a power tiller, but I think hobby gardening should provide modest exercise and teach patience.

Maybe I should begin with a summary of what this section is about. The process will be easier if you know where we are going.

(1) We start by selecting a site. There are several points you might consider, but the most important decision should be where you want to have your garden. Almost any site is feasible; some will require more compromises than others, but life is full of compromises.

(2) You will need to decide where the runoff water will go. No matter how good the soil, there will be some excess water after a heavy rain; standing water can cause serious problems.

(3) In the middle of the summer you will dig what is going to become the topsoil, not very deeply, just about four inches or so. Because there is no reason to rush this, you can work at it early every morning.

(4) Then you will cover the entire dug-up area with a sheet of clear plastic and let the sun's heat kill weeds, weed seeds, and nematodes. Why fight weeds when the sun will do it for you?

(5) After the weeds are killed, you will spread lime over the soil, work it in, and build raised beds. Fertilizer (organic, compost, or commercial) will be added as a narrow strip under the raised beds.

(6) Now you are through. Cover the garden with leaves and wait for the lime to do its work.

How to Do It, Leon's Way

Everyone loves to start gardening in the spring; you have been indoors for too long and want a little exercise. The garden centers are having sales and all of your neighbors are working in their yards. Well, maybe you should join them. Psychologically, early spring is the best time to start gardening—and who am I to argue with psychologists? Realistically, however, spring is too early, or possibly too late, to begin your garden. The best time is late July or early August, when you are sick of hot humid weather and do not want to even think about gardening. Try working at it a little every morning or late in the afternoon. There is no real hurry, and you will soon understand why summer is the best time to start.

Begin your garden by selecting a site (figure 1). The first priority should be sunlight. A good garden should have at least six hours of full sun, preferably in the middle of the day. Anything less will limit the selection of plants you can grow. If the shading is from deciduous trees, you may have to grow leafy vegetables or a summer cover crop and emphasize the winter garden. If you are growing ornamentals, the winter garden could have pansies, sweet peas, and maybe some of the ornamental leafy vegetables. Consider the problem of trees being too close to the garden. Tree roots extend well beyond the extent of the limbs (called the *drip line*); if a few roots find the loose, fertile, well-drained soil, they will proliferate until all of your efforts are going into the

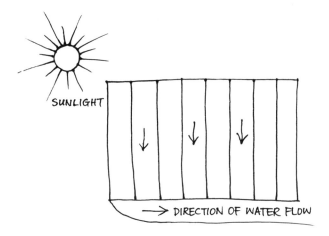

Figure 1. Selecting a site.

production of a larger tree. Maybe I should give that more emphasis: If you have large trees nearby, the beds will become so full of roots that an annual "derooting" process is necessary. The other option is rather harsh, but you might decide to cut the tree down. After all, this is your garden and your tree: which is more important to you?

If you still have choices after considering the above factors, look closely at surface drainage patterns. It rains down here; even with a well-drained soil there will be excess water, and you should now decide where it will go. Try to avoid locating the garden in an area where your neighbor's yard drains into yours and, with your added water, goes to the next neighbor. (You might decide to build a low levee at the upper end of the garden, but that is a bit of trouble.) The primary question at this time is, where can the water from your garden go?

You will need to put a very gentle slope in the water furrows. If you are new to the Deep South, *water furrow* may be a strange term. In Iowa the furrow is where you plant corn. Here it means the drain between raised beds where the plants will be growing. The water furrows are also the walking paths: the area where you can get to the plants without compacting productive soil. These furrows will be covered with leaves (to help you avoid getting muddy feet) and will empty into a shallow, grassed-in trench at the lower end of the garden and on out to somewhere. Ideally, the trench will extend out to the street; this is not a ditch, just a broad shallow area that you can easily mow over. One more point that you may have missed: you want only a very gentle slope in the garden because you will also use those water furrows for irrigation during dry weather.

Now take a spade and see what the soil is like, hoping it is not some strange fill-dirt that the contractor hauled in. For practical purposes, consider that the top four inches is topsoil (it probably is not, but will be in a few years) and the next eight inches is subsoil. We discuss topsoil in more detail later (see chapter 15); it is a vague term that means only what you want it to mean. For now, rub some moist soil between your fingers and estimate the texture. Clay is very sticky, silt is smooth—like talcum powder, and sand is, well, sandy. Loam is a good mixture of sand, silt, and clay, but it probably is impractical to add sand or clay to your topsoil. Look at the color of the subsoil; a rich red or brown subsoil shows that you will have good internal drainage. The most poorly drained subsoil is white, or sometimes blue, grading into yellow. (We also discuss subsoil drainage in chapter 15, explaining why white soil means poor drainage.) These steps are taken just to evaluate your problem; they give suggestions as to how long it will take to have a good garden, but will not affect the way you get there.

Decide on the size of your garden; for my example it will be 20 feet by 22 feet. This may seem large, but I chose it to make the calculations simple: 440 square feet is roughly 1/100th of an acre. Stake off the exact limits and take a soil sample. Actually, you will take one topsoil sample plus another of the subsoil, and each of these will represent a composite from several points (figure 2). Select about ten sampling sites scattered evenly over the area; the exact number is not important. Using a trowel, take a sample (not much, maybe a very small handful) to the four-inch depth. Remember that we defined topsoil as being four inches deep, regardless of what it looks like. Put that soil in a pan and take a sample of the subsoil (four to eight inches deep) at the same site. Put it in another pan and repeat this at the eight or ten sites, pooling all the topsoil samples in one pan and the subsoil in another. Then carefully mix the soil from all topsoil samples, and then from all subsoil samples, removing debris and breaking all clods. Take about a pint of soil from each composite sample to your county extension agent's office to be sent in for analysis. Ask for a complete analysis of the topsoil sample, but ask only for the lime requirement of the subsoil. This is a good first step because it may be a while before you get the results.

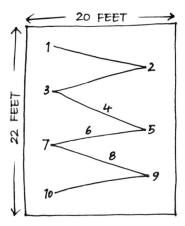

Figure 2. Taking soil samples.

On cool mornings spade the entire garden area to a depth of about four to six inches. Try to be consistent with the depth, not going too deep. This kills the established weeds by exposing them to the hot sun; digging more than four inches just makes the work go more slowly. Repeat the spading every week or so for a while. The time required will depend on the weather; weeds die more quickly in hot dry weather than during rainy spells.

Here is a little trick that will speed things along. If you cover the loose soil with a sheet of clear polyethylene, the soil surface temperature will rise to over 130°F every afternoon. (Remember that we are talking about a sunny day in July or August.) If the hot weather continues for about a week, the heat will kill all weeds in the upper two inches, most of the weed seeds, and all active nematodes. Now I need to add some "yes, but" cautions. Simply spreading the plastic over the soil will not work very well. To keep the heat confined you must dig a shallow trench around the area and bury the edges of the plastic (figure 3). Do not substitute black plastic, which will not heat the soil as well. Bermuda grass and nutsedge (nutgrass, coco grass) will be killed, but only those parts in the upper two inches. Portions of the weeds below that zone will be warmed enough to start growing faster. If you have hot clear days through-out the week, this will not matter much; shoots will grow up into the heat zone and be killed. The hazard is that a hard afternoon shower will cool the soil so much that it will not reach 130°F again for several days. During that time the nutsedge shoots can grow so rapidly that they will punch holes in the plastic

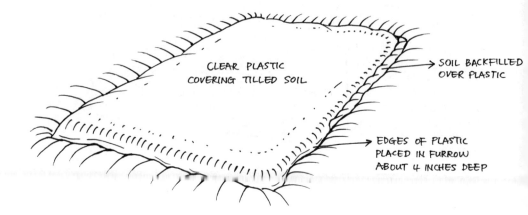

CLEAR PLASTIC
COVERING TILLED SOIL

SOIL BACKFILLED
OVER PLASTIC

EDGES OF PLASTIC
PLACED IN FURROW
ABOUT 4 INCHES DEEP

Figure 3. Covering a garden area with clear plastic to kill weeds.

and keep growing, and those holes let hot air escape. Another problem is that the moist heat will promote rapid decomposition of the (already low) soil organic matter. You would rather not have that happen, but it is better to kill the weeds and nematodes first and then rebuild the organic matter levels. Raising the amount of organic matter is not difficult, if you accept the fact that the organic matter is continually breaking down; nonbiodegradable organic matter is useless.

Now, back to work. Even if you use plastic, Bermuda grass and nutsedge are hard to kill; plan on some degree of failure. When everything else has died, you might decide to spot treat with a broad-spectrum, postemergence herbicide. Or you may want to simply dig up the shoots that have escaped the heat treatment. My argument is that you should try to kill all established weeds before planting a crop. If the plot is badly infested, Bermuda grass and nutsedge may keep coming up throughout the fall. Just keep digging up or killing the new plants; they cannot last forever.

Regardless of how well-drained your soil may be, raised beds are essential for surface drainage; it rains down here. The only real question is how wide the beds will be. The decision for bed width is largely a compromise between space and labor efficiency. The bed is going to end up as a trapezoid, flat along the top and sloping at something like a 45° angle on each side (figure 4). Assume that each sloping side will take about one foot of space. If the bed has a one-foot flat surface, it will have another two feet of slope for each side, making it three feet from water furrow to water furrow. If you increase the flat surface to two feet, the bed will now take four feet of space. That way you can have two rows of plants on one bed. The practical limit of this expansion is about three feet of flat surface—a five-foot bed. You can get three or more rows on such a bed, but reaching the center for harvesting or pulling weeds becomes more difficult. So, take your choice: land efficiency favors a wide bed, and labor efficiency is greater with narrow beds. For this example I use four-foot beds with two rows per bed.

By now (maybe) you will have gotten your soils report back and the county agent will probably have translated the recommendations to garden-size proportions. If so, the report will recommend the amount of lime needed per 100 square feet and the amount of fertilizer per 100 row feet. The lime requirement is based on liming the top 4 inches of your garden, expecting that some excess will wash down into the subsoil. For this illustration I assume you will need about 10 pounds per 100 square feet or around 40 pounds for your 440 square feet. In farming terms, this is two tons per acre.

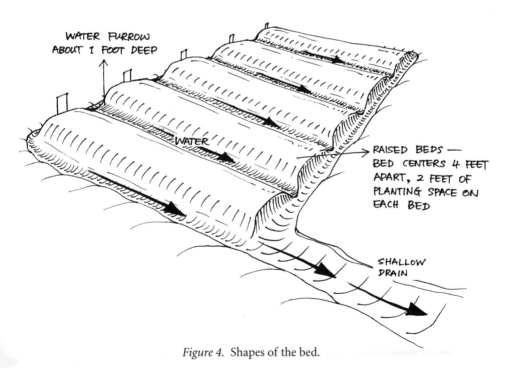

WATER FURROW
ABOUT 1 FOOT DEEP

WATER

RAISED BEDS —
BED CENTERS 4 FEET
APART, 2 FEET OF
PLANTING SPACE ON
EACH BED

SHALLOW
DRAIN

Figure 4. Shapes of the bed.

Now we come to the fertilizer recommendation, which is different. Lime requirement was given for a *broadcast* application, spread uniformly over the entire area. The fertilizer recommendation will probably be given in pounds per 100 row feet; this is based on the assumption that fertilizer will be applied as a band beneath and slightly to the side of where the seeds are planted. It is probably based on the rows being spaced 40 inches apart. Our rows are 4 feet apart but the difference is unimportant.

Besides telling how much fertilizer to apply, the county agent's recommendation will suggest a certain kind of fertilizer, such as 13-13-13, or possibly 3-8-16. These numbers refer to the percentage of nitrogen, the percentage of phosphorus, and the percentage of potassium, respectively (chapter 16 gives more detail).

Now, why should you apply the fertilizer as a band instead of simply mixing it into the soil, as you do with lime? Nitrogen and potassium would be just as effective if applied broadcast, as the lime was. Band application of fertilizer is done (almost) entirely to have the phosphorus used more efficiently. If the phosphorus were mixed into the soil, most of it would become nearly insoluble and of little value for plant use (see chapter 16). By applying it as a band you reduce the amount of phosphorus fertilizer needed. Phosphorus fertilizer is cheap and plentiful but it is a nonrenewable resource.

By now most of the weeds are dead and the soil has settled a little. It is time to lay out the rows. Figure 4 shows that the water furrows are four feet apart and the flat surface of each raised bed is two feet wide. The sloping sides of the bed and bottom of the water furrow take up the remaining two feet. Maybe I should add some terminology here: a *row* refers to the four-foot distance from one water furrow to the next. *Bed* means only the flat portion of the raised bed. Measure off four-foot units at the upper and lower ends of your garden. *Upper* and *lower* are arbitrary terms here because you will create the slope you need. The first four-foot unit should be only two feet from the edge of the garden because you are laying off points for the center of each raised bed. There will be a small water furrow between the first bed and the garden edge. Put a marker (a stake or stick of some kind) at the center points for the upper and lower ends of each raised bed. Later you will need two good stakes and some string; these temporary markers are used only as general guides. You might consider the orientation of the garden. There are good arguments for a north–south bed direction to take advantage of the sun, but convenience is important, too.

Now is a good time to lime the topsoil. Spreading lime uniformly over the garden is a bit tricky; you tend to put too much in some areas and run out before you get to the other side of the garden. I have fair success by applying it to each one-row strip. The example row is 22 feet long and 4 feet wide, or 88 square feet. The recommendation suggests 10 pounds per 100 square feet, so you will need about 9 pounds per row. Weigh out two units of around 4.5 pounds each. Using the stakes that mark rows, spread the first 4.5 pounds over the entire 4 x 22 foot strip. You may not come out right, but you will get a good idea of how to spread the rest of it to have a fairly uniform strip. Notice that we say "about" and "fairly uniform"; liming is not a very precise operation, but you should be as careful as possible, especially while you are getting the feel of it. Do not worry too much about errors; plus or minus 20 percent is good enough. Continue to lime each row over the entire garden. There is no real need to work it into the soil because the next step, building rows, will accomplish that.

My next suggestion is not a common practice; Ed will complain—but he is wrong. I want you to push the topsoil aside and apply lime in the subsoil. (Remember that you took a subsoil sample and asked for lime requirement only. The lime requirement of subsoil is often higher than that of topsoil but, for simplicity, I am assuming that it is the same.) Going back to the stakes for the first raised bed, take the spade and dig a strip four inches deep (down to the firm subsoil) and two feet wide (one foot on each side of the center point of the bed), throwing the soil off to one side. Now that you are down to the subsoil, spread the 4.5 pounds of lime uniformly over the strip. This is the same rate that you were using for the topsoil; it is only half as much total lime because you are liming only half of the area (two feet wide instead of four feet). Using the spade, work this into the soil to a depth of about six inches and smooth the soil surface. Apply the recommended amount of fertilizer as a uniform band about two inches wide and on top of the subsoil (figure 5). Now replace the topsoil over that strip and spread it smoothly with the rake. Do the next row if you feel like it, or wait until another cool morning; you have plenty of time.

By September or October it is time to build raised beds. October is often a

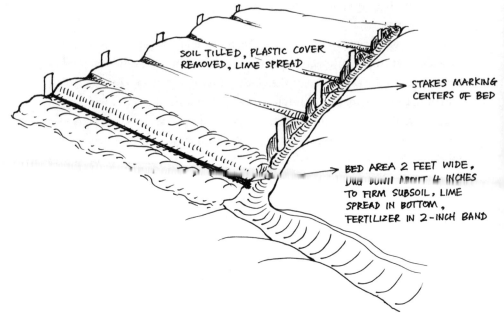

SOIL TILLED, PLASTIC COVER
REMOVED, LIME SPREAD

STAKES MARKING
CENTERS OF BED

BED AREA 2 FEET WIDE,
DUG DOWN ABOUT 4 INCHES
TO FIRM SUBSOIL, LIME
SPREAD IN BOTTOM,
FERTILIZER IN 2-INCH BAND

Figure 5. Liming the subsoil beneath beds.

fairly dry month; the process is easier with dry soil, and spading wet soil invites trouble. Check carefully for more Bermuda grass and nutsedge: if you find any, dig it up.

There are several ways to build beds. An easy way is to move each of the bed center stakes so that they mark the centers of where the water furrows will be. Using that as a guide, dig out a strip about a foot wide down to the depth of the firm subsoil. Throw that topsoil onto the two-foot strip where the bed will be. No need to be too prissy about the smooth water furrows or beds; you can straighten them out later. When you get through, smooth the top of the beds with your hoe and rake, then wait for a rain. The rain will probably show where the low spots of your water furrows are, but you need to be a little more precise than that. You need a 0.5 percent slope on the drains: this means a 6-inch drop in 100 feet, or just over an inch in the 20 feet of your row. You will have about a 50 percent idiot factor in building it: Half an inch will do, and 2 inches is almost too much. Take the two good stakes I mentioned earlier, the kind you can put pencil marks on, and drive one at the upper end of the furrow and the other at the lower end. Now make a pencil mark on the upper-end stake—about 8 or 10 inches from the surface of the water furrow. Tie a string exactly at the pencil mark on the upper-end stake and pull it to the other stake. While someone else holds the string tightly against the lower-end stake, use a bubble-type carpenter's level to make the string horizontal. Mark that point on the lower-end stake and put another mark 1 inch lower. Now tie your string to that lower mark. This gives you a guide for a gentle 0.5 percent slope from the upper to the lower end of the garden (see figure 6). Check the height of the string at several points along the furrow to find where you should add soil or cut the slope down a bit. Do this for every furrow, throwing the excess soil on the beds or taking from them as necessary. Then smooth the beds out with a rake and cover the entire garden with leaves, pretty deep. The beds will settle with winter rains, and some areas of the water furrows will settle a little. Smooth everything out, but try to keep a leaf cover over the soil. The leaf cover is your weed control, erosion control, and source of new organic matter.

You have invested nine months of occasional work and have not yet planted a seed. You now have a garden that will allow plants to grow well, will

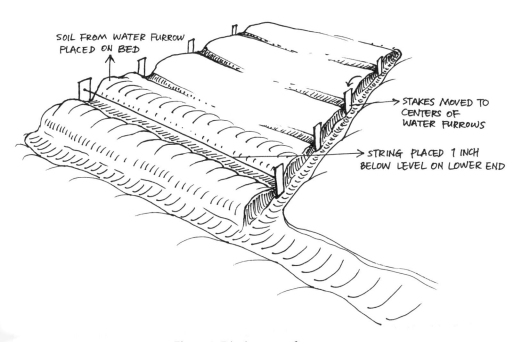

Figure 6. Digging water furrows.

improve each year, and will require little maintenance. The water furrows remain in place permanently, draining excess water away and providing a walkway between the rows. During dry weather you can block the lower end and fill the furrows with irrigation water. That trapezoidal shape of the beds provides more soil surface area. This is important because the plant roots will be most active close to the soil surface, especially on the sloping sides. The roots farther into the bed will be less active and, during rainy periods, may die because of low oxygen levels. As dry weather returns, the roots will start growing throughout the interior and some will develop down to where you loosened and limed the subsoil.

You have the potential for a very good garden. Just how good it is now depends on what the soil was like when you started. If it had good internal drainage, organic matter, and fertility you should be able to grow a good winter garden in the first year, although it might be best to wait until spring. If you started with white, acid, low-fertility soil, your garden will take a while to develop. Good soil structure requires organic matter, fertility, moisture, oxygen, tillage, and time. There is no substitute for time. Gardening teaches patience. Even if your original soil was very bad you can probably have a pretty good crop the next spring, but the soil will improve gradually over a three-year period, with each crop better than the previous one.

With a garden like this, maintenance is critical but not very difficult. Obviously, you should never let any weed produce seed. Annual plants should be cut off at the soil level and put in the compost. Periodically scoop up the soil that has washed into the water furrow and put it back on the bed; this is good soil with most of the fine clay particles and weed seed gone. You may want to keep a leaf mulch in the furrows: it prevents muddy feet. About twice a year you should dig in the raised bed down to where you put that fertilizer band and replace it. You may also want to add compost there (it will help to hold the phosphorus). Occasionally you should completely renovate the bed; dig down to (not into) the subsoil, loosen it up, check the pH, and rebuild the bed. "Occasionally" may mean twice a year if the soil is bad or every other year with better soil. Do not even consider just moving the bed over to where the water furrows were: they are the key part of your garden.

Maybe I should mention here that periodically you will get tired of year-round gardening. Just cover the unused beds with a leaf mulch, or plant a cover crop on them; if you let weeds grow you will be taking yourself back to square one.

Ed's Equal Time Discussion

Leon is a modern Don Quixote, the impossible dreamer. Nobody, not even Leon, would spend nine months preparing a garden. Here are the things wrong with his approach.

(1) He does pretty well in the part on selecting a site and deciding where the water will go. Then he has you hand spade the entire area! Borrow a tiller from your neighbor or go to a rent-all store. The tiller does a much better job than you can do with a spade, and it can be adjusted to work uniformly to a preset depth.

(2) Don Quixote wants you to kill weeds using only the heat of the sun. Lay out the plastic as he says, dig the trench, and apply a fumigant under the plastic: methyl bromide and Vapam® are good. The Environmental Protection Agency may put these on a restricted-use list, but other fumigants probably will be introduced. Such chemicals, under plastic and in the hot sun, will kill everything, weeds, seeds, and nematodes, in one day—three at the most. The fumigant will kill nutsedge tubers to a depth of about eight inches; this is not deep enough to get them all, but the few that are deeper might stay dormant for years.

(3) Soil tests are almost useless except for determining the lime requirement, they are expensive, and they take forever to get back. Ask your gardening neighbors how much lime they use and how often they lime; probably about five or six pounds per 100 square feet, every three or four years. Try that for the first year, then go to the garden center and buy whatever they sell to determine pH—a stick-it-in-the-ground meter or maybe some pH indicator paper. You want something that works in the range of about 5.0 to 7.0. A pH reading of 5.5 to about 7 is acceptable. If it is a little lower than 5.5, add more lime. Later (see chapter 16) we explain why knowing the soil pH tells only whether you need to lime, not how much to add. In general, sandy soil becomes acid more rapidly but requires much less lime for adjustment. Organic matter and clay require more lime and slow the acidification substantially.

Forget all of that foolishness about paying for a soil test and fertilizer recommendations. With our high rainfall you will need to add nitrogen for every crop. If this is a new garden, Leon's 13-13-13 fertilizer is probably good. The rate should be around three or four pounds per 100 row feet. But if you have limed the soil and grown crops for two or three years, that amount of fertilizer will raise the soil phosphorus level to an extremely high level. Over the years the LSU soil testing lab found that most of the soil samples from home gardens had phosphorus levels so high the instruments could not measure them. Leon is talking from both sides of his mouth. He tells you that you should apply phosphorus as a band to save a nonrenewable resource, but wants you to keep using 13-13-13 continuously. We explain the why and wherefore later (see chapter 16), but large amounts of phosphorus can accumulate and be slowly released by organic matter. After two or three years you can cut back on the phosphorus—the middle number of the analysis. Select a fertilizer that is high in nitrogen (first number) and low in phosphorus, and moderate in potassium (the last number). Should you have a soil test run to check on the phosphorus levels? Well, maybe, but later (in chapter 16) we give you some suggestions on eyeballing nutrient problems.

(4) With most of our soils in the humid South, it really is necessary to build raised beds. But Leon tries to make you think the process is difficult, like building high-quality furniture. Forget the tape measure; make your beds about three or four feet apart, and around a foot or so high. Now for the slope of the water furrows: eyeball a slight slope in the right direction and wait for a rain. After the rain, fill in the low spots and adjust the slope to something that works right.

(5) I can (almost) agree with Leon's idea of loosening the subsoil beneath each row, but liming it? Leon is still trying to hang this on saving phosphorus; even if the phosphorus level is low, the plant will get enough if you put the fertilizer in a single band where only a few roots can reach it. The roots that are down in the subsoil are useful for taking up water during a dry spell. Feeder roots in the raised beds can get all the nutrients a plant needs.

(6) Starting your garden in the middle of the summer: It is your garden, so start it when you please! Midsummer is the best time to kill weeds and nematodes under plastic. If you already have a garden, do not bother to work the beds up. Cut out the crop plants, spread the plastic, use a fumigant if you can, bury the edges in the soil, and wait.

(7) Year-round gardening, using leaves as a mulch: well, maybe. Leon is right that you should never leave the garden idle long enough for weeds to

produce seeds. Covering the soil with leaves provides weed control, prevents soil erosion, and adds organic matter. During the winter it protects the delicate little insects from winter kill—but you are not gardening for the welfare of insects. Sometime during the winter or the hottest time of summer you should leave the soil exposed; it would be better to loosen the beds so that more insects will die.

Leon's Rebuttal

As Martin Luther said: "Here I stand." I am still on the moral high ground. I am *right*. Do the job right the first time and patching things up will not be necessary. It takes only a little more effort to measure the row width exactly and get the slope right. Maybe I went overboard with the string and carpenter's level to determine the slope. You may not have a carpenter's level. You must surely have a hose. Fill it with water and get a friend to hold one end at the top of the garden (with his thumb over the end so that water does not drain out). Take the other end to the bottom of the garden and adjust the height until water just begins to run out. Now, each end of the hose is exactly level with the other, and you do not need the carpenter's level.

You really should loosen the subsoil under each bed, although liming it may be a bit much. And I may have overemphasized the soil test idea. Soil testing is extremely valuable for farmers but you will not see much economy in your 1/100th-acre garden. If you were to save fifteen cents in fertilizer costs, it would not amount to much for you. A farmer would see it as fifteen dollars per acre, or fifteen hundred dollars on 100 acres.

Soil pH is important for reasons other than phosphorus economy, and you really should monitor it. Any soil, sandy or clay, will become acid under our high rainfall conditions. If the pH drops down to about 5.0, you can expect serious nutritional problems. But the garden center will have a device for you to measure it.

Ed: I can't let that joke slip by. Folks, the garden center won't have a device for measuring it; what they sell will cost an arm and a leg, and won't work. Get some pH indicator paper.

Back to Leon's rebuttal: Old "get-it-done" Ed is right in saying that a fumigant under the clear plastic will make the sun's action much more effective. Fumigants are messy to handle and I question whether they will remain available for home use. We always will have the summer sun.

End of the arguments: We began by saying that the principles of raised beds are applicable for all rapidly growing plants; in fact, they apply for all plants. Roses, planted in a raised bed with loose subsoil, will grow faster and produce more flowers than if they are planted on a flat surface in your yard. The same is true for almost any perennial. Even slow-growing plants like azaleas and camellias will respond to the better drainage of raised beds.

The large garden that we have described is land and labor efficient, but you may want to have several smaller beds scattered over the yard. Large trapezoidal beds require maintenance several times a year; you are either scooping up the soil that has washed into the water furrows or adding more mulch for weed control. Permanent raised beds can be held in place by landscaping timbers, lumber that has been treated to retard decay, or old railroad ties. Initial control of Bermuda grass and nutsedge is critical regardless of the size of the bed. With permanent raised beds you should be concerned about turfgrass stolons growing under the timbers and into the beds. Another problem is that of tree roots. They can be a nuisance even in gardens where the beds are frequently reworked. We have no suggestions other than to dig into the beds and cut the roots out every year or two. Someone, sometime, will surely find a way to construct a tree-root barrier around beds.

Landscaping crews like to work the soil up with a power tiller, work some bedding material (made of bark, peat moss, a little soil, and some sand) into the soil, and then place landscaping timbers around it all. That is not a bad approach. It is fast, effective, and expensive. (If you have nutsedge, as you probably do, it will not come up through the mix for a year or two; by then the contractor will not be responsible. Maybe nutsedge infestations come under the heading "Acts of God.") You will probably have to lime the mix pretty often. The bark and peat moss will decompose slowly, and their high carbon/nitrogen ratio means that you should apply nitrogen frequently (see chapter 3). Another problem is that frequent rains cause the bark, peat moss, soil, and sand mix to separate: bark at the top and the sand/soil at the bottom.

Annual plants would grow better in a bed of real soil. We understand the argument in favor of hiring a contractor: If it might take three years to build a real-soil bed, three days for a new bed sounds much better. If you plan to grow annuals in a bedding-mix soil, it is a good idea to have a compost pile. You can dig a trench in the mix, fill it with good compost, and grow the seedlings in that.

Another compromise is that, if you plan ahead, you could spend one summer and fall killing the weeds, working up the soil, subsoiling, and liming. Then the landscape contractor could build a permanent bed on top of your good soil. Another advantage of these permanent beds is that you can avoid the use of a leaf mulch for weed control and soil protection. If you cover the mix with black landscape fabric, it will provide pretty good weed and moisture control: water will go through it but evaporating moisture does not move up through it very well. This does not make an attractive bed but the fabric can be covered with ornamental bark.

Chapter 2

TOOLS AND TRICKS OF THE TRADE

Every visit to the garden center takes you past a wide array of new tools and gadgets that seem to be just what you need to make gardening easier. By now you should realize that we are old-fashioned; we think you need only a few tools to have a good garden. The first part of this chapter is a summary of our thoughts and those of our gardening friends as to what you really need. In compiling this we discovered that there is no real uniformity about what the various tools should be called. It seems likely that the tool manufacturers have their own set of terms. Well, they did not write this chapter, and we use terms that local gardeners know.

Beginning with Basics

The first laboratory session of a general horticulture course includes a lecture on caring for tools. It is usually a simple demonstration on using the right tool for the job, washing it when you finish, oiling it, and sharpening dull edges. We discuss more than that here because these are your tools and they should have been expensive.

"Should have been expensive" is a good place to start. Always buy the best quality, and buy only tools that you really need. That is sound advice that we all tend to forget. "That's an interesting tool and it's on sale." You take it home and discover why it was on sale; it breaks easily, does not do the job, or you do not really need it. With expensive equipment, such as a power tiller, consider how often you will use it and the storage space it will occupy. You will probably decide to rent rather than buy. An even better idea is to borrow one from your neighbor.

With basic tools such as shovels, hoes, and rakes, you should look for quality. Soft metal will need frequent sharpening, and spot-welded tools often break. Before making a shopping trip decide what you really need, then look at several stores, comparing quality and price. "But a shovel is a shovel, why pay more?" There are many kinds of shovels, and some of the better ones may be too heavy or inconvenient for your use. Often the best advice is that if it feels right for you, buy it; but look for quality. We will give some other suggestions when discussing specific tools.

First, some thoughts on maintenance. Develop the habit of cleaning the tool before putting it away. You may be tired, running late, and have a hoe that is caked with mud. Take the time to clean it off, partly for appearance but largely because mud will rust the sharp edge and make hoeing more difficult the next time. Many good gardeners dry the tool after washing and wipe it with an oily rag. Some have a bucket of oily sand to dip it in a few times, which is a messy procedure but it protects the metal. At the very least, you should wash your tools before putting them away.

Keep all tools sharp, because a dull tool makes the work twice as hard. Each of your tools—hoe, shovel, or lawn mower blade—has a cutting edge bevel. The angle of this bevel differs with the tool, and when sharpening you should usually keep that original bevel. Making the angle smaller will result in a sharper tool but the edge is more likely to be nicked. A shovel will come with a wider angle than that of pruning shears, but the shears are for cutting wood and are not likely to be nicked on a stone or bit of metal.

For sharpening you can use an electric bench grinder, which sharpens tools rapidly but not very accurately and may heat the metal edge enough to reduce the temper. Usually a good file and a little patience is best for home tools. It is convenient but not critical to hold the tool in a vise while sharpening. There are many kinds of files; you will probably want a simple eight-inch, flat, single-cut file. The double-cut files tend to take too much metal off. Then there are four grades of coarseness: coarse, bastard (sorry folks, that is the standard term), second, and smooth. Generally, the grade called second is best for garden tools; the smooth file is too slow. The bastard grade is good for sharpening really dull tools. It is a good idea to have a wire brush for cleaning metal particles from the file and to keep the file lightly oiled; everything rusts down here.

Some gardening books have a short section on repairing tools. Our advice is not to break them. Use each tool properly, and if it breaks, buy a new one. Cracked handles on a spade or hoe mean that you were prying too hard and probably should have been using a heavier tool. But when you do break a handle the question is whether to repair or replace. Compare the price of a new

Figure 7. Shovel.

handle with that of a new shovel; you will probably decide to replace the shovel. Unless you are very good at woodworking, the new handle will not fit quite as well as the original.

We consider that the bare essentials for gardening are shovel, hoe, rake, trowel, one or more hand pruners, and loppers. Unless your yard is very small you will need a power mower.

SHOVELS AND SPADES

As nearly as we can tell, the difference between a shovel and a spade is that shovels have a cant and spades do not. If you put a shovel blade on the ground and the handle sticks up at an angle, it is a shovel; if the handle lies on the ground that shovel is a spade. Well, so what? For most gardeners, the terms are interchangeable, but gardening shovels are usually the pointed general purpose shovel (see figure 7). There are round-nose shovels and a square-nose scoop shovel. The latter is useful for scooping up loose material such as compost, but a general purpose shovel will do pretty well. Spades are essentially heavy-duty tools for use in heavy, compacted soil. You can do the same thing with a standard shovel if you just take smaller bites from the soil.

HOES

There are several types of hoes but you will probably need only one, two at the most. The hoe has three main purposes, which conflict slightly. After digging a bed you may want to break large clods before raking it off smoothly. If the soil

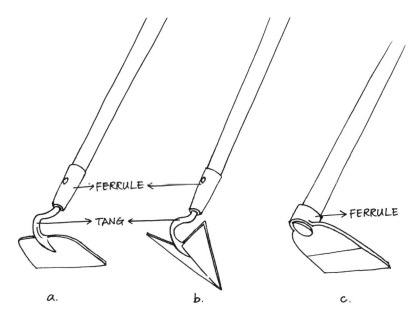

Figure 8. Types of hoes: (a) general garden hoe; (b) triangular hoe;
(c) eye hoe *(changol).*

has poor structure, you will want a rather heavy hoe for this. Breaking the soil
crust after a hard rain can be done with a heavy hoe, but a lighter one makes
the work easier. Weeding should require only a light hoe if you are consistent
enough to have only small seedlings.

For all of these purposes you need what is called a general garden hoe. It
has a slightly angled blade to make weeding easier. With the better hoes this
blade is part of a solid, forged socket into which the handle fits. Most hoes are
made with the tang and ferrule method. The tang is the goosenecked rod that
is welded to the blade and sticks into the metal ferrule where it fits onto the
handle (see figure 8). The tang is held in place with a rivet through the ferrule
and handle. This is a satisfactory hoe if it is given reasonable care. With abuse,
the tang can become loose due to a broken rivet or a cracked handle. In
cheaper hoes the blade is riveted or spot-welded onto the tang; these are satisfactory for very light use, but that junction will break easily.

Both the heavier and lighter types are known as general garden hoes. They
differ in the kind of metal, thickness of the blade, and size of the blade.
Thicker blades made of carbon manganese steel will remain sharp longer, but

you may not want to swing that much weight. All hoes seem to have the same angle, but the diameter and length of the handle vary. Try them for comfort at the store. There is a triangular hoe, which is not quite a triangle but has a tapered end that is useful for tillage in hard soil. The Warren hoe really is triangular and useful for opening furrows, but the corner of an ordinary hoe does about as well. So, take your choice but do not buy more hoes than you will use.

The Pick Mattock, the Eye Hoe, and the Pick

Sometimes the soil is so compacted that even a strong shovel (or spade, if you like that word) will hardly dent it. Frequently, the soil is so wet that a shovel will only pull up a batch of mud. You will not use a pick mattock often, but when you need it this is a great tool. Manufacturers do not seem to like the name pick mattock; that is a gardener's term. A pick mattock is a double-ended tool with a heavy-duty hoe on one side of the business end and some sort of pick or axe on the other. These are opposite ends of the tool, not of the handle (see figure 9). The pick can be used to start digging in hard soil, then you can turn it over and use the mattock end to continue digging.

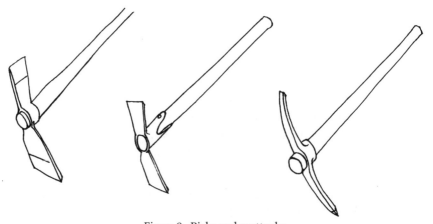

Figure 9. Picks and mattocks.

Leon also wants to make a pitch for what seems to be called an eye hoe, also known as a Scovil hoe. During his hitch in Malaysia he learned to love that tool. It was called a *changol* (pronounced "chunkle"), which does not sound like a Malay or Chinese word. The Malaysians think it was introduced from Europe. In the old painting of *Man with a Hoe* a peasant is leaning on a *changol.* This tool is called an eye hoe because the metal part has an eye, a hole, at the top. This hole slips over the narrow end of a tapered handle and slips down until it is tightly fixed (see figure 8c). It is the very best implement for digging a wide ditch in wet soil, which means it can be useful down South. The eye hoe is what a pick mattock would be if it had no pick at the other end. (Leon feels a lot safer when swinging a heavy tool that does not have a sharp end pointed at his backside.) The eye hoe can dig into hard or very wet soil, it can pry up stones, and, if you keep it sharp, can cut through roots. It is better than a heavy hoe for breaking up heavy clods and it is adequate for light weeding, but is so heavy that you get tired quickly. The eye hoe is not a common item in hardware stores, but if you find one, consider trying it.

Now for the pick. It is best for breaking up really hard soil and is good for prying stones or cutting roots. After using a pick, you can shift to a shovel and finally to a hoe for breaking the clods. A pick is useless in wet soil.

Rakes

There are several kinds of garden rakes. The most common and versatile is called a bowhead rake, attached to the handle by tangs coming from each end of the rake head. It is strong enough for breaking soft clods, leveling the seedbed, or light tillage. The flathead rake is attached like a hoe, with a single tang going to a ferrule on the handle. It is not as strong as the bowhead but is often lighter and easier to use. There is a heavier rake called a cultivator or potato fork; this may be more nearly a hoe than a rake. It has four or five long tines and is useful for breaking large clods (see figure 10).

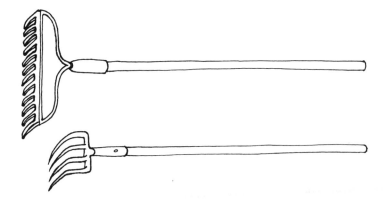

Figure 10. Bowhead rake and cultivator.

You should not try to use a garden rake for leaves on the lawn. It is hard work because the tines fill up with punctured leaves. The simple approach is to run over your lawn with a power mower, collecting the broken-up leaves in the grass catcher. But if you really want to rake leaves, both the steel-tine and polypropylene lawn rakes are very good. We lament the passing of bamboo yard brooms. Back in the days beyond recall proper southern homes were surrounded with large trees that kept the house cool and prevented grass from growing. Once a week you swept the twigs, leaves, and debris with a yard broom.

Now that we are into the discussion we remember that only affluent people had bamboo yard brooms; the common folk made their own from brush. The hard packed soil hardly ever got muddy but probably slowed tree growth substantially. It also made a wonderful place for little-boy games: pitching washers at holes in the ground, cutting small roads and building miniature towns for the toy cars, playing marbles, and let's not forget the old favorite: mumble-peg, or maybe it was called mumbly-peg.

TROWELS

We have not seen a good trowel in years. Apparently, manufacturers follow a planned obsolescence program for trowels. The cheap ones last two weeks and the expensive ones last two months. Seriously, our poll of gardeners brought in very few suggestions on how to select a good trowel. They all seem to bend at the tang or the folded metal that substitutes for it. This may mean that, in our wet compacted soils, we expect more of trowels than other gardeners do, but it does seem that trowels used to be stronger. Leon has a World War II entrenching tool that fits into the transition between trowel work and shovel work. The date 1943 is stamped into the metal. He has replaced the handle twice, but only because stores do not sell good entrenching tools.

As you wander through a hardware store you will see many other useful hand implements, but we must stop somewhere. Now for the expensive tools.

Power Equipment

LAWN MOWERS

Regardless of what we might prefer, every home has a lawn and the grass must be mowed. The simplest, most inexpensive mower of them all is the old push-type reel mower. It is excellent exercise for upper arms, general muscular strength, and endurance. It is pretty good for the cardiovascular system but, as heart exercise, it does not compare well with a brisk walk. This type of mower has five to eight spiral blades attached to reels at each end. These blades push the grass against a fixed blade called the bedknife. A rear-mounted roller adjusts the cutting height. This scissorlike system makes a fine smooth cut on each grass blade, and the cutting height can be precisely adjusted. Golf green mowers are reel type, which is why the greens look so good: each grass blade is cut smoothly and lacks the brown edge caused by the slash of a rotary mower blade. The disadvantages, whether with the push type or power version, are that the lawn must be very level and that it is important to mow regularly. Cutting tall grass with a reel mower is not impossible but it is difficult. Another problem with the reel mower is that of frequent adjustment. The bed knife must contact all parts of the spiral blades as they rotate. Adjustment is not difficult but is time-consuming.

Ed used a power-driven reel mower for fifteen years and switched to the rotary because his reel mower was so old that he had to make replacement parts for it. Leon has not used a reel mower since high school days: the push type. Power reel mowers are good but expensive and heavy.

The most common inexpensive power mower is the rotary type. It is the kind you already know about; a motor on top drives a rapidly spinning blade that shears the tall grass and throws it out a discharge chute. The better versions have a belt drive that decreases vibrations somewhat. The greatest disadvantage with a rotary mower is that it will pick up rocks or bits of metal and sling them away like bullets. At best, the rotary mower is dangerous; but do not operate it without a mulcher attachment or grass bag over the discharge chute. Otherwise, that chute is like the barrel of a rifle.

The blades of a rotary mower should be sharpened periodically, but even sharp blades will not make as clean a cut across the grass as a reel mower. To sharpen a blade, remove it from the mower and file the cutting side of each end to a sharp bevel. Then put a large nail through the bolt hole and suspend the blade to check the balance. An out-of-balance blade can shake the entire mower. If the blade is reasonably well balanced, it will remain horizontal when suspended by the nail; if one end dips downward you should file more metal from it.

Leon notes that sharpening of a mower blade has gone out of style in this throw-away society. A sharp new blade is pretty cheap. Check the price and decide what you want to do. You should either sharpen or replace the blade two or three times each mowing season. This is the advice of our turfgrass friends, who say that a dull blade is the most common cause of grass problems.

Riding Mowers

Unless you have a very large lawn, you probably cannot justify the investment in a riding mower. But we do not pretend that gardening is a commercial enterprise. If you want a riding mower, get one. There is an adage that the primary difference between adults and children is the price of their toys. A good riding mower will cut a wide swath, has adjustments to increase the speed of the blades while slowing the forward motion (a great help when you have postponed mowing for too long), and has room for a large grass or leaf catcher. If your lawn has many trees or small shrubs, check the mower for a sharp turning radius. Riding mowers come with either rotary or reel-type blades, but the rotary ones are more popular and much less expensive.

Trimmers and Edgers for the Lawn

You probably do not need any of these, but they are inexpensive labor-savers. The old-fashioned hand trimmers looked like sheep shears and were used to trim the grass growing out of the sidewalk or driveway, but they were so slow and tiring that people usually resorted to hoes. There are better scissor-type trimmers now, but they also are too slow unless you have a small lawn. The garden center will probably have a turf edger, which looks like a cut-off shovel. It does a good job, but cuts a little soil each time you use it. There is also a push-type rotary edger that will do a nice job of trimming along the walkway, but modern gardeners usually buy an electric or gasoline-powered type. Leon has an electric one and often wonders why he ever deserted the hoe. All models seem to be similar and equally dangerous; always wear safety goggles when using them. The nylon grass trimmer is pretty good for edging along the walkway and very useful along walls or the edges of flower beds. The greatest hazard is that you will decide to use it in weeding around small trees. This damages the cambium layer (growing cells just below the bark); with consistent damage the tree will certainly die.

Pruners and Loppers

If you have any shrubs or trees you will want one or two hand pruners and a lopper to cut larger branches. The best type of hand pruner is called a bypass type; these are much like scissors except that one blade is narrow and curved (see figure 11). The largest of these can cut three-quarter inch or larger branches. We should note that the most common damage to these pruners is having the blades sprung out of alignment by someone trying to cut a branch that is too large. Look at several sizes and styles before deciding what fits your needs and price range. The blades can and should be sharpened with a whetstone.

Anvil-type pruners consist of a single cutting blade that pushes down against a soft metal anvil. These are good for many purposes and are often cheaper than bypass pruners. The problem is that they tend to crush the branch on one side rather than producing a smooth cut. Also, the anvil makes it impossible to cut a twig off very close to the parent branch.

Loppers also come as bypass or anvil types. They will easily cut branches up to two inches in diameter and much larger if the lopper has a rachet for extra power.

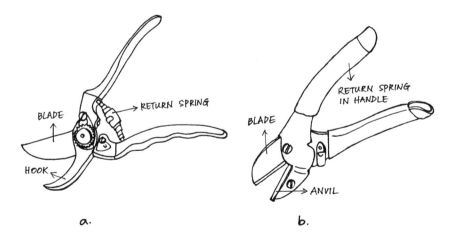

Figure 11. Pruners: (a) bypass-type pruner; (b) anvil-type pruner.

Saws

It is a good idea to have a pruning saw or two in your arsenal. These saws are specially made to cut green wood with a minimum of binding. The two we suggest are a crescent-shaped saw with a wooden handle and a bow saw with replaceable blades for larger cuts. The crescent saw cuts on the pull stroke (this is important because it is the opposite of a carpenter's saw, which cuts on the push stroke) and can handle quite sizable limbs (up to five or six inches in diameter). Bow saws come in different sizes; one with about an eighteen-inch blade should handle most needs. In cases of storm damage or other circumstances requiring larger cuts, you should probably call for outside help, but those of us who are determined (stubborn) gardeners may want to rent or borrow a chain saw. These can be quite dangerous and are recommended only with strong reservations and emphasis on safety precautions. The small chain saws seem to be even more dangerous than larger ones, or perhaps the operators are more careless.

Sprayers and Spraying

CALIBRATION

The following discussion is complex and not absolutely essential for home gardeners but we (Leon) would like for you to understand the principle.

We will explain calibration using the metric system because it is much easier. The commercial use of pesticides is based on application rates: pounds of pesticide per acre. We will use kilograms per hectare, which means about the same thing. One pound per acre equals 1.12 kilos per hectare. A hectare is 10,000 square meters, and a kilogram is 1,000 grams. If you build rows 1 meter (about 3 feet) apart, then a single row 10,000 meters long will cover 1 hectare. So a row in your garden that is 10 meters long will be 1/1000 of a hectare. If you want to apply the chemical at a rate of 1 kilogram per hectare, you would apply 1/1000 of a kilo, or 1 gram, on the 10 meters of row.

To apply 1 gram uniformly over 10 meters you must dilute it with water. The amount of water is unimportant as long as it can be put out uniformly. Assuming you have a nozzle that will spray a uniform swath 1 meter wide (you probably do not but it makes the illustration easier), assume also that you want to apply the kilogram of chemical in 1,000 liters. This would be one-tenth of a liter (100 cubic centimeters) for the 10 meters of row. Here is something you can measure. Back in the old days, gardeners used baby bottles for measuring in cubic centimeters or ounces. This is not a good idea. The garden center probably has a plastic measuring container. You can fill your sprayer with water and, holding the water pressure constant, measure the time required to deliver 100 cubic centimeters. This is the speed at which you should walk the 10 meters: go 10 meters in x seconds.

Now we can make our point. *Tablespoons per gallon of water* is a sloppy term because it refers only to concentration. Commercial vegetable growers and greenhouse growers must apply all pesticides by rate: the amount applied per acre or per 100 square feet. This would be fairly easy in our illustration because we were applying the pesticide only to the soil surface. Most insecticides and fungicides are applied to cover the leaves. The surface area is much greater for an acre of large plants than for an acre of small seedlings. We checked the Environmental Protection Agency (EPA) regulation on this. Essentially, it says the dilution rate is your problem. EPA simply says that for safe pesticide usage you must not apply more than x pounds per acre. They do not care how much water you use.

You want to be a responsible, ecologically minded gardener, but the insecticide label says to put two tablespoons of the chemical in a gallon of water and spray the plants. Huh? We do not like that sort of compromise but it exists. Our best suggestion is this: wetting the plants means to use a fine mist and spray until the leaves are glistening but no solution is running off. The plant probably will not be hurt by excess solution running off onto the ground, but you are using too much insecticide. Broadly speaking (very broadly), covering plants just to the point of runoff is equal to about 40 gallons per acre.

Basically, this explanation is meant to show that gardeners should not bother with applying a herbicide on a small garden, and that the rates of insecticide application are much more of a guess than we would like them to be.

TYPES OF SPRAYERS

There are four kinds of sprayers available for home use.

Trigger-Type Sprayers

This sprayer is the kind of plastic bottle that liquid soap comes in. Your garden center sells one that is a little better, but a soap bottle will do. It has two nozzles: squirt and spray. The spray produces the kind of mist that you need for good coverage of the leaves. These sprayers have short lives and your hand gets awfully tired of pulling the trigger. But they are pretty good for houseplants.

Hose-End Sprayers

The theory of this is sound. This is a pesticide container with a siphon tube that attaches to the end of a hose. The more expensive ones have a dial to vary the water to chemical ratio (concentration). But hose-end sprayers cannot be calibrated beyond a simple guesstimate. We do not like sloppy pesticide use.

Compression Sprayers

This is what you probably will buy. It is relatively inexpensive and easy to find but is not the best sprayer. A compression sprayer is simply a tank with an air pump built into the top of it. You unscrew the pump, pour the pesticide mixture in, and use the pump to push air into the tank. This forces the solution through a rubber hose at the bottom, past a shutoff valve, and through a nozzle. Most compression sprayers are now made of a good plastic that does not break or corrode easily. Some have pressure gauges. Check to make sure the gauge is replaceable, because pressure gauges do not remain accurate. Another good feature to note is whether the nozzle is replaceable. You might want to use several types of nozzle tips. Finally, look at the size. A one-gallon sprayer actually has a half-gallon capacity because you need a lot of air space to keep reasonably uniform pressure. The largest, four gallons, is good for two or three gallons, but it gets pretty heavy.

Back-Pack Sprayers

These are the best for a serious gardener, but the price is steep. The tank has two shoulder straps and is carried like a book-pack. Make sure it is comfortable for you. This sprayer has an internal pump that forces the solution into a *surge chamber.* This is simply a closed tube with an air cushion at the top to allow for uniform pressure. A handle extends out for the left hand to pump while the spray wand is held in the right hand. The shutoff valve usually has a spot where a pressure gauge may be placed. The solution then goes through the wand, to the nozzle body, and into the nozzle tip, which produces the spray pattern (see figure 12). The volume of water going through the nozzle is governed by both the pressure and the nozzle type. With a little practice, while

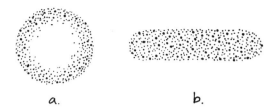

Figure 12. Spray patterns from a cone nozzle (a) and a flat fan nozzle (b).

watching the pressure gauge, you can develop a pumping rhythm to hold a constant pressure.

Nozzles

We should begin this with terminology. Your sprayer may not have these parts, but we think it should. The nozzle body should screw onto the wand, preferably with a quarter-inch pipe thread. A small filter should fit inside this body. Filters usually come in two sizes: 50 mesh and 100 mesh. The finer (100 mesh) filter is used for spraying a fine mist. Most sprayers have a fairly coarse screen where the solution is poured in, but that is not good enough to protect the nozzle. Regardless of how careful you are, something will get into the tank. The filter will keep it away from the nozzle tip. There is nothing quite as irritating as to have the nozzle stop up. You must carefully remove the pressure, drain the hose, unscrew the tip, take it apart, and hope you can remove the obstruction. Try to get a sprayer with a nozzle body that has a good filter. If it does not, and uses a pipe thread, you can replace it with a good commercial nozzle body.

Cone Tips

A cone tip, which is the kind of nozzle tip most garden centers will have, is excellent for application of insecticides and fungicides on garden plants and shrubs. It is not as good for spraying turfgrass and is useless for reliable herbicide application. As the name implies, this tip delivers a cone-shaped spray pattern. Particle size can be adjusted by screwing the outer cap down closer to the pointed disperser. Until recently, the only reliable nozzle tips were made of brass, but they are now available in a good grade of plastic. Be sure to buy one that will adjust the spray particle size. If you want to go first class, you can buy individual nozzles for various particles, from a fine fog to nearly raindrop size.

Flat Fan Tips

This is primarily a nozzle for applying herbicides, but it is also rather good for spraying insecticides on turf. Look back at what we said about the cone nozzle. It produces a cone pattern: at any given distance from the tip it is a circle. Although the distribution pattern within the circle is uniform, consider what it is like as you move the nozzle along a row. You have a circle of spray moving in a straight line; the actual distribution is a bell-shaped curve with much more solution at the middle than on the edges. That produces an error, but in spraying a mist on plants the error is overshadowed by the leaf arrangements. If you are applying the pesticide to a flat surface—herbicide on bare soil or insecticide on turf—this is a more important error. The flat fan nozzle produces a triangular sheet of spray, hitting the ground as essentially a straight line. As it moves along the row it will produce either an absolutely uniform application or one that narrows out at each edge. The latter type is used with a boom sprayer on a tractor. On a boom, the nozzles can be adjusted for a slight overlap, still giving a fairly uniform application.

Most homeowners will have no need for a flat fan nozzle. However, some of you may want to apply herbicides or turf insecticides, which cannot be applied accurately with a cone nozzle.

Flooding Nozzle Tips

The problem with using a flat fan nozzle for applying chemicals to the lawn is that the best accurate band width is about twelve inches, and twenty is the absolute maximum. If you spray a twenty-inch band across the lawn, it is very hard to make the second round without missing a strip or overlapping the first one. The design of a flooding nozzle is different from that of a flat fan, but essentially it delivers a fairly uniform pattern in a fan shape that is parallel to the ground. Because of this the nozzle can apply a swath of as much as five feet. It will still be difficult to avoid overlapping, but this is much better than a twenty-inch swath.

Pesticide Safety

This is a serious topic that we must begin with a policy statement. We believe in stopping at stop signs and slowing down when the traffic light turns yellow.

We are not tolerant of people who do not, and we are not going to change. We believe that laws should be obeyed until they can be changed. The alternative is anarchy.

We think many EPA regulations are bad. A few are too strict, but most of the bad ones evade the problem. However, before the EPA was established, pesticide use was chaotic. Pesticide regulations, both good and bad, are intended for the protection of us all.

The enforcement of EPA regulations on home pesticide use is all but impossible. Most articles on pesticide use say: read the label and handle pesticides with caution. This is sound advice that you should follow, but it bypasses some problems.

PROTECTIVE CLOTHING

As a general practice you should always wear rubber boots when applying pesticides. Even relatively safe pesticides will soak into canvas or leather shoes and, over a period of time, there can be a high concentration in contact with your sweaty socks. The label for the particular pesticide will advise whether you should wear rubber gloves, a long-sleeved shirt, goggles, or a respirator. Wearing a respirator is a real hassle on a hot day but is less trouble early in the morning. Early morning also is best to avoid wind disturbance of the spray pattern.

Incidentally, studies have shown that cotton fibers retain pesticides much longer than do the polyesters. You may want to use that horrible long-sleeved Christmas present as a pesticide shirt.

Cleaning Up after Spraying

This can present serious problems. Assume you want to spray two camellia bushes with an insecticide. How much solution will you need? With experience, you can make a pretty good guess, but a good idea is to spray with water first. Measure what you put into the tank and what was left over; the difference is the amount of insecticide solution you need. But you still cannot hit it right on the button. To avoid running out before finishing with the second bush, it is better to mix a slight excess. EPA regulations say that the excess should be sprayed in the same area. If you have other shrubs that might need an insecticidal treatment, put it on them. The other option is to spray the excess on the lawn. That is termed a biological filter. We are not particularly happy with the idea; it seems that the mulched soil in your raised bed is a better filter, but either is acceptable. After spraying that out, the spray tank is still dirty. Rinse it twice, spraying the rinse water on the grass each time. Then hang the sprayer up so that the tank will drain. Do not even consider saving the leftover solution to spray again in a few days. It could ruin the sprayer, settle out, decompose, or all three.

When you use the last of the pesticide, wash the container three times and add that to the rinse water, then break the bottle or punch a hole in it so you will not forget and use it for something else.

What should you do with leftover pesticide? The best advice is to buy no more than you will need for a few applications, or plan to share with a neighbor. Most pesticides can be stored safely through one season but many cannot be kept over the winter. So, if you bought the large economy size bottle and used only half of it during the whole year, you bought too much. Do not pour the mess down the drain. Our sewerage disposal system is not designed to clean up pesticides. But will only one bottle matter? Absolutely! It is against regulations—that is all the reason you need. It is becoming increasingly important for communities or garden centers to have pesticide disposal days. Brace yourself for a shock. It may cost you more to return the unused portion than you paid for the new bottle. The garden center must pay a waste disposal company to destroy it for them. One more point: never lose the pesticide label. Unless the disposal company knows what it is, they will not know how to dispose of it.

Now for a few standard points. Keep pesticides locked and away from children. Never pour a little in another container for your neighbor to use. There are several horror stories about people who poured some in a soda bottle and the tragedies that were caused.

So, with regard to pesticide safety we paraphrase the National Rifle Association slogan. Pesticides do not damage the environment, gardeners do.

Irrigation

SPRINKLING CANS

There are many kinds of sprinkling cans and most of them are not very good. You cannot find the old-fashioned watering can—the kind that you could use to water one plant well and uniformly—in gardening centers. The garden center would sell too few to justify stocking them. They are available from nursery supply houses but are fairly expensive.

A good sprinkling can for outside work should hold about two gallons of water and have a large sprinkler head (called a rose) with many (a hundred or more) holes in it. This may be hard to find, so a fan sprayer head (called a hose divider) for your garden hose does pretty well. Try to find a fan sprayer with a lot of holes. There is also a misting head that fits on hoses; it can be adjusted from a coarse spray to a fine mist.

For potted plants in the house, small plastic waterers are pretty good. The copper ones look better and cost more. The trigger type plastic bottles that liquid soap comes in also work.

Hoses

Before shopping for a hose you should indulge in some honest self-analysis. With tools you learn that if you do not take care of them the work becomes much more difficult. But water is water; if it runs through the hose and gets to the plant, that is fine. Some people take very good care of their hoses; Ed rolls his up and hangs it in the tool room. Leon leaves the hose out because he might need it again tomorrow. In rainy weather he coils it in a corner of the yard. Ed buys a good hose; Leon buys what is on sale and replaces it frequently. He has plenty of broken hose pieces to use as small tree supports. The summer sun will cause any hose, rubber or vinyl, to deteriorate. Running over a cheap hose with your lawn mower is not nearly so bad as running over an expensive one.

Hoses come in four sizes: three-eighths inch, one-half inch, five-eighths inch, and one inch. These sizes make more difference in the amount of water they deliver than it would appear; this has to do with the friction of water against the walls of the smaller sizes. The three-eighths inch is awfully small for most purposes, and the one inch is very cumbersome. Most people choose the five-eighths inch for yard and garden uses. *Ply* refers to the number of layers in the hose. The cheaper hoses are usually two-ply vinyl, with an inner vinyl core and a thinner vinyl skin. This is a bit too cheap even for Leon because it will kink easily and is hard to straighten out, especially during cold weather. The three-ply kind is only a little more expensive; it has a vinyl core covered with a nylon mesh, and a vinyl outer skin. The really good hoses have a rubber core, covered by two layers of some synthetic mesh, and a tough skin of rubber. The really good ones are also really heavy. You pays your money and takes your choice.

Hose-Ons

A hose-on is a handy gadget that allows you to add fertilizer while watering plants or lawns. It is a small brass fitting that attaches to the hose at the faucet. There is a small rubber tube that goes into a bucket of water containing soluble fertilizer. As water goes through the hose it sucks up a uniform amount of the fertilizer solution. In theory, this is very accurate—but actually is not—because a hose does not apply water uniformly. On the other hand, it is a lot easier to use than applying fertilizer by hand.

Nozzles and Sprinklers

You will need an adjustable hose nozzle for hand watering when you are bored, frustrated, or mad and there are no weeds to hoe. We still like the old-fashioned brass kind, but the pistol-grip versions are just as good and easier to hold. For efficient long-term watering you should have some sort of sprinkler. They come in many types, but none of them produces the uniform patterns you would like. The fixed sprinkler is simple; it has a pattern of holes to water in a circle, rectangle, square, or fan shape. Some have several patterns that you change by turning a knob. Oscillating sprinklers rotate to produce a long rectangular pattern; it is not quite uniform because the center gets more water than do the ends. The revolving sprinkler has two revolving heads that produce a rather uniform pattern, but in circles. It was the long-time favorite for nurserymen because it is simple and reliable. The impulse sprinkler is a scaled-down version of the one commercial vegetable producers use. This sprinkler also produces a rather uniform circular pattern but can be adjusted to cover a half or quarter circle. This is convenient for watering near the house or sidewalk. The large commercial versions are extremely dependable but the yard and garden versions often become a repair nuisance. We suspect that the water pressure is not strong enough for those moving parts.

There was a time when only very rich people could have their lawns watered automatically with pop-up sprinklers. However, that type of equipment is getting cheaper, and you can install your own with a little patience. You need a good in-line filter so nothing goes through to stop up the sprinklers. It is also very helpful to have a timer so that the lawn is watered at night or in the early morning. Because the air is more humid at night you waste less water and your friend does not get wet walking by your house. On the other hand, during a long-term drought nearly everyone waters when they get home from work. The water pressure will be much better if you can set the timer for early morning.

Before digging in the yard to put in a sprinkler system be sure you know where the electrical, telephone, and television cables are buried. The exact pattern and spacing of the nozzles will vary. Dig a trench about ten inches deep to bury the primary hose, which is simply a half-inch diameter polyethylene pipe, much cheaper than a garden hose. After that, follow the manufacturer's instructions for your type of system.

There is another very good permanent watering system for beds. This has essentially the same requirements except that you will need a water pressure regulator, and the in-line filter is even more important. This is because the system uses very fine (small aperture) nozzles. The polyethylene tube is buried, as with a lawn system, a little deeper than you plan to work the soil. At uniform distances you punch a hole (there is a special tube) in the main tube and insert a smaller tube that extends upward. Because this tube is so small, a support is required to hold it up. The nozzle is screwed into the upper end of this tube. Nozzles are available to produce sprays with different patterns. A full circle (360°) is used in the center of a bed; with the main hose running along the edge of the bed you can select a 180° nozzle. More narrow patterns would allow for overlapping sprays. The height of the small supported hose is determined to some extent by the type of nozzle and plants to be watered; do you want to spray under or over the leaves? Obviously, the area to be covered depends partly on water pressure, which is adjustable. Detailed instructions come with the equipment, of course. We are simply showing that installation is a bit of trouble, but it takes much of the bother out of watering.

Drainage

Over the past ten years agricultural engineers have been studying the use of a ten-inch-diameter polyethylene pipe for subsurface drainage. This is a flexible pipe with folds like an accordion. Within those folds are small slits to allow water passage, and the entire pipe is covered with a thin fiberglass sleeve that filters out sand and larger silt particles. The engineering research was conducted in farmland where internal drainage was poor but probably not as bad as the nearly white subsoil in your yard. They buried the pipes about three feet deep to avoid damage from tractor implements and spaced them either fifty or one hundred yards apart. All of this was designed with a uniform gentle slope, draining the pipes into pits at the lower end of the field. The pits had several purposes, as you will see later, but were primarily a device for measuring the water that drained out. The drainage, even with pipes one hundred yards apart, resulted in substantial crop yield increases.

We have no direct experience with home use of this pipe but have seen it at a garden center, and the price seems reasonable. We discussed our ideas with an agricultural engineer and a landscaper who has used the pipes in flower beds. But we should emphasize that the following are simply ideas. You can probably develop better modifications.

As an example we use the same twenty-foot garden with four-foot beds that we discussed in chapter 1. We also assume that your soil has poor internal drainage and the lot is nearly level, with a slight slope toward the street. In the South you must always plant on raised beds, and the soil in the water furrows between them will be tightly packed. This seems to mean that you must put a drainage pipe under each bed, but you might think of a better approach. Dig a trench in the bed deep enough so that you will not damage the pipe with standard tillage, probably so that the top of the pipe is at least a foot below the settled bed. The engineers mentioned in the previous paragraph dug an absolutely uniformly sloping ditch using a laser beam, and they lined the ditch with sand. But you can just dig the ditch so that it looks pretty good and slopes gently toward the lower end. You may want to use a tight string to assure a uniform slope. The garden center will have large T connectors for attaching each pipe to a central collecting pipe at the lower end. They also have caps for the upper end. After you have laid pipes under all the rows, or all you want to bother with, run the collection pipe to a pit at the lower end of the garden. It would be more convenient to have it draining into a ditch but that would be difficult to maintain. The pit should be large enough to hold a plastic garbage can with a hole cut about halfway up to admit the collection pipe. You could cover the can with its lid but would still need a wooden platform over it so that nobody stumbles into the pit at night.

Now for the operation. During a heavy rain most of the water will surface drain off the beds, into the water furrows, and out into the grass. The excessive water in the beds will slowly flow into your drainage pipes and down to the garbage can, where you will have to pump it out. A small suction pump (a more efficient version of the hose-on that we described) that attaches to a hose will do the job. The water will drain into the can slowly, but the plants can stand a day or so in wet soil.

This system has one other benefit. During dry weather you can fill the garbage can with water and slowly subirrigate your entire garden. Because this is a back-pressure system you should keep water trickling through your hose and into the can. The engineers included this feature in their research and it worked beautifully. Obviously, when laying the pipe you should keep the slope as gentle as possible if you plan to irrigate also.

Vegetative Propagation

Someday, we would like to write a (much smaller) book on grafting and rooting of cuttings. Maybe it will be called *Graft and Similar Schemes.* For here and now, we think a chapter on tricks of the trade should at least have a short account of some innovations that make propagation easier.

ROOTING OF CUTTINGS

You probably realize that plants vary in their tendency to produce roots from cuttings. Stems of coleus and fig have what are essentially root initials (preformed on the stems), and given a little moisture and shade they will root easily. At the other extreme, blueberries are slow to root and present a real challenge. Most evergreens require some measures to prevent moisture loss while rooting. The so-called rooting hormones will usually improve your chances of success. There is another extreme group that just will not root. Our resident propagation expert says he would rather try rooting barbed wire than work with pecan, citrus, or oak cuttings.

Current technology has improved the chances of success in rooting difficult cuttings. Greenhouses with automated mist systems and bottom heat are important for some species, but simple home recipes often work. In most cases you should use this year's wood, take small cuttings (maybe six inches long), make a sharp diagonal cut at the base, and dip that in the rooting hormone powder. Remove a few leaves from the lower part and stick the cuttings in clean, washed, moist sand in a plastic pot, and slip a plastic bag over the pot.

Ed's Tale about Rooting

Knowing when to take cuttings for rooting can be the secret of success. Japanese magnolia *(M. soulangeana)* once was considered nearly impossible to root. A Japanese nurseryman in Alabama knew how to get consistent rooting but he wouldn't tell his secret. After a substantial amount of undercover investigation, the competition learned that cuttings had to be taken when they were very tender—a stage that everyone else had considered too delicate for rooting. Back when I was the gofer of an experienced nurseryman, he sent me out at specific times to cut branches of certain shrubs. He then took the branches and selected parts from which to make cuttings of a certain size, with a definite number of leaves—or sometimes just half-leaves. He then entrusted me to line them into a trench made in washed sand. I *hammered* them in: placed a board next to the row of cuttings and pounded the board with a mallet. All of this was done in a hot, partially shaded greenhouse that was *syringed* every hour to keep the humidity near 100 percent. I sweated a lot and chewed large quantities of salt tablets. Together, the boss and I rooted over 90 percent of the cuttings, very consistently, and this was before the advent of rooting hormones. The key to all of this was the boss's knowledge of when to take cuttings and how to prepare them—and how to keep other nurserymen from knowing his secrets.

It helps to make a wire frame to hold the plastic away from the plant. If this little tent is exposed to direct sunlight, the plant will get too hot: slip a paper bag over the plastic to provide shade.

GRAFTING

Even if you can propagate from cuttings, it may not be the best approach. Some plants do not grow well "on their own roots." Part of this may be genetic; a plant might produce good flowers or have interesting leaves and not make a very good root system. Another aspect is that most young seedlings have a juvenile vigor—they grow very fast. Whatever the reason, it is often better to graft a bud or a stem cutting (called a scion) onto a better rootstock.

For camellias and other evergreens, grafts on a seedling may be covered with plastic over a wire frame (to reduce water loss through the leaves). If you want to graft onto a branch of a more mature bush, a plastic cover is impractical. There is another technique called *green wood grafting.* For this, the leaves are removed from a small cutting, and the entire graft, including the cutting and bud, is wrapped with a paraffin film. After the graft takes, the bud will begin to grow and will penetrate the film. We realize that this does not sound revolutionary, but the use of paraffin film on grafts can give you the reputation of being an expert.

Garden Stakes

We grew up in the time when it was easy to stake tomatoes and grow pole beans on tripod poles. First you go out into the woods and cut some oak saplings, about an inch or so in diameter. You cannot do that any more. Finding stakes is a hassle—and they will last for only about two years before rotting. The modern term for stake is *rebar.* This is the slang term for reinforcing bar, the sort of thing contractors use to reinforce concrete slabs. The rough ridges on rebars make them hard to handle, and they rust easily, but we think they are worth the trouble. Your building supply store will have them in lengths of ten feet and up. The best size to use for stakes is called a Number 3, which is about four-tenths of an inch in diameter. Number 4 is just a little larger (half an inch); it will do but is a bit heavy. The bad news is that your friendly building supply probably will not cut rebars to the size you want. Maybe they will change the policy, but our approach is to rent a large bolt cutter, take it to the store, and cut what we need. You should cut the rebar to a length that will allow you to drive it about twelve to eighteen inches into the ground and still have about four feet for staking tomatoes.

So, how do you drive rebars into the ground? The building supply store will sell you a fence post driver for not very much. When you see what it is you may decide to make one. Take a short length of half-inch metal pipe, thread a T-fitting at the top, and thread short lengths of pipe on the two lateral openings. You slide the pipe over the rebar and pound downward. Each light stroke lowers the rebar a bit; keep at it until you get the height you want.

The ordinary half-inch PVC pipe is another modern device that can replace stakes and poles. We like to slide a PVC pipe over the rebar because it gives a smooth, clean surface for tying the tomato or cucumber plants. After your last harvest, it is easier to slide the vines and tie strings from a smooth surface.

The greatest value of PVC pipes is as tripod poles for pole beans. Use them just as you would wooden poles, except for one modification. A half-inch PVC pipe is not strong enough to withstand a windstorm when it is covered with bean vines. As a precaution, drive a rebar in the center of the row and slip an approximately six-foot PVC pipe over it. Now, use six-foot pipes to make the tripod and, at the top, tie these pipes together around the upright one that is held steady by the rebar.

Cold and Bird Protection for Strawberries

Back in the days before clothes driers it was easy to find large coils of eight-gauge clothesline wire. We used to buy a fifty-foot coil and cut through one side of the coil. This produced about thirty strong hoops that we could push into the ground over strawberry plants. It formed the supports for a long tunnel that could be covered with clear plastic to warm the plants on cold days, row-cover cloth to protect plants from overnight frosts, or bird netting to keep birds from harvesting our crop (see figure 13). Maybe we should explain that a row-cover is a fine netting material, designed to keep insects away from a crop, that also holds some heat around the strawberry plants on cold days. Using clear plastic on a cold sunny day is risky because the plants might get overheated, but you can reduce the risk by leaving each end open during the day.

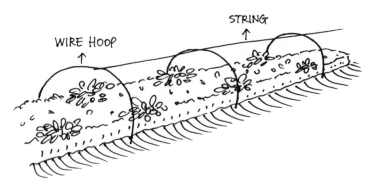

Figure 13. Covering strawberries.

It is very hard to find clothesline wire now, but you can create the same kind of tunnel using half-inch PVC pipe. When using this for bird netting you must anchor the edges to the soil. Garden centers sell wire pegs called ground cloth anchors that serve the purpose well. The pegs are simply large wire staples. You could make them from old coat hanger wire, but that is a lot of trouble. (Ed suggests that Leon's row-cover support idea is less than efficient and that Leon is simply in love with PVC pipe. A good hardware store manager, Ed says, can get you some wire. Make the hoops and you will save a lot of trouble and a little money.)

We recently read of a good technique for protecting early tomato plants from cold. Put wire cages over the plants, but wrap a layer of row-cover fabric around the cage, leaving the top open. We think this also may help to prevent the movement of thrips from plant to plant, and thus help lessen tomato spotted wilt virus, which is spread by thrips and can be devastating.

OTHER COLD WEATHER PROTECTION IDEAS

These ideas are more dreams than actual how-to. On cold afternoons when we are hustling around to find things that might protect the camellias, cycads, satsuma trees, and so forth, we think about "what might have been." Suppose you had kept the satsuma and camellia bushes pruned to around five feet high. Suppose you had dug holes at the four corners and slipped in a short section of large PVC pipe—one that a section of half-inch pipe would slip into. Using those four PVC uprights you could attach crosspieces, tying them together and forming a framework. Now you would have a way to give wind protection and hold the heat, without having the cover resting on the bush. You would have built a temporary greenhouse. For a cold, clear night, with little wind, you could cover this with a polyethylene film. A strong wind would cause problems, but maybe sheets of Styrofoam™ insulation would hold up.

You will notice that we said "suppose." This means that we have not tried the ideas yet, but they sound good over a cup of coffee.

Chapter 3

COMPOST, EARTHWORMS, AND PRODUCTIVE SOIL

There is an old saying about home remedy medicines being "good for what ails you." Compost is good for what ails almost any plant: vegetable, outdoor ornamental, or indoor potted. Every gardener worth his or her salt should have a good compost pile—or maybe two. We realize that you can buy compost at the garden center, but that stuff simply cannot compare with the homegrown variety.

Maybe we should begin by giving some examples of how compost can be used. These are just broad, working ideas; we will have a more detailed discussion in chapter 16. Compost is not quite, and is much more than, natural fertilizer. As compost breaks down it does release plant nutrients, or fertilizers. In the same process it releases a gummy, sticky material that binds soil particles together, improving the soil structure. Good compost is a fine, loose material that can serve as a seeding mix. If you are planting small seeds in a bed, it is a good idea to dig a narrow trench, fill it with compost, and plant the seeds directly in that. A little compost is useful for adding to potting mix. Spreading some compost on soil with low organic matter will "seed" it with the proper bacteria and fungi to hasten the breakdown of dead plant material. The stuff is good for what ails you.

We could add a few more uses, but you get the idea: compost is a valuable tool for gardening. Before getting into "how to," we should say something about what compost is and how it came to be. Compost is decaying organic material in the process of being broken down to the end products: carbon dioxide and a few minerals. For practical purposes, humus and compost are the same material; maybe composting is the process and humus is the product, but we will not quibble over terms. It is important to say that dead leaves and slimy grass clippings are not compost, they are just the raw material. These materials are broken down by microorganisms—bacteria, fungi, and similar buglets. These microorganisms do most of the work.

Making Good Compost

We are discussing a backyard compost pile in which you want to maximize the amount produced from your limited materials. Commercial composting methods focus on decomposing large amounts of material quickly. They are reducing the bulk of organic material, with compost as a by-product. Do not buy a book on how the Big Boys make compost—the right way. Their system works, is fast, but is wasteful. Making backyard compost the right way is easy; avoiding the wrong ways is a little more tricky. We begin with "how to" and then point out flaws in some of the more complicated methods.

Find a shady spot to pile leaves, grass clippings, watermelon rinds, and butter bean hulls. Do not put weeds there if they have already produced seeds. It would help to add a little fertilizer and a little lime occasionally. Extra nitrogen makes the composting process go faster but has little effect on the end product. Ideally, you should add the nitrogen as ammonium nitrate, but ordinary mixed fertilizer such as 8-8-8 will do; the extra phosphorus will help a little. The amount of fertilizer to add is something of a guess. Mix in a handful or two every week or so, maybe a little more if the pile is large. If you start smelling ammonia going off as a gas, you are adding too much; cut back a little. Lime should be added because the better microorganisms work efficiently near a neutral pH, slightly acid but not much. Add about half as much lime as fertilizer.

The next point is a little more important than whether to add fertilizer. Oxygen, water, and temperature are critical for microbial growth. If the compost pile gets too wet, or is very large, rapid microbial activity can use up most of the oxygen, especially in the center of the pile. During the summer you should stir the pile about once a week and add a little water if it seems to be dry, but be cautious about adding water because it might rain tomorrow.

Honestly, that is all there is to making compost: find a shady spot; pile leaves, grass clippings, and any other kind of plant residues; stir it occasionally; and wait. How long do you wait? That depends on a lot of things, but a good rule of thumb is that the compost is ready when you see earthworms growing in it.

There are several things that you need to know about the composting process. First, there is the carbon/nitrogen (C/N) ratio; this is not complicated and is very important for understanding compost. Microorganisms break down plant residues (leaves, grass, vegetable scraps, etc.) to obtain energy and nutrients for their body tissues. This is a key point: the energy comes from carbohydrates (sugars, starches, and cellulose), but nitrogen is also important for building amino acids and proteins. Roughly, the body tissue of microorganisms contains about 1.8 percent nitrogen on a dry weight basis. (The amount of carbon in microorganisms varies but is around 40 to 60 percent.) If the plant residue contains 1.8 percent nitrogen, it is suitable for fairly rapid microbial breakdown, meaning that there is enough nitrogen to produce new microorganisms. Because plant material is mostly cellulose, there will always be enough carbohydrate for microbial breakdown; nitrogen is the element most likely to be in short supply. This is the meaning of the C/N ratio, which should be the carbohydrate/nitrogen ratio but nobody calls it that because carbon is easier to measure. The point is that the C/N ratio is a fairly good estimate of how suitable the plant material is for microbial decomposition. The standard critical level for the ratio of C to N is 10 or 20 parts of carbon to 1 of nitrogen. The ratio of most grasses is higher than this (too much carbon); they will decompose slowly unless extra nitrogen is added. Gardeners will tell you that if you work hay into the soil it will *tie up* the nitrogen for a while. This means that the microorganisms have used all available nitrogen to decompose the carbohydrates; there is no more nitrogen in the soil for the microorganisms and absolutely none for plants. Plants will get only what the microorganisms do not need. The hay or grass you worked into the soil will decompose only as fast as more nitrogen is produced by nitrogen-fixing bacteria or from rainwater that washes nitrogen out of the air. Eventually the grass will decompose, leaving compost with about 1.8 percent nitrogen—which is a good natural fertilizer. What about the dry manure that you can buy at the garden center? It has an extremely low C/N ratio (high nitrogen); manure makes good fertilizer, but if you compost it the excess nitrogen will be lost as ammonia.

So, C/N ratio sounds very professional but it is also vague. You can only estimate whether the material you add to the compost has a good C/N ratio. The best guess is that most plant material will decompose faster if you add extra nitrogen. The good news is that it is not that important; if you add too much the excess will go off as ammonia. Regardless of what you do, the final composted product will have about 1.8 percent nitrogen. Here is the reason: good compost contains some of the more resistant parts from decaying plant residues, but it is mostly dead microorganisms. Yep, dead buglets. They are very small but there are billions of them in the pile.

There is one more critical point: microorganisms produce heat when decomposing organic material. Unless you stir the pile occasionally, it can get very hot. From a standpoint of efficiency, a temperature range of 40 to 85°F is best for composting. The organisms working at those temperatures lose less organic matter as carbon dioxide and keep more of the nitrogen, which means that more compost is produced from the amount of plant residues you have. If the compost temperature increases (as it will with rapid microbial activity) to the range of 100 to 170°F (it cannot go much higher), some high-temperature microorganisms take over. These are different species of microorganisms that work much faster but are more wasteful. We suggest that you stir the compost pile frequently, both to maintain a lower heat and to add more oxygen. The plant residues will break down faster if you let the pile get hotter, but you will be wasting compost.

Consider the story that composting kills weed seeds. Well, yes. Seeds without hard coats will probably take up moisture from the damp compost; moist seeds are killed if exposed to about 130°F for several hours. The hard-seeded ones (meaning that the inner portion is fairly dry) will survive higher temperatures, but not 170°F. So the answer is yes, if you manage the pile so that it uses high temperature microorganisms, composting material in the center will get hot enough to kill all weed seeds. High temperature is a wasteful approach to composting; you should not allow it to happen, but even if it does you will never be quite sure that the pile was mixed often enough to move all seeds into the central portion, which has the lethal temperatures. Bottom line: do not add weed seeds to the compost pile because some of them will survive.

You will notice that the system we described builds only one compost pile. And although it is possible to add plant material at the top of the pile and use compost from the bottom, that does not work very well. So perhaps you should have two piles: one for making and the other for using.

Now for a few idle thoughts. Periodically you will see articles saying a compost pile is wasteful, that you should work the organic matter directly into the garden. Technically this is true. In those early stages of decomposition microbial gums and released nutrients may simply leach out of the pile and into the soil. The argument against digging compost directly into the soil is that the plant residues are too bulky and materials such as leaves and straw will cause microorganisms to take extra nitrogen from the soil. It is usually good to have an organic mulch covering the soil surface in your garden but this is for erosion and weed control. Well, it also keeps your feet from getting muddy; most gardeners use leaves or partially decomposed grass clippings. The mulch will require a little extra nitrogen and the released gums and nutrients will leach directly into your garden.

Some magazines carry ads for a compost-starting inoculum. The theory is sound, but you should be more patient. If you add that kind of inoculum to a new pile, those organisms will work pretty well for a while. Gradually, native microorganisms will take over from the store-bought kind. The ones that remain will be those kinds that are best adapted to the way you like to manage your compost pile, and to the temperature, the rainfall, and the kinds of plant residues you use. We think the idea of adding compost inoculum to fresh plant residues is fine, but caution against getting it from the garden center. The soil beneath your new compost pile has the microbes necessary for decomposition, but the population is not very high. Be patient and let it build up. When you add new residues to the pile, it is a good idea to throw some compost from the old pile (full of decomposition microbes) on top.

This discussion has been directed primarily at composting plant residues: grass clippings, leaves, stems, and vines. Most of you will not have access to animal wastes such as cow, horse, or chicken manure. That material is much higher in nitrogen, and mixing it with plant residues will usually accelerate the composting process. But . . . (you knew there would be a *but*). Animal wastes are notorious carriers of human disease organisms. Salmonella is common but there are others. The easy answer to this problem is to say that good composting will kill most of the organisms. Here you meet the same argument we gave against adding weed seeds to compost: Good, uniform composting is difficult to achieve, and some disease organisms simply cannot be killed by it. The hazard is from vegetables that are eaten raw and are in contact with the soil or close enough for splattering by raindrops: tomatoes, bell peppers, lettuce, spinach, and so forth. If you use composted manure, rinse the vegetables in a dilute chlorine solution. It will not affect the taste and may avoid some problems.

Earthworms

Regardless of what you might read in some magazines, earthworms do not make the soil rich and productive. Earthworms thrive in good soil with plenty of organic matter. They will often accelerate the decomposition process and probably help to improve soil structure. To restate this, the presence of earthworms indicates that you have made a good garden or good compost, but do not give them the credit for your work.

There are several species of earthworms, but for our discussion there is little difference among them. Earthworms obtain nutrients and energy by ingesting soil (eating is not quite the correct term). They grind the material finely, digest some of the organic matter, and pass the rest out of their bodies in structures called worm castings. Because the grinding process promotes microbial activity, these castings are often high in available plant nutrients, microbial gums, and a wide range of microorganisms.

Earthworms are nearly aquatic organisms. The soil must be very moist because earthworms cannot survive unless they maintain a thin water film over their bodies. Worms have no specialized breathing organs; they take dissolved oxygen from the water film and transport it through the skin into the area of digestion. Fish use the same system but are more advanced, using gills to extract oxygen. Because earthworms can take oxygen only from water, if the film dries they suffocate. We are discussing this to make two points: the soil must be moist and well aerated. If a field is wet long enough for plants and microorganisms to use up the oxygen, earthworms will die. If the soil becomes very dry, they burrow down to a moist area. If they hit any type of hardpan, they curl into a tight ball, conserving moisture. During long droughts worms die, especially if the soil has a hardpan (see chapter 15 for a discussion of hardpans).

Occasionally someone says that commercial fertilizers kill earthworms. This means that a fairly concentrated salt solution will remove the water film, suffocating the worms. Salts washed from manure will do the same thing. The only fallacy in such a statement is that worms usually can move away from a salt solution before it kills them. In our fertilizer application procedures Leon suggested that you apply a concentrated band to conserve phosphorus. This is valid whether you use commercial fertilizer or fresh manure. It probably does not bother the worms because they will stay away from it.

Ed's Worm Casting Tale

An earthworm grower asked me if I thought he could market earthworm castings as a soil additive, since he had read that the material could improve soils. Even though no regulations governed the sale of potting soils or additives (fertilizers are regulated), I knew that heavy metals can be concentrated in the castings, so I recommended testing before marketing. The tests showed cadmium levels several hundred times what they usually are in soils. Most plants will take up cadmium passively but usually not in amounts that would be toxic (to the plants). I was not very concerned over the safety of these castings for ornamental plants but wondered what would happen if someone tried to use the additive around vegetables. Would the cadmium levels be toxic to humans? Apparently the worm farmer decided not to market his new material.

A few years later another eager earthworm producer came to me with samples of his castings. He had already printed up a label for the wonder product: Atomic Soil! He listened to my tale, had the castings tested, and found there were no serious levels of heavy metals. I agreed to use the castings in a class lab project, adding various amounts to a mixture of peat moss and using tomato seedlings as test plants. In every pot containing any amount of the castings all of the plants died, brought down by a soil-borne fungal disease. Earthworms accumulate strange combinations of things. I suggested that he steam sterilize the castings before offering them for sale, but do not know whether he did. It is a shame that there must be so many regulations, but I think fertilizer regulations should extend to potting mixes.

Should you worry about what is in the potting mixes and soil additives at the garden center? Probably not; a successful garden center will not risk its name on some new product that has not been adequately tested.

Chapter 4

Ed enjoys giving potted plants to friends, though they always tell him "Ed, honestly, plants come to me to die. I try to take care of them, but it never works."

We want you to know that there is no such thing as a green thumb. Be patient, give your plants consistent care, and recognize that the environment of a potted plant is substantially different from what it would be out in the flower bed. This chapter will help you to understand the differences. Make yourself a fresh pot of coffee, take a few sips, and read for a while.

Potted Plants

We begin with a point that seems to dabble in semantics but is very important. Consider the question of whether you actually want to grow potted plants in your home. With a few exceptions the answer is no; you enjoy caring for the plants but your goal is to maintain them at about the same size and attractiveness. Occasionally, you might get a small cutting from a friend and want it to grow, but for the most part you want houseplants to remain as they are. This is a reasonable goal; with occasional pruning, a sensible watering schedule, and maybe just a little fertilizer you can keep some plants at the same size for many years. You should also recognize that most plants will slowly outgrow their pots, and many will eventually die under home conditions. A good assumption is that, with some care, you can keep most plants healthy and attractive for several years; do not try to make them live forever.

Now, consider the plant you bought at the garden center. Very recently it came from a commercial greenhouse producer who makes a living by growing plants to sell to you. But you do not want the plants to grow, or at least, not by much. That producer designed the potting mix, the fertilizer program, and the watering schedule around a single goal: making those plants get up and get with it. He used the "root-hog or die" system: plants that do not grow rapidly get thrown out.

When you buy a plant, the rules change. It will be under less intensive lighting, watered less frequently, and will need much less fertilizer. However, there is no need to worry that the plant will die when you shift it from the growth program to one of health maintenance. Our point here is that plant care in a house should be built around your personal needs and the environments that you have available. Do not try to duplicate greenhouse procedures. The new plant is in for some culture shock, but most of the popular house-plants can adjust to the changes very nicely; otherwise they would not be popular plants.

Now we can discuss some of the options you have for making the necessary adjustments. Broadly, these are the kind of potting mix, watering routines, light quality and intensity, and fertilizer.

Potting Mixes

Back when Ed was teaching, he used to devote a full lecture to techniques for preparing potting mixes. A few gardening experts still prepare their own, but most of us buy a forty-pound bag of mix at the local gardening center. The do-it-yourself approach requires you to have bags of peat moss, perlite, pine bark, and vermiculite, plus some real soil and a pile of good sand. We have decided that our book should tell how to make a potting mix, but that sort of thing belongs in an appendix. So if you want to try it yourself, see appendix B.

When Grandma repotted her houseplants, she usually went out to the flower bed and got some rich soil with plenty of organic matter in it. Of course, Grandma used what was available because she did not have access to a garden center. Rich garden soil does not make a good potting mix: It will not drain well enough, and the soil surface will puddle badly from frequent watering. If you do not want to try making your own potting mix, you should use one of the mixes sold at the garden center. The question is which one. A wide selection of potting mixes is available for many special uses, but there are two broad categories of mixes: seeding mixes and potting mixes.

Seeding mixes are generically called "Jiffy mixes" (in the same sense that we make "Xerox copies"). Jiffy mix is the trade name for a fine-textured mixture of peat moss, perlite, and vermiculite. It is important to use if you are going to sow small seeds to transplant later, because seeds would fall down into the cracks of a coarser mix. Though good for starting seedlings, Jiffy mix is too fine and holds moisture too well to maintain potted plants properly.

Now we get around to describing real potting mixes. We can start with a broad guideline: a good potting mix should be a mixture of coarse material, such as bark, a little soil, possibly some sand, and a little peat moss to hold moisture. You should choose a mix that fits your situation, including the kinds of plants you have, your watering schedule, lighting conditions, and humidity. The type of mix you need for your houseplants depends to a large degree on the kind of watering schedule you want to follow. If you are able and willing to water frequently, it is best to have more bark so that the excess water can move down through the pot, flushing out carbon dioxide and excess salts. If you do not want to water too often, the mix should have more peat moss. All mixes should have a little soil to provide some protection against fertilizer burn in case you get too ambitious about using it.

At your garden center, try to find an open bag and look over the stuff inside. If it contains a lot of soil or finely ground peat moss, you may want to add some bark and a little perlite to it. The general mix should be a ratio of 1:1:1 soil, peat moss, and perlite or bark. It might be a good idea to buy the bag, take it home, and try potting one plant in it before committing all your houseplants to this new mix.

Watering

The only reasonable answer to the frequent question "How often should I water this?" is "When it needs watering." Watering frequency depends on the location of the plant in your house, the kind of plant, the kind of potting mix, the characteristics of your water, and the schedule you want to follow. It is important to understand why you are watering: to replace water and to flush out excess salts and carbon dioxide from the potting mix.

What does a houseplant do with water? A plant's roots take water and a few nutrient salts (fertilizer) from the potting mix and move this water/salt solution into its stem and leaves, where the nutrients are used in the normal growth process. Most of the water in the leaves evaporates. The amount of evaporation depends on the air around the plant: how dry it is, its temperature, and its movement or air current. These will vary depending on the plant's location in your house and at what temperature you set your thermostat. A good bit of water will also evaporate from the surface of the potting mix, and this soil-surface evaporation removes no salts at all. Since the amount of salts taken up by a houseplant is minute, you can assume that all the salts from your tap water will remain in the pot. Tap water usually has a large amount of salts, which means that more salts are being added to the potting mix every time you water. The problem with adding plenty of fertilizer is that the mix will eventually become too salty for the plant to draw enough water from it. If this happens, the plant will start wilting even though the potting mix is moist. (See the upcoming section on water quality.)

Grandma told you that plants inhale carbon dioxide and exhale oxygen, but she was wrong. Plants breathe the same way you do. Their roots take in oxygen, which reacts with carbohydrates to produce energy, and carbon dioxide is released as a waste product from the roots. Photosynthesis is the process in which leaves take in carbon dioxide and emit oxygen as a waste product. But the roots do not work that way. Moving water and plant nutrients from the potting mix to the stem and leaves requires energy, which the plant gets when oxygen reacts with carbohydrates. The roots take oxygen from small air pockets in the potting mix, and they deposit carbon dioxide in those same air pockets. Unless you empty the carbon dioxide from the mix, oxygen cannot move in, and the roots will begin to suffocate. The plant will start to wilt because the roots cannot send up enough water to its stem and leaves.

At this point you begin to wonder what went wrong. The potting mix feels moist, so you think you should add some fertilizer—the last thing it needs. That poor plant needs love, affection, and a good purging. If you add water until it runs from the bottom of the pot, the water will have filled all the air pockets in the mix. Technically the pot is now water-logged, but this process has forced the carbon dioxide from the air pockets and out through the drainage holes. The excess water will drain from the air pockets, creating a vacuum, and fresh air will be forced in. *Voila!* The plant is happy again. It does not take much to make a houseplant happy.

"But how often should I water?" Actively growing plants in the high-light conditions of commercial greenhouses may need watering twice a day, but in the reduced light of your home, once a week or even less frequently may be often enough. Outdoors, some potted plants need daily watering. In both cases, the plant should dry out some between watering. The kind of plant will influence the frequency of watering; hydrangeas in bloom will lose a lot of water, while a cactus loses little water at all. The cactus has a waxy coating and many small spines, which protect the plant but also create *microclimates* by disturbing the air flow. Young leaves and stems do not yet have the water-resistant (waxy) coverings that older ones develop, so they need more water in proportion to growth rate. Location in the house is critical: plants directly in the air flow of central heating and cooling will have a higher water requirement than identical plants in a sheltered part of the same room.

The safest way to judge when to water your plant is to follow these recommendations. First water the plant until the water drains from the bottom of its container. A guideline for the proper amount is that a six-inch pot usually needs about twelve to fourteen ounces of water, if has been allowed to dry out properly between waterings. You may want to move small indoor pots to the kitchen sink while they drain. Larger pots can be located in trays or waterproof saucers on beds of gravel to allow drainage but prevent the roots from standing in water. After drainage stops, pick up the pot and get a feel for its weight (or weigh it on a scale and write down the number). Allow several days to pass, then pick it up again. Remember, you do not want to keep the pot well watered: It needs to dry out so that you can water it heavily and flush out the carbon dioxide. When weight loss is easily detectable—when the pot weighs about one-half to one-third of its weight the last time it was watered thoroughly—you should water it again.

Consider all the variables—air movement, humidity, temperature, light intensity, growth stage, kind of plant, size of plant, kind of potting mix—check the weight of the plant when freshly watered and after a few days or a week. Only you can decide when to water your houseplants. It is an art that you will develop for your plants and home situation.

Repotting

With very careful management you can control the growth of potted plants so that they sustain themselves with essentially no size increase. Bonsai trees live to be hundreds of years old growing in the same pot, but they demand almost constant attention. Your plants will gradually outgrow their containers. *Potbound* usually means the root growth has become so dense that water does not percolate into or out of the soil mix. When this situation develops, you should first consider whether you want to keep the plant. If it has lived to a ripe old age, you may want to let it die with dignity and buy a new one. If you want to keep it, in that pot, it is time for surgery. Tap the sides of the pot gently, and the plant will (usually) slip right out when you pull. If it does not, tap some more. When you get the plant out, cut the root system back severely, especially the roots that have coiled around the pot surface and at the base of the pot. Prune the top growth to about the same degree; this is to reduce water demand until new roots grow. Ideally, you should do this when the plant is relatively dormant, during cool weather, or at least under shaded conditions.

Another option is to repot the plant into a slightly larger container. Avoid the temptation to move that plant into a much larger pot so you will not have to repeat the process next year. When you move the plant into a large pot, the root system (even if you spread it out) will occupy only a small volume in the middle of the new soil mix. Water in loose soil mixes does not move laterally very well. The root system may reduce the water content of that small portion to a point at which it requires irrigation. You can have a situation in which the plant needs water but most of the pot does not. Adding water can produce symptoms of overwatering. As a precaution, it is always best to move up to the next size pot rather than skipping to a monster one.

Water Quality

We are not going to discuss the quality of water used for drinking and cooking; water that is safe for humans may not be good for plants. Well water can have some special problems for houseplant use. Rainwater was once an old standby, but who knows what sorts of pollutants might be in the rain now?

Most city water is chlorinated, and some is also fluoridated, but the amount of chemicals in your city water is seldom high enough to cause problems. Sodium and chloride levels can be too high for many houseplants if your water comes from aquifers near the coast, where the intrusion of salt water has increased to damaging levels. Well water sometimes contains very high levels of naturally occurring fluorine, to which plants in the lily, agave, and maranta families are particularly sensitive. If your water is from a well that is high in fluorides, it may be almost impossible for you to grow airplane plant (*Chlorophytum*) without leaf scorch.

High levels of calcium and sodium in your water can cause problems.

Boron can cause damage, and then there is the matter of water pH. Do not be frightened by these warnings: the hazards are real but uncommon. Most city and well water is satisfactory for houseplants if you water them well enough to flush out the carbon dioxide and excess salts.

We strongly suggest that you get an analysis of the water you use for your plants; it will probably turn out to be fine, but why worry? All municipal water systems monitor water chemistry. Though they may not be "happy to send you a copy," they will do it if you persist. The report lists various chemical components as parts per million and will give pH. (See chapter 15 for our detailed discussion of pH.) Look also on the report for *titratable alkalinity,* which is related to pH. Alkalinity refers to the capacity of the sample to neutralize acids (H ions). A high value for titratable alkalinity means that this water can make the potting mix very alkaline. If you are lucky, the report will tell about alkalinity in terms of both carbonate and bicarbonate. As an example we will describe New Orleans water. The Crescent City's water treatment system often results in a pH of around 10 and occasionally up to 11. This is far too high for plant growth, since anything above 7 is usually bad, but it does not matter for watering houseplants because the high pH is due to carbonates, which are easily neutralized by acidic materials in the potting mix. A high pH due to bicarbonates would be disastrous. Unfortunately bicarbonates are rather common in well water and in much of the artesian spring water.

Look for these critical levels in the analysis:

(1) Titratable alkalinity should be less than 100 ppm. If it is higher than 150 ppm, you should treat the water with a little vinegar before using it.

(2) Soluble salts should be less than 1,000 ppm (if this is given as a conductivity reading in your report, less than 1 mmho/cm is good), and less than 60 percent of the total dissolved salts should be sodium (if this is given as sodium absorption ratio, or SAR, it should be 2 or less).

(3) Boron should be less than 1 ppm and chlorides less than 70. Occasionally—though not often—water can be too pure. If total soluble salts are less than 150 ppm, you might need to add some calcium and magnesium, but only if the potting mix contains no soil.

What should you do with bad water? Dilute it with distilled water, which is available at many stores. Get a large container to use as your potted plant water supply, and add enough distilled water to bring the important elements below critical levels. You could decide to use only distilled water, but that would get expensive if you have a lot of plants. If you want to use the pure spring water that is delivered to your house, get a water analysis first: "pure spring water" does not mean "pure water." It could be very high in bicarbonates. We do not recommend using filtered water, either. Grandma used to catch rain water to use on her houseplants. That is still a good approach. Air pollution might complicate matters, but you could wait until it has been raining for a while before catching any.

Light

It is impossible to make generalized statements about the light requirements of plants because they have evolved under widely differing light conditions. Many of the best household plants originally grew as understory plants in rain forests, where light is not only of low intensity but also of different quality (wavelength) from that of the upper canopies. For example, bromeliads grew in the upper parts of tall trees and philodendrons developed as understory plants. Obviously, philodendrons and bromeliads will not grow equally well in the same light conditions.

Most plants have adaptations that enable them to grow to some extent with unfavorable light. When you bring plants into the house after they have been growing outside they might drop the lower leaves. When light conditions change, most of the stored food materials will be moved out of those leaves and into the active growing points. The old leaves will drop off and the newly formed ones will probably be much farther apart under lower light conditions. This system reduces the overlapping of leaves and allows them to intercept light more efficiently. In very low light the plants may be able to make only enough food to maintain their respiration, with little energy for new growth. With slightly better light conditions the plant will make new growth but will not produce flowers. If there is enough light for respiration and new growth, the excess food will be diverted to flowering. As a general rule, most plants do not flower well in a home because they cannot be supplied with enough light. African violets are popular because of their ability to produce flowers in the home and remain small at the same time. They were originally adapted for growth under very low light conditions.

The more popular houseplants have two characteristics in common: (1) They endure indoor conditions (light, humidity, and neglect) better than most

Bromeliad *(Tillandsia stricta)* on tree fern stem piece.

other plants, and (2) commercial producers can grow them profitably. For these same reasons popular plants are often overused in homes. If you are interested in some of the less popular houseplants, there are standard references that categorize plants by their light-intensity requirements. Most of these ratings were made for greenhouse production, but they will provide you with reasonable guidelines. The tremendous range of plants grown somewhere as foliage plants may be seen in A. B. Graf's *Pictorial Cyclopedia of Exotic Plants,* published by the Roehrs Company of East Rutherford, N.J., which contains 12,000 illustrations; or *Exotic Plant Manual,* a guide to the more common foliage plants, published by Florists' Transworld Delivery Association, with more than 100 photographs. Both publications have cultural information and general plant suitability for various environments.

Light requirements are not the only considerations in selecting indoor plants: texture, color, shape, and ultimate size also are important. The light environment of a plant is more complex than a simple question of whether it gets enough light.

Plants near a window usually get enough light even during the winter, but you should occasionally turn the pot to assure even growth. If you feel that a plant is not getting enough light from the window, try artificial light. The timing and duration are critical to a degree; if you are away from home all day it will help to turn a light on the plant for a while at night. If possible, use a fluorescent light, because the quality (color spectrum) of incandescent light bulbs contains too much red and too little blue, gradually causing the plants to become elongated and pale. Most fluorescent bulbs will keep the plant attractive. The plant growth tubes contain more red and blue than other fluorescent lights and really are a little better, but they are not worth the bother for home use. However, there is one point that you should consider: the colors in cool white, warm white, and daylight tubes affect the appearance of the leaves and flowers. This has nothing to do with growth, but if the light makes your plant look strange, try another kind.

Many recommendations regarding plant light conditions specify the intensity in foot-candles (abbreviated f.c.). This is a measure of the radiant energy within the wavelengths that the human eye can perceive. But plants respond to some wavelengths that humans cannot see. This is especially important in the far-red area. Also, there are visible wavelengths that have little effect on plants. The most obvious is green; plants appear to be green because that color is reflected from or transmitted through them. So, after many arguments, a new plant standard was developed: PAR (photosynthetically active radiation). This is measured in energy (microwatts per square centimeter); equipment for measuring it is expensive. Foot-candles is a more practical measure of light intensity for home use. But how can you measure foot-candles? Your local camera store will have a table to convert camera settings to foot-candle readings.

When the light intensity is such that a plant can synthesize only enough food to sustain itself without the accumulation or depletion of food reserves, that intensity is known as the *compensation point;* anything less than that will starve the plant. (Note that *plant food* does not refer to fertilizer, but rather to proteins and carbohydrates that plants make through the process of photosynthesis.) Unfortunately, compensation point is not an absolute figure. A plant can adjust somewhat according to available light. A study of foliage plants in Florida showed that the compensation point of shaded plants was lower than that of sun-grown plants, even those of the same species and variety. This meant that shade-grown plants could remain stable, without using food reserves, at a lower light intensity.

Fertilization

Plants in low light need less fertilizer as well as less water. Notice that we are now talking about fertilizer (nutrients) instead of plant food. Fertilizer supplies minerals and nitrogen that a plant also needs.

In general, the lower the light intensity, the less fertilizer plants can use efficiently. In practice, this means that a potted plant in the house needs less fertilizer than the same plant would need if it were growing in the same container and potting mix out on the patio with more light. Also, if plants need to be watered more often, this extra water will remove some differences in fertilizer needs among the foliage plant species, which most houseplants are.

Now we return to the original point; you probably do not want to grow houseplants. In most conditions, fertilizing indoor plants every two or three months will be sufficient to maintain them, if they are growing in soilless mixes. If the mix has some soil, the plants may not need fertilizer for years. Garden centers offer fertilizers sold especially for houseplants, together with recommendations for use. While reading the fertilizer label, remember that it was written by people who like to sell fertilizer. Experienced interior landscape people (they take care of plants in expensive offices) say that more of our houseplants are killed by overuse of fertilizer than by deficiencies. If your plant is not growing well or has strange-looking leaves, it probably needs repotting rather than more "plant food." Fertilizer is not food for plants.

Are organic fertilizers better for potted plants? The old-timers swore by it. When Ed was a young fellow, one of his first greenhouse jobs was to prepare manure water, which involved placing horse manure from the stables (yes, Virginia, horses were still being used for transportation) in burlap bags, which were hung in barrels of rain water for aging; it was ready when the bag had rotted. The manure water was then ladled onto foliage plants. The greenhouse had huge numbers of philodendron "totem poles" that thrived on the manure water, as did ferns and other foliage plants. For some reason the old-timers did not like to use cow manure.

Leon notes that back in Mississippi they had milk cows but could not afford carriage horses, and that cow-manure tea was a good starter fertilizer for tomato transplants.

A few years ago Ed was visiting with a grower who had an excellent crop of ferns. These plants were growing in containers on a concrete floor and were fertilized with slow-release granular fertilizer broadcast over the potting mix. The plants were every bit as good as those that grew on manure water, but were using a synthetic source and at a lower cost. The ferns did not care about the source of the nitrogen. Of course, the pleasures of making manure tea were denied the young man working for that grower, but he seemed to be surviving without the experience.

One more tip: do not be tempted to use leaf shine materials, which simply add to your light-intensity problems. Besides that, they can collect dust and plug up the stomates (the minute openings on leaves and stems through which gases are exchanged). If the leaves look dusty, wipe them gently with a damp cloth or tissue paper. A little mild soap in the water may help, but do not scrub. You also might try a little skim milk in the wash water to produce a more natural shine.

Acclimatizing Plants for Moving

With the coming of spring you may want to move the houseplants outdoors. Remember that the plants must be gradually adapted to higher light intensities. Keep them in open shade for a week or two. Some houseplants cannot be adapted to full sun, and open shade is the greatest amount of light they can utilize.

Note that plants probably need more water while outdoors. This is particularly important during hot, dry weather. With full-sun plants you may want to put the entire container in garden soil. The root system will be cooler and may have more uniform watering. However, the roots may grow through the drainage holes and into the soil. You can avoid this by twisting the pots about once a month to break the unnecessary roots. In some gardens there is no open soil area, or in some spots such as patios, both containers and plants will be exposed to the drying air. Unglazed clay pots will lose water through the walls. It is sometimes helpful to *double pot,* placing the clay pot into a larger glazed or plastic container and filling the space between with sphagnum moss.

In such a case, water is applied to the plant and the sphagnum moss as well, but be sure that no standing water is allowed to accumulate in the bottom of the large container. Remember not to allow plants to stand in water-filled saucers.

Cold-hardy plants can be grown outdoors in containers all year, but winter can bring on low humidity and drying winds even in our normally moist environment. Be careful about letting potted plants suffer from drought in cold winter weather.

Tender plants that were grown outdoors in summer and early fall should be prepared for moving back indoors with a reversal of the acclimatization methods used when moving them outside. Some of them may have grown larger than you would like them to be for their indoor spots. If you have time, prune them back until they fit, and consider the possibility of repotting to a larger size. Frequently, the cold snap will come unexpectedly and you will not have time to let plants adjust to reduced light. In that situation you can expect some leaf drop, but the plants will recover.

Container plants can fall prey to insects and diseases in the house as well as outdoors; careful inspection before bringing plants in from the garden, or from the garden center, can avoid many problems. Institute a quarantine period to watch for pest problems. The dry atmosphere of the home may foster the attacks of mites and thrips, which might not have been a serious problem outside. Scale insects and mealybugs are frequent uninvited guests on our indoor plants. However, most houseplants attained their popularity by being tolerant of the low light, the dry atmospheres of the home or office, and also by being fairly resistant to insect and disease problems.

You might be interested in some results from a foliage plant clinic serving commercial foliage plant growers that was established at the Agricultural Research Center in Apopka, Florida, in 1976. The hundreds of samples submitted were categorized as to the cause of any problems—cultural, pathogenic, entomologic, or phytotoxic—and the ten species most frequently found in each category were listed. Although these foliage plants were being grown commercially, the results show which of our common houseplants are most prone to troubles. For example, 13 percent of the samples submitted with problems were philodendrons, but philodendrons made up about 28 percent of the foliage plants grown in central Florida during that time. *Epipremnum* and *Peperomia* constituted 11 and 10 percent of the samples, respectively, but only about

Succulents *(Peperomia scandens variegata)* in hanging baskets.

4 percent each of the foliage plants grown, so these two species appear to be much more prone to problems than philodendrons. Philodendrons are popular because they have few problems. Most of the many other plants represented in the samples showed a frequency very like their market shares, or an indication that they were not especially trouble-prone. Does this mean that you should shun *Epipremnums* and *Peperomias?* No, but do not be surprised if they present interesting challenges.

Our examples in this discussion have been ornamental plants, but this is only because they are the most commonly grown in pots. Using the same principles, you can grow a wide range of vegetables in pots, including some herbs. Do not stereotype all potted plants as ornamentals.

Chapter 5

BULBS AND THINGS THAT ACT LIKE BULBS

One gardening event you can rely on if you have ever bought seed or garden supplies by mail order is the arrival in the fall of spring-flowering bulb catalogs. Then, in late spring, you will get another flood of catalogs for fall-flowering bulbs. These always have pictures of beds with masses of beautiful blooms, designed to tempt you into saying "maybe I will try one more time." The catalog has done its part when you put the check in the mail—you ordered the bulbs and they sent them. Why do catalog people not realize that disappointing results will kill future sales?

Although many catalogs forecast the chances of success with seeds or bulbs according to the different climatic zones, they should be more cautious about bulbs. The production of bulbs seems to have evolved as a mechanism for plants to survive harsh environmental periods—either severe cold or long dry spells. Down here in the humid South the living is easy, which means that bulbs developed for hard times are poorly equipped to grow here. Many of the plants from cold climates succumb to lack of winter chilling or to wet soil conditions. Bulbs from tropical areas are killed by our occasional hard freezes.

Some Definitions and Examples

Basically, a bulb is simply a squashed plant. There is a stem with swollen leaf bases or scales enclosing the next season's bud. At the base there are some stubby roots or root initials, developing on what is called the basal plate. But there also are things that act like bulbs, but are not—quite. Corms are the bulblike structures produced by plants such as gladiolus, crocuses, and freesias. Tubers are similar to corms, except they have no scales or leaf bases. With tuber-forming plants, roots and shoots grow from *eyes* located on the surface. Potatoes and caladiums are common examples of tubers. Rhizomes are horizontal stems that have thickened and stored food materials. Roots will grow from the lower part and shoot buds will grow from the upper part. Then we have some structures called tuberous roots: things that are enlarged roots but look like tubers. Dahlias, sweet potatoes, and some begonias make tuberous roots. New shoots form from buds on the base of the attached stem. If you are dividing tuberous roots, be careful to retain part of the stem with at least one bud. Lumping all of this under the heading of bulbous plants, there are around three thousand species of bulbous plants being grown for food, aesthetic value, or profit.

Considering the growth cycle of the tulip can clarify why some of the pretty things we would like to grow will not grow here—at least not very well. The tulip bulb is called a *periodic* bulb; it lives one year if all goes well and is replaced by one or more daughter bulbs that develop at the bases of the leaves or scales (which are modified leaves) at about the time the flower reaches full bloom. Under proper conditions, seed can develop. However, when bulbs are grown for sale, such as in the production fields of Holland, the flowers are removed to prevent seeds from competing with the developing daughter bulb. Growing plants from seeds is not profitable because the offspring will be different from that of the original bulb. In good growing areas, tulip leaves remain functional until summer, then begin to deteriorate toward death. When the bulbs are dug, one or more daughter bulbs will have grown to the size of the original bulb. These bulbs are then dried. Some will shrink, but the larger ones will be sold and the small bulbs stored to plant in the spring.

The daughter bulb you bought at the garden center is now a new mother bulb, which already has the beginnings of leaves and a rudimentary flower on a short stem. If the weather is too warm, this rudimentary flower will not form. In the humid South you cannot expect to get a repeat bloom from daughter bulbs even though they may be almost as large as those you bought last year. In our warm climate the leaves die before a flower is formed.

In the right conditions, this new flower continues to develop within the dry, apparently inert, bulb. After the flower reaches a certain stage of development, it requires a chilling period at about 40°F for as long as 12 weeks. Without chilling it will not bloom properly after it is placed in growing temperatures. "A certain stage of development" means that if cold treatment is started before that stage the flower can abort. High temperatures also can cause flower abortion. Stored bulbs should be kept dry and cool—about 60°F—until the chilling stage is reached.

Now for what happens in the Deep South: if bulbs have not been chilled long enough they will produce flowers on very short stems. Or, if chilled bulbs are planted too early during a warm winter, some of the chilling may be nullified by the high temperature of the soil. If warm weather continues until Christmas, do not plant bulbs unless they are beginning to sprout. This also means that the garden center should avoid exposing chilled bulbs to heated conditions. If you notice that the tulip bulbs are in a warm sales room, try to find out how long they have been there.

Actually, most garden centers do not have the facilities to treat and store bulbs properly. In our part of the country, chilling and storing tulip bulbs is a do-it-yourself project. Try to buy tulip bulbs in early November and get the largest, cleanest bulbs you can find. Do not skimp on this; smaller bulbs will be much cheaper but they will not do well at all. Store your bulbs in the food crisper part of your refrigerator—it should be around 40°F. Check the bulbs every couple of weeks after mid-December. If you see shoots and/or roots beginning to emerge, plant them immediately even if you have not chilled them for 12 weeks. This growth indicates that, somehow, the bulbs have been chilled enough.

A few years ago, some tulip bulbs were sent to the LSU horticulture department for testing, with a specific statement that they had been prechilled. As a precaution, the man running the test chilled half of them for 12 weeks and got striking results. All of those he chilled bloomed, but very few of the prechilled bulbs did. We need to hedge a bit here because we do not know just how the prechilled bulbs were stored while the others were being chilled. We can only assume that they were held at near-freezing, but may have warmed up in shipment.

This is the first time we have mentioned that temperatures at or below freezing have no effect on the chilling requirement of plants. This point will come up several times in the book: 40°F appears to be a suitable temperature for chilling all plants.

Having to store bulbs in your refrigerator is going to limit the number of tulip bulbs you can chill, unless you want to devote an entire refrigerator to your project. We hope this discussion has shown you what we meant by calling them periodic bulbs. No matter how careful you are in bed preparation and handling of bulbs, tulips will not establish themselves and bloom every year in the Deep South. In our part of the country, tulips are annuals. But there are other bulblike species that do well here—some that will not grow in tulip country.

Another point we need to make is that most bulb advice is intended for the upper United States. Just ignore it—plant only deep enough to cover the bulbs with about an inch of soil.

Bulbous Species That Grow Well in the Deep South

It is encouraging to see that professional gardeners, people who landscape commercial buildings, have been using more agapanthus in our area. This is called the "blue lily of the Nile," and has both white- and purple-flowered forms in addition to blue. These are robust plants, producing flowers in summer on three-foot stems. There are some dwarf forms available for other landscape uses or for containers. These plants do better in partial shade than under our intense sunlight. After about five years (in a good location) the plants will become overcrowded; divide them and share with your neighbors. Agapanthus is a hardy plant that is seldom frozen in the Deep South; farther north you risk cold injury.

Amaryllis (botanists like to call it *Hippeastrum*) differs from tulips and other periodic bulbs in that it has no built-in life span, but is theoretically immortal. These bulbs are composed of fleshy bases of large, strap-shaped leaves and a conical basal plate, sometimes with dried, but functional, roots. Left to its own devices the amaryllis is evergreen; the bulbs that you buy at the garden center were dug and dried for easier shipping. In the growth cycle of the bulb, there are four-leaf increments produced, with the bases of three leaves completely surrounding the basal plate and short stem. The base of the fourth leaf in each growth unit only partially surrounds these parts. The flower bud begins in the axil of this fourth leaf. This develops within the bulb and emerges later in response to some unknown stimuli. A large amaryllis (around three or four inches in diameter) may have several of these potential flowers, ready to emerge when things are right.

Amaryllis that you see at the garden center are usually hybrids that originated in England many years ago from several South American species, sent there by plant explorers back in the heyday of that activity. Dutch bulb growers, having long experience with tulips, bought the hybrids from the English firms and began exporting what is called the *Dutch* amaryllis. Dutch growers began large-scale production of amaryllis bulbs in South Africa. You can find these South African bulbs for sale in the fall, ready to bloom at Christmas time in our area. This is because they were grown in the southern hemisphere, where Christmas is in the spring. After the first year the bulbs will reset their internal clock and begin blooming during our spring rather than in the South African spring. Dutch amaryllis hybrids produce massive scapes (flowering stems of bulbs), usually with four flowers. You may get more or fewer than that.

Until now, we have been talking about the Dutch hybrids. The amaryllis species offers a range of flower forms, colors, and sizes. The first known amaryllis hybrid *(Amaryllis x Johnsonii)* used to be common in the humid South and was known as St. Joseph's lily, probably because it usually bloomed in mid-March outdoors, near St. Joseph's feast day. Several untimely hard freezes over the past twenty years have made it a rare plant here. Most amaryllis bulbs will survive cold snaps if they are well mulched. In colder areas, they should be taken up in late fall and stored cool and dry until the danger of temperatures below about 25°F is over.

Amaryllis *(Hippeastrum hybridum)* in flower.

Caladiums, mostly grown commercially on muck soils in south Florida, represent the other end of the climatic adaptability scale—they are tropicals. With reasonable care you can get several years of good performance from them. These should not be planted until the soil temperature is about 65°F or above. The tubers will not have roots at this time but you can tell which end is up: the bottoms are smooth and rounded, and there are several pointed buds on top. However, if you plant caladium upside down you will just get more, somewhat smaller, leaves than if you plant right-side up.

When greenhouse growers want caladiums to make more leaves for full pots, they often cut out the central, largest, bud. This allows the lateral buds, which would have been kept dormant by the large bud, to sprout. This central bud sometimes produces one large leaf, followed by the flower, which has a typical jack-in-the pulpit shape. Some of the flowers are quite pretty, but if you do not want flowers, break them off early. When the leaves mature and begin to die back in summer (they have a genetic tendency to do this), lift the tubers and let them dry in a cool place until the old dry leaves can be pulled off easily. Then store them in ventilated containers (old stockings or mesh bags are good) in a warm, but not hot, place until the soil warms up in spring.

There is a group of caladium varieties called strap-leafed; their leaves are lanceolate rather than heart-shaped. These have thicker leaves and are better suited for open sun. Those with heart-shaped leaves do better in partial shade (even though they are grown under full sun in south Florida).

Several kinds of irises are well adapted to the humid South; one group originated in Louisiana. The bulbous irises are called Dutch iris. The parent species are native to Spain and northern Africa; it seems that everything the Dutch grow is called Dutch. Some selections of Dutch irises will establish and persist in our climate, but many are no happier here than are tulips.

Louisiana irises have a color range surpassing that of other groups. Hobbyist breeders have improved the form and colors far beyond those you see in our swamps. These are very tough plants with relatively few problems and will grow despite poor soil drainage that would kill many bulbous plants. This does not mean that they require poor drainage; like most plants they respond to care. They grow well in partial shade but need full sun to bloom. The bloom period is from early spring into early summer. After several seasons of growth the rhizomes usually branch, older leaves are shed, and bare sections of the

Louisiana iris, variety "Colorific."

rhizomes appear between newer leaves. This is a good time to dig, divide, re-plant, and share the extra rhizomes with friends.

Japanese iris also thrives in the South, producing large, relatively flat flow-ers. These vary in color and form, with some having wider floral segments than others. Like the Louisiana irises, they grow from rhizomes as well as from seed. Hobbyists have made great improvements in these also.

You will see lots of *Lycoris radiata,* the red spider lily or hurricane lily, which blooms in the fall before its leaves emerge. Other species of *Lycoris* are not as well adapted to the coastal South but will do well a bit farther north. These include yellows, flesh colors, coral shades, and in the case of *L. squami-gera* (surprise lily), pink flowers on two-foot stems in July. It seems to us that, with only a little effort, breeders could improve the climatic range of these at-tractive plants.

Narcissus can be well adapted or very picky, depending on the kind. There are many types, derived from several original species, native to mountainous regions of such places as the Caucasus. Enthusiasts have divided them into strict categories, based on floral form and habit, but not on adaptability. You frequently see clumps of yellow jonquils still growing on old home sites; the houses and people are long gone but jonquils remain. Where the land starts to rise from the coastal plain, you will find naturalized trumpet daffodils, such as the variety King Alfred. Few daffodils do well south of that line. Some varieties that do are Ice Follies, Fortune, Thalia (white), Tête-a-Tête (dwarf yellow), February Gold, and Baby Moon, which has branched flower stems with one-inch yellow flowers. Some of the old white narcissus that bloom in midwinter in the coastal South have been passed along for generations. Paper-white narcissus, often forced during winter, need no chilling period and, if they are properly handled during shipping, are almost certain to bloom the first season from dry bulbs. After bloom these may be planted into the garden and, after a year to make new leaves and initiate new flowers, can repeat for years.

A longevity and performance study done at LSU identified several small-flowered bulbs that perform well and persist in south Louisiana and in other areas of the coastal South. These include *Brodiaea laxa,* which sends up striking blue flower clusters on stems about twelve inches tall before leaves grow in late spring. *Scilla campanulata,* sometimes called Canterbury bells, produces stems about a foot tall with clusters of one-inch, nodding, bell-like flowers. They can be blue, white, or pink.

Triteleia uniflora sends up leaves in early winter, then one-inch star-shaped flowers on six-inch stems in early spring. These increase from offsets as well as seeds, and may invade the lawn near beds where they grow. Most people find this desirable, especially as it is too early to mow the grass. Later on, just mow over them.

One invader that can be troublesome is star-of-Bethlehem *(Ornithogalum umbellatum).* This grows about eight inches tall, with leaves emerging in early winter, and flowers in spring with clusters of white blooms with dark centers. Charming as they are, they produce huge numbers of offsets that spread throughout the bed, defying efforts to remove them.

Rain lilies, species of *Habranthus* and *Zephyranthes,* can border beds without becoming a nuisance. These got the common name from their habit of responding to rains, especially after dry spells, with a profusion of flowers. Some bloom as early as April in the humid South—some as late as September. Most are native to Mexico or to Central or South America—a few are native to the Gulf crescent from south Florida through coastal Texas. Severe cold limits the range of most. Flowers are usually from one to three inches across, lilylike on stems up to eighteen inches tall. Colors range from white and yellow through rose and pink; apricots and pure reds are known.

Cannas used to be more popular back in the old days when most of us lived in the country—cannas take up a lot of space. There is a *leaf roller* insect that turns up wherever cannas are grown. This little critter presents a constant challenge to anyone who tries to keep canna foliage looking good.

Callas are old-fashioned plants that have been dramatically improved by breeders in recent years. We grew up thinking of calla lilies as the tall, white *Zantedeschia aethiopica* with three-foot stems. We also thought of them as plants for funerals, but the newer forms and species, especially *Z. elliotiana* (yellow) and *Z. rehmannii* (red), have some really "hot" colors and smaller plants—they would look out of place at a funeral. You can now choose from colors such as coral, pink, burgundy, or yellow—some with attractive white-spotted leaves. All of these will be damaged by hard freezes, but mulching will protect them into the mid-twenties, or they can be lifted and stored over colder periods.

We almost forgot to mention *Leucojum aestivum*—the snowflake. This small spring-flowering bulb can substitute for lily-of-the-valley *(Convallaria)*, which does not do well in hot weather. Snowflake makes stems about a foot tall with clusters of nodding, bell-like blooms, which are white with a distinctive green dot at the ends of the floral segments.

We have not mentioned lots of others, but remember that we began the chapter with an estimate of three thousand bulbous species. Look around at other gardens to see what succeeds if you are just starting out with bulbs.

Chapter 6

ANNUALS AND HERBACEOUS PERENNIALS

If looking at bulb catalogs gives you feelings of inadequacy, turning to the seed catalogs may make things worse. It seems as if every year the professional photographers surpass themselves in presenting amazing specimens with colors that are beyond anything you will ever be able to achieve. But, occasionally, you really do succeed in matching the picture: for a few days with a few blooms. Do not be discouraged by the failures and partial successes; remember that photographers do not go into the field or greenhouse and randomly pick a plant or flower to photograph. They care enough to select only the very best. Seed companies have good merchandising programs, but they produce a good product and, in the long run, it is to their advantage for gardeners to be successful. Read the instructions on the package. The plant breeders continue to make advances, and the fruits of their efforts show up in the ever-more-beautiful offerings. A few years back we saw an article in a bedding plant magazine that suggested (but not seriously) that breeders should incorporate a gene into pansies that would cause them to self-destruct after one month. Pansy varieties have been improved to such a degree that they last too long in spring, and there is no room in the bed for plants that used to "come in" after pansies.

How to Select Bedding Plants

Where can one find advice on which of the huge number of ornamental bedding plants will perform satisfactorily in a given area? Can one rely on seed and plant catalogs, or articles in home and garden magazines, or in garden books? Often these sources are pertinent to areas far different from ours. We could all benefit from results of trials conducted close to our gardens or in areas with similar environments. We (Leon and Ed) are happy to have seen a few more testing programs started in the South over our working careers.

Your local county agent's office is a good place to start. Ask the staff there to provide you with any recommendations they have and ask if they can obtain results of testing programs from areas similar in climate to yours. Often the horticulturists at the land grant university in your state will make lists of publications available to the public.

Newspaper articles on gardening often have little value outside of limited areas and, unfortunately, many magazine articles are just as restricted. Ask your garden center manager to provide information about bedding plant performance.

The Economics of Buying Plants versus Growing Them from Seed

There was a time, not many years ago, when Ed told students that they might want to consider the commercial production of bedding plants, but only as a sideline. Ed was wrong—over the past few years the bedding plant industry has mushroomed beyond anything he imagined. One reason for the growth is related to the introduction of plastic products: flats, packs, pots, labels, etc. Equipment that automates the seeding and growth of small plants in individual cells of plastic flats is mind-boggling. The small plant, with its root system and growing medium, is referred to as a *plug*. Some companies specialize in the production of plugs for only one plant species. For example, they may be in the pansy plug industry. They have their own seeding mix and a machine that plants only one pansy seed per cell. Conveyor belts move the flats into a germinating room, with the correct temperature and humidity. After a programmed time period the flats are moved into a growing room and then into the hardening room. The plants are then just the right height to allow the flats to be stacked and moved onto trucks that haul them to the garden center, untouched by human hands. The bedding plant business is very competitive; if the garden center offers varieties that you like, you cannot possibly save money by growing your own plants.

Now that we have paid homage to an efficient industry, it is time to add a bit of caution. The garden center often has very small bedding plants that are already blooming. This is a good sales gimmick in that you can see what kind of flowers you are buying. But ask yourself, why are such small plants blooming? In most cases, this is because they have been treated with a growth retardant that made them bloom early. After you put those cute little plants in a bed they will remain stunted for a long time—and may even stop blooming.

As a general rule, you are better off buying small *green* plants: those with no buds or blooms. If you want to know what the blooms will be, look at the label or color photos.

Maybe we can soften our criticism a little. Some people buy plants to get instant color. If you have been to Walt Disney World, you were probably impressed that all of their plants look great and are at the peak of blooming. They have a nighttime crew that pulls out the old plants and replaces them with new color.

Granted that buying small plants at the garden center is simple and inexpensive; but they may not have the plants you want, or you may simply enjoy growing your plants from seed. The challenge of trying something new is important to gardening. We can offer useful tips and a few cautions. Some plants are extremely hard to grow from seed. Be prepared for occasional disappointments—even Ed has failed, more than occasionally. Sometimes the seeds you purchase have been stored too long or under poor conditions. Those used by commercial growers are vigorous and are often preconditioned for rapid 100 percent germination. There is a big difference between viable and vigorous. The seeds you bought are probably viable and might show a 90 percent germination rate, if they are tested under ideal conditions. Seeds with high vigor will germinate more uniformly and under a much wider range of conditions. Because there is no commonly accepted rating system for vigor, you should assume the worst when dealing with small seeds. (Large-seeded varieties usually retain their vigor much longer than the small kinds.) Read the planting instructions carefully. Seeds of different species (or even different varieties) can vary substantially in germination requirements. Many of the major seed companies include detailed handling instructions in the catalogs. Studying the instructions will give you better insight regarding the needs and range of adaptability of the plants you want to grow. Germination of small seeds (even those with high vigor) is strongly affected by soil temperature, light exposure, and time.

Even under optimum conditions, some seeds take a long time to germinate. Do not give up and quit watering regularly; that will only make things worse. The temperatures for best results will be given on the package, which also should tell whether the seeds must be kept in light and or in the dark. Most small seeds require some light but the amount usually is not critical.

There are situations in which the best germination conditions may not be

Table 1. Best Temperatures for Germination

Temperature	Plant
85°F	Torenia
80°F	Ageratum, amaranthus, aster, balsam, basil, browallia, celosia, cineraria, coreopsis, cosmos, dahlia, exacum, fuchsia, gaillardia, gerbera, gomphrena, helichrysum, heliotrope, heuchera, hibiscus, kalanchoe, lantana, lavandula, lobelia, marigold, nierembergia, petunia, poppy (oriental), pyrethrum, rudbeckia, salpiglossis, salvia farinacea, sanvitalia, scabiosa, solanum, stocks, thunbergia, tritoma, vinca, zinnia
70°F	Alyssum, arabis, aquilegia, begonia, calceolaria, calendula, candytuft, carnation, centaurea, chrysanthemum (annual), coleus, cynoglossum, daisy (shasta), dianthus, digitalis, cineraria, euphorbia, geranium, gloxinia, gypsophila, hypoestes, impatiens, kochia, matricaria, nasturtium, nicotiana, pepper (capsicum), poppy (oriental), portulaca, primula, salvia splendens, statice, verbena
60°F	Dimorphotheca, doronicum, centaurea (dusty miller), flowering cabbage and kale, geum, hollyhock, lunaria, nemesia, phlox, schizanthus, snapdragon, viola
55°F [A]	Delphinium, larkspur, lupine, myosotis, sweet pea
Alternating warm days (80°F) and cool nights (60°F)	Bells of Ireland, cleome, liatris
Improved germination in light	Aquilegia, basil, begonia, browallia, calceolaria, coleus, daisy (shasta), digitalis, cineraria (dusty miller), exacum, flowering cabbage and kale, fuchsia, gloxinia, heuchera, hibiscus, impatiens, kalanchoe, lavandula, liatris, lobelia, matricaria, nicotiana, pepper (capsicum), petunia, primula, salvia farinacea, salvia splendens, snapdragon, solanum, stock
Improved germination in darkness [B]	Cynoglossum, centaurea (dusty miller), gomphrena, larkspur, myosotis, nasturtium, nemesia, pansy, poppy (Iceland), salpiglossis, schizanthus, statice, sweet pea, vinca, and viola

Note: Some seeds with cool germinating temperature requirements may be helped by chilling in the refrigerator for about a week, then planting immediately on removal. In this group are such plants as carnation, cleome, delphinium, larkspur, pansy, and snapdragon. For seeds with temperatures above 60°F, avoid the use of cold water.

[A] Several days at high temperature kills seeds.
[B] Cover seeds to a depth perhaps twice that of the seed size. Putting the entire seed flat in the dark may result in forgetting to check frequently so that the plants can be moved to light as soon as germination occurs, resulting in rapid stretching of the seedlings.

good for growth of young seedlings. For some seeds germination occurs most rapidly under fairly low light intensity, which means that you must shade the seed flat. After the seeds have germinated, the young seedlings must be moved to higher light intensity to prevent *stretching*. If you are not watching the flats carefully, the seedlings can quickly develop into tall, spindly plants that take weeks to recover.

Until now we have been assuming that you purchased seeds from a catalog. A more common situation is that you have collected seed pods from a friend's garden and there are no package instructions. See table 1 for optimum temperatures for various annual seeds and the light conditions that are most effective; see table 2 for the approximate times for them to germinate. Try to look on these as guides rather than absolutes. Commercial producers follow them more rigorously than you will, but that is because their livelihood depends on getting the seedlings up and growing—uniformly. If you come pretty close, the seeds will germinate, maybe a little more slowly. Our calendar (see the appendix) suggests planting times for various annuals throughout the year. These are necessarily generalized because they are based on optimum germination temperatures—and nobody can predict our climatic conditions with

Table 2. Seed Germination Times (at Proper Temperatures)

Germination Time	Seed Type
One week or less	Ageratum, alyssum, aster, balsam, basil, browallia, calendula, celosia, centaurea, cleome, cosmos, dahlia, dianthus, flowering cabbage and kale, gerbera, geranium, helichrysum, marigold, nasturtium, nemesia, pepper (capsicum), petunia, poppy (oriental), portulaca, rudbeckia, salvia farinacea, sanvitalia, snapdragon, stock, torenia, zinnia
Up to two weeks	Amaranthus, arabis, annual chrysanthemum, coleus, cineraria (dusty miller), euphorbia, exacum, gomphrena, gypsophila (annual), hollyhock, hypoestes, impatiens, kalanchoe, lobelia, lunaria, matricaria, myosotis, nicotiana, pepper (solanum), phlox (annual), scabiosa (annual), schizanthus, statice, sweet pea, verbena
Up to three weeks	Calceolaria, cineraria, coreopsis, daisy (shasta), gaillardia, heliotrope, heuchera, kochia, larkspur, nierembergia, pansy, pyrethrum, salpiglossis, salvia splendens, thunbergia, tritoma, vinca, viola
More than three weeks	Aquilegia, begonia, bells of Ireland, fuchsia, geum, gloxinia, hibiscus, lantana, lavender, liatris, lupine, primula

great accuracy. For example, plants needing several weeks at temperatures below 60°F can be exposed to such outdoor conditions only in spring or in early winter. On the other hand, if they germinate too early they will be killed by a late freeze. Some seeds need several weeks of warm soil temperatures. For example, torenia seedlings never show up as volunteers until midsummer; they need soil temperatures around 86°F for about a week.

Seeds of most annuals germinate well in loose, well-drained soil. If they are small seeds, it might be a good idea to sieve the soil so that the small particles will have good contact with the seeds. The soil should be free of disease organisms. An easy way to assure this for a small amount of soil is to put it in shallow pans so that you can heat it in the oven to about 180°F, for about half an hour. Be careful not to overdo this with higher temperatures or longer time periods. This can cause serious soil nutrient problems—which we will discuss later.

Leon: Ed, I have sat quietly while you pontificated about grow-your-own seedlings, which are dirt cheap at the garden center. I must, however, rise in protest about your idea of do-it-yourself seeding mix. Who is going to sieve soil and bake it for thirty minutes at 180°?

Ed: Folks, Leon's attitude shows that he has never lost an entire planting of pansy seedlings because the commercial seeding mix was just a bit too salty—maybe had a little too much starter fertilizer. It is safer to use sieved, heat-treated soil with sensitive seedlings because the soil will have enough nutrient salts for the seedlings to grow—at least for a while. Because soil is better buffered than the synthetic mixes, those salts will not hurt delicate seedlings.

The special seeding mixes that you find at the garden center are pretty good, for general use. The problem is that they tend to be a little too general. The principle is that, after a seed germinates, the seedling will need a little starter fertilizer to get it up and running. The key here is to have a little starter but not too much. Small seedlings often are sensitive to salt concentrations; if the delicate roots are killed the plant will die. Why do the companies sell mixtures that are too hot for the seedlings? To some extent the answer is that the mix has enough starter fertilizer for most seedlings but not for the salt-sensitive ones. But quality control is often very sloppy. Back when Ed was teaching students about using the commercial mixes he began measuring the salt content of various brands over a period of years. The results were amazing; with some of the well-known brands, salt levels varied substantially from batch to batch. The differences were not enough to damage seedlings from larger seeds but were occasionally disastrous for a small-seeded species. If you plan to use garden center mixes, it is best to assume they added too much fertilizer for sensitive seedlings. Leach the mix thoroughly and repeatedly with water, then let it drain and dry out. Now you know that the mix has essentially no starter fertilizer. Sow the seeds and watch for germination. Then apply a very dilute soluble fertilizer to the seedlings, about a teaspoon of soluble 13-13-13 in a gallon of water. This is because very small seeds have almost no nutrient reserves to get them going; they need to be fertilized quickly.

The new kinds of seeding flats can make seedling production much easier. You can get flats that have plastic liners providing about ten small furrows per flat; this allows you to sow tiny seeds in separated rows. Besides being more orderly, this system isolates the effects of disease organisms (called damping-off), which might get started in one spot. You may want to use flats that have clear plastic covers that fit snugly over the top, providing the high humidity that promotes rapid germination. When using plastic covers, be very careful about leaving the flats in a spot that might get direct sunlight; the temperature can rise very quickly, killing all of the seedlings. If you do not have a shady spot, you can make one with something as simple as a layer of newspaper placed over the flat. As soon as the seeds germinate, lift the cover to reduce the humidity, then increase the light intensity. You do not want spindly plants.

There have been many other helpful innovations in recent years that make seed growing more fun and easier. If you have not tried it, or have not tried it for some years, look around the retail outlets or browse through the growers' supply catalogs—your garden center should have copies to lend to you—and see what is now available. Growing your own plants is something of an adventure: try it, you might like it.

You may want to plant annual seeds directly into the garden where they are to grow. The larger-seeded kinds will usually do well in the open but, with smaller seeds, rain can dislodge or bury them too deeply (remember that most small seeds require light for germination) or the rain might cause the soil surface to crust over. With direct seeding, there is a greater hazard of soil-borne diseases that damp-off the young seedlings. Besides the disease problems, you also will find that many small creatures enjoy eating young seedlings.

Ed's Suggestions for Annuals You Might Like

Recommendations prepared by extension horticulturists for southern conditions list about fifty kinds of annuals—combining that with the numbers of varieties for some of them, you will find that the range of size, form, color, site adaptability, and season is large. Most of the annuals listed are best adapted to sunny locations, but there are a good many that will succeed in open shade, such as occurs under tall trees. The group that will succeed in shade includes impatiens, begonia, coleus, alyssum, arabis, balsam, dianthus, lobelia, and pansy. This is not a very long list, but it gets much longer when you consider that many varieties are available for each species. Impatiens varieties are probably the hottest item on the list for the past several years. The New Guinea impatiens, found by plant explorers a few years ago, has a wide range of varieties; some of them have attractively colored foliage. The impatiens are available in various heights, from only six or eight inches to several feet tall under good conditions. Impatiens will reseed and you may find them invading other beds. Essentially, those invaders are weeds but they are not difficult to control.

Coleus plants will do well in shade or sun—the leaves will be thicker in the sun and the colors will be different. Seed-grown coleus will produce a wide variety of colors, with different tendencies to flower. Some of these plants will *bolt:* that is, they will flower early in the season. Cull them out, because coleus leaves are attractive but the flowers are sad looking. The same lot of seeds that produced bolting plants will have some that continue to have attractive leaves until the first frost. Make cuttings of these plants and pot them up. When freezes are predicted, bring them indoors. In the spring your plants can be increased by cuttings.

Begonias can be grown in sun or shade; plants started in the shade will be set back and leaves may scorch if moved to direct sun.

Petunias are probably the most popular bedding plant annual in the country as a whole. Down South, they are good early spring plants, but you should not expect them to last as long as they will farther north. There are several reasons for this, all related to weather. The soil-borne fungus, *Phytophthora*, attacks petunias and rots them off near the ground line; we have problems with this fungus almost year-round. Most petunias are susceptible to damage by rain, and our rainfall frequency almost ensures that you will run into trouble. During the short days of early spring, petunias tend to stay compact and produce side branches. With our mild springs you are able to set petunias out much earlier than would be possible farther north. The best advice is to plant petunias early and remove them when they start dying; sprays and protection from rain are not worth the effort.

Marigolds offer a wide diversity of types, flower form, size, color, plant height, and shape. Some are excellent for dwarf borders, others get tall enough for background plantings in beds, and some are in between. There was a time when breeders placed heavy emphasis on producing larger, double flowers. One company held a contest, encouraging amateur breeders to produce a white marigold. Later, there were efforts made toward deodorizing marigolds. The current interest seems to focus on single-flowered marigolds, whether they have a bad odor or not. Some marigolds are sensitive to day length; if these are set out in early spring or late fall the plants will bloom while they are very short. The same variety, set out in the longer days of summer, will make large plants before blooming. On the other hand, some varieties are insensitive to day length. Seed catalogs usually have information concerning adaptability of the various kinds of marigolds they offer for sale.

Geraniums are very popular in the Northeast; in the West they will grow like weeds on dry hillsides. Down here, they die in hot weather. However, breeders have been producing some new types that do better in our climate. You might want to have a go at these. Many colors are available, along with plant form differences. You can get seeds for a few full-double types—the sort that you could only get from cuttings a few years back. Geraniums suffer from the same sorts of problems as do the petunias. Plant them in early spring beds or in containers that you can put under overhanging eaves for rain protection.

For plants that perform well with little care, I would include ageratum, antirrhinum (snapdragons), cosmos, dahlia, dianthus (pinks), hypoestes, nierembergia, petunia (multiflora types), portulaca, rudbeckia, salvia, *Tagetes* (marigolds), verbena, vinca, and zinnia (with seed treatment). Within these kinds are many varieties, affording a sizeable menu for selection.

Herbaceous Perennials

This chapter is supposed to be about annuals, but terminology as to annuals and perennials is sloppy. *Annual* means that the plant grows as an annual in this specific climate, usually. Perennial means that it grows or can be grown as a perennial in the area, except when we have unusual weather conditions. When we put this problem to the coffee-table authorities, one wag said that he grows citrus as an annual: He buys new plants every spring and they are killed the following winter.

There are only a few kinds of plants that are true annuals. Corn is the classic example: it flowers, produces grain, and dies. This is programmed genetically, and there is nothing you can do to make it live longer. Petunias will continue to grow and flower for years if the plants are not exposed to temperatures that are too hot or too cold. Then there are some plants that are neither annuals nor perennials. Biennials are plants that grow vegetatively the first year, flower in the second year, and die. Hollyhocks are supposed to be biennials, but our growing season is so long that they are frequently annuals. Classifications are convenient but you should not accept them as absolutes.

If you start reading about the culture of herbaceous perennials, you will see many comments such "requires good drainage in winter"; "wet soils, especially in winter, are fatal"; "the North American midsummer sun is detrimental"; or "it is unable to survive in a wet soil during winter." Down here we are going to have wet soil in winter and hot sun in summer. Many (perhaps most) herbaceous perennials are described as being *hardy*; well, maybe so, but not in the humid South. Many of them are hardy within a narrow habitat range. A typical English garden includes many herbaceous perennials, but this is because the climate is mild—neither too hot nor too cold. Do not try to duplicate an English garden.

But neither can English gardeners duplicate our gardens. We have some herbaceous perennials that survive long enough to be called truly perennial, and a few that are so well adapted that they need very little care. The survival of perennials usually depends on site preparation. Herbaceous perennials will do much better in raised beds; in fact, many of them will survive only in raised beds.

When growing perennials in the South you must also consider cold injury. Because the hot summers reduce the range of temperate zone plants available to us, we tend to choose more tropical plants. Hibiscus is a good example of a plant beautifully adapted to our conditions—except for cold tolerance. Acalypha, the copper plant, is another that, like hibiscus, must be *carried over* in a protected place during the damaging cold spells. Some gardeners try to keep the large plants alive by moving them inside a building during the several freezes of our average winter. This is a masochist approach; it is easier to root cuttings during the fall and hold those small plants through the winter. Rooted cuttings of most tropical plants will grow rapidly during the warm spring and act as mature plants by summer. Getting tropical plants through the winter is a hassle, but they do help to provide a changing landscape. Try to look on tropicals as our compensation for not having the seasonal changes common to the upper United States.

Here are some choices for dependable herbaceous perennials: hemerocallis (daylily), Shasta daisy, perennial phlox, Louisiana iris, German iris, Japanese iris, canna, calla, hibiscus, acalypha, hedychium (butterfly lily), curcuma (hidden lily), hosta, tritoma, liriope, verbena, and mints of various kinds.

Most perennials may be propagated by division or by cuttings to ensure keeping the same kinds. Many are propagated easily by seeds. The main problem with using seeds is that you may get a wide diversity of seedlings, including some that are unkempt. Other species produce plants that are uniformly similar to the parent plant.

Many zinnias now suffer from seed-borne diseases caused by a bacterium and a couple of fungi. Try soaking seeds in a solution of one part bleach and four parts water, air-dry, and plant. If you dust the dry seeds with a fungicide before planting you can reduce the danger of damping-off caused by soil-borne fungi.

Chapter 7

WHAT ABOUT TREES?

This chapter was originally called "Choosing Your Trees." We were not comfortable with that because you may not actually have a choice of trees. For instance, if you move into a house with existing trees, that is what you have. Or you might build on a site that was cleared of thick forest growth. In that case it would seem that you could simply decide which trees to cut out and leave the rest. But after doing so you will realize that the remaining trees are tall and produce very little shade; even if you have the tops cut out, they will never become good shade trees. Or, your new subdivision may be in what was once a pecan orchard, with large trees in orderly rows. These are good shade trees, but straight rows do not make for good landscaping. If your lot has no trees at all, you will be choosing the kinds of trees to plant, what size to buy, and whether to buy bare-root, balled and burlap-wrapped trees, or trees growing in containers.

We hope this chapter will tell you more than how to choose the best tree for your home. On the other hand, we cannot tell you all about trees; that would require an entire book unto itself, even if we knew that much. We can tell you a lot about when and how to transplant trees, common problems with the more popular trees, and we can offer suggestions for helping your trees live long and happy lives.

We will share some thoughts on the characteristics of common landscaping trees, but that will not cover every tree that you might want to consider. The LSU Cooperative Extension Service has published a fine bulletin, *Trees for Louisiana Landscapes: A Handbook*. It is a good reference on the ultimate size, shape, and other important characteristics of more than 100 kinds of trees. In New Orleans the Metropolitan Horticultural Advisory Committee of the LSU Extension Service has gone a step further and rated some of those trees according to their performance in New Orleans. We hope other cities will follow their example. The Advisory Committee for New Orleans is a group of horticulturists, landscape architects, and nursery managers who share their experiences. Another good source of information is *Plants for Designers: A Handbook for Plants of the South* by LSU landscape architects Neil Odenwald and James Turner. It is a comprehensive book, covering trees, shrubs, and bedding plants.

So, let us begin. When we discuss characteristics of the various trees you may notice that we tend to stress the bad aspects of a species more than the advantages. Sorry about that. Our logic is that, because every kind of tree has some drawbacks, we can best serve you by pointing them out before you have bought a tree, planted it, and waited while it grows large enough to become a problem.

On the other hand, we do not want to accentuate the negative; we need to begin with emphasizing why homes in the Deep South need trees—in spite of the problems. Trees are extremely valuable to a home environment. The cooling protection of a shade tree in July is wonderful. Trees can reduce the utility bills for cooling in summer, and deciduous trees drop their leaves in the winter and allow the sun to warm the house. Trees can filter dust and noise and serve as windbreaks (evergreen trees in the proper location can help to reduce that winter heating bill as much as the use of deciduous trees in other locations). Trees also increase the value and sales appeal of houses if you make sound choices about the kind and placement of trees.

But trees are more than utility bills and real estate sales value. The sound of a breeze blowing through pine needles is more relaxing than a tranquilizer. Trees are for kids to hang an old tire swing under. They are for the dignity of towering oaks and the patterns that moonlight traces through the leaves. The spiritual value of trees is beyond description; it more than balances out the trivial problems we will describe.

Street Trees

Street trees, those planted along the front of the lot to form a tree-shaded street, can cause angry outbursts after the tree-trimming companies go through to clear around the utility wires. The companies often call themselves tree experts; they are butchers, dedicated to clearing the wires in the shortest period of time without actually killing the trees. There is a better way to trim around utility lines, but it would require studying each situation, which would make the process more expensive.

We have always hated tree butchers and are too old to change. But we will admit to some minor efforts being made at improvement. Most cities have begun to require certification courses for butchers. They are learning better ways of trimming: We have not seen evidence that they are practicing what is being taught, but maybe that will come with time.

The front of your lot may have a designated right-of-way, which means that the utility company can do pretty much as it wishes. If you are choosing trees to go under utility lines, consider those that remain rather small: the utility people (usually) do not butcher small trees. Another reason for using small trees in an area close to the street is based on the restricted root systems resulting from having much of the area paved. When Ed moved to Ithaca, N.Y., for graduate school he was impressed by the huge elm trees located between the streets and sidewalks. A few years later western New York suffered through the first hurricane that anyone could remember. Most of those big elms had roots only in the area between the street and the sidewalk. Hurricane force winds cut them down, and the trees sliced through nearby buildings like giant knife blades. Here in the Gulf South we have more frequent exposure to storm winds. We know what will happen if the trees do not have room for strong root systems.

Choosing Which Tree Stays, Which Goes

If you are building on a heavily wooded site, the choice of which trees to remove can be difficult. Trees that have been too crowded will be tall and will not have any lateral branches until quite high up the trunk. This competition for light is paralleled by the root competition, so the trees may not be well-anchored either. When the surrounding trees are cut out, the remaining tall spindly trees are vulnerable to winds, especially hurricanes. It may be a painful decision, but you should at least consider replacing all of them with smaller trees that will have a better chance to develop in a more open environment. You may be tempted to simply *top* the tall trees. They will never develop the spreading habit that you hope for; remember that if the limbs are not spreading, neither are the roots.

The Life Span of Trees

All county agents have stories of being called out to look at a tree that is dying. "Why is my fine old tree dying, and what can I do about it?" Trees die for many reasons, but if the fine old tree really is old, that is probably why it is dying. The life cycle of a tree is that it grows, matures, and dies. Trees such as redbud, dogwood, and tallow are typically short-lived. If your tree is in good soil and getting loving care, it will live longer than others; but it will eventually die from being short-lived. Live oak, pecan, most pines, and sweet gum are long-lived; if one of them is dying, something is probably wrong. Another possibility is that the tree might simply be dropping its leaves. New residents in the South sometimes get upset at seeing the fall of large, leathery leaves from the beautiful magnolia tree or the drop of live oak leaves or pine tree needles. Evergreen trees are not really evergreen. They drop leaves on a seasonal schedule even though they do not remain bare for very long.

Choosing Trees for Your Property

Trees vary not only in their ultimate size, but in their shape—some are upright and narrow, some conical, some spreading; these are important distinctions to consider. Trees also vary in the overall leaf color, shape, and size. The bark of some trees is quite attractive and may be used for winter accents in the landscape plan.

Spring bloom is another feature for consideration. Many of the standard spring bloomers of farther north do not grow well here. We get good blooms from swamp maple; several hawthorns; some pears; some crab apples (the spectacular flowering crabs do not grow well in the southern Gulf Coast states); silverbell; dogwood; smoke tree; fringe tree; and redbud. The golden rain tree can be beautiful but is occasionally hurt by cold. Look around your neighborhood to see what is blooming in spring. The "Japanese" magnolia (*M. soulangeana*) makes a brilliant display in spring, and the Taiwan cherry has become very popular for its spring bloom in recent years.

You will notice that we used the botanical name for the Japanese magnolia. We are opposed to pomposity, but occasionally the botanical name is important. A plant may be known by several common names, plus a horticultural name, and a botanical name. Of the three, the botanical name is the most precise. Common names can vary from place to place even in the same language, and when you try to discuss plants with someone from another country, common names cause even more confusion. Horticultural names are mostly cultivar names. The term *cultivar* is fairly recent, and we still have problems about using it. In the old days we spoke of varieties, but taxonomists were also using that word with a different meaning: describing variants in native plants. Horticulture fell back to the term *cultivar,* which means "cultivated variety." Botanical names are typically binomials; that is, they consist of two names, genus and species. Some botanical names will follow the species with subspecies, and occasionally with a variety term. From a practical viewpoint, there is no real difference between the terms *variety* and *cultivar;* it is just a technical device to keep taxonomists happy. Having said all of that, we are not going to use the term *cultivar* anymore; we speak of varieties because that is the way we learned it. You will notice that garden center people speak of varieties instead of cultivars; we will use botanical variety only when it is absolutely necessary.

Having gone through terminology, we are back to the Japanese magnolia *M. soulangeana.* It is also called oriental magnolia, but there are several other oriental magnolias. Actually, the Japanese magnolia originated in France. A man named Soulange had collected specimens of *M. liliflora* and *M. denudata,* from China and Japan. These hybridized in his garden, and he planted the seeds and got a new plant that he modestly named after himself. In the above paragraph, we avoided the common name problem by saying *M. soulangeana.*

Sometimes the species part of the botanical name is descriptive. The *Magnolia grandiflora* is a large-flowered magnolia, but the botanical name is used so often that it is also accepted as a common name. If someone is using *Magnolia grandiflora* as a common name, it will not be italicized.

Moving on from spring color to fall color, in the Deep South we cannot come close to the display seen farther north. In some (most) years our tree leaves go from green, to dirty brown, to dead. Occasionally, if the weather is right, some trees can be spectacular. The sweet gum and tallow can have brilliant leaves, especially in a dry fall. Why dry weather? Primarily because frequent rains in the late summer and early fall promote leaf diseases on sweet gum, prompting the leaves to drop off before any color can develop. Some oaks and hybrid pears are good fall color candidates, in a dry cool fall. Dogwoods can be brightly colored in some falls. And although the crape myrtle is grown for its summer bloom, it occasionally produces vivid fall color.

Trees, like children, are wonderful to have around the house, but even the best of them are sometimes a nuisance. Trees drop things, either twigs, leaves, fruits, or all of them at once. Squirrels live in trees and are continually cutting things off. In the cities, where squirrels are protected from hunters and hawks, they are fat, sassy, and a frustrating fact of life. When we discuss fruit in chapter 8, we deal with squirrel depredations and offer some suggestions about lessening them. We realize that squirrels bring up nice images of the beauty of nature and saving nuts for the winter, but we also wonder if it might be possible to start calling them tree rats.

A range of diseases and insects attack trees. Most trees eventually grow beyond the reach of home garden spray equipment, so it is good to know ahead of time whether a tree will need regular spraying to keep it from becoming unsightly. You can contract to have trees sprayed, but it might be better to choose a more hardy type.

Trees can cause serious problems for plants that grow under or even near them. The combination of shade and water stress may affect lawn grasses so badly that you will have to substitute ground covers. Contrary to what you read in some books, tree roots usually extend well beyond the drip line and can take water as well as nutrients from plants growing in raised beds, even those far away from the drip line. If the arable soil is shallow because of a hardpan, tree roots can bulge above ground; this makes the mowing process exciting. In shallow soil, tree roots can lift up driveways and sidewalks (the hydraulic pressure generated by a root is impressive). Some tree roots grow under house foundations and cause them to crack. In New Orleans, trees can pull so much water from the ground that the soil will subside from around the house foundation. In extreme cases buildings have almost collapsed. The solution to these problems seems to lie with root barriers. Some progress is being made with reliable barriers but, for the present, you should remember that tree roots will grow where they can get water and nutrients; they do not care whether the water was intended for them or for your flower bed. When Leon taught a class on plant growth responses he used the idea of hydrotropism (roots being attracted to water) to illustrate an apparent response that does not exist. Technically, there is no such thing as hydrotropism, but tree roots do seem to grow straight toward water and nutrients in flower beds. In Ed's yard they grow up through the drainage holes of flower pots left on the ground to the extent that the pots are firmly attached masses of tree roots.

PROTECTING EXISTING TREES

When trees are already growing on your potential home site, once a choice is made about which (if any) trees to keep, protecting them from damage during house construction is important. Even small injuries to the trunk can have major effects on tree survival. Keep in mind that a thin sheath of tissues beneath the bark, surrounding the trunk and branches like a skin, is the actual living, growing part of the tree's framework. This sheath creates the parts of the trunk and branches that do the work of transporting water and nutrients up from the roots and food materials from the leaves to the roots and other parts. If the trunk is injured, this transport is partly interrupted until new tissues can grow over the injury.

Sometimes a barrier can be built to keep trucks, concrete mixers, and so forth away from tree trunks. Of course, a determined truck driver can damage both the barrier and the tree, so it may be a good idea to convince the overall general contractor that your trees have real value (in real money) and illustrate that with an example. The contractor needs to understand that damage to the trees could reduce his profit from the job. It probably would surprise most people to learn of the values that have been placed on trees and upheld by courts.

Tree values in landscapes are far more than they would be for comparable trees in wood lots or forest situations. There are guidelines for establishing monetary values of trees and recognized authorities for making the estimates of value. A county agent or your state forestry office can supply the names of such authorities who are recognized by the courts. Several years ago in New Orleans a homeowner had damaged five live oak trees growing as street trees (on the right-of-way), and the city brought damage claims in court. The value was approximately $10,000 per tree. Because this was long ago, the figure would be higher now, but $10,000 is enough to get the attention of almost anyone. If you can use such an argument to persuade the contractor that your trees should be protected, this is progress.

You may face a situation in which soil must be removed or added to a low spot where a tree is growing: this can be tricky. Adding or removing more than about two inches of soil under the tree, the area where most of the active roots are growing, can kill the tree. It will go into a slow decline and take a year or more to die. You might even forget that soil had been added or removed and start wondering why the fine shade tree died just when you started taking care of it. We would like to be more specific on how much soil you can add around a tree but it varies with the species, soil type, and drainage patterns. If you must add soil be very careful, adding about one inch per year. This will allow roots to occupy the new soil layer before more is added.

Removal of soil from around a tree can be dangerous. This is a common problem when you need to put a sidewalk or driveway close to a tree. The best compromise is to build a masonry or wooden wall to hold soil close to the remaining roots. After four or five years the root system will have adjusted and the wall can be removed. If you must remove a lot of soil, the tree may have to go. It is not a good idea to simply leave the tree there until it dies; tree cutting people do not like to take chances with their lives by climbing a rotten tree.

We discuss fruit trees in detail later (see chapter 8), but in some cases a fruit tree may also be used for its landscape value. You should consider a location that will afford easy access for the needed pruning, spraying, and harvesting operations.

A Word on Pruning

Most trees will require some sort of pruning, either to develop a strong framework in young trees or to repair damage from wind or other causes. In fruit trees the objective is usually to improve production. After a tree reaches a height that cannot be safely reached from a short ladder, you should probably leave pruning to professional tree people. We wince at the term *tree expert* because it reminds us of the butchers who attack trees under utility lines. But there are licensed tree workers who know how to do the job properly. We will cover pruning in chapter 8, because many of the pruning objectives that apply to fruit trees apply to shade trees as well.

Planting Trees

MOVING THE TREE

Back in the old days most gardeners knew how to ball and burlap a tree; they also knew that it was hard work and very expensive. The era of ball and burlap is over; the new tree-digging and transplanting equipment is nearly mind-boggling, but so is the cost. Maybe we should hedge there; the cost is amazing to those of us who still think in the economics of the late 1950s. But the new equipment also will dig and move large trees, the sort that we ball-and-burlappers would not even consider attempting.

However, having the right equipment is not enough—you must still know how to transplant trees. We have seen some very large trees dug, moved, planted, and allowed to die. The situation is becoming rare as the specialists begin to learn about the sorts of root systems that allow moving large specimens with some degree of success, and which trees should not be moved. Much of the root system is lost in moving large trees or shrubs. Heavy pruning of the top growth helps to compensate for the loss but may also ruin the value of the plant. The tree will go through a period of slow growth while producing new roots.

When transplanting young trees it is helpful to wrap the trunk with water-resistant paper. In the case of shrubs, you may want to spray the foliage with a water-resistant material that reduces water loss without damaging the leaves; the garden center will have this compound.

Good nurserymen use a procedure called root pruning. For about two years before a row of trees is ready to be sold they disk the field (run a tiller over the upper five or six inches of soil) frequently, about two feet from each side of the row. This causes the trees to produce more roots close to the trunk. Those trees may be smaller and more expensive than some of the same species that were grown rapidly without root pruning. Within a few years the smaller, root-pruned tree will have outgrown the bargain tree. Ask the garden center or grower about root pruning before you buy an expensive tree.

There is a current trend to grow some rather large trees in containers, partly due to the introduction of large plastic pots. These are fairly inexpensive trees that can be transplanted safely if you handle them properly. Roots of such trees usually begin to curl around in the shape of the container. Try to straighten them out, at least to some degree. If they are too large and woody, it might be best to simply cut them out so that new roots will exploit areas beyond the original *ball* of media. The potting mix used in containers is usually amended to provide rapid drainage for frequent watering and fertilization (as mentioned in our discussion of houseplants). If the mix is substantially different from the soil you are planting into, this can cause long-term problems. Unless you manage things properly, the new roots may never grow out of the old potting mix. The tree will just sit there, not growing and not dying. In most planting situations it is best to simply knock that loose mix out of the ball and plant what is essentially a bare-root tree. This is a good approach only if you plant immediately. Do not let those small roots dry out—they can die within a few minutes.

We know that you are getting tired of listening to what can go wrong. Stick with us because we have some good ideas about transplanting.

Proper Soil Condition

You can usually get away with sloppy planting methods if the soil is in good condition and well drained. Good soil produces brilliant gardeners, but poorly drained soil develops character. Assuming that you do not have good soil, it is best to dig the hole before buying the tree. This is partly because you should dig when the soil is not too dry or too wet. It is particularly important with heavier soils, which have high clay content. Digging in wet soil can destroy the structure and cause problems for up to a year. The best test is to mold some soil into a ball; if it falls apart the soil is dry enough to dig. If it remains in a ball, wait a while.

When the moisture is right, dig the hole carefully, trying not to press the shovel against the sides of the hole. This can cause compaction. After you dig the original hole, you should *dress it up* by working the edges to remove any compressed soil.

The hole should be a little larger than the extent of roots in the ball. In the dressing-up process, leave rough sides to promote root penetration. Now for the mound of loose soil that you should leave in the bottom of the hole—the hump on which you will place the ball. Grandma taught you to make this mound with organic matter—leaves or compost—but she was wrong. Such materials hold water too well, and in hot, wet weather they use up oxygen (remember our discussion on composting). Build the mound of loose soil high enough so that the tree will be at about the same level as it grew in the nursery; it should be a little higher to allow for settling. Spread the roots out and start adding loose soil carefully. Occasionally use the handle of your spade to pack soil around the roots. When the hole is about half full, add water to that level and let the soil settle. Then add loose soil and pack until the hole is full. Using the extra soil (or get more if you need it), make a berm (a narrow circular levee) around the tree and just outside of the hole area. Add water carefully and slowly. A strong stream will puddle the soil and ruin your work. Fill it to the rim of the berm, and repeat this a day later if it seems necessary. The tree will need frequent watering for a few weeks, but you should break the berm during a rainy spell; too much water is always bad.

Using Fertilizer

There is some question about whether fertilizer should be applied at planting time or later. One advantage of applying it at planting time is that you will not forget to do it later. We do not know whether it is better to put the fertilizer in the bottom of the hole or on top; both have advantages and disadvantages. Some people hedge a little by putting half in the hole and the rest on top. Another choice is between soluble fertilizer, applied in water, or dry forms. There are slow-release types and regular dry forms. People continue to try different approaches and sometimes new fads become evident for a while, but we have not seen good research evidence to support one practice over another. We do feel that the tree will benefit from fertilizer in most areas of the lower South, and that this should be applied soon after transplanting. How much to apply? Some books give detailed information on this, which is amusing in view of how little reliable information is available about fertilizing transplanted trees. With established trees the common recommendation is to apply a pound of a complete fertilizer (containing nitrogen, phosphorus, and potassium) per inch of trunk diameter. Our tree people say this should mean the diameter at about three feet up the trunk. Even this can be debated, but remember that tree roots extend far beyond the legendary drip line, and when you fertilize the lawn or garden you are fertilizing nearby trees. It may be impossible to overfertilize a large tree without killing the grass around it.

Leon: Ed, I need to have my say about fertilizing for transplanted trees. I think you should decide on a planting spot about three months before you are going to plant. Dig the hole properly, sprinkle some fertilizer in the bottom, add some more soil and sprinkle more fertilizer, continuing until the hole is full. Or, you may want to mix in some good compost instead of, or with, the fertilizer. All of this will equilibrate over three months of waiting.

Ed: When Leon interrupted, we were talking about how much fertilizer to add. He didn't mention that.

Leon: I don't have any idea about how much—just how to do it. The amount will probably depend on the soil type and the kind of tree you are going to plant. It seems logical to sprinkle the fertilizer about as you would do in making a raised bed. The actual amount shouldn't be very important if you aren't going to plant for three months anyhow; the excess will probably wash out.

WHEN TO TRANSPLANT

Transplanting time depends on the weather and type of tree. It is probably better to transplant deciduous trees when they are dormant, to reduce water loss, because the roots will be growing even though the tops are bare. Most evergreen trees go through spells of activity (flushes of growth), and should not be transplanted at those times. If you are using container-grown material, and are careful with the operation, you can transplant trees (or shrubs) at almost any time that is convenient. But remember that there are times when the plants will do better with less careful management and that the weather in some seasons is easier on the plants.

Now for a point about root competition: Grass will not grow well under large trees because of root, light, and moisture competition. If you have a small tree and want it to grow rapidly, do not make it compete with lawn grass. This is partly because of grass-root competition but there is another problem: allelopathy. We explain more about this in chapter 14 but, as a working definition, *allelopathy* refers to chemicals that act as natural herbicides. Most grasses, and many other plants, produce compounds that kill or stunt other plants. We are not suggesting that the grass around a young tree might kill it, only that it may slow the growth substantially. We know that a lawn looks much nicer if grass is allowed to grow up close to the new trees. But if you want the tree to grow rapidly, leave a bare, mulched circle around it, a foot or two wider than the extent of the planting hole.

Trees of moderate to large size will probably need staking after transplanting. Small trees can be supported adequately with a single stout stake located near the central stem; larger trees may need two or three stakes to which the trunk may be fastened with wires. Take care that the wire is padded (a piece of old garden hose works well) to avoid injuring the bark and do not make any tight fastenings that could force the new tissues to grow around them. This would girdle the stem and could kill the tree.

A Short List of Recommended Trees

One problem with listing recommended trees is that there will always be exceptions: someone will have great success with plants that usually do not grow well in an area. There will be examples of consistent failure with "recommended" plants that should grow in a particular site. These exceptions can usually be traced to green-thumb or brown-thumb factors, but sometimes the matter is just a puzzlement. Please understand that this list has shortcomings but is the best we can do. Several pages back we mentioned the rating of trees and shrubs in New Orleans through cooperation of interested gardeners. This is a valuable guide to people there and to people located in areas with similar environments. A number of the trees that we list are well suited to New Orleans, but some are not. We also have tried to list some of the strong and weak points of the various trees but have probably have missed some.

EVERGREENS

Pines

Evergreens are trees that always have green leaves, which does not mean that they do not drop leaves. Pines drop two-year-old leaves every fall; actually, they drop some during the spring and summer, too, because the new needles grow in flushes. But pine needles are not very difficult to rake.

There are six species of pine that will grow rather well here, but probably only the spruce pine and slash pine will be sold at your garden center.

Spruce pine differs from the others in holding its branches near the ground, whereas others tend to drop branches, resulting in bare, long trunks. Spruce pine also has short needles and small cones, about two inches long, that persist on the tree for years. Especially important about spruce pines is their tolerance for soils that are not well drained. Although they can get scale insects with the accompanying sooty mold, they are fairly resistant to the leaf-chewing beetles that can turn other pines brown. Another point in favor of spruce pine is that the limbs are a bit more sturdy than those of most pines. When hurricane force winds hit pine trees, limbs start breaking. Spruce pine limbs hold up a little better.

Slash pine is the standard lumber tree in the Deep South and the most common in home plantings. It grows rapidly in a wide range of soil conditions. In contrast to spruce pine the mature trees have long, bare trunks. This makes a good planting area for azaleas and camellias. Slash pine is susceptible to fusiform rust, which causes large wounds on the trunk with a yellowish powder coming out of them. This looks awful and can eventually kill the tree. The infection is rare and is usually not worth attempting to treat. Another (fairly rare) problem is colaspis beetles, which usually attack in early summer and cause the needles to turn brown. The tree looks bad for most of the summer but probably will not die. Do not spray; most insect populations go in cycles, so the infestation probably will be much smaller next year.

Loblolly pine looks very much like slash, differing largely in the appearance of the bark. The bark of slash pine has thinner plates on it, but there is no real need to distinguish between them. Both are good yard trees. Slash grows a little faster in good soil, and loblolly tolerates wet soil better. They have the same insect and disease problems.

Having grown up in southern Mississippi, Leon loves the longleaf pine, but it grows very slowly for the first few years and requires good soil drainage. The botanical name is strangely misleading—*Pinus palustris,* which means "pine of marshlands." Loblolly will grow in marshlands but longleaf will not. The needles of longleaf pine range from eight to eighteen inches in length, whereas those of slash and loblolly seldom reach more than ten inches.

Japanese black pine is an interesting tree that eventually will die unless you have extremely sandy soil or plant it in a large raised bed. It simply cannot stand our wet soils.

Cedars

Our eastern red cedar is technically a juniper, but it is really a cedar because that is what people call it. Various authorities give differing accounts of the soil requirements for cedars. Our observation is that it will grow rather well in low fertility soil, whether it is acid or alkaline, wet or well drained.

We have also noticed that there is a lot of variation in the shapes of cedars, and possibly in soil requirements also. Cedars are difficult to transplant and usually grow slowly. In our coastal areas the cedar is a very common large tree. Some trees become columnar as they mature and others are pyramidal or rounded. From our (not very detailed) observations this seems to be more a matter of genetics than of the surrounding conditions. To be sure of the shape of the mature tree, obtain it from a nursery rather than using seedlings. Cedars form a dense, very dark element in the landscape, and the limbs spread so that it is almost impossible to grow plants under them; cedars require adequate space. Spider mites can cause the foliage to turn brown, and they can be host to cedar rust, a fungus disease that produces large, orange jellylike masses on the cedar tree, called cedar apples. Another stage of this fungus attacks some fruit plants, notably the hawthorns and crab apples, in which it causes lesions on the leaves and young fruits.

Broad-Leaf Evergreens

The pines and cedars are often referred to as coniferous, meaning that they bear cones, but how do we account for magnolias, which also bear cones but are usually referred to as broad-leaf evergreens? We could try calling the pines *needle bearing,* but would have to put the cedars into another group because their leaves are mostly scalelike. This illustrates the fun that people have with classification and the reason that there will always be something for taxonomists to argue about.

Magnolias

The southern magnolia *(M. grandiflora)* is so often associated with the Deep South that it is difficult to believe they are not rated highly as shade trees. But when you see beautiful magnolia trees in the wild they are probably the survivors from large numbers of seedlings, the ones that happened to find well-suited (fairly well-drained) sites. The primary objection to them as yard trees is leaf drop. The large leathery leaves fall off throughout the spring, summer, and fall. They stick to your rake and are difficult for the lawn mower to shred. Also, the tree is attacked by several beetles and scale insects, the leaves get algal spot, the roots are subject to rot, and the tree is very sensitive to changes in the soil levels around the root system. The flowers are beautiful on the tree, but be careful about touching those white petals. Within a few hours the flower will develop brown "fingerprints." Encourage your neighbor to plant a southern magnolia that you can enjoy from a distance.

One more little throwaway about magnolias. Some of the *M. grandiflora*s, both in the wild and grown in nurseries, are actually sweet bay, *M. virginiana.* They look very much like *grandiflora* but the flowers are smaller and the leaves are slightly different. This sometimes becomes a taxonomist's argument. *M. grandiflora* varies considerably in flower size but so does sweet bay. There is a middle point at which a large-flowered sweet bay could be a small-flowered *grandiflora.* Then you should compare the leaves; but they vary too. None of this really matters; they are both pretty trees and we still think they look best in our neighbors' yards.

Big leaf magnolia *(M. macrophylla)* is another interesting native tree. It is deciduous, but the strikingly large leaves are not as difficult to rake as are the leathery ones of *grandiflora.* The flowers are smaller but very attractive. Nurseries occasionally stock container-grown big leaf magnolia, but there is no great demand for it. The real negative is its environmental requirements. In the woods you usually find it on the east side of sloping land. Transplant them into well-drained soil where they receive only morning sun. Probably because those large leaves lose water rapidly on hot afternoons, big leaf magnolias will die if they get afternoon sun.

Hollies

Within the broad-leaf evergreens are the hollies, with the American holly, dahoon holly, and yaupon providing very useful material for gardeners. The hollies have female flowers on separate trees from male flowers, and berries are produced only on the females. Obviously, there must be a male tree somewhere close by, but it does not have to be in your yard. Bees will bring pollen from several blocks away.

Maybe we should digress for a minute on names. Many species of holly are grown as ornamentals down here, all of the genus *Ilex*. The name *holly* should probably be reserved for English holly, which does not grow well in the Deep South. Because it was used extensively for Christmas decorations, the long-ago English began calling it a holy tree, which then changed to "holly." American holly is I. *opaca* and yaupon is I. *vomitoria*. Thereby hangs a tale. The leaves of yaupon contain a strong caffeinelike stimulant. Back in the days before we foreigners invaded America, the Indians used the leaves to make a tea that they drank before going into battle. This gave them a real high and an extra kick of courage. The story goes that when the price of British tea began to rise, the colonists began to use yaupon as a substitute. British naturalists then spread the word that yaupon was poisonous, and named it I. *vomitoria*. This is a taxonomists' beer-drinking tale but it may be close to the truth. Another possibility is that the Indians liked very strong tea, so strong that it made the colonists vomit. We do not know the procedure for making yaupon tea; we have heard that it does not taste very good but will wake you up very fast.

Then there is a deciduous holly that is native to Louisiana, *Ilex decidua*. It is known by the typically southern name of possum haw but makes an attractive landscaping tree. During the winter the leaves fall off, exposing the beautiful red berries.

All three of these hollies are tolerant of wet soils (not standing water, although they can even stand being submerged for a while if the water is not stagnant—moving water has enough oxygen to prevent the roots from dying). All are subject to scale insects, and yaupon seems to be especially prone to harbor leaf miners. Dahoon holly may occasionally be mistaken for yaupon, but its leaves are much larger. The berries also are larger and not as tightly clustered around the stems. There are weeping forms of yaupon in the trade, all from one tree growing on a small hill in Folsom, La.; and there are slow-growing, dwarf forms of yaupon, useful as hedges because the plants grow slowly.

Live Oaks

It can be argued that live oaks are deciduous because they drop all of their leaves in the spring and, for a few days, are completely leafless. Well, yes, but that is getting a bit picky.

Like magnolia and cypress, live oak is part of the southern image. They are long-lived trees but, in good soil, they grow to a reasonable size in ten to fifteen years. The best-publicized live oak in Louisiana is the Evangeline oak at St. Martinville. Longfellow's poem of Evangeline's search for Gabriel reaches its climax when she finds him, dying, under a tree on the banks of the bayou. (The real-life Evangeline did find him there, and discovered that he was already married.) The plaque on the tree says that this is the spot where she found him; it does not say that this is the tree. Old-timers around there think the tree is about 100 years old. It is growing in good soil, on a good slope, and, with such good growing conditions, is not nearly large enough to have been there in Evangeline's time.

As with any native tree, there is substantial variation in the final size and shape of live oaks but, in general, they are good yard trees in a large yard. Most of the trees become quite large and will dominate a small yard. Large live oaks near a house contribute to the cooling in summer but also contribute to the cold and dampness during a cold winter. Given adequate space and full sun on all sides, the live oak is a beautiful tree. The lower limbs hang downward until they touch the ground, forming a large, shaded play area beneath them. In time, this will occur naturally, but some people encourage the process by hanging weights on the ends of the limbs and pruning for uniformity. Another reason for promoting the process is that limbs touching the ground are more stable in a windstorm; massive limbs do not break off, leaving a big gap in the tree.

There are seldom serious problems with live oaks. As with most trees, they drop dead limbs. It is difficult, but not impossible, to keep grass growing under them; you will need to water and fertilize rather frequently. Along the Gulf Coast, salt water intrusion is killing some beautiful trees. On the LSU campus the tramping of student feet is having the same effect, but more slowly. Several trees have already died from what is called "Texas decline," which seems to mean that the already-stressed trees died from some disease or increased environmental stress. It is very difficult to loosen the compacted soil under these trees. The approach being used at LSU is to add a few inches of mulch each year, hoping that new feeder roots will develop in that layer.

As we said earlier, live oaks drop their leaves in the spring just before the new flush of leaves begins. Within the same yard, some trees may drop leaves and begin new growth before others begin the leaf fall. This seems to be genetic variation and is not a cause for worry.

Stinging (buckmoth) caterpillars are right at home on live oak trees, just as they are on all oaks. This can get exciting while young children learn to avoid those prickly things.

We have an old tale relative to insects on oak trees. The bark louse spins a network of fine-textured webs over the bark of some oak trees. Like most insects, they appear in cycles, so years may pass between invasions of bark lice. Although the insects come much earlier, the webs appear in November and December. One of our favorite county agents had a stock answer for people who called in, asking what to do about the webs covering the trunks of their trees. "Get three large floodlights and position them to light up all sides of the trunk, and turn the lights on every night until after Christmas," the agent advised. "Will that kill the insects?" the tree owners asked. "No," the agent replied, "but the webs will be beautiful for the Christmas season!" Bark lice, and many other insects, do not harm trees at all.

Palms

Another evergreen group that deserves consideration from us in the lower South is the palms. If they fit into the landscape design, several palms were widely adapted over most of Louisiana and the Gulf states until the "great freeze of 1989." The main limitation to growing palms in our area always has been low temperature but, during the past few years, a disease called lethal yellowing also has hit some species very hard in many parts of the world. Palms are classified as having leaves that are featherlike (pinnate) or fanlike (palmate).

One feather palm, the jelly palm or peach palm *(Butia capitata)*, was found throughout the Gulf states until the freeze of 1989. Since that time we have not

Butia capitata, the jelly palm.

seen any survivors even in the areas closest to the Gulf. This palm got its common names from the fruit that it bears. The seeds, or nuts, are surrounded by
a layer of somewhat fibrous orange flesh perhaps three-eighths of an inch
thick, which is soft enough to be eaten fresh, but they are better as a jelly fruit.
The tree produces pinnate gray-green leaves that characteristically curl back
toward the trunk and will grow to a diameter of over a foot.

Another feather palm, some of which survived the freeze, is the Canary Island date palm, *Phoenix canariensis.* This is fairly fast growing and eventually

Canary Island date palm *(Phoenix canariensis).*

makes a stately, thick-trunked tree with leaves ten feet or more long, and will produce bunches of colorful dates, considered edible by small boys and other scavengers. This palm regularly survives temperatures into the midteens and makes a good container plant.

A smaller feather-type, the pygmy date palm, *Phoenix roebelenii,* is well suited to containers if the weather does not get too cold, or if the container is small enough for determined palm enthusiasts to drag it into a garage or other protected place during really cold weather.

Fan palms are well represented—the cabbage palm, *Sabal palmetto,* is native to the southern United States. It produces big green leaves up to eight feet across on old plants and will (slowly) make a trunk up to twenty feet high. It can stand almost anything in the way of cold that the South can throw at it, and it can grow in poorly drained soils, a real advantage in much of the South.

The Mexican blue palm, *Erythea armata,* grows slowly to a height of forty feet, can stand cold down to about 18°F, and has silvery leaves that appear almost white in sunlight. These took a beating in the 1989 freeze, but it is such a beautiful plant that you might consider the gamble of replanting.

Trachycarpus fortunei, the windmill palm, is the most common container palm in this part of the country because it will survive temperatures near 10°F. Most of these seem to have survived the freeze of 1989. They make a slender trunk, larger at the top, growing ultimately to thirty feet or more.

The Mediterranean fan palm, *Chamaerops humilis,* has been known to survive a temperature of 6°F and is often seen in clumps that grow to heights of twenty feet or so. It is also used as a container plant and as a hedge, which is very hard to penetrate.

In contrast with most trees, palms are more safely transplanted in midsummer than during the winter. The root systems are divided clearly into a lower portion, which seems to be largely for anchorage, and densely branched upper root, called *coralloid* (resembling coral). Coralloid roots do not extend far from the trunk and seem to be involved in the uptake of nutrients rather than support.

Deciduous Trees

Deciduous trees make the coming of fall interesting. Trees begin to go dormant in August. As the days become shorter the leaves quit producing sugars and gradually start sending nutrients (minerals, proteins, and some sugars) into the stems and on down to the trunk. The green chlorophyll decomposes, and the leaves show fall color. Down here, the fall color will never be as striking as what you see in Vermont, but a few trees do pretty well—if the fall is cool and dry.

Cypress

Cypress growing in a swamp, covered with Spanish moss, is one of the great images of many southern landscapes. Our species *(Taxodium distichum)* is called bald cypress, possibly because the trees growing in the swamp have dead stubby limbs. In favorable conditions cypress will grow rapidly, producing a large pyramidal tree. This good cypress looks nothing like the tall scraggly specimens that you see in swamps.

Favorable conditions for a cypress tree are about the same as those for any other tree: deep, well-drained soil, fertility, and occasional rains. The reason we associate it with swamps and marshes has to do with the seeding mechanism. The seed coat of cypress is impregnated with a resin that prevents germination by keeping water out. (If you soak fresh cypress seed in alcohol for a few minutes it will dissolve the resin and the seeds will germinate quickly— not in the alcohol but after you plant the seed.) This resin decomposes while the seed is submerged in water or mud for a few months, but the seed will not germinate in very wet (low oxygen) conditions. So, trees growing in a marsh drop seeds during the fall and dormancy is broken (the resin breaks down) underwater during the winter and spring. As the marsh dries during the summer, the seeds germinate. Cypress trees are associated with swamps because the water is both a distribution method and a means of breaking dormancy.

An old-time ecologist at LSU used to say that cypress doesn't grow in swamps—it just lives there. Cypress roots, like those of other trees, need oxygen to take up nutrients. So cypress growth is limited to those times in the summer when the soil is relatively dry. Cypress roots tolerate long periods of submersion much better than those of most trees, but our LSU ecologist friend contends that the tree is only surviving, rather than growing.

Cypress knees, which are produced when the tree is growing in poorly drained or wet soil, also are produced in well-drained soil, but not as profusely. The popular explanation is that the knees are structures that allow the roots to get oxygen, much as rice does with its leaves and stems. But no one has so far been able to show that the knees function as an oxygen source. The best guess among people who study cypress is that the knees function somehow in gaining physical stability for the trees. Cypress is not a deep-rooted tree, but it stands up well in heavy windstorms. Another possibility is that the knees do not have a function and are simply a characteristic of the tree.

From a practical standpoint, a cypress tree in your yard will have a nice pyramidal shape and give rather interesting fall color. It will grow very rapidly for the first ten or fifteen years. Unless the soil is very sandy, the tree eventually will produce knees; mowing will become increasingly difficult. Some homeowners keep a sharp hatchet handy and chop off any root that starts producing a knee.

Swamp red maple *(Acer rubrum)* in fall.

Courtesy LSU Cooperative Extension Service

RED MAPLES

The swamp red maple is another wetlands tree that usually is found where cypress is growing. This tree is frequently the first real sign of spring in swampy areas, with the swelling buds and red flowers in very early spring, followed soon after by the red winged fruits. It is not long-lived, but is fairly fast-growing. Because the wood is somewhat weak, you should prune the young tree to avoid weak side branches. When the tree matures, limbs growing out away from the trunk may be broken in wind storms.

The Drummond red maple is a variety of the swamp maple. Its leaves are whitish underneath, the fruit is somewhat larger than that of the swamp red maple, and it has a slightly different overall look. Swamp maples bear fruits on the female trees only. If you want to dig a tree from the woods (which is not a good practice), look for fruits to prove its sex. Neither the ordinary swamp maple nor the Drummond produces very good fall color, but they do change somewhat.

The southern sugar maple is a native plant that makes a good yard tree. The fall foliage is an attractive yellow. It grows in well-drained soil and is easily reproduced from seed; do not dig one up from the woods. Technically, it is not the real sugar maple that is used in Vermont to make syrup. The botanical name is *Acer barbatum,* var. *floridanum,* but that is getting a bit picky. The two species are almost identical, although this one stays somewhat smaller. You could probably make syrup with the sap, but it would be a lot of trouble. The main problem with this tree is that it requires moist soil and good drainage, very much like the requirements of dogwood.

Oaks

The oaks are what you might call sexually promiscuous. They hybridize and rehybridize among species. Taxonomists enjoy arguing over their classifications. We will describe three species that are used as yard trees, but remember that it is common to find a tree that fits precisely between two species. The red oak is *Quercus falcata.* It is the one with deeply lobed leaves. This is an excellent shade tree that becomes very large and has no shortcomings other than those of all oaks: falling limbs, stinging caterpillars, and so forth. The cherry-bark oak is a variant of red oak with a smoother bark; it is a little better adapted to wet soil. The chestnut oak is another species, *Q. michauxii.* It has leaves that look like those of the chestnut, with small serrations along the margin. This is another good yard tree that gets very large. It grows in a range of soil conditions, has large acorns, and sometimes gives good fall color.

Now we come to the bad one. Water oak *(Q. nigra)* has generally narrow leaves that may or may not be lobed; there is a wide range of leaf shapes on the same tree. The tree grows rapidly in many soil conditions, and the acorns germinate more readily than do those of any other oak. It is a very good yard tree for the first fifteen to twenty years, but after that you should sell the house and let someone else worry about the tree that has a big hollow in the trunk and is beginning to die. This tendency to rot is the tree's biggest drawback. The rotting begins as a result of borers and continues until the entire tree dies. There is nothing you can do to stop it, and the cost of having a twenty-year-old tree removed safely is horrendous, largely because tree cutters are leery of climbing up into a rotting tree. On the other hand, there is a lot of variability in water oaks and some of them do not rot.

Sweet Gum

Almost everybody wants to bad-mouth the sweet gum. It has a beautiful genus name *(Liquidambar)*, grows well in almost any soil, gets very large, and usually has good fall color. It is the exception to our rule about the impracticality of topping tall trees that developed in a densely wooded area; the sweet gum often branches out nicely. The primary problem with sweet gum is that it drops round, spiny "gum balls" in the fall—thousands of them. They are woody, and the lawn mower just throws them around instead of picking them up. Tent caterpillars love to work on sweet gum in the fall. Although they make the tree look bad, in contrast with the stinging caterpillar on oaks they really cause no trouble.

We have some good news: someone has found a sterile clone that does not make gum balls. It is a recent introduction, and we do not know much about it. But this should improve the status of sweet gum, which is really a very good yard tree.

Pecans

If you have a big native pecan growing on your lot, it makes a nice shade tree, so leave it there. Do not plant one of the wonderful new varieties expecting to have an annual crop of pecans. Back in the olden days this was a good idea, but over the last forty years the extensive large-scale plantings of pecan orchards has developed pests that make the protection of backyard trees too much of a hassle. Maybe we should reword that: the pests were probably around all of the time, but monoculture has promoted large population increases. Pecan trees are plagued by scab, a couple of leaf spot diseases, two kinds of webworms, and two kinds of phylloxeras (gall-forming insects).

These can all be controlled by timely applications of various sprays, but the trees are too tall for spraying with your home equipment. You can hire a specialist to spray regularly, and usually get a good crop of pecans (except for the ones the squirrels get).

Everything Else

Green ash makes a fast-growing shade tree that reaches heights of forty to sixty feet, and it is rated fairly high as a city tree. It has shallow roots and somewhat weak wood, so it is another candidate for preventive pruning in its early years.

Chinese elm is a small-leafed elm that performs well as a yard tree, but it is sometimes confused with Siberian elm, which is not as good. The young trees are so difficult to tell apart that you must depend on the integrity of the nurseryman. Unlike many trees, they fruit in the fall, but the fruits are not conspicuous.

Crape myrtles (*crape* is the proper spelling, but that is just the anglicized form of *crepe,* so you are reasonably correct with either spelling) are widely planted and generally deserve to be. They have some problems, but are our best answer to the lilacs that are so beautiful in northern areas. To have lilac flowers you must first endure a long cold winter. Lilacs bloom early and are a sure sign of spring; but then they quit blooming. The crape myrtles (which will not grow in the North) bloom all summer. For colored leaves in the fall, lilacs are not even in the same class. Crape myrtles get leaf spot that can be serious enough to defoliate them in late summer and sometimes requires spraying for control. Because crape myrtles stay fairly small, a home gardener can use the trusty little pump-up sprayer for this treatment. Aphids seem to love crape myrtles, and they can get thick enough to cover all the plants (and automobiles or other things) under the trees with honeydew and sooty mold. Spraying can be used for aphids, but the entomologists tell us that a slurry (thick paste) of insecticide applied with a brush to the trunks in bands several inches wide will be translocated to the leaves and kill aphids. It is an easy enough treatment to warrant a try.

Silver-bell trees are becoming a popular substitute in soil where the flowering dogwood does not grow well (people try to grow dogwood, and when it dies they try silver-bell). This is a small native tree that produces clusters of

The silver-bell tree *(Halesia diptera)* is covered with white bell-shaped flowers in spring.

Courtesy LSU Cooperative Extension Service

white flowers in spring. They are not like dogwood—the flowers are pendant and smaller than the dogwood bracts—but the trees are attractive as smallish shade trees in addition to the spring flowering, and they grow well in a wide range of soil types. Flowers are a bit sparse if the tree is growing in the shade. Silver-bell leaves usually produce a nice fall color, yellow instead of the red leaves of dogwood.

Maybe we should elaborate on our disparaging remark about dogwood. It is a good yard tree, where it will grow well. The flowers are spectacular, and it fits into most landscapes well. It requires very good internal soil drainage, acid conditions, and frequent watering. It will survive under lesser conditions, but will eventually die from some minor disease—meaning it was too stressed to withstand the added problems.

Mayhaw is a small tree or bush that is excellent in poorly drained soils where dogwoods do not stand a chance of surviving. In nature they grow in places that usually flood in spring when the fruits are produced, and the fallen fruits are dipped up from floating accumulations, similar to the way cranber-

The golden rain tree *(Koelreuteria bipinnatum)* exhibits salmon-colored seedpods in autumn. Summertime flowers are yellow.

Courtesy LSU Cooperative Extension Service

ries are harvested. They grow well on dry land and are worth having for the spring bloom even if you do not want to make mayhaw jelly (which Leon enjoys not only for its tart flavor, but also because it is one of the few gourmet foods that has not been promoted under the name of Cajun cooking). The little fruits are too acid to eat fresh, but squirrels like them.

A related tree (both are in the genus *Crataegus*) is the parsley hawthorn, so called because of the leaves that are divided at the edges like parsley leaves. This tree also blooms in spring but, whereas mayhaws fruit in late April, the parsley produces its red fruits in fall and early winter. Birds like them, and squirrels like everything.

More than twenty-five years ago we were struck by the beauty of the Taiwan cherries that were introduced around Mobile, Alabama, and since that time they have been widely planted all over the southern part of our range. They are fast-growing, fruit at an early age, and bloom in late winter in various shades of red. They are in the same genus as plums and peaches and are subject to many of the same pests, notably borers and fungus diseases as well as that old nemesis, oak root fungus. They are not long-lived, but they grow fast. Right along with the Taiwan cherries you can expect to see the various hybrid oriental magnolias blooming—often before winter is over, unfortunately, so the beauty is transformed overnight to brown, dead flowers by the later freezes.

Redbud trees are beautiful in the spring, and they make a good yard tree in drier areas of the South. In the humid South they seem to always look a little ratty: dead limbs, leaf spot, or dead areas on the trunk. These are largely disease problems, but we do not know why they are worse in the South. Even in drier areas the trees are short-lived, but they grow rapidly and never get very large.

Golden rain trees are another of the short-lived trees. There are two kinds of these; if you live in a northern part of the Deep South, look for the more hardy kind. South of that, the more tender types do well and are prettier. These produce golden showers of blooms in spring (you do not want to park under them if you can avoid it; they drip) and later produce winged seed pods that color in the fall. Freezes and scale insects are the main limitations to their growth.

The redbud tree *(Cercis canadensis)* blooms pinkish-purple in spring.

Courtesy LSU Cooperative Extension Service

Japanese persimmons are good dual-purpose trees, making medium-size shade trees. The leaves color somewhat in the fall but the attractive orange, edible fruits remain on the tree after the leaves have dropped. We will say more about persimmons in chapter 8, but want to make a pitch for them here also.

The weeping willow is a nice yard tree. Despite their problems of weak wood and invasive roots, willows have a form that is hard to duplicate (sure, there are weeping mulberries, but who needs that messy fruit?). The tree has interesting uses; a willow shoot makes the best kind of pop gun when used with hollowed-out elderberry stems. Called a plunger, this kind of toy was the mainstay of children's summer entertainment back in the old days. The end of the willow stem was chewed and pounded to make it airtight inside the tube. The other end was finished with a wooden spool (most of our mothers still sewed), and ammunition was gathered from another tree—the chinaberry. This fruit has a slippery outside covering a substantial inner part. Placed into the elderberry tube, just as the early settlers set their lead balls into Kentucky rifles, it could be propelled with great force and considerable accuracy when one hit the spool of the plunger with the flat of the hand. The end of the plunger was kept moist by spitting on it, of course, and the sound made when the plunger was withdrawn will never be forgotten by veterans of the pop-gun wars.

Incidentally, the chinaberry (*Melia azeradach*) is a nice small yard tree. As a bit of trivia, it is the only mahogany tree that grows well in the United States. The tree grows very rapidly and has beautiful purple flower clusters in the spring and deep green leaves. The problem is that those chinaberries that we kids loved are produced abundantly. When ripe, they are messy and smelly.

A number of places are named for the trees that must have impressed early settlers, such as the Acadians who came in from the Gulf and were probably yearning to see some sign of solid ground after the trip from Nova Scotia and up through the marshes they found. There is Cypremort Point (Dead Cypress Point); you can imagine the grim forebodings it put into those early visitors. Much of the higher ground in the marshes consists of ridges thrown up by hurricanes of long ago. These were colonized by live oak trees, becoming known as *chenieres:* oak ridges, or maybe oakeries is a better translation.

Chapter 8

FRUIT TREES AND SMALL FRUITS

Back in the olden days (1960) Ed wrote a bulletin called *The Home Fruit Garden in Louisiana*. Periodically the Cooperative Extension Service has published it with a few changes and some added author credits. When we started writing this chapter Ed pulled out the original bulletin and compared it with the current modified and improved version. It has not changed all that much: the situation was not very encouraging back then and is still pretty bad. With the exception of a few small areas, there is still no fruit industry in the southeastern United States.

Why, with our long growing season, is it so difficult to produce good quality fruit consistently? This is a reasonable question with many reasonable answers. Hang in there with us while we give a few discouraging answers. We will end with a discussion of fruits that often do well in a home garden. We will not suggest that you try a commercial project, but you can produce good fruit.

The original bulletin said that at least twenty-five kinds of fruit can be grown with variable success in Louisiana; the important word is *variable.*

The Right Conditions for Growing Fruit

What makes a fruit adapted to a given area? This is largely a combination of weather and soil conditions, plus the characteristics of the variety being used. But do not ignore the expectations of the grower; if he is satisfied, the plant is growing well. Those are generalities; we want to help you in understanding the problems that will limit success with the various kinds of popular fruit.

Because most of our fruit trees originated in the temperate zone, they have a kind of dormancy known as the *rest period*. This is usually in the winter and is associated with another kind: *enforced dormancy*. A basic difference between the conditions is that enforced dormancy is caused by external factors, such as low temperature, and the rest period is determined by genetics. A plant in rest will not grow even when the weather is favorable for growth. This is not an absolute because the plant may eventually begin straggly growth in June, but it will probably die.

It seems (to us) that plants evolved this mechanism to allow survival in areas where fluctuating temperatures occur, either at the beginning or at the end of winter. Consider that if only low temperatures inhibited a plant from growth, a few warm days could prompt the buds to start growing—only to be damaged by the next freeze. If the plant is in rest, it will not respond to the warm weather and will not get killed. This rest dormancy disappears slowly when the plant is exposed to temperatures below about 45°F but above freezing: temperatures below freezing have no effect at all. During an average year, for a given location, there is a summation of hours with the temperatures in this 45 to 32°F range.

For our purposes (avoiding a few ifs and buts) the dormancy of rest is broken only within the range of about 45°F to freezing; this range is called the *chilling temperature*. The *chilling requirement* of a plant is the number of hours

Ed's Tale about Fruit and the Eye of the Beholder

I have a collection of color slides that I used in class to show the kinds of fruits that are occasionally grown in Louisiana. These included papayas fruiting in New Orleans (not very often); the Canary Island date palm with huge clusters of fruit in City Park, New Orleans; and other examples of the diversity in gardeners' interests and successes. Among these slides was a shot of a gentleman gardener standing proudly beside his Concord grape vine. I would point out the debilitated condition of the vine, with several leaf diseases, uneven fruit ripening, grape berry moth depredations on the scattered clusters, and ever-present black rot on some of the grapes. However, the most important aspect of the slide was the obvious pride the gentleman had in his grapes. Who am I to tell him that Concord grapes cannot be grown successfully in Baton Rouge? He was growing grapes for his pleasure, and very successfully. Although I say it usually isn't worth the effort, in this case growing grapes was very much worth the effort.

that it must be exposed to the chilling temperature before the dormancy of rest is broken. For example, if a peach variety has a chilling requirement of one thousand hours, the rest period will not be broken until it has been exposed to at least that long in the temperature range of 45 to 32°F. Temperature below freezing does not count. After the plant has received one thousand hours of chilling, its rest period is gone but enforced dormancy takes over until the temperature rises to the proper growth range for that variety; maybe above 60°F.

There is an old southern saying that spring has not really come until the pecan trees bud out. Pecan trees have such a long chilling requirement that, by the time their buds swell, there probably will not be another frost.

The safety factor of a chilling requirement usually works with plants that are well adapted to the area. The winter of 1948–49 is a classic example for demonstrating the meaning of "usually." Throughout the Deep South that winter was so mild that fall-planted tomatoes were never killed. This sounds wonderful, but it was devastating for the peach growing region around Fort Valley, Georgia, then the most southerly commercial peach growing area in the country. There had been just enough chilling to break the rest of the flower buds, but the leaf buds on peaches have a higher requirement. (This is fairly common with fruit trees; you may have noticed that they flower before leafing out.) The Fort Valley trees bloomed and set small peaches, which used up the small food reserves in the branches, and the trees died. This was not just a matter of a few trees dying. Entire orchards had to be uprooted and replanted.

This is why you should not order fruit trees from that wonderful nursery back home in Iowa, and why Iowans do not plant southern-adapted peach varieties. Plants developed for areas farther north usually have long chilling requirements that cannot be met in the South. Even if you were to artificially chill them in cold storage, most would not do well. Besides the longer chilling period, they also need cool weather for successful growth and fruiting.

In the far, far north, where alternating warm and cold spells do not occur, there is no advantage to having a long chilling requirement. Ed used to grow the Siberian crab apple *(Malus baccata)* in south Louisiana, where it would bloom and leaf out with the first warm spell, often in January. Then would come the light frosts and some hard freezes; the thing was never able to set fruit. It seems strange that the Siberian crab, which could withstand the winters of gulag country, would be racked up by the bitter cold of south Louisiana. It makes sense if you understand what the rest period is and how it works in various climates. Ed used to give this as a test question: Explain why the Siberian crab tree is sensitive to winter injury in south Louisiana.

Maybe we should add some thoughts about how plants are damaged by cold weather. Winter injury may be due to temperatures that are not particularly cold but occur when the plant is not conditioned to stand them. During bloom the flowers are especially vulnerable. Later, when the young fruits are large enough to store a little heat, they can go through exposures that would have killed the little threadlike styles (which connect the pollen tube to the ovule) in the flowers. With deciduous plants, the onset of rest dormancy moves from the top down, and the last part to become dormant is the lower trunk (or crown) near the ground. Sometimes an early severe cold spell can injure the trunk. The tree may then die because of a poor connection between the top and the roots: food materials cannot move into the root system. The remedy for saving such damaged trees is called bridge grafting: portions of small shoots are grafted across the damaged area (see figure 14).

Fully dormant plants can stand exposures that would damage or kill them if the cold were to come while the lower trunk area was still growing. For reasons we do not quite understand, young trees are particularly bad about continuing to grow in late fall. A Chinese proverb says "the young seedling is foolish." That explanation is as good as any we can think of. Fall down here is usually rather dry, but if a rainy spell comes, young trees will simply continue growing. When this happens, you can help a bit by using a spade to prune some of the roots. This seems to produce an artificial drought, which helps to induce dormancy.

After a few mild winters, we are tempted to try growing some tropical

Figure 14. Bridge grafting.

fruits, hoping that "maybe we are getting into a warm weather cycle." Maybe, but warm cycles end, and those trees are probably going to die in a hard freeze. On the other hand, your home garden is not a commercial enterprise; you can probably find protected niches in the yard where citrus may survive long enough to make planting and nursing it through the juvenile stages worthwhile. Citrus trees mature fairly quickly, and picking citrus from your backyard is a lot of fun. In chapter 17 we give some hints about protecting sensitive trees, but you should plant citrus with the expectation that, if you live north of Alexandria (or, say, San Antonio, Hattiesburg, Dothan, Valdosta), it will eventually be winter killed.

The other side of the temperature coin is hot weather. Our summers are just too hot for many fruit species to do as well as they will in the better-adapted areas: cherries, apricots, most apples, and many bunch grapes are not able to fruit or grow well in our hot, humid summers.

Would it be possible to develop fruit varieties that would do well in our area? Yes, but the problem lies with breeding and selection, which is a slow, unrewarding process in the early years. Most fruit trees require four to ten or more years to grow from seedlings to mature plants; apple and pear seedlings may take as long as twelve years. A good plant breeder who plans for a thirty- to forty-year professional career can develop only the beginnings of a sound program. In this era of publish-or-perish, intelligent young fruit breeders concentrate on crops that have shorter times between generations. There is a lot of good work being done with bush fruits. There have been some good new blueberry varieties developed in recent years and a handful of grape varieties, but hardly any apples or pears. A few new peaches are being released, but the breeding of peaches has two advantages over working with apples and pears. First, peaches are precocious, often fruiting in the second or third year from seed. The other advantage is partly political. Because peaches are largely self-fertile, the seedlings produced are homozygous for the more important physical characteristics. The pome fruits (apple and pear) usually require pollination from a different variety to set fruit. This makes the new progeny much more variable and lengthens the breeding process. This, plus the fact that apple and pear seedlings have longer juvenility periods, means that the pome breeder cannot grind out new varieties very fast. The political aspect of this is that a planting of nearly homozygous peach seedlings looks very uniform and neat. Seedlings of pears and apples will look awful during the first few years;

some are short, some tall, some thorny, and some have strange-looking leaves. When an administrator decides to take a tour of the research plantings, he is impressed when the peach breeder casually points out his orderly peach plantings in comparison with the irascible plantings of pome seedlings. (You might remember that Ed was once involved in the breeding of apples, pears, and figs. He left it in favor of growing ornamentals.)

We are not trying to persuade you that there are no fruit plants worth growing in the Gulf South. We are suggesting that you should try to grow those that have been selected for our conditions.

Before we get too much further along in talking about fruit, we should revisit the discussion about the importance of sunlight in locating the various garden plants you may want to grow. In general terms it takes more light energy for plants to produce flowers than to produce leaves, and still more to produce fruits than flowers; fruits are produced when there is more light energy than is needed to maintain the needs of respiration and modest growth. It follows that the vegetable garden, in which some of the plants will be leafy vegetables and some fruiting vegetables, needs more sun than an area where only foliage will be growing. Fruit trees should have full sun; at a minimum it should be as much as the vegetable garden.

How about space? Strawberries probably take as little space as any fruit crops, with plants only about a foot apart; for comparison, some pecan trees may cover an entire yard. The good news is that even commercial fruit trees do not grow as large as they once did. The use of dwarfing rootstocks for some varieties and selection of types that will fruit on smaller plants has improved your possibilities for having an urban fruit planting. Blueberries have been developed that produce excellent fruit in the Deep South. More importantly, you can grow them in containers; blueberry plants in fifteen-gallon containers can produce up to five pounds of berries a season.

POLLINATION REQUIREMENTS

Most tree and bush fruits benefit from having other varieties that bloom at the same time to pollinate them, whereas some will not produce any fruit with their own pollen. Extension publications on recommended varieties usually provide advice on pollination needs and suggest fruitful combinations. If you have room for one tree only, give your neighbor a tree of a recommended pollination variety.

Fruits That You Can Grow (Maybe)

APPLE

You probably should not try to grow apples in the Deep South, but we will hedge on this statement later. In chapter 12 we explain the problems of fire blight and of protecting leaves from fungal spores by maintaining a layer of fungicides. Most apple varieties are very susceptible to fire blight and several fungal diseases. In commercial regions growers reapply the fungicide after ten hours of rain. During a particularly long rainy spell they may be spraying while rain is falling. Our frequent rains and humid weather make disease control of apples very difficult. Another problem is that, with most varieties, ripening apples do not develop an attractive color or good flavor unless the weather is cool.

Now for the hedging. There are thousands of apple varieties and only a small fraction of the total have been tested in the Deep South. We realize that this point is of no real value to you, it is just the first step of our hedging. The good news is that several rather good varieties are reasonably well adapted even to warmer southern areas. If (you knew we would say "if") you are the only person on your block growing a few apple (or crab apple) trees, they should grow well and produce large crops of good apples for maybe ten or twelve years, provided that they pollinate each other or tend toward self-fruitfulness. You need not do a lot of spraying, just a dormant spray for scale insects and maybe a couple of fungicide applications. Some people will be lucky and never need to spray at all. The flavor of apples grown here is pretty good in comparison with the tasteless things you can buy at the supermarket.

You will recognize that our "if" is based on isolation. Bitter rot and various other diseases will eventually find your tree. When they begin to decline, cut them down and tell your neighbors that you got tired of growing apples.

PEARS

The disease problem is almost as bad with pears. Fire blight, caused by a bacterium, is the main problem, but some resistance has been introduced from crosses with the oriental sand pear. Along with the resistance came the grit cells that gave sand pear its name. We will discuss a solution later.

The varieties that have fire blight resistance may still be susceptible to early or late leaf spot, or both, caused by different fungi. Early leaf spot can defoliate the tree when it is trying to make new growth and develop fruit at the same time. That puts a real strain on a leafless tree; it is much like losing your job while your children are going to college. Late leaf spot defoliates the tree in late summer or early fall, when the tree's internal clock is inducing dormancy in the buds. The loss of leaves exposes the buds to the heat of the direct sun, which can break their rest, so that in addition to producing a late crop of leaves at the expense of stored foods, the trees often bloom. In mild winters you may sometimes see full-grown pear fruits at Christmas time, even though the trees are almost leaf-less.

Another rest period–related problem occurs with pears (and sometimes with apples) in our area. During winters when the upper buds do not have enough chilling, some of the latent buds on trunks near the ground will sprout and begin growing. When you see a tree with *water sprouts* on the base of the trunk, what went wrong is that it should not have been planted so far south. Water sprout production is fairly common with pear trees so far south, but is not much of a problem unless you let the sprouts grow and become weedy. Break the sprouts when they appear as tender shoots.

Now for tips on how to get good pears from your backyard tree. Pears

White flowers bloom in spring on an Oriental pear *(Pyrus bretschneiderii)*.

ripen best at around 60°F. Over most of the South, daytime temperatures are not nearly that cool at the time pears are maturing; accept the fact that you are not ever going to be able to pick a lush ripe pear directly from the tree. If you take pears from the tree when they first begin to change from grass green to yellow-green and bring them into a cool place, they will ripen more quickly than those on the tree and will have far fewer grit cells. Ed used to ripen pears in a cold storage room at 60°F and give them out as samples of what can be done if you handle the fruit properly. This system works pretty well if you just store the pears in the kitchen. The temperature may not be 60°F but even 70 to 75°F is better than leaving them outside. An advantage of ripening pears like this is that you can pick only the amount you need, and leave the rest on the tree. Because they will not ripen on the tree, the green fruit will remain hard and firm until you are ready for more ripe pears.

Oriental pear varieties do not produce the buttery flesh prized in European pears, but develop crisp, juicy fruits that do ripen on the tree in our area. Some pear species do not produce edible fruit (for people) but are good wildlife food sources and may be beautiful in bloom and again when fall leaf color develops. The "Bradford" pear, derived from *Pyrus calleryana,* is one, and *P. bretschneiderii* has very showy flowers. You might consider trying one of these.

STONE FRUITS—PLUMS AND PEACHES

Several varieties of plums are recommended in publications of the Cooperative Extension Service. In addition, many of unknown origin may be found growing throughout the South—some with obvious partly Japanese plum parentage. Plums are precocious, compared to pears and apples, but usually are not long-lived due to insect and disease problems. Few are grown commercially.

Peaches are grown commercially in a number of southern areas, and a number of breeding programs have been supported in several states. This has provided a wider range of varieties than is the case with plums.

PERSIMMONS

Persimmon is a tree you should consider for both the ornamental value and the fruit, the ornamental value being primarily in its attractive orange-to-red fruit. In the yard it provides a colorful substitute for our rather pitiful fall foliage. After the fruit is picked, it makes an attractive addition to autumn table centerpieces. The larger fruit can be sliced into thin cross sections for display on an hors d'oeuvre tray.

As an edible fruit, some people enjoy persimmons while others consider them to be quite attractive, but inedible. The genus name, *Diospyros,* means "food of the gods," from Greek *dios* meaning godly or divine and *pyros* meaning grain. There are two species of edible persimmons: the American persimmon, *D. virginiana,* and the Japanese or kaki persimmon, *D. kaki.*

Persimmon connoisseurs tend to smirk when we include the American persimmon as being edible: "Persimmon is an excellent food for wildlife, but who else is going to eat it?" Who else? Anyone who grew up in the depression South loves the native persimmon. Back in the really olden days Choctaw Indians dried the ripe persimmon fruits and kept them as choice delicacies for feast days. The native persimmon tree grows well in a wide range of soil types; it grows best in fertile, well-drained soil but will do the best it can if you plant it in poorly drained clay soil. Under good conditions it makes a reasonably large tree, perhaps thirty or forty feet high. It has a few leaf diseases, but nothing serious. The tent caterpillar likes to build massive webs on it in the fall, but that bug likes almost any vigorous tree. As for fruit quality, it would probably (maybe) be as good as the kaki if somebody would put a little effort into a breeding program. (The Japanese have been developing persimmon varieties for hundreds of years.) Fruit of the native persimmon is a little bigger than a large acorn and is mostly seeds. There are several cultivars, which are simply chance selections, that have larger fruit, and some are seedless. All of the native selections are astringent until they are completely ripe; we will talk about the mouth-puckering tannins later.

Now for the other species: the Japanese, oriental, or kaki persimmon. It is classified in two ways, which we will only mention. One classification is by pollination constant and pollination variant. In the variant group changes, the flesh darkens and becomes coarse in texture if it is pollinated. The other does not. Another meaning of this classification is that pollination is nearly always undesirable: pollination produces seeds, and seedless persimmons are better than seedy ones. The other classification has to do with astringency: whether the not-quite-ripe fruit has mouth-puckering tannins. There are more than a thousand kaki persimmon varieties (cultivars) in Japan. Of these, the commercial persimmon producers in California use about a dozen. It seems likely that many of these will soon be available at your garden center.

Figs

Maybe you have to grow up in the South or in Mediterranean areas to like figs. There is a wide difference of opinion as to whether it is worth the trouble to grow them. The trees often get rather large in a small backyard, but they grow well throughout the Deep South and have only minor disease and pest problems (except for squirrels, birds, and little boys).

The biggest problem for fig trees is cold weather, especially an early freeze before the tree has become fully dormant or a late spring freeze when the new growth is tender. The soft wood breaks easily when the tree has a heavy fruit load, nematode problems are fairly common, and there are a few fungal diseases. Generally, fig trees can live for twenty to thirty years in our area, producing heavy fruit crops with little or no care. The varieties that are most common here are those that can survive the occasional severe winter. We will describe them in later paragraphs.

Many articles about figs say they are pollinated by a specialized wasp that carries pollen from the male flower to the female fig flowers. We do not have that wasp here, and it would not matter if we did. The larvae overwinter in small immature fruit; our winter cold snaps would kill them. Those articles are about California figs, the kind that you usually get as dried fruit. The only real difference between our figs and those of California is that, because our figs are not pollinated, they do not produce seeds. The nutlike oil of those seeds is responsible for part of the flavor of dried figs. This means that our figs are very good when eaten fresh but are not much good as dried fruit. But that is not important because we could not dry figs outdoors in this humid climate. You can dry figs in the oven, but they will not quite have that dried-fruit taste.

Figs are easily propagated by rooting cuttings. They will root at almost any time, but late winter is good; just stick a few twigs in the ground and wait. The new trees will grow beautifully during that first year but will not go dormant with the approach of winter. A hard freeze will kill the plant, roots and all. A plant that survives the first winter will be mature enough to go dormant by the next fall. To encourage dormancy, in late July of the first year you should try slowing the tree's growth. Do not water or fertilize. If the fall is warm and rainy, prune the roots in a circle about a foot from the tree. This is simple; cut the circle with a sharp spade, sinking it to the full depth, maybe ten inches. If the tree continues to produce new leaves, repeat this in two or three weeks. As a last resort, cut all the roots on one side of the tree, push it over, and cover the trunk with soil and cover that with leaves. This will get it through almost any cold we have in the South.

For the first four or five years prune the tree to a convenient shape in late winter, after the last freeze and before the leaves begin growing. We strongly suggest that you cut the upper branches back to a height you can reach for picking. Children love to climb in trees to pick the figs that are up high, but the branches break easily. Arms and legs break just as easily; all of us old-timers remember falling out of fig trees at least once. Eventually the tree will get too large for its allotted space, especially if you keep topping it. Then you should start pruning new growth in July or early August, which will have a stunting effect because you are removing leaves and branches that would produce food materials for the coming year. Late summer or fall pruning is risky because it makes the tree more sensitive to cold injury. It is common in figs that some wood dies back after you prune. Painting the cut stump will not help. Do not leave a long stump, or cut so close that you leave no stump at all, which would cause a wound in the parent limb.

Pecans

In the minds of us more mature types, pecans are associated with huge old trees that were around when our grandparents were mature types. However, it is hard to get pecans like that now. The main reason is phylloxera, a gall-forming insect that lays its eggs in young pecan nuts and kills them. A contributing factor is that phylloxera, like many other insects, has population cycles of about ten to fifteen years. We assume a virus kills the high phylloxera populations. If you were young during a low part of the cycle, when the phylloxera population was small, you will remember having massive pecan crops. But even the high part of the cycle did not hurt crops as badly as it does now. This is because the state experiment stations have been such a help to pecan growers. Well, actually, we are being too hard on scientific progress. The problem, one shared with many other crops, is that of monoculture. What this means is that most of the earlier pecan trees were seedlings: grown from seeds rather than having been grafted. Some trees leafed out and produced flowers early, some were much later. There were differences in the size, quality, and shell thickness of nuts produced. Differences in flowering time had a large influence in reducing the extent of insect damage, but there were probably other factors that made some trees less attractive to insects. The new improved varieties of today are mostly selections from wild seedlings, grafted onto other seedlings. At the garden center you will find three or four varieties, all of which are recommended for home use, and most of them will flower at the same time. Although you might have only one tree in the yard, your neighborhood is practicing monoculture: growing a few varieties that are almost identical. Commercial growers do the same thing. They have more varieties available but, for economic reasons, they must plant large blocks with varieties that produce nuts at the same time.

So phylloxera is the primary reason for your having a big tree that never produces very many pecans. There are also some diseases, such as scab and some leaf problems. It is possible, but very expensive, to control these problems with several spray applications. If you do that, the tree will produce large crops, which the squirrels will eat while the nuts are still green.

Pecans make excellent shade trees, and you will occasionally get pretty good crops of nuts. If you are in a low phylloxera population cycle, "occasionally" can mean almost every year for maybe ten years. We do not have a solution for controlling squirrels. We should add that pecans tend to have a two-year cycle for producing large crops, whereas squirrels are prolific every year. This means that when a tree produces its large crop most of the food reserves are exhausted. During the next year the poor tired tree will not produce nearly as many flowers, the yield will be skimpy, and the tree will build up food reserves to have a big crop next year. The pat answer to this is to fertilize during the heavy crop year, but that does not work.

Blackberries

You can remember picking luscious, sweet blackberries from the wild, but it is easy to forget how tired you got of trying to fill a molasses bucket with them, and the thorns, and the chiggers if you did not take a hot bath right away.

The new lines of blackberries taste less sweet, or maybe it is just our memories. After you learn how to pick dead-ripe berries, you will agree that the flavor is excellent—and they get almost as big as strawberries. As with the wild berries, the red ones are unripe—but just being black does not mean that they are ripe. The fruit must be plump and have a dull sheen. The blackberry is an aggregate fruit, meaning that it is a cluster of many tiny fruits: fruitlets. If you look closely, you will see that each fruitlet has a small dimple on it. This dimple disappears when the fruit is fully ripe. We know that you are not going to examine each berry that closely, but it is a useful guide while you learn to recognize ripeness.

Propagation is usually by root cuttings—not rooted stem cuttings. You cut a root about pencil-to-finger thick into pieces six inches long, then plant them about an inch deep. Be patient and keep them watered, and shoots will develop. Select the biggest shoot on each piece and break the others off.

For good yields, blackberries need full sun, good drainage, fertility, and water. It is best to build a raised bed. It is also a good idea to sink some sort of root barrier to a depth of about a foot, all around the bed. A vigorous berry plant will send roots far out into your lawn—and then make a shoot. Those shoots are good for propagation, but in the lawn they are weeds. You can dig up a few and give them to your neighbor, but next year he will be trying to give some away.

Now, some information on pruning, which is also related to disease control. Blackberry stems (called canes) live for two years. On established plants, shoots emerge from the base (crown) of the plant. These grow rapidly, producing leaves and some side shoots, but no flowers. These shoots are called primo (first-year) canes. They will initiate flower buds in the fall, then go dormant and become fruiting canes in the next spring. Now comes the trick. After the berries have been harvested from fruiting canes, those canes should be cut out. They still have green leaves but contribute nothing to the plant. Well, actually they contribute something that you do not want: some blackberry varieties have a disease called double-blossom. Control of this disease is the main reason for our pruning techniques. Double-blossom is a fungus disease that develops and overwinters in the young primo canes. When spring comes, the fungus is already growing within the flower buds. When a diseased bud opens, it produces large, impressive flowers—except that the flower has no pollen. The stuff that looks like pollen is disease spores. (We do not know why diseased flowers are larger than the healthy ones, but suspect a growth promoter produced by the fungus.) These spores fall on the lateral buds of tender young primo canes and set up housekeeping. When the mature primo canes set flower buds in the fall the fungus is already there and you cannot do anything about it. The control method is sanitation. The best system is to cut out any primo canes that develop while the fruiting canes are flowering. An easier method is to wait until you have made the last berry harvest and simply cut everything back to the ground. Because of our long growing season new primo canes will sprout and mature before the first frost. Do not let wild berries grow near your plants—they will be a source of inoculum.

Now we need to hedge a bit because many of the new varieties have fairly good resistance to double-blossom disease. Realistically, you could just reach in and cut out the old fruiting canes and leave the large, healthy primo canes. Just as realistically, such selective pruning is not a fun job because the new primo canes have vicious thorns. To borrow advice from foresters: clear cut and burn. Use gloves, wear long sleeves, and cut everything back to the ground. This may reduce your yields a bit but, besides convenience, there is the logic of disease control through sanitation. Just because the variety is resistant does not mean that you can be sloppy. Plant diseases are notorious for developing new strains that bypass the resistance mechanisms; sloppy practices will accelerate the process, and sanitation will slow it.

A bad aspect of some blackberries is that they tend to trail along the ground instead of growing upright. Building and maintaining trellises is a nuisance. A system that works pretty well is to drive a stake beside the established plant and cut everything back to only four primo canes. Tie them to the stake and start cutting the tips back when they reach a height of about five feet. During the winter you should prune all side shoots (on the four canes) to lengths of about a foot. Plants like this, spaced about six feet apart, will yield at least a gallon of good fruit every season. That is a lot more than you got from one wild blackberry bush.

A few thornless varieties are available and we hope to see more if breeding programs are supported. Early thornless varieties were not well adapted to the lower South, but the newer ones show promise.

BLUEBERRIES

Discussing types of blueberries reminds us of the old song about the highland Dutch and lowland Dutch; there are many kinds and the taxonomy is a mess. For practical purposes there are the wild (lowbush) blueberries that grow much farther north, and the commercial (highbush) that also grow farther north. In the lower South all of our blueberries were of the *rabbiteye* type up until a very few years ago, when breeding efforts began to allow introduction of some of the highbush blueberry traits into hybrids. The rabbiteye blueberry itself was a hybrid complex, usually involving several native species that differed with the area of the South in which the wild hybrids originated. The southern part of the Florida peninsula had several native evergreen blueberry species, and breeders for that area used evergreens in their program. Breeders in other states have used species better adapted to their soils and climates. This mix of blueberry species grown in the South is still called rabbiteye, but for practical purposes they can be grouped as highbush; the terminology arguments will continue forever.

Blueberries as a whole are closely related to rhododendrons (azaleas) and do best in conditions where azaleas grow well, often in well-drained soils with high levels of organic matter. In Louisiana the native species are seen only where the land begins to have a little elevation; they seldom occur in the alluvial flatwoods soils. In the chapter on fertilizers we discuss more fully the forms of nutrient elements that plants take up and use from the soil (see chapter 16), but here we need to mention forms of nitrogen used by blueberries. Nitrogen in the soil exists (primarily) in two forms, and plant species differ in which of these produces better growth. The plants in the heather family (blueberries and azaleas) grow best when most of the nitrogen available to them is in the form of ammonium rather than as nitrate. Part of the reason for azaleas growing better under acid conditions and in decomposing organic material is that this tends to keep nitrogen in the ammonium form.

What does this mean to those of us who do not have acid soils and well-drained land but still want to grow blueberries? Earlier we pointed out that blueberries in large containers can produce as much as five pounds of fruit per season. That, like all stories too good to be true, has a flaw: you will have to water the plants frequently during hot weather. If your soil has bad internal drainage, try to improve it in the way you would for any other crop: use raised beds and incorporate organic matter. Adding sand to the soil will not help at all. Some of the newer varieties (highbush hybrids) will grow well only if they are in almost pure organic matter: peat, bark, and so forth. In growing blueberries, always be sure that the surface water can drain away. Find out what the pH of the soil is by having the soil or mix tested, and mention that you want to grow blueberries or azaleas in it. The testing agency will recommend additions to reduce the pH (increase the acidity)—usually sulfur or aluminum sulfate. After amending the soil and planting the blueberries, put on a mulch. An acid pine bark mulch works well here, and blueberries can stand fresh grass clippings if they are not too high in fertilizer materials (most home lawn clippings are not). Use an ammonium form of nitrogen as fertilizer when applications are made. These same recommendations will apply to acid soils except that there is no need to adjust the pH. Blueberry plants tend to make a lot of small, twiggy growth, and it is a good idea to cut most of this out during the dormant season so that more light gets into the center.

When the fruit begins to turn red, long before it is blue-ripe, the birds will arrive. It is absolutely amazing that so many kinds of birds love blueberries. The only solution is to purchase bird netting to hang over the entire plant. Hanging bird netting is not a fun thing to do and it makes harvesting more difficult. You may want to consider building a frame of posts and wires high and wide enough for you to get inside for harvesting. We do not know of any alternative to netting, if you want to harvest blueberries. Even commercial berry growers have to contend with birds. In a large planting, birds take about one-third of the crop; with your single bush they will take three-thirds. The effect of bird netting on ripening of blueberries is a real garden phenomenon. Covering a bush will result in a profusion of ripe berries in a few days (at the right time of year, of course), whereas uncovered bushes will not even show red berries.

Blueberry bushes covered with bird netting.

GRAPES

We still do not have bunch grape varieties well enough adapted to our area to cause any sleepless nights in California. Most of the commercial grape varieties were developed for less humid areas; some varieties can be grown here but are not worth the trouble to the average home gardener. Some truly dedicated wine makers have small plantings.

Now for the good news. Muscadine grapes are native to our part of the world. They take a few years to establish a good root system, but after that they grow like weeds. Your biggest problem will be keeping them pruned. The good thing about muscadine fruit is that the tough, thick, bitter skin makes it resistant to insects and diseases. The bad thing about muscadine fruit is that the tough, thick, bitter skin is inedible. If you want to eat muscadines as fresh fruit, you must squeeze the inner flesh and juice into your mouth and throw the skin away.

Leon would like to point out here that Ed was being delicate to speak of the "inner flesh." It is really called the *frog's eye;* it is so tough that you have to chew on it to get the seeds out.

Eating frog eyes is not nearly so much fun as popping a few grapes into your mouth. However, many new muscadine varieties have excellent flavor, produce great quantities of fruit, and have seeds that are more *free floating,* to use a grape term. So, what can you do with great quantities of fruit that must be eaten one at a time? Squeeze them out for the juice. Back before the era of frozen orange juice the stores sold orange juice squeezers; maybe you can find one. Maybe you can get a small apple juice press. Anyhow, squeeze the juice out and serve it as a chilled drink, bottle it as grape juice, freeze it, make jelly, or make wine. Our main point is that you should decide what to do with the fruit before you simply decide that it might be good to have a muscadine vine for low-maintenance fresh fruit.

So, how do you grow muscadines? They will grow pretty well in almost any soil but do best in well-drained soil, if they get plenty of water. Muscadine vines use a lot of water. After they get established they will do well regardless of what you do. Having said that, we get tangled in the matter of the real purpose for growing a muscadine vine. Back in the days beyond recall, muscadines were the favorite for making the old-time poor folks' gazebo. We have not seen a good muscadine arbor in a long time but, back then, the arbor was a wonderfully cool, shady place for kids to play on long summer mornings. In the afternoon, the place belonged to the old folks, who would sit in comfortable chairs, drink iced tea, and solve the political problems of the day. The fruit would begin to ripen in August or September, which was the time for everyone to move out and turn things over to the birds and squirrels. A muscadine arbor bears much less fruit than a vine on a standard grape vine trellis. However, a good arbor will produce enough fresh fruit for the birds, the squirrels, and you. But the fruit of an arbor should be considered as lagniappe; the real product is a thick cool shade that is much more pleasant than that of the store-bought gazebos.

For real fruit production you should trellis the vines like a commercial grape planting. Our sketch (figure 15) shows how it should be arranged and how severely you should prune it every winter. For good production, you should prune back to a few short spurs on the large leader vines.

Maybe this is a good time to explain the general principles for pruning muscadines and most other fruit-bearing plants—or, for that matter, any flowering plants, such as azaleas, roses, or camellias. If a plant (in this case a vine) grows in good conditions, it will produce large succulent shoots called *bull shoots*. These shoots will have mostly vegetative buds in the next year.

Leaves of grapes are produced on nodes, but on the other side of each node is a group of active cells (not yet buds) that can become flower or tendril buds. Precisely what will happen depends on the balance of nutrients, water, and foods within the vine and on the way they are pruned. With excessive water,

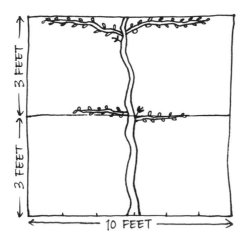

Figure 15. A grape vine after pruning.

nutrients, and food, they will produce tendril buds. If the supply is extremely low, the cells will produce no buds at all. With the proper balance flower buds are produced. It is easy to see this relationship on a productive grape shoot: Buds in the middle of a shoot will form flower buds, whereas those at the extremes (far end and close to the trunk) produce leaves or tendrils but no flowers. Early in the growth season, food is usually in short supply but water and nutrients are excessive. At the end of the season everything is in short supply. When you start to prune a grape vine, look at last year's growth and decide whether it was too vigorous or a little weak. If it was vigorous (the grape term is *bullish*), you should leave more buds on a shoot—to drain the food/nutrient balance. If last year's growth was weak, you should cut it back more severely to reduce the drain on the balance. This is the meaning of *balanced pruning.*

The trellis system also will influence your approach to pruning. Many grapes are trained on two-wire trellises, with the upper wire about six feet high and the lower at three or four feet (see figure 15). In this system the vines are trained and pruned to have a central trunk with four branches (arms). Vines are spaced to allow around ten feet of trellis per vine. Each winter the previous season's growth is cut back to leave about forty buds per vine—assuming moderate but not excessive vigor. A shoot (called a cane) that you leave for production should be about the size of a pencil and have buds spaced six to eight inches apart.

Because the exact amount of pruning varies according to the vigor of that plant, you must decide how to prune your vine by trial and error. This pruning problem is the reason muscadine arbors will not produce nearly as much fruit as vines growing on a trellis and pruned regularly. The vine on an arbor is very hard to prune. You will probably have no serious disease or insect problems. The birds and squirrels will get more fruit than you do, but there should be plenty to go around.

You can use these same principles for flowering shrubs. Each individual azalea, rose, or camellia bush should be pruned according to the vigor of the previous season, and with some idea of how much flowering you really want. Azaleas grown as hedges are pruned severely just after the blooms fall off, and they usually form a solid mass of flowers the following year. A more vigorous azalea, growing without the competition of a hedge, would be pruned somewhat less. Of course, if the plant is getting too large for its space, prune it to what you like—it will cost you a few flowers the next year. (See also chapter 9 for more information on pruning shrubs.)

In choosing muscadine varieties, be aware that some have perfect (self-pollinating) flowers and others have only female flowers. If you have a female variety, it will grow a beautiful arbor, will flower every spring, and will never produce any fruit. You will have to go back to the garden center and get a perfect-flowered variety to keep it company.

Strawberries

You can grow some pretty good strawberries in your backyard garden, much better than the beautiful, flat-tasting, or far-too-acid berries that you get at the supermarket. Strawberries in the lower South are handled as annuals, with new plantings in October or November. Most are grown in California, Michigan, or Canada, and only a few varieties are available now.

As for planting methods, it depends on how traditional you are. Strawberries have that name because everybody used to tuck straw around them to control weeds and to protect the ripe berries from lying on the ground. The traditional straw in many southern states is pine straw, the stuff you can now get by the bale at the garden center. The absolute truth is that black plastic is better and easier to handle.

Place the plastic over standard raised beds, water furrow to water furrow. Dig a small trench in each water furrow so that you can bury the edge of the plastic and cover it with soil. Cut small planting holes in the plastic at intervals of about a foot. "Small" planting holes means that you should make X slits just large enough for a hole to set the plant with the crown just at the soil surface, not too deep nor too shallow. If you bury the crown, the new shoot might push up or it might not. If you set the crown up where it can dry out, it will die.

Two rows of plants spaced about one foot apart, with plants about eighteen inches apart in staggered rows, will give adequate spacing. After planting, fit the plastic slits back in place to provide as much weed control as possible. If desired, a drip-type irrigation tube can be placed down the middle of the bed between the two rows of plants before the plastic is put on. After one short cold snap the plants will think spring has come and will start growing. With a bit of luck you can have rather large plants by Christmas. They should begin flowering in late January or early February, and you will start hoping for warm weather. If you are really into early production, you can make frames from half-inch PVC pipe and cover the plants with a polyester insulating cover during cold nights. We give details about the covering material later (see chapter 17), but it is essentially a thin blanket that will hold warm air around the plants. We discuss using wire and PVC frames in chapter 2.) Strawberry plants do not need protection from our cold, but a cold snap of about 26°F will kill the delicate flowers, similar to the cold damage of peach flowers discussed earlier.

As the berries begin to ripen you need to protect them from birds. Insulating cover or bird netting, placed over the frames, provides excellent bird protection. You also need to pick all ripe berries about every other day. Take particular care to pick and discard any rotten berries and dead leaves. Put them in a container and dump them in the compost pile. By practicing this kind of good sanitation you avoid any need to spray with a fungicide.

We believe the first, big, juicy berries are not nearly as sweet as the small, late-season fruit, but they are all good eating.

Citrus

Growing your own citrus is tempting in the Gulf South. When we get four or five mild winters, we are encouraged to try some citrus again. Well, why not? You will probably get several years of good fruit before the trees get zapped. If you plan ahead for cold protection, you might win for ten or fifteen years. The following discussion is primarily about what to grow and how to grow it (see chapter 17 for tips on cold protection).

Broadly, citrus can be divided into four groups: mandarins, sweet oranges, grapefruits, and the acid citrus. The terminology gets confusing, but satsumas are mandarins that have zipper skins, a mild flavor, only a few seeds, and are very cold hardy. There are several varieties of sweet oranges that will take moderate cold snaps, if you give them some degree of protection. Of the acid citrus, kumquats (which have sweet skins) are nearly as cold tolerant as satsuma and, because they tend to be small trees, they are easy to protect from the cold. Lemons are questionable, but some people do well by growing them as potted plants; the large-fruited Meyer lemon is popular. Then there is grapefruit, the real challenge. This is a big vigorous tree that bears large crops but is badly damaged by freezes. Some gardeners pile leaves around the trunk to protect it from being killed in very cold weather and brag about the good grapefruit crop they get during a series of mild winters.

Except in Florida, for a citrus tree to survive in the South it is almost essential that it be budded on trifoliata rootstock. The full name is *Poncirus trifoliata Rubidoux*. You will notice that this is not just a citrus species. It is from another genus, which means that grafting is difficult except when the rootstock is very young. The key point is that the trifoliata rootstock goes dormant during the winter. This will slow growth of the citrus you have budded on it, and will give the plant a degree of cold protection. It is not enough to get you through a hard freeze but is a good start. For best results, the bud should be located about six inches above the soil line. Some people like to place the bud a little higher, on the assumption that it gives more cold protection. It probably does, but it also tends to slow tree growth and makes it difficult to protect the trunk above the graft before hard freezes. If part of the grafted portion survives, you can get pretty rapid regrowth of the citrus. If the plant is killed down to the graft, regrowth will be a useless, thorny, trifoliata tree; the fruit of trifoliata is very bitter. Regrafting on that rootstock is extremely difficult.

Satsuma trees sold at a garden center may already have some small fruit on them. We know how difficult it will be to pull those fruits off; bite the bullet and do it. Besides drawing food materials that should be going to building a stronger tree, the ripe fruit will be almost tasteless.

During the first few years you should provide some protection on nights when the temperature is predicted to get into the mid to low 20°s. Mounding soil around the bases of trees is a good practice. This can be a problem with high-budded trees, but if they are not too large it can be done. Some sort of windbreak around the tree, or on the north side, and perhaps a large light bulb hanging in the main branches can afford a great deal of protection. The use of a kerosene lantern or heater also can get trees through the cold spells. Ed keeps several lanterns just for that purpose. You can still buy the nice red kind at discount stores.

Commercial growers use heaters in the orchard on occasion when the trees are bearing size, but usually to save a crop that has not been picked. Freezes severe enough to kill the large trees are usually too severe for the grove heaters to be effective. Sometimes fruit may be picked in advance of a freeze even if it is not fully ripe, but most of the green fruit must be written off. Satsumas are hardier than most kinds of edible citrus except for the kumquats (which some people consider inedible), but how many kumquats can one family use?

How far north can you plant satsumas, navel oranges, and grapefruit? How cold will our winters be over the next ten years and how willing are you to protect the plants if it does get very cold? Do not let this prevent you from growing citrus. Accept the fact that the tree will eventually be killed, and enjoy the fruit while you can.

We are frequently asked why satsumas and navel oranges drop small fruit. This is because they are largely seedless, setting fruit parthenocarpically (from the Greek word *parthenos,* or virgin, and *carpus,* or fruit). Seeds produce hormones that enable developing fruits to compete with other parts of the plant for food materials. In many fruit species the few-seeded fruits drop in waves—the June drop in peaches, for example. When fruits have no seeds they develop only when there is an excess of elaborated foods over that needed for vegetative growth. This seldom occurs in juvenile, rapidly growing plants. This situation is encountered with many seedless or few-seeded fruits.

Loquats

The loquat or Japanese plum *(Eriobotrya japonica)* is not a plum, but more closely related to apples and pears. The trees are found throughout the South, occasionally being injured by cold in the more northerly parts, but usually not fruitful except in the southerly parts, because they bloom in early winter and the flowers or young fruits can be killed by freezing weather. They are often found near the sea coast and are quite salt-tolerant.

In favorable conditions they produce a profusion of attractive yellow or orange fruits—quite variable in size because most of the trees are grown from seeds. The skins are slightly fuzzy, and the seeds are large, but the tart flavor appeals to many people, especially small boys (who grudgingly admit that girls may like loquats, too).

Even where they seldom bear fruits they are attractive evergreen trees, with large, leathery, glossy, dark green leaves, fuzzy and whitish on the bottom, and when in bloom are fragrant. Their main problems other than cold are fire blight and the soil-borne disease oak-root fungus. Resistance varies in the seed-grown population, and if the tree you plant is resistant, it can live for twenty-five years or more and grow to twenty feet or so in height and spread.

Chapter 9

SHRUBS

I (Ed) seem to keep running into definition and classification problems. A shrub, according to the dictionary, is "a low, usually several stemmed, woody plant." Now what? Within the bounds of this definition are hundreds, perhaps thousands of plant kinds, each with some special need or characteristic that could make somebody want to plant it or to avoid planting it. And then, there are the categories of shrubs; some are described as having *creeping* or *upright* forms; an upright form may reach a height of twenty feet. Is it still a shrub?

Some Definitions—And a Few Complaints

One author described shrubs as plants that are in between the vines and the trees. That is a good beginning: shrubs fill several important needs in a landscape, including screening out unwanted views, either incoming or outgoing; forming backdrops for the display of flowers; and forming windbreaks where wind is a problem. Shrubs develop rather quickly; a bare landscape site can look almost finished in a few years as the shrubs develop. This concept helps a little, but it describes a shrub's uses rather than defining it.

Some of the better publications about the use of shrubs were prepared by landscape architects. As a get-down-and-do-the-work gardener, I often (usually?) criticize these landscaping authorities but will admit to their expertise at fitting shrubs into an overall design. Some but not all of them seem to regard plants as design objects that should grow wherever they are put. I prefer architects who address fundamental problems that influence the selection of shrubs for a particular home landscape. Some obvious points are the need for drainage, effects of soil acidity, and the light requirements. Then there is the matter of cold requirements. Consider a plant that needs four hundred hours with temperature below 40°F to break dormancy. It may do well in an exposed part of your yard or die slowly if planted close to your brick house. In selecting shrubs for your home, location should mean more than simply how it will look; if it will not grow, it cannot look good.

Another complaint I have with some books on shrubs is that the authors tend to lean heavily on the natural forms and sizes. They say that if plants need to be pruned to control their form or size they were chosen poorly. Well, maybe, but what about hedges? God did not make plants that grow with attractive flat surfaces. I am being facetious, but I get disgusted when reading articles about famous gardens. How many of those gardens are the size of your yard? Usually it is Lord Somebody's estate of a thousand acres, or the Rothschild's little place that takes up most of a county. In such a setting you can admire the beautiful form of a shrub, perhaps imported from Nepal when the British raj was in full flower, or you can see the effect of a few hundred feet of shrub border across five acres of lawn. Those make beautiful pictures but have no relationship to the problems of choosing shrubs that will have a chance in your soil conditions, judging how large they will get in a few years, or how they will survive the amount of care that you are able to give them.

There is a lot of interest in the use of native plants for the home landscape. I think the best reference book is *Plants for Designers: A Handbook for Plants of the South* by LSU landscape architects Neil Odenwald and James Turner, which describes a large number of native plants. Their book has stimulated interest in more frequent use of native plants by homeowners and landscape architects. In general, I agree that native plants can fit well in a home setting and that they offer alternatives to the dull selection of popular shrubs that you find in many garden centers. I want to add a bit of caution: do not assume that all native plants are better adapted to the local environment than are the introduced species. In the chapter on trees we said that the big-leaf magnolia and dogwood are beautiful landscaping trees, but only within a narrow range of conditions. Many other native plants are narrowly adapted; they may require excellent drainage on the side of a sunny slope, continuously moist soil in a shaded location, or something in between. Most native plants produce large numbers of seeds each year. If you see a single attractive plant growing in the woods, ask yourself why there is only one. Also ask whether you should take that plant to your yard, where it might die, or leave it for others to enjoy. Ask around the garden centers about native plants; it might encourage them to start carrying some. But you should also consider why the local garden centers carry the lines of shrubs that they do. There are several aspects to their choices, and an obvious one is that the plant must be easily propagated either from seeds or cuttings. Another is that it must be reasonably well adapted to general home conditions of the area; they do not like to make refunds because the plant died. Finally, there is the old god of the marketplace: they sell what most people want to buy. You can influence this to some degree by asking why they do not have a certain plant; perhaps they did not realize that it might sell or had not tried to locate a supplier. It is more likely that they have found the plant did not grow or sell very well.

Pruning Shrubs

Before digressing to native plants, I was working toward the point that many good landscaping plants are so vigorous that they must be pruned to the required size. Now I want to run through some principles of pruning. The first point is that any pruning operation ultimately dwarfs the plant, meaning that pruning is both a system for controlling size and for shaping the plant according to your taste. Unless the plants are used in hedges or in topiary work (a beautiful art form that went out of style with the era of being able to afford several full-time gardeners), the natural shape is more desirable than what you can produce by pruning. This means that most pruning should strive to remove entire branches from their point of origin (which may be from another branch or from the main branch, or trunk). This will result in a *thinning-out* type of pruning. If you want to thicken up an area of the plant, where perhaps breakage, poor light, or just chance caused an open space, you should use what is called *heading back*. This means the removal of the shoot tips, which allows several lateral buds to grow. Too much heading back results in a hedge, or an artificial shape, whereas too much thinning out will produce a living pole. Balancing the two types will allow you to hold down the ultimate size and approximately maintain the natural plant shape.

Back when I was a graduate student at Cornell University, the department head (a stiff Prussian gentleman of the old school) had a ritual of having the entire teaching faculty follow him into the orchard for lessons on pruning. His complaint was that too many of the students did not understand the principles behind pruning. In his mind, this meant that the faculty were not teaching it correctly. When they had gathered in the orchard, he would select a person at random and have him explain how a specific tree should be pruned. Then he would go over each proposed cut and demand justification for it. After the victim explained the cut, the department chair would point to branches with equal forks, either one of which (or neither) could reasonably be removed. Although we considered him a sadist (which he was), his criticism demonstrated that pruning is an inexact science but that it must be based on clear objectives and a knowledge of the growth habit of that plant. With that kind of understanding you should be able to withstand criticism of your reasonable choices.

Pruning is not easy to teach as a definite system because every plant presents an individual case, but the principles can be taught and applied to all plants. Pruning is a means of size control and a means of shaping plants for definite objectives. You may want to keep the tree low so that all the fruit can be picked from the ground, or you might decide to provide a better light environment where the foliage has become too dense, or the plant might need heading back to allow more leaves in a space that is underutilized.

Flowering shrubs are a different challenge. Pruning them at the wrong time may remove the flower buds. The best way to decide when flowering shrubs should be pruned is to divide them into the kinds that bloom on new shoots (produced the same season as the flowers) and those that bloom on shoots produced the previous season. Plants that bloom on wood produced the same season (the term is *current season's wood*), should be pruned in late winter or early spring before new growth starts. If you are pruning cold-sensitive plants, it is a good idea to wait until the danger of damaging cold is over. There are two reasons for this: (1) A late freeze could further reduce the living material left after pruning, and (2) pruning can reduce cold hardiness. Plants that bloom on wood grown the previous season should be pruned immediately after bloom. This will allow the new shoots to grow and initiate the new flower primordia for next season. Azaleas are examples of plants that bloom on previous season's wood. If an azalea is becoming too large, you should prune immediately after it blooms.

You should have no trouble determining the blooming pattern of a shrub by simple observation during flowering season; it is easy to see what kind of wood is producing flowers. Examples of plants that bloom on current season's wood, or new growth, are abelia; althea; hibiscus; hydrangea; hypericum; indigofera; lagerstroemia (crape myrtle); michelia (banana shrub); bush roses; spiraea; vitex; and oleander. Those that bloom on last season's shoots include azalea; flowering quince; magnolia; mock orange; climbing roses; viburnum; camellia; raphiolepis (Indian hawthorn); and some kinds of spiraea.

Choosing Shrubs for Your Yard

The following paragraphs include some examples of shrubs that are useful in the humid South, categorized by some of their attractive characteristics.

Shrubs with fragrant flowers include daphne; gardenia; hamamelia; jasminum; lonicera (honeysuckle); magnolia; philadelphus (mock orange); and viburnum.

Shrubs that make good hedge plants include aucuba; berberis; buxus; deutzia; elaeagnus; euonymus; ilex; lonicera; pyracantha; podocarpus; rosa; viburnum; ligustrum; cleyera; *Camellia sasanqua;* and azalea.

Shrubs with conspicuous fruits include spring-fruiting types: blueberry, leatherleaf mahonia *(Mahonia bealei),* and winter honeysuckle. Summer-fruiting types are blueberries, French mulberry *(Callicarpa),* cleyera, goumi *(Elaeagnus multiflora),* and huckleberry. Winter-fruiting types are *Ardisia crispa;* golden dewdrop *(Duranta); Euonymus americana;* hollies; *Photinia serrulata;* podocarpus; pyracantha; and viburnum tinus (black-fruited).

Some shrubs have variegated foliage, making them good accent plants. Some of these are aucuba; elaeagnus; euonymus; gardenia; hydrangea; ligustrum; osmanthus; and pittosporum. Nurserymen often discover variegated *sports*, which they propagate and offer to home gardeners. Most of the variegated plants also are available as the usual green-leaved types. These are usually better known than the variegated forms.

Other characteristics of shrubs that are important in evaluating them for use in your yard are texture; color of foliage (summer and fall); whether deciduous or evergreen; blooming or fruiting habits; ultimate size; growth rate; longevity; susceptibility to disease or insects; adaptability to the proposed planting site; maintenance needed; and availability.

In chapter 7 we mentioned publications that rated trees and shrubs adapted for the New Orleans area. Shrubs that were given the top rating included small-to-medium, medium, and large-growing plants. In the small-to-medium group were dwarf Chinese holly, dwarf yaupon, Chinese mahonia, and dwarf Burford holly. Medium-size shrubs included leatherleaf mahonia, nandina, and Reeves spiraea. Large-growing shrubs included Russian olive; pineapple guava; oak leaf hydrangea; Burford holly; Chinese witch hazel; sweet olive; tea osmanthus; cleyera; and Japanese viburnum. Notice that some of the more popular shrubs did not make the better ratings. Roses were given a low rating of 4 because of the special requirements for drainage, pruning, and pest control: roses are a lot of trouble. Azaleas and camellias did not make the top grade. Most azaleas produce spectacular flowers for a short time in the spring, but the bush is there for the entire year—some are rather attractive but many are not. In chapter 12 we explain some of the serious pest problems of these plants.

This said, Leon suggests that you might still consider such camellias as "Pink Perfection" and "Purple Dawn." They grow slowly and get scale insects. With careful sanitation you can hold petal blight to a minimum. The flowers are beautiful and the foliage is attractive throughout the year. Camellias require care, but they are worth the trouble.

Transplanting Shrubs

One of our extension agents says that if homeowners would transplant shrubs properly the nursery industry would lose half of its business. So here are some tips on transplanting shrubs.

Transplanting should begin with soil preparation, done before you buy the plant. But if you bought some plants on sale, the soil can be prepared on the same day. We can start with the assumption that your soil is tightly packed and poorly drained. Loosen the soil to a depth of about a foot over the entire area where you expect the roots to grow within two years. Now is the time to lime and fertilize if the soil needs it. If the soil is very poorly drained, consider digging a trench to a lower spot for water to drain away from the new transplant. You will not be able to drain to the entire one-foot depth, but try for at least a few inches of surface drainage. Remember that without somewhere for the water to go, you are essentially planting in a closed pan. There is no need for this drain to be an open trench; refill it with loose soil for slow drainage, or you could leave a shallow V ditch.

From this point on I am discussing the preparation for any soil, whether it has good internal drainage or not. Dig a hole slightly larger than the plant container and not quite as deep. Despite the helpful advice from your neighbor, do not put compost, leaves, or any organic additive in the hole. It will simply hold water that you want to have draining away.

Your new plant is probably in a plastic container, growing in a loose bark-mix soil. If you have a choice at the garden center, select a plant with healthy green leaves, full foliage, and no broken branches. If it has dropped many leaves or they have a yellowish color, you should suspect root damage; someone neglected watering or messed up the salt concentration. The plant will probably recover after transplanting, but it may die slowly.

In transplanting, remember that you are moving the roots from a loose, well-drained (probably excessively drained) medium into the natural soil of your yard. Pull the plant from its container and wash away as much of the bark-mix as possible. The nursery used bark-mix because it drains well and is light, but your plant has graduated from the nursery and is on its own. A solid stream of water from a hose might do the job. Soaking it in a bucket of water will help if the ball is not too compact. You may need to physically straighten out the roots in the ball mass by twisting it with your hands. Breaking a few roots is allowed if it helps get rid of the old bark-mix and spread the roots for better contact with the soil. If roots have coiled around the bottom of the nursery container, cut those roots completely. New roots will develop above the cuts and grow into the new soil area. I want to emphasize this point: the most common cause of dwarf azaleas dying after they are planted is that someone dropped the tight root ball mass into a hole and covered it up. If the poor little plant is watered regularly and not exposed to long rains, it will adjust and live—but with very little growth. A year later you can dig the plant up and see that the root system still consists of that tight ball.

In planting, hold the bush so that the root-stem junction is slightly above the soil line, and tamp soil all around the roots. This will leave the plant growing high enough to promote some runoff of water from around it. If it is at all feasible, try to transplant during October and November, our two most nearly dry months. This plant will be developing a new active root system with a high oxygen requirement; excessive water could kill the young roots. Obviously, the plant will require frequent watering during this dry period but the goal should be to keep the soil moist rather than wet.

Do you really have to be this careful with transplanting? No, but this approach will result in more rapid recovery and fewer losses of plants. Your poor nurseryman may lose half of his business.

Chapter 10

VINES ARE FASCINATING PLANTS

In this chapter we explain why, and how, vines are not quite like other plants.

Back in the shrub chapter we mentioned an author who described shrubs as being those plants between the vines and the trees. That is not good enough to describe vines or shrubs. Some vines can serve as ground covers and some, when trained upward for a few years, make stems stiff enough to serve as small trees. You have seen wisteria trees that were made like this. Vine stems are indeterminate; they keep on growing as long as external conditions do not make them pause (permanently in extreme cases). This is an obvious similarity with trees and shrubs, but vines differ in the stiffness of the stems. During the juvenile stages vines are not rigid enough to keep the plant upright. Most of the successful vines have developed some means of growing upright so that the leaves are exposed to light. The only alternative would be that they must compete with low-growing plants.

Some vines climb, usually on other plants (unless you provide artificial support), by means of twining stems. These stems coil around things, some in a clockwise fashion, some counterclockwise, as they elongate. Some climb by means of adhering roots. They may adhere so tightly that removing them from painted surfaces pulls off the paint. Grape vines produce tendrils that wind around anything they touch. Then there is the cat's claw vine, which produces gadgets that look like claws. Those claws take advantage of any small indentations in surfaces they encounter.

Once the twining stems or tendrils encounter objects, the coiling action seems to be due to a response similar to that caused by the plant growth hormone *auxin,* with the tissues in the stem on the opposite side expanding more than those on the side in contact. Based on a Greek word meaning "to grow," auxin is produced primarily in the stem tip. It usually moves uniformly down the sides of the stem, causing all the cells to elongate. However, most of the auxin moves away from sunlight, to the other side of the stem. The cells on the far side grow longer, so the plant appears to lean toward the sun. You often no-

A white-flowering wisteria *(Wisteria sinensis)* that has been pruned to form a tree.
Courtesy LSU Cooperative Extension Service

tice this with potted plants that seem to be growing toward the window. If you rotate the pot occasionally, the plant will grow more uniformly. Another characteristic of auxin is that it moves downward in response to gravity. This response keeps the stem growing erect; if the plant leans a bit, the cells on the lower side will elongate more, which straightens it up.

But how do a vine's tendrils find something to grow on? Old-time gardeners say that young stems are attracted to objects. Maybe this is because of radiating heat waves or reflected light. At any rate, tendrils seem to sense the nearby object and reach out for it.

We should mention one other basic point about auxin. It is also the hormone that prompts new cells in mature plant tissues to form roots. This is why roots form at the bottom of a stem cutting. It is also why you should dust the cuttings of some species with a root promoting compound, which is a dilute mixture of auxin and talcum powder. Notice that the auxin still moves downward by gravity, but the cells form roots rather than simply elongating.

Many vines attain their mature stage only when growing upright. Some of the tropical vines, such as philodendron (the name means "tree lover") and *Epipremnum* (our old "pothos vines"), will produce large vines and large leaves after climbing only a few feet. Lower down, the juvenile leaves are smaller and simple (entire) instead of having the lobed shape of adult leaves. The adult leaf shape seems to be more wind-resistant. This adult shape is not due to vine length, because prostrate vines remain juvenile regardless of length. It is not light intensity or temperature. It does not help to say that the plant can detect its upright position from auxin movement, because what happens after that is not known. This matter of juvenile and adult plant stages is fascinating, but no one has developed any sound ideas of how and why it works. It is one of the areas in which horticulture is very much an art; but art is fascinating.

Fruiting responses of plants are another aspect of this juvenile/mature situation: juvenile plants grow; mature plants flower and produce fruit. We do have some thoughts on the fruiting response in vines. Often gravity and wind will pull some of the large stems of upright vines loose to a horizontal position, which causes them to produce fruit. It seems probable (at least to us) that the bending causes a kind of girdling (an old practice for making fruit trees switch from vegetative to fruit production), and the accumulated foodstuffs induce the blooming stage. When the climbing fig vine *(Ficus repens)* starts growing up walls or trees, it has small leaves and stems. These become larger with height; this is called an arborescent (treelike) form, with large leaves that are substantially different from those on the juvenile parts. This arborescent part will fruit and produce purple figs up to three inches long. Ed used to get strange calls from people, saying that their cedar trees were producing figs. They seldom mentioned that the cedar tree had a vine growing in it. There is an old brick church at Paincourtville, Louisiana, with a fig vine covering one entire wall but producing fruit only at heights above twelve feet. The figs are edible (although not very tasty), which leads to the tale that there are ripe figs above twelve feet because that is the height to which a Cajun can reach when standing on the cab of his pickup truck.

Choosing Vines for Your Site

Southern gardeners are faced with the same temptations toward tropical vines as with shrubs and trees. We love to plant attractive vines that might make it through mild winters but will be killed or severely injured by freezing weather. Sometimes the vine will survive if it is growing on or near a brick wall that will protect it (for a day or two) with radiant heat. If you want to grow tropical vines, try rooting cuttings every fall and keeping them over the winter as potted plants.

At the other extreme, there are vines that do not grow well without some winter chilling or do not tolerate hot, humid weather. Trying to grow those vines in the Deep South is difficult, and why bother? There are enough well-adapted vines to let you choose something for most uses: shade, privacy, flowers, or fruit. In the case of fruiting vines, your selection of grapes is pretty

Table 3. Vines Suitable for the Deep South

Annuals	Hyacinth bean *(Dolichos lablab)*, morning glory, sweet pea, cypress vine *(Quamoclit pinnata)*
Very sensitive to cold	Bougainvillea, Dutchman's pipe *(Aristolochia durior)*, bleeding heart *(Clerodendron thomsonae)*, cat's claw vine *(Doxantha unguis-cati)*, creeping fig *(Ficus pumila* or *F. repens)*, Mexican flame vine *(Senecio confusus)*, moonflower *(Calonyction aculeatum)*, wood rose *(Ipomea tuberosa)*, firecracker vine *(Manettia glabra)*, red passionflower *(Passiflora coccinea)*, butterfly vine *(Stigmaphyllon ciliatum)*
May die back but resprout	Coral vine *(Antigonon leptopus)*, potato vine *(Dioscorea* spp.) kudzu, rangoon creeper *(Quisqualis indica)*, mirliton (vegetable pear: *Sechium edule)*, potato vine *(Solanum jasminoides)* (deciduous), bengal clock vine *(Thunbergia grandiflora)*, black-eyed Susan vine *(Thunbergia alata)*, Confederate jasmine *(Trachelospermum jasminoides)*
Cold hardy [A]	Akebia *(Akebia quinata)* (D, N. La.), Boston ivy *(Parthenocissus tricuspidata)* (D), cross vine *(Bignonia capreolata)*, trumpet vine *(Campsis radicans)* (D), New Zealand clematis *(Clematis paniculata)*, Japanese clematis *(Clematis dioscoriefolia)*, painted trumpet *(Clematis virginiana)*, Argentine trumpet vine *(Clytostoma callistegioides,* also called *Bignonia speciosa)*, Carolina jessamine *(Gelsemium sempervirens)*, Algerian ivy *(Hedera canariensis)*, English ivy *(Hedera helix)*, climbing hydrangea *(Hydrangea petiolaris)*, Spanish jasmine *(Jasminum officinales)*, Hall's honeysuckle *(Lonicera japonica halliana)*, coral honeysuckle *(Lonicera sempervirens)*, Virginia creeper *(Parthenocissus quinquefolia)* (D), Lady Banksia rose *(Rosa Banksia)*, smilax *(Smilax lanceolata)*, wisteria *(Wisteria sinensis)* (D), evergreen wisteria *(Wisteria megasperma)*, muscadine grape (D) *(Vitis rotundifolia)*

Note: Many of the vines listed here are rare, and you may not be able to find them at garden centers. You may have to resort to buying seed from a catalog. Also, it is safer to order by botanical name than by common names, which may vary according to the region.

[A] D=deciduous.

much limited to muscadines, but they produce well with very little care (see chapter 8). There are similar substitutions possible with the ornamental kinds. You may want to choose deciduous vines such as grape and wisteria, or something that is evergreen. After vines become established they need almost no care except for pruning to keep them in bounds, and occasionally some renewal pruning to invigorate old, woody vines.

Some Specific Recommendations

In selecting vines, you should consider these factors: (1) Can they be grown as annuals? (2) Some vines that are cold-tender enough to be killed back in severe winters may survive mild ones, or in protected places. (3) Some vines that are killed back in cold weather will sprout from the roots when spring comes. (4) Finally, there are the "no hassle" vines that are cold-hardy throughout the Deep South. See table 3 for a list of vines that fit in those categories.

Now, we should mention some of our favorite vines. They are arranged, roughly, into the cold-hardiness categories. This is difficult because Mother Nature does not like having her plants forced into absolute situations.

Among the vines that we grow as annuals, try hyacinth bean, morning glory, sweet pea, and cypress vine.

Cypress vine *(Quamoclit pinnata)*, an annual, flowering in summer.

Courtesy LSU Cooperative Extension Service

Bougainvillea, an ornamental tropical vine suited to protected areas.

Courtesy LSU Cooperative Extension Service

Cat's claw vine *(Macfadyena unguis-cati)* with spring flowers.

Courtesy LSU Cooperative Extension Service

Vines that are cold sensitive but will make it through mild winters include bougainvillea, Dutchman's pipe, *Clerodendron thomsonae* (bleeding heart is a common name, but this creates confusion because *Dicentra* has the same common name). *C. thomsonae* has a white tubelike calyx with protruding red petals. It is also called red beans and rice. In Cuba, it is "heart of man." Cat's claw vine produces clusters of three perfect little claws that can dig into trees

Creeping fig *(Ficus pumila)* will even climb on glass.
Courtesy LSU Cooperative Extension Service

or walls. Creeping fig (the climbing fig that we mentioned earlier) is another cold-sensitive vine that is popular. Mexican flame vine produces clusters of orange daisylike flowers all spring and summer until the first frost of fall kills it back. Moonflower vine has striking white morning glory–like flowers that open at night. Wood rose has attractive seed pods that resemble tan roses carved from wood. The hummingbird or firecracker vine produces masses of red flowers on shiny green foliage. The red passion flower is an attractive vine. Butterfly vine produces clusters of small yellow flowers in summer, followed by tan seed pods that resemble small butterflies about three inches across.

Now we come to tropical vines, which need protection from cold but will make it in protected nooks. They may or may not come back from the roots. Two of these are the coral vine (sometimes called "rosa montana") and the potato vine, which has striking, large, heart-shaped leaves, shining and with depressed veins (this vine produces aerial tubers that can be used to propagate more vines).

The kudzu vine comes under this heading, if you really want that sort of thing. It was introduced as the solution to badly eroded fields but became a terror that completely covers trees. It is killed every winter and resprouts from crowns.

There is quisqualis, the Rangoon creeper, and the mirliton (or chayote or vegetable pear) treasured by cooks (and eaters) in south Louisiana. *Solanum jasminioides* is a deciduous vine that grows quickly and produces a profusion of yellow flowers like potato flowers—they are in the same genus as the po- tato. The Bengal clock vine, with its surprising trumpet-shaped blue flowers

Butterfly vine *(Stigmaphyllon ciliatum)* shown with its butterfly-shaped seed pods in late summer.

Courtesy LSU Cooperative Extension Service

that are two to three inches across, is known botanically as *Thunbergia grandiflora,* for its large flowers. *Thunbergia alata,* the black-eyed Susan vine, sometimes has orange flowers with black centers. Variants have flowers that are solid orange, yellow, or almost white. It is often grown from seed and will reseed each year from seeds that drop to the ground. Confederate jasmine (*Trachelospermum jasminoides),* a native of Asia, is dear to the hearts of unreconstructed southerners. Its close relative, Asiatic jasmine, makes a good ground cover but will not bloom unless it has something to climb on.

Finally, the following is a partial list of vines cold-hardy enough to endure our winters (see table 3). *Clematis paniculata* is a vine from New Zealand sometimes sold as Japanese clematis, which it is not. The Japanese clematis is a different species that produces larger flowers. Both kinds have white blooms and are well adapted to our area. *Clematis virginiana* is native to the eastern United States and very hardy.

The painted trumpet vine has two botanical names; the old name was *Bignonia speciosa* and the new one is *Clytostoma callistegioides.* Under either

Argentine trumpet vine *(Clytostoma callistegioides)* shown with spring flowers.
Courtesy LSU Cooperative Extension Service

name it produces an evergreen vine with pretty, shiny, dark green leaves and pairs of dark lavender flowers in summer, trumpet shaped and about three inches long. Its flowers are very like those of the cat's claw vine, except that the latter are yellow.

Carolina jessamine (it is a jasmine, but the common name is spelled differently) seems to be used more these days, especially on rural mailboxes. It was hurt badly during the great freeze of 1989 but it did eventually recover. This vine is notable for the very early bright yellow flowers in late winter and early spring. Its foliage is poisonous, which reminds me of a story. Long ago, one of our horticulture faculty learned about its poisonous leaves the hard way. His grandchildren were visiting on Easter and somebody gave them a cute little bunny. The only green foliage he could find to feed this new pet was Carolina jessamine. On the following morning his grandchildren had a dead bunny. We never let him forget that blunder.

Algerian ivy can be used very much like English ivy, but it is somewhat more cold-tender. Where it clings to walls or trees, the heat from the supporting structure often protects it during freezes. Algerian ivy makes a good ground cover if it gets a little cold protection. English ivy is best known for its wall-climbing propensity. It can damage mortar between bricks and often damages trees, if the growth gets very dense. There is a climbing hydrangea that is attractive and quite rare. Most garden centers do not carry it, but I see it occasionally advertised in catalogs. We like Spanish jasmine and Hall's honeysuckle, which has white flowers that turn yellow as they age. Coral honeysuckle, with red flowers, is not quite as vigorous as Hall's. Virginia creeper is one of the few vines that may provide autumn foliage color in our area. This is the plant that is occasionally mistaken for poison ivy; it has five leaflets and poison ivy has only three.

There is a related vine appropriately called "bush killer vine" in the New Orleans area, where it has completely overgrown and killed many shrubs despite the efforts of gardeners. It is much more aggressive than Virginia creeper, but most of the "well-adapted" vines can cause serious problems in yards. Uncontrolled wisteria can overgrow and kill shrubs. It may also invade the very structures of houses, growing into small crevices of the wood or walls. However, an evergreen wisteria is available (ordinary wisteria is deciduous) that is not so invasive.

The Lady Banks rose *(Rosa banksia)* makes a showy display in spring with its yellow blooms, but it gets large and needs space plus lots of light. Smilax, or bull briar, is known by many names, some of which are not commonly used in polite society. It can become a nuisance weed but it has attractive shiny leaves, especially when it climbs a bit and changes to the more arborescent-type growth. Smilax is widely used in Christmas decorations in some parts of the country.

We mention muscadine grapes here as well as under the fruit category (see chapter 8), because they are relatively trouble-free, well adapted, and make good subjects in the landscape, especially when trained overhead on arbors.

If you look around, you will find a surprising diversity of vines growing in sheltered places throughout the humid South. Part of the fun of gardening is trying new things to see whether they will succeed at a specific spot in your own yard.

Chapter 11

A SOFT GREEN CARPET

Maybe we should begin this chapter by assuming that you have bought a new home, that landscaping was not included in the purchase agreement, and the "yard" is bare soil that has been compacted by the contractor's trucks running over it.

A turfgrass contractor will say, "No problem, I can just smooth out the ruts and lay sod over the entire thing." To be honest (and if I do not say this Ed will laugh at me) the contractor's method is generally effective. Homeowners are usually well satisfied; if they were not, the contractor would have to replace dead grass. Good sod placed on top of badly compacted soil grows rather well provided there is a good slope for drainage and the grass is watered frequently. This seems to indicate that turfgrasses are naturally shallow-rooted plants and do not need a loose subsoil. But research plots in carefully managed, well-drained sandy soil show that our two most popular grasses will produce roots to depths of seven feet; with roots like that they should never need watering. The realistic answer is that our grasses will survive in very shallow soil if they are watered frequently, and within a few years the roots will probably penetrate the compacted subsoil and you will not need to water quite as frequently.

Ed: Folks, please note that Leon is setting you up for another "why don't you do it right, even if you don't have to" lecture.

Leon: Yep, and here I go.

Is there ever a reason to prepare soil well for a good lawn? Maybe. You are planting a crop that will grow for twenty or more years. It will be exposed to many kinds of stress: long droughts; hard freezes; insects; diseases; and baseball, football, and soccer games. Consider also that you will mow the crop at least once a week for about forty weeks per year. With a small lawn it will take maybe thirty minutes, or as much as two hours for a larger one. Twenty to eighty hours per year for twenty years begins to add up. There are estimates that about 60 percent of your monthly water bill is the cost of watering the lawn, much of which would not be necessary if the soil had been prepared properly. Do you want to make that much of an investment in a lawn that will never look very good?

Go back to fundamentals. To the extent you can, you should prepare the soil well before planting a lawn. This is true whether you are starting a new lawn or renovating an old one. Take a soil sample and adjust the pH and fertility levels according to the kind of grass you want to have (we discuss types later). Kill the perennial weeds if you can. Subsoiling would be helpful but you probably cannot do that. Slope the yard so that there are no low spots and the water drains smoothly in the direction you have chosen. Rent a power tiller and pulverize the soil as deeply as you can. Rent a lawn roller and smooth the soil as well as you can. If centipede grass seeds are sown thickly and watered frequently, they will probably crowd out all weeds except perennials, but centipede is the only good turfgrass that can be seeded. All of our grasses can be successfully *sprigged* (propagated by planting stolons or rhizomes) on about four to six-inch centers, but you should also apply one of several good pre-emergence herbicides at the same time. This will give you four to six weeks of weed control, and you may decide to spray one more time after that. Hand weeding of large grass plots is tedious work.

After considering the problems of seeding and sprigging, you will probably decide to have the lawn sodded even though it will cost an arm and a leg. That is the only way to get an instant lawn. But remember that the grass will look better and withstand droughts much better if the soil is prepared properly before sodding. Also remember why you worked the soil so well: do not drive a car on your wet lawn. If you did a good job of soil preparation, the car would probably get stuck, which is just what you would deserve.

Our suggestions about which grass you should select for your lawn are almost as simple as the ones on land preparation. Centipede is a very good turfgrass that has moderate shade tolerance and fairly good drought and chinch bug resistance. St. Augustine grass develops a deeper green color, has good drought resistance, and is the best selection for grass in the shade of trees. Much of it will be killed in extremely cold weather but patches will survive and spread rapidly. It can be badly damaged by chinch bugs, and both grasses have disease problems. You may choose other grasses but, because these two are the most popular, we explain their insect and disease problems first.

Chinch bugs are the primary reason for the large dead areas that you often see in St. Augustine lawns during the summer. (Brown patch, caused by a fungus, is more likely during cooler weather from fall to spring.) Chinch bugs vary in size; the largest are only about one-eighth of an inch long. You will probably notice their effects before you see the bugs. These insects eat away at the grass roots during warm weather; when a drought hits you can see what has happened. Despite all your watering the runners turn yellow and die because they have no roots. If you resod the dead patches, chinch bugs will eat the new grass. When infestations are heavy you may see the small dark-bodied bugs with whitish wing covers scurrying about on concrete walks or driveways near the edges of lawns. Do not crush them—they smell like crushed stink bugs. If you suspect a chinch bug infestation, cut a plug of grass (roots and all) and put it in a pail of water. Chinch bugs will desert the sinking grass and float to the surface.

Chinch bugs are easily controlled by any of several chemicals. If you ask at the garden center, you will find that most people choose an insecticide especially for chinch bug control rather than a multiple purpose product.

Brown patch kills leaf blades in the lawn in roughly circular areas from one to as much as fifty feet or more across, and the areas turn brown. Sometimes you get an interesting design when the grass puts out new growth where the fungus is no longer active. This creates a ring of dead grass with healthy-looking grass in the center. (Fairy ring mushrooms do the same thing for the same reason.) The brown patch fungus is inactive at high temperatures, so you will not have it during the summer. Dollar spot is the fungus of hot moist summer weather. It attacks all grasses but is worse on Bermuda and zoysia. As you might guess, this begins as a group of small spots in which the grass blades die. Then the spots grow together into large dead spots. Another fungus called gray leaf spot might attack St. Augustine grass in warm moist weather. The first signs are gray spots on the leaves and, later, the grass appears to be scorched from high light intensity—except that this occurs in damp, shaded areas. Fortunately, all of these diseases can be controlled by applying a fungicide. Ask at your garden center.

On the other hand, the disease may be gone next year. Leon has a theory: diseases come and go, usually due to some climatic condition. During rainy spells the wet spots in the yard frequently show signs of disease, but the long-term solution is to improve surface drainage rather than pouring more pesticides into the yard. Obviously, if the infection is so bad that great patches of grass may die, you should treat. But fungicides will not kill all of the fungal spores in your yard. If you can put up with a little dead grass, things may improve next year.

There are some harmless fungi that appear occasionally. Slime molds can develop during warm, moist weather as black or gray crusty coverings on leaf blades, coming off like soot on shoes or clothing. This is not really a disease; the fungi use grass blades to support the fruiting structures and can be brushed off or washed off with a hose. Fairy ring is a fairly harmless disease that fascinates children. Large whitish mushrooms appear in rings, usually eight or ten feet in diameter. They come up overnight and persist for a week or so. The grass near the mushrooms is often greener than the rest of the lawn, whereas that in the center may show signs of stress. Tell your children that fairies come out at night and dance on the mushrooms. If you have no children of the proper age, pull the mushrooms up and get rid of them before they begin spreading spores. The only method of control is to dig the soil out to a depth of two feet and replace it.

A virus disease, called St. Augustine decline (SAD) has been isolated from grass in some areas. Affected grass has a mild mosaic symptom, less green color, and may die out over a period of some years. When SAD was first noticed, pathologists predicted the elimination of St. Augustine as a lawn grass. Much like Mark Twain's death, the claims were greatly exaggerated. But if you have a sunny area with the acceptable soil pH for centipede grass, and you are going to establish a lawn, why not use centipede? You may have heard of something called *centipede decline;* pathologists now believe that it is only a reflection of poor conditions for grass establishment and/or poor culture. Taking everything into account, St. Augustine grass and centipede grass are probably the best choices for lawns in our area for the average homeowner.

Shade Tolerance

The relative shade tolerance of different turfgrass varieties is easier to understand if you recognize that tolerance has two aspects. The most obvious is that grass growing in the shade of a tree is surviving on hand-me-down light. The sunlight has already been filtered through tree leaves that use the same wavelengths (for photosynthesis) as the grass leaves need. The light intensity (total amount of light) under the tree is less important than how much of the red and blue wavelengths are left. If the leaf canopy is not thick and the wind blows frequently, the grass will get more light. Also, grass under a tree will often get early morning or late afternoon direct sunlight. With the less shade-tolerant varieties such as Bermuda grass the leaves become long and narrow, and are often yellowish; the plants are starving. This is where the irony of the popular term *plant food* comes in. The plants are starved for real food—carbohydrates and proteins that are end products of photosynthesis. Adding fertilizer will not help and may make things worse. Growth reduction is due to low levels of photosynthesis, so the plants eventually will die. We should also point out that it is very difficult to establish grass even in moderate shade unless you sod it. Sprigging just will not work.

There is another, equally important, aspect of shade tolerance. This is one that you can help to correct. Grass growing in the shade of a tree is also growing in competition with tree roots for water and nutrients (fertilizer, not food). Large trees use a tremendous amount of water on hot summer days. Well-established tree roots are usually more competitive about obtaining water than are the shallow roots of newly planted sod. Unless you water the grass well it will die, but this will occur only to the edge of the tree, which is where most of the tree roots are competing for moisture. If the grass under the tree has died, and that away from its canopy continues to grow, it seems obvious that the variety is not shade tolerant. But the grass under the tree probably died from the double stress of low sunlight and low moisture.

Sprinkler irrigation is probably the best solution for drought stress under a tree. Because a tree does use a lot of water, and you want it to grow also, you might consider putting a permanent irrigation system under large trees. Some people water trees by digging holes at several spots, filling the bottoms with gravel or sand, and inverting a bottomless plastic jug in each hole. You can fill the jugs with water every day in dry weather, giving the tree a constant supply of water. Whether this helps both the grass and the tree is not clear, but you might want to try it.

Turfgrass Selection

CENTIPEDE

This is the grass you will probably choose. Centipede is a medium-textured grass, coarser than zoysia and finer than St. Augustine. It grows best in slightly acidic soil (pH 5 to 6) and with lower fertility than is required by other turfgrasses. It has fewer pest problems than the others. The primary shortcomings are that it requires more frequent watering than does St. Augustine and does not stand up as well under heavy use (such as children's football and baseball). Even when it is well managed, centipede does not develop the deep green color of other grasses. We have noticed that centipede grass turns brown with the first heavy frost; St. Augustine has considerably more frost tolerance. This effect is striking where your lawn contains a mix of the two species.

St. Augustine

This grass seems to do better than centipede in the shade of trees, but the difference may be entirely one of drought tolerance. St. Augustine will continue to grow well in drought conditions that will make centipede go dormant.

St. Augustine is still a very good lawn grass if you maintain it well and control chinch bug infestations. As you walk around the neighborhood you will notice that the new houses with plenty of sunlight have centipede; it is easy to identify by its narrow uniform leaves, which look almost like artificial turf. St. Augustine is around the older houses with large shade trees. It has broader leaves, is less uniform, and more vigorous than centipede. St. Augustine requires a pH of 5.8 to 7.2 and a little better fertilization than does centipede, but the grass has a deeper green color, and it usually grows back over home plate and first base before football season begins. This assumes that you water and mow frequently. In general, St. Augustine grows a little faster than centipede but both grasses do well with weekly mowing, allowing you an occasional lapse for vacation or wet weather.

Zoysia

Emerald zoysia is a hybrid of two *Zoysia* species, *Z. japonica x Z. tenuifolia.* The El Toro zoysia is a selection from *Z. japonica.* The Meyer zoysia that you see advertised in some magazines is of the same species but it does not do well in our area. There is also a variety of the very fine-leaved *Z. tenuifolia* called Mascarenegrass that is beautiful in small areas, but it is difficult to find and very difficult to maintain. So, for our purposes—and for the present—zoysia means the hybrid Emerald zoysia.

Zoysia is a very fine-textured, dark green grass. Shade tolerance is probably less than that of St. Augustine, but this is hard to determine because zoysia has a high requirement for frequent watering. Established zoysia has good drought resistance, meaning that it will survive with about the same watering as St. Augustine but cannot compete with the other grasses unless it receives more water. With good fertility, adequate soil drainage, and frequent watering it will slowly crowd out the weedy grasses. You will also have to mow twice a week throughout the summer. Zoysia stands up well under traffic and easily covers home plate after baseball season is over.

Zoysia sod is expensive. It can be established by sprigging but the process is slow. Do not try to establish zoysia by planting the small plugs that you might see at the garden center. Those plugs do spread but they also produce humps where each plug was planted. If you buy plugs, use them for sprigging.

For about twenty years Leon had a thick zoysia lawn except for the St. Augustine that grew under the large live oak trees where he did not water frequently enough. To be honest, Leon mowed only once a week after the grass was well established, and fertilized every other year, but the grass did not have a dark green color. Zoysia grows such a thick carpet that thatching can become a serious problem. Leon's solution was to mow several times during late winter, progressively dropping the cutting height until the thatch had been removed. The grass recovered slowly each spring but there were never any weed problems. This approach works only if the lawn is uniformly smooth.

Hybrid Bermudas

During the late 1950s a U.S. Department of Agriculture plant breeder in Tifton, Ga., began making selections from, and crosses between, several species of Bermuda grasses. His original objective was to develop good pasture grasses, but he also noticed that some would make good lawn or golf course grasses. He began releasing these as varieties under the prefix "Tif." An important point about these hybrids is that they do not produce viable seeds; this keeps the lines pure. The primary objection to Tifton Bermudas is that maintenance is even more demanding than that of zoysia, but they are beautiful grasses for someone who has time to care for them.

Tifway

This is a selection that was developed for use on golf fairways. It has slightly coarser leaves than those of the other Tif varieties but it is very attractive.

Tifway grows rapidly from sprigs and will quickly provide a nice, inexpensive lawn. It requires frequent fertilization, watering, and mowing.

Tifgreen

This is the Bermuda grass used on most putting greens in the South, but it is also a good lawn grass if you maintain it well. It has a finer texture than Tifway but grows more slowly during establishment. Both hold up well under traffic.

Tifdwarf

This was selected as a mutant from Tifgreen. It has fine, small leaves and fits well in small areas, but it tends to thatch if mowed at common heights for lawns. It can be established from sprigs about as fast as Tifgreen.

CARPETGRASS

This is a somewhat inferior low-maintenance grass that grows well on wet, poorly drained soil. It can be seeded or sprigged, but it never makes a dense lawn and seems to always be producing new seed heads. It does not hold up well under traffic and is often damaged by cold. As of now, it is more of a lawn weed than a turfgrass, but there has never been any breeding and selection program for this grass.

BAHIA GRASS

Although there might be some justification for deciding to use carpetgrass for low-maintenance, do not let anyone persuade you to try Bahia grass for a lawn. It grows on almost any kind of soil, has low fertilizer requirements, and can be seeded. It forms thick, fleshy rhizomes, grows in bunches rather than producing a turf, and is very difficult to mow. This is a pasture grass and not even very good for that.

WINTER GRASS

All of the grasses we have mentioned will be killed to the ground by the first hard freeze. Your lawn will take on a lovely beige coloration until springtime. The beauty of this is that you will not have to mow it for several months. If you want to have a green lawn throughout the winter, overseeding with perennial ryegrass *(Lolium perenne)* is the best bet. In the Deep South, perennial ryegrass grows as an annual because it is killed by summer heat. Several varieties of this grass have been selected as good lawn grasses, and this is what is used in the winter on golf greens. Annual ryegrass is a different species *(L. multiflorum)* that also grows as an annual but was selected for use in winter pastures. It makes a coarse-looking lawn. Seed winter grass at a rate of around five to ten pounds per thousand square feet and mow at heights of one and a half to two inches. You probably will not need to add fertilizer, but extra nitrogen will give it a deep green color—and you will have to mow more often.

Mowing and Thatch

Mowing is a cultural practice that affects all lawn grasses, and it involves several variables you can control—with a bit of self discipline. The kind of mower used, frequency of mowing, height of cutting, and disposal of clippings are all involved. Lawn grasses are able to stand being handled as lawns because of the way they grow and adapt to hug the ground, but some are coarser than others and have different growth habits. A widely used rule-of-thumb is to remove no more than one-third of the leaf blade length in each mowing. This, in theory at least, spares the runners, or stems, and enough intact leaf area remains to carry on photosynthesis. The inherent size of the grass determines cutting height, but you should set the lawn mower height while it is on the grass. The concrete driveway is more convenient but it does not allow for wheels to sink into the turf and can lead to scalping the grass. For St. Augustine grass the best cutting height is usually from two to three inches, depending on the sponginess of the turf: If the wheels sink down, use the higher setting; if the lawn is solid, use the lower one. Centipede and carpetgrass lawns are usually cut at one- to two-inch heights, common Bermuda from three-quarters to one inch, and hybrid Bermudas and zoysias from one-half to one inch. The finer textured grasses are usually mowed with reel-type mowers and the coarser grasses with rotary mowers. (See chapter 2 for a detailed discussion of the merits of reel-type mowers as opposed to rotary mowers.)

Mowing frequency will depend on how fast the grass grows, and this is affected by temperature, moisture, and fertilizer. You will probably want to mow about once a week. With a little practice you can adapt irrigation and fertilization for your grass to grow at the proper rate.

A couple of interesting observations come to mind here. A noted agronomist (noted as an agronomist but not for expertise on lawns) once observed that if you only mow occasionally (no fertilizer or water) you will end up with a pretty good Bermuda grass lawn. A landscape architect friend (who may not have had any more expertise with lawns than the agronomist) says that he rates lawns based on the speed at which the observer is passing. For example, the agronomist's Bermuda lawn might look fine to somebody driving by at thirty-five miles per hour, but an observer strolling by it could see that it had lots of Dallis grass, stickerweeds, clover, and other plants in it. Turf areas along the interstate highways are "70 MPH lawns" that look pretty bad if you slow down. Our warm-season grass standbys, St. Augustine and centipede, are probably the most satisfactory for most of us.

Now, what about clippings? Will they cause the dreaded thatch we are often admonished to avoid? Ed removes clippings from his grass because his wife thinks it is lazy not to. He is usually told to put the clippings in plastic bags and dispose of them properly in the garbage collections. Environmentalists are welcome to try, but Ed does not think they will be able to convince her otherwise. If you are really lazy, let the clippings filter down among the leaves. If you mow often enough at the proper height, the clippings will not hurt the grass, but actually can help by returning nutrients. Another tip: thatch does not build up as badly if the lawn is limed regularly. Apparently, the fungi that decompose thatch work more effectively at a pH of about 5.6 to 6.0.

We need to talk about what thatch means. Thatch is a mass of living leafless stems, dead stems, and dead leaves that accumulate on the soil surface. In a sense it is a minicompost layer, and a little of it is good. As it gets thicker the grass tends to start making roots in it, water will not move through it well, and insects and diseases thrive in the environment. Thatch is not a problem unless it becomes more than three-quarters of an inch thick. If the lawn is excessively spongy underfoot, it can indicate a thatch buildup (or it can be due to tunnels made by moles, mole crickets, or other pests). A rough check for too much thatch is to pull on the sod; if it feels loose, the thatch is a bit thick.

If you or your consultants decide that thatch is a problem worth correcting, dethatching makes a good early spring project. You can rent dethatchers or core aerifiers for the weekend. A dethatcher is something like a vertical mower, with small blades that cut through the thatch, which you then simply rake up. Core aerifiers punch holes through the thatch and into the soil. The cores are removed and scattered over the soil surface. After dethatching, it is a good idea to scatter sand over the lawn and water it in. On golf greens they simply scatter sand on top of the thatch and make it part of the soil.

With most grasses, thatch accumulation means that you have been mowing too high or fertilizing and watering too much for your mowing practices. Look at the recommendations on mowing heights and fertilization for the different grasses. Because zoysia thatches excessively, it should be mowed short every spring. Mowing short will also work with Bermuda grass but not with St. Augustine or centipede. Zoysia and Bermuda grass produce rhizomes: underground stems that send up new shoots in the spring. The others spread by stolons, which grow primarily at the soil surface.

The idea that you can avoid thatch by collecting the cut grass in a catcher attachment on the mower seems to make sense, but research has shown otherwise; the clippings increase the thatch accumulation by only 10 or 15 percent. The best argument for using a catcher attachment is that the clippings are unsightly and make good compost. If clippings are piled up too deep when still wet, they undergo an anaerobic decomposition, which makes a smelly mess. In the compost pile, adding thin layers of leaves alternated with coarse, fibrous materials keeps the process aerobic. Under shrubs, follow the practice of spreading only thin layers of clippings to avoid the same mess.

Watering

Most turf recommendations say that lawns need an inch of water a week during the growing season. If your area does not receive that much rain, you should consider watering. The garden center will have a wide array of sprinkler types: none of them are very good (see chapter 2).

Remember that the amount of water going through the hose has little relationship to what the grass gets; a lot of the water evaporates during the sprinkling process. Take four or five cans and arrange them in the area covered by the sprinkler. After about fifteen minutes of watering measure the amount of water in each can. You will be disgusted with the uneven application pattern of your sprinkler, but you also will have an idea of how long it takes to apply an inch of water. Also, if you start watering in the afternoon after getting home from work the water pressure will gradually drop as everyone else begins to water. This means that the time required to collect an inch of water will increase. You might try attaching a timer to the faucet so that watering begins at about 4 A.M. when the pressure is better and evaporation is at a minimum. One other point: if you decide to water, do a good job. Watering a little every few days will encourage the development of a shallow root system that will make the lawn even less drought tolerant.

Remember that at the beginning of this discussion we said you might consider watering. You also might just want to take a break from mowing and wait for a rain. This is not to say that our droughts will not kill lawn grass. But that depends on how bad the drought is, how bad your soil is, and whether the soil is compacted. You might want to hold off watering until spots of the lawn seem to be dying.

Late on hot summer days it is interesting to study the drought-stressed patterns in newly sodded lawns and wonder what caused them. Some are obvious, such as the drying grass near a tree, which is probably trying to compete for water that tree roots are getting. You can usually see the straight-line tire marks where construction workers parked along the roadside, with two wheels on wet soil that would later be sodded. Circular patterns in the yard could be from insects or disease, or where the cement truck was washed out. Occasionally the circle represents a low spot where the grass roots were too wet during a long wet season. Low oxygen killed the deeper roots, and drought has taken moisture from the shallow roots. Grass growing over concrete culverts often dies during a drought because there are no deep roots. With St. Augustine grass, circular patches usually indicate that chinch bugs have killed the deeper roots, with the same effect as grass growing over a culvert. With centipede, the patches that died during a drought will sometimes grow back with Bermuda grass, which means that it was a weed in the sod you bought; Bermuda grass is more drought tolerant than is the centipede.

Should you complain to the contractor who sodded the yard? Sure, but it will not help. He will show you a lawn of the same age just down the street. It was put out in the same way but that man watered almost every day. If you had watered it often enough, the grass would not have died. Then you can point out that most of the grass lived with minimal watering and only died in the bad spots. But you will not win an argument with the contractor.

Fertilizing

There are many "best" fertilizer recommendations for home lawns, but they may not be practical. Also, you should consider not fertilizing very much or very often; more lawns are injured by too much fertilizer or poorly timed applications than by not fertilizing. For warm-season grasses, an application of one pound of nitrogen per thousand square feet in April, June, and August on St. Augustine grass or one-half pound nitrogen in April and August on centipede grass, usually will be enough. If the grass remains off-color or does not grow well, you might suspect low phosphorus or potash, but insect or disease problems are more likely. The nitrogen can be put on as a form containing nitrogen only, such as ammonium nitrate, or urea, but those are hard to find: try getting a mixed fertilizer with low phosphorus and potassium, especially for the spring applications. Most mixed fertilizers are pelletized, made in small grains or balls to minimize hardening or *setting up*. Application is best done with a mechanical spreader that you can rent from the garden center, either a drop type or a rotary type. With either of these, take some pains to get the material spread over all the grass without making double applications on part of it. The day after mowing is a good time to apply fertilizer if the grass is dry, so that the particles can sift down away from the leaves. Always water the material in to prevent burning of the leaves. There are slow-release materials that are not as liable to injure the grass, but they cost more and may not offer much advantage. (See chapter 16 for a more detailed discussion of fertilizers.)

Every fall we see signs at the garden center saying that it is time to "winterize" your lawn with potassium. There must be test results in the coastal South showing that a fall potassium application will reduce winter kill of turfgrass, but the tests we've seen show no improvement—zilch. The principle is fairly sound; grasses with high levels of stored food reserves (carbohydrates and proteins, not fertilizer) will hold up better under severe cold conditions. If you manage your lawn well during the summer (fertilization, irrigation, and consistent mowing), the plants will accumulate reserves. In the fall you should continue to mow but avoid fertilizing and watering. This will reduce the amount of new growth, the tissues that are more sensitive to cold damage. The logic that we see about adding potassium in the fall is that, if you have added too much nitrogen in the summer, the extra potassium might reduce plant growth somewhat. That is a pretty weak "if." Winterize your lawn by not watering or fertilizing it in the fall.

Weed Control

There are several "weed and feed" fertilizers that contain a little herbicide to control certain weeds that have gotten out of hand. In general, you do not need herbicides for a well-managed lawn. We will skip the details here because chapter 14 is devoted entirely to principles of weed control. Turfgrass—watered, fertilized, and mowed regularly—provides a dense mat that competes well with any weed. The best weed control program for lawns is fertilizer, water, and a lawn mower.

One of you is saying, "But it won't control nutsedge." Yes, it will, but not immediately, not the first year, or the second, but each year you will notice that the nutsedge is getting weaker, and in time it will quit producing new shoots. Notice that we did not say good management kills nutsedge; it is still there after the shoots disappear. If insects or disease kill a spot of your lawn, the nutsedge will sprout and you will begin the fight all over.

Bermuda grass is a weed that management will not control, and you will be forced to hand-dig it out or spot spray with an herbicide. Another serious weed of turf is Bahia grass. This has long been a good low-fertility, low-management grass of pastures. For this reason most old pastures have at least some Bahia plants and a lot of dormant seeds in the soil. With the popularity of solid sod planting for new homes, farmers who once raised grass for cattle are deciding to raise grass for profit. They disk the pasture well, plant some turfgrass, and become sod farmers. Some states have a state sod certification program under which the fields are checked for disease, insect pests, and weed problems. Because the legal aspects are difficult, your state may not have such a program yet. In that case, you will have to rely on a good garden center or sod contractor; otherwise you may spend a year hand-digging to remove Bermuda grass and Bahia.

As we said earlier, weeds are usually best controlled by having a thick, vigorous grass cover. There are herbicides to prevent seedling growth, but the fundamental problem is that the grass cover is too thin. Take care of your lawn and you will not need herbicides.

Stickerweed is a good example of weeds in poorly maintained lawns. This plant probably has other names. It is an annual that was once called *Soliva ses-silus* but is now *Soliva pterosperma.* The seeds germinate in February and, if the grass covering is sparse, the soft green plants will grow throughout the spring. They produce pretty little white flowers and you may begin to think that it might make a nice ground cover. With the first hot, dry spell in May or June the plants die, but the seeds remain. Each seed has a long sharp spine on it. This is not like the sand spur that will go through rubber-soled shoes, but stickerweed seeds will stick into your hands, knees, or bare feet—and hurt like everything.

Back in the good old days almost every lawn had at least one patch of stick-erweed. The stickerweed contest among barefoot boys was to see who could run farthest into the patch—remembering that you also had to run back out. Woe unto the little boy who tried sitting down to pull the stickers out—they go through pants, too.

Stickerweed makes a good story but it also illustrates the lawn weed prob-lem. A preemergence herbicide applied in January will control stickerweed for that year. Eventually you will realize that the stickerweed is there because grass is not growing well. Correct the problem, which could be compaction, fertil-ity, pH, or possibly drainage; then the stickerweeds will disappear.

The pretty little moss that grows in damp bare spots during the spring is a similar problem. It makes an attractive ground cover in shady spots, but only if you keep the soil damp all summer. What about spring violets in your lawn? Are they really weeds for you? Better care for the grass will eliminate them but they are pretty in the spring and no trouble during the summer.

Renovation

Most of this chapter assumes that you have a new house and are ready to es-tablish a new lawn. But many of you already have an old lawn that you inher-ited or established long ago. In this section we assume that you do not like your lawn; it has low spots where water stands after every heavy rain, high spots that the mower scalps most of the time, and the grass is a mixture of St. Augustine, carpetgrass, common Bermuda, nutsedge, buttonweed, and stick-erweed.

If your lawn is large, divide it into manageable units, fairly small areas that you can concentrate on one year at a time. If you have a friend with a transit, it might help to survey the lawn and decide which way it should drain—a decision you must make whether you can get a transit or not. By watching after a heavy rain you can mark the low spots and get a good idea of the general slope. You should contract with someone to bring a load of fill dirt for those low spots. He will call it rich topsoil, but what you get will often be river silt: a mixture of silt and fine sand with no organic matter, no structure, and many weed seeds. Spread this fill material in the low spots and wait for a rain to settle it. You will probably need to refill several times before the water drains off properly.

If you are satisfied with the grass, or grass mixture, already in the yard you may decide to simply fertilize, water, and mow until the lawn improves. Grass will grow up through the fill dirt and you will no longer have the low spots. We are assuming you want to establish a good new lawn of St. Augustine, zoysia, or centipede. Select a manageable area and check to see if anyone has buried the TV cable, telephone line, or gas line there; this may decide how deeply you can work the soil. Take a composite soil sample just as you did in the garden spot and send it off for analysis.

In chapter 14 we explain why the best time to kill weeds is in July or August. For the present, trust us. The easiest approach will be to spray that work area with a broad spectrum translocated herbicide, wait a week, and rent a power tiller. Alternatively, you could just till the soil and hope that hot, dry weather will kill everything. Regardless of the approach to killing weeds, you will probably need to till the soil well on two successive weekends. Before the second tillage, apply the lime and fertilizer suggested by the soil test and for the kind of grass you will grow. After tilling, rake it smooth and wait for a rain to settle the soil. The spots where you applied fill dirt may settle and still be low, but that can be corrected with a hoe and rake. Now, rent a lawn roller, which is simply a metal tank designed to be filled with water and rolled over the soil to firm it. The lawn must be sloped properly and the low spots filled before you roll it.

If you are tired of the inconvenience that comes with sprigging, you may decide to buy sod now. But we will assume that you are a real do-it-yourselfer. Sprigging is much cheaper and results in a smoother, better-established lawn, meaning that you can water less frequently. If you choose an easily established grass, such as St. Augustine, and sprig closely you will have a muddy unsightly lawn for about two months. If you decide on something like zoysia, look forward to a year at least: with bad weather it could take two years for really good coverage.

Minority Statement

To round out this discussion of turfgrass we should admit that neither of us maintains our home lawn this way. Ed once had a St. Augustine lawn, but when chinch bug damage became frequent he plugged centipede in the full-sun areas. He never fertilizes, and he mows when the grass seems to need it. Leon has a relatively new yard (ten years old). He sprigged St. Augustine in for a fast cover and is starting zoysia in the full-sun areas. The ground is covered and it looks pretty good. He waters the zoysia plots but ignores St. Augustine except during extremely dry weather.

Our reasoning for the way we handle our grass is largely that the lawn is not a great concern for us, but we can make other arguments. Unless the subsoil is badly compacted, most established turfgrass will survive a drought and still look pretty good. It seems strange to advocate water conservation in Louisiana, but much of our municipal water is from deep wells where the water is replaced slowly. If the report is sound that 60 percent of a homeowner's water consumption goes into watering the lawn, why should we waste so much? The argument about fertilizer wastage is less sound. In some areas the runoff of excess nitrates will pollute groundwater, but recent studies in our nitrogen deficient conditions show that, even with frequent fertilization, most of the nitrate is retained by the grass or decomposing organic matter. Nonetheless, we still contend that unless you enjoy a beautiful lawn, heavy fertilization is a waste of resources, requires more frequent mowing, and promotes thatch formation.

Ground Covers

We originally had this discussion of ground covers in the chapter on trees because ground cover is a good option when the shade or water competition is too great for grass. But now we have decided that ground cover is a type of turf. Well, we had to put it somewhere!

A ground cover can be living (plants) or some aggregate, such as crushed stone or coarse pine bark. Ground covers also can be useful in full sun: you may want to cover a slope that is difficult to mow. Although we usually think of ground covers as low-growing plants, some that grow to several feet in height can used as covers; for example, some of the junipers do well on slopes. Ground covers include a wide range of plant types, including some that are evergreen and hardy, some that occasionally may be killed back by freezes, some that are grasslike, some that are vines, and some horizontal-growing shrubs. We cannot think of any trees used as ground covers, but if you want to stretch things a bit, some of the dwarf fruit trees are grown low enough to the ground that they might qualify.

Ground cover plants can be less demanding than lawns in that they do not need frequent mowing. Most of them will require some maintenance at times, at least the removal of leaves dropped by trees growing above them. Some will look better if they are trimmed occasionally. String trimmers work very well on most, or you can raise your mower to its highest level and simply mow the cover. A few will stay fairly well within bounds of height without maintenance, but most of them will get too tall unless they are trimmed occasionally.

One of the more popular plants used as a ground cover in our area is Asiatic jasmine *(Trachelospermum asiaticum)*. There is also a variegated green and white form, but most variegated plants are not as vigorous as the green forms and are less tolerant of high light intensities because only the green area contains chlorophyll. Asiatic jasmine can climb and cover fences, trellises, or bushes unless you keep it trimmed. You may remember from our chapter on vines that most will flower and fruit only after climbing. If this jasmine climbs, it will usually flower in late summer and produce masses of white, fragrant flowers like its cousin, the Confederate jasmine, which came from China long ago (it is a "Confederate" plant only because it is not cold hardy enough to succeed in the far north). Liriope, a member of the lily family, makes a fine ground cover but takes a little longer to establish than does jasmine, largely because it produces clumps of plants rather than vines. It comes in a number of varieties, differing in size and also in the number and color of its flowers. Some are not very showy, but others, especially if they are watered, make a spectacular show in summer. Some varieties have white blooms, but most are lavender-purple. There also are variegated liriopes that produce showy leaves and have purple flowers in summer.

Monkey grass and mondo grass are related to the liriopes but usually have smaller leaves. Mondo grass is very dwarf, making plants only about three inches high, which gradually spread to cover the ground. These produce less showy blooms than liriope, and the flowers are usually hidden in the leaves. Monkey grass produces startling sky-blue berries that sometimes extend above the leaves. These are tough plants, but cannot take the abuse from traffic that turfgrasses endure. All of these liriope-like plants gradually will spread and invade flower beds or spread out into lawns unless edging materials are used. A former horticulture professor used to caution Ed about planting monkey grass, because it had taken over a large part of his yard. Ed did not bother to point out that regular mowing was the solution to that problem.

Two *Vinca* species are popular ground cover plants—*Vinca minor* and *Vinca major.* These are hardy, perennial plants, related to the periwinkle, which is often called a vinca, but is not (it is *Catharanthus roseus*). Periwinkle is so badly damaged by moderate cold that it does not make a good ground cover. The others are cold hardy and can be propagated by cuttings or runners. *V. major* gets pretty large and rank, whereas *V. minor* usually stays below a foot in height.

You can find many types of English ivy, varying in leaf size, shape, variegation, and vigor. Before deciding on ivy as a ground cover, consider the various problems. Most varieties are subject to serious leaf and stem diseases. These can be controlled by spraying but that adds to the trouble of maintaining an area. Established disease-free ivy is extremely vigorous, climbing up trees and shrubs and into beds. As with diseases, this can be controlled, but it requires attention and sweat. We do not consider ivy to be a low-maintenance cover.

As you might expect, not all ground covers grow well in all sites; look around the neighborhood to see if any ground covers appear to be well and happy, or which ones look sick. Among other candidates (for some locations) are holly fern *(Cyrtomium falcatum),* which grows about three feet high and can be winter damaged even in Baton Rouge. Turkey ivy *(Lysimachia nummularia)* is a low-growing, light green plant for areas where the ground cover should not get taller than about six or eight inches. Dwarf ardisia *(Ardisia japonica)* makes a good ground cover; but do not confuse it with *Ardisia crispa,* which is a taller-growing plant with conspicuous clusters of red berries in season.

In sunny areas, where height of the ground cover is not a problem, daylilies, junipers (some of these remain quite short and spread along the ground), and some honeysuckles are useful.

There are many attractive, but troublesome, ground covers: Ajuga, euonymus, dwarf gardenia, hosta (this will grow better in more northerly areas than in the coastal South), and strawberry geranium, which is hard to keep attractive in hot weather. With a little effort, and by using plants in the proper location, there are many other plants that you could grow successfully as ground cover. You will notice that we favor those that are largely trouble-free.

Poison ivy is often a serious weed in ground covers that are growing under the shade of trees. Birds love the fruit of poison ivy, so the seeds fall with their droppings. This makes a nice planting system, with its own starter fertilizer. Careful spot treatment with a herbicide is usually the best solution, but get some advice from the county agent—herbicides also kill ground covers.

Chapter 12

INSECTS, DISEASES, AND COMBINATIONS OF THE TWO

We hope you have noticed our frequent promises to explain things in later chapters. This is the first of those later chapters. We are now switching from "this system works (usually)" to "this is how it works (maybe)."

Insects

Controlling insects in your garden is difficult because the bugs will not stay put; insects fly, they develop resistance to insecticides, and are kept somewhat in check by predator insects, which are also killed by insecticides. We can illustrate this by giving you two imaginary neighbors with large gardens. (We will be talking about a vegetable garden but this applies to any type of garden.) One of them hates insects. He sprays every few days with the same kind of insecticide. When insects become resistant to that chemical he switches to another kind. The neighbor on the other side of you plants enough for herself and the insects. She picks her crop a few times and leaves the rest to the bugs.

You have one neighbor who is building up insecticide resistance and making things worse by killing off the predator insects. You will not get many insects from his garden but those few will be difficult to control. The other neighbor lets a heavy population build up and when they eat everything in her garden they will move over to yours. If you had no gardening neighbors in the entire block, you might be able, with sanitation and minimal amounts of insecticide, to manage the populations that move into your garden. If you were to buy populations of predator insects and release them in your garden, most of them would fly over to your neighbor's yard where there are many more insects to feed on. Some will fly in the other direction and be killed by sprays.

The situation is not really that bad, but we wanted to get your attention before defining the problem: insects have been thriving in this world long enough to have developed many survival devices. A sound control program requires careful, consistent management and the realization that you will not be able to control all insects in your garden.

The most important approach to insect management is sanitation. Although most garden insects can fly long distances, they would rather not. If an insect population gets out of control in your garden (the large, mature insects are difficult to kill), cut the crop out and put it in the compost. Be sure to cover the infested plants with more compost. In general, it is not a good idea to keep a crop until the last flower or fruit is ready; it wastes garden space and promotes higher insect populations. So, sanitation usually means that you should cut the crop out quickly and compost it.

The next point for consideration is insect-resistant crop varieties. Where you have a reasonable choice, go with varieties or crops that the insects do not seem to like. But consider that *resistance* has several meanings. Usually it means that there is something about the plant that makes feeding on it difficult for insects; it may mean that the leaves are too hairy to feed on easily. Or, taking corn as an example, the shuck may be so tight that it is difficult for the worm to reach the kernels. The variety may have an odor or taste that the insects do not like. In these illustrations *resistance* refers essentially to preference; the variety is not very appealing but a hungry insect will eat it. This is probably the safest kind of resistance; if something in the crop kills the insects you may begin wondering what it will do to you.

Sanitation and insect resistance are fundamental, but we still must face the question of how you are going to protect against insects that are already eating on your plants. Maybe this is a place to list some rules: just a little old-fashioned common sense. First, personal observation is critical; you should look over the garden almost every day and study it carefully about once a week. Look for any differences, such as a plant with less green color, or plants that were blooming a week ago and now have no flowers while others of the same kind still are blooming.

Once you have noticed something unusual, look for a cause. Insects have survived over the millennia by clever adaptations, including camouflage, mobility, concealment, and feeding at night when most of their predators (including us) are sleeping. For instance, you may become aware of aphids in trees when you notice a sticky exudate on the automobile that was parked under them, or when sooty mold growing on the exudate turns the roof of your house black. Sometimes the leaves of plants growing under aphid-infested trees become entirely covered with the coatings of exudate and sooty mold, which not only is unsightly but also reduces photosynthesis. Aphids are not the only insects to produce exudates; scale insects and mealy bugs also do this. These insects are frequently accompanied by ants. You may remember some fanciful article about ants acting as "herdsmen" and "milking" the aphids. The less colorful truth is that ants feed on the sugary exudates.

Crape myrtle trees are often heavily infested with aphids, and with another insect that can come to your attention because it seems to be "raining" under the crape myrtles when it is obviously not raining anywhere else. Regardless of what you might think the insects are doing, the rain is mostly water; insects known as *sharpshooters* suck the sap from the tree and forcefully eject the water after removing most of the soluble material from it. These are sometimes called *squirrel bugs* from their habit of scurrying to the hidden sides of branches when they see you coming.

Remember that many insects feed on the undersides of leaves or specialize on the unopened buds. If you jostle a ligustrum plant, you might be surprised by a cloud of whiteflies that were feeding under the leaves. So do not just walk through the garden, but instead also poke around at the leaves.

Caterpillars have a host of devices for concealment, although you may only notice droppings or chewed leaves. Hidden slugs also can cause serious damage to plants. To control an insect you must first find it, somehow.

Sometimes you simply cannot find what is affecting the plants: insects, disease, nematodes, or nutrition. Many state extension services maintain clinics to help you solve such problems; contact your local county agent to find the schedule for these clinics. If your garden center operator is on the ball, the staff there should be able to help you in identifying the problem.

Identification of the cause is important because the control measures will depend on it; insects differ in their feeding habits, either sucking sap from plants or chewing and ingesting tissues. Thrips lacerate the tissue and appear to lap up the juices, whereas other sucking insects puncture the tissues with various sorts of probes to suck out the juices. Worms, beetles, slugs and snails, and some ants also chew up leaves and other plant parts. Strictly speaking, mites are not insects, but that does not matter. They act like very small sucking insects.

Ed's Tale about Thrips

An earlier-generation horticulture professor at LSU was showing a New Orleans nurseryman through our collection of magnificent rose bushes. The nurseryman was a flamboyant character, wearing spats and smoking a large cigar. I had worked for him during my high school days, and was watching this meeting with much interest. The nurseryman, in his unique New Orleans accent, asked, "Got any t'rips?" The rather austere professor replied, "No, I haven't seen any." The nurseryman bent down and blew a fog of cigar smoke into a rose bud, whereupon a cloud of thrips, no doubt coughing little thrip coughs, erupted. The nurseryman grunted, "No t'rips, eh?"

So, you have found and identified the little critter. Now what? You might ask someone at the garden center for suggestions or you may consult a chart on insect and disease control. The county agent's office has a good one.

TYPES OF INSECTICIDES

You have not yet decided whether to use an insecticide, but it is time to discuss what insecticides do. Some chemicals act on contact with the insect, either through some toxic action or simply by suffocation. There are also *systemic* insecticides that are taken up by the plant and kill (or strongly discourage) the insects that feed on the leaves. As you will see later, this creates the same situation as having a genetically insect-resistant plant; we think the genetic insecticide is safer because you cannot make a mistake and apply too much. There are some effective biological controls; the most popular are various preparations of a commercial preparation called BT *(Bacillus thuringiensis)* that is a bacterial disease of many caterpillars. It can be sprayed on plants to poison caterpillars without any danger to mammals. More about that later.

Recommendations for use of insecticides often are quite specific about the dosage and timing of applications. Both are important. Timing and dosage are designed to kill the insect at its most sensitive growth stage. For example, insects are usually most susceptible to an insecticide in the young adult stages but are resistant when in the egg. If the life cycle is such that the time from egg to young adult is seven days, it is important that you spray carefully to contact as many adults as possible in the first application. You will probably miss some, but the main problem is that those in the eggs will not be affected. This means that the first treatment is useful only if you apply a second spray to control insects that hatched from surviving eggs and before they can lay more eggs six days later. Two applications would do the job if you could be sure that no adults escaped your treatments; a third application six days later is a good precaution. So: Use the right dosage, try to spray so that the entire plant is covered, and repeat the applications at the correct intervals. It is important to know the life cycle of the particular insect you are trying to control.

Most pesticides are applied as sprays, some as dusts, some as drenches, and a few as aerosols, fogs, or smokes. The equipment you need often depends on the amount to be applied. For a few houseplants a one-pint plastic spray bottle will do nicely. For larger gardens you may need to use a pump-type pressure sprayer, of one or two gallon size, or a hand duster. Because many insects hide under leaves, the sprayer should have a nozzle that you can adjust to spray beneath the leaves. You may decide that a duster would be better for getting good under-the-leaves coverage. For large-scale applications you might want to consider a power sprayer that would give coverage to young trees. You will probably decide against that; they are expensive and take up storage space. Alternatives are renting the sprayer or getting a contract spray company to do the job. Lawn pesticides can be applied with irrigation sprayers, but it is difficult to maintain an even pattern, so some areas might get too much and some not enough.

Some pesticides recommended by extension entomologists may be listed for "restricted use," meaning that application is legal only for people certified to use them. Because they are not all that strongly restricted, you can probably figure a way to get the pesticide without having a permit, but resist that temptation. Many of those chemicals are pretty dangerous, and you should not need such strong treatments. The garden center will have shelf after shelf of special chemicals for this and that. Also, remember that you do not really want a wide array of pesticides; two or three will probably do the job for you. Some of these chemicals are very good on ornamental plants but not safe enough for plants you are planning to eat. Generally, the chemicals that can be safely used on vegetables require that you wait for a reasonable period before harvesting the produce for food. All of this information is on the instruction label, so read it carefully.

Predator Insects

We know that you would really rather not use insecticides, and we agree with you completely. The idea of using predatory insects for control of the bad guys is interesting, and we hope the techniques can be worked out. However, the popular term *beneficial insects* does not seem to be quite accurate. Insects are beneficial for pest control only if they really kill the pests you have. The ladybug beetle is widely advertised as a predator insect, which it is: up to a point. It eats a wide range of garden pests, but only if they are small and soft-bodied: that is, young and tender. Remember that the ladybug is in your garden for easy-to-get food. When the supply of small, soft insects runs low the ladybugs leave. When they leave, the pest population builds up again and the ladybugs return. They have no real interest in protecting your garden, of course; their only concern is for good food. The other side of this argument is equally true; if you apply a hot, broad-spectrum insecticide it will kill everything, ladybugs and all. Predators will return when the pest population builds up again.

Our main point here is that ladybugs are very good, but they must have food. Suppose you see a few pest insects in the garden and buy a box of ladybug eggs. The eggs will hatch and produce larvae, which will become beetles and fly away unless you have a serious pest problem. Consider this: If you do have enough insects to justify ladybugs staying around, the native ladybug population will build up and keep the populations rather low. We realize you have heard some amazing anecdotal reports of how one year someone released ladybugs in the garden and had almost no insect pests. Sure; but did you talk to your friend a block away who did not release ladybugs and had almost no insect pests? Natural pest populations vary tremendously from year to year. This usually reflects weather conditions, such as a very cold winter, but long-term population cycles are probably caused by diseases.

We are not trashing the whole idea of predator insects. The point is that the use of predators is not an absolute answer. A lot of good research is being done on the subject, and commercial growers in California are using predators successfully on some crops.

Fire Ants, the Master Predators

Having wounded one sacred cow, we will try to consecrate another one. Have you ever wondered what fire ants eat and why their mounds grow so rapidly? The fire ant is an excellent predator. We need to stop here for our new-to-the-South friends. All ants that sting are not fire ants. The kind we are talking about builds large mounds in lawns and flower beds. If you stand on, or even very close to, a mound for very long they will attack you, and the stings burn like fire. This is often called the Argentina fire ant because it seems to have been introduced from Argentina on a boat that docked in Mobile, Alabama, sometime in the 1930s. For years it was an interesting example of an insect that did not move north because of climatic conditions, probably cold weather. But the ingenious little creatures learned to thrive in their adopted country; they became able to survive in cold soil and began spreading northward. Cattlemen would find young calves covered with fire ant stings. There was always a question about whether the ants had actually killed calves, but there also were other easily demonstrated problems. Cows being stung by fire ants are not very content. The same can be said about tractor drivers when the mower blades hit a big mound.

Years ago cattlemen began pressuring entomologists for control methods. There are several insecticides that will kill fire ants, but long-residual insecticides are serious hazards to the environment. The relationship between these two points is that fire ants swarm, not precisely like bees, but the effect is the same. When a queen leaves the mound to mate she flies high into the air. The male who can fly that high gets to mate with her. She then flies to the ground and starts a new colony. If the wind was blowing when she mated, that new colony may be many miles from the original one.

The best example of how fire ants can be used as good predators is in sugarcane country. Fire ants are extremely effective in the control of sugarcane borers. Fire ant stings hurt cane farmers just as badly as they do you, but nobody tries to control fire ants in a sugarcane field. Our picky bug friends would want us to add that fire ants cannot eliminate all cane borers. After the borer gets into the stalk and behind a leaf sheath, it gets so fat that the fire ant cannot pull it back out, or perhaps the ants cannot sting through the sheath.

So, what can you do about fire ants in the yard? No matter what you do they will keep moving in, but they can be easily controlled with granular insecticides from the garden center. If you can find a way to coexist with fire ants, they will almost eradicate ticks and fleas from your yard. The plants around fire ant mounds always look better than where you controlled them. As predators, ladybugs are not in the same class with fire ants. These feisty little critters will eat any insect they can catch. They will take on big tomato hornworms and stink bugs that would terrify ladybugs. The key to this is their venom. They sting anything that fights back, and then call for help in carrying it to the mound. Notice that we are making a distinction between stinging and biting. They sting you in defense of the mound and they sting large insects. They bite food.

Managing fire ants safely is a difficult problem. We cannot quite bring ourselves to say that you should keep a fire ant mound for insect control, or that you should not try it. We know of one gardener who coexists with fire ants by laying down firm rules. The mound living in the half-of-a-whiskey-barrel pot can stay. Any ants trying to set up housekeeping in the lawn are zapped.

And *zapped* seems to be the right word for using various chemicals to "control" fire ants. Kerosene, used motor oil, soapy water, cigarette slurry, and most commercial insecticides will kill fire ants, at least to the degree that they will abandon their mound. The bad news is that the mound was only a doorway to the maze of tunnels that the ants have built. In many cases the tunnel system extends beyond your yard and over to the neighbor's. You will see insecticides that promise to eliminate fire ants because the workers will carry poisoned food to the queen. Well, maybe it does kill the queen and that colony, but maybe there are several colonies in your yard. Take it from us, who have tried and failed: you cannot eliminate fire ants from your yard. The best you can hope for is to make their life miserable.

Fire ants are dangerous because dogs and children never seem to learn to stay away from the mounds. But honey bees are also dangerous and many people learn to coexist with a hive in the backyard.

Bees and Wasps

At best, these creatures are a nuisance, but some people are extremely allergic. We do not have any surefire control methods, but here are some thoughts.

Begin with an attitude adjustment. These insects do not view property rights in the same way as you. They find some vacant space, build a nice house, and consider it to be their property for the rest of the year. It does not matter that you bought and grew the azalea or blackberry bush. We could argue that most wasps are insect predators, but that has nothing to do with their territorial claims. If your hand comes within a specified distance of their home, you will be stung. They have decided where the property line is, and you must not trespass. If they come after you, move away, without running or slapping if at all possible.

But it is still your bush and you want to reassert property rights. To control wasps, first locate the nest. The safest way is to use a long pole, at least the length of a rake. Before poking your hands into an unknown bush, shake it gently with the pole—gently, brother, gently. If the wasps come out, you have found a nest; leave them alone until tomorrow. There are many good one-shot cans of insect spray being sold. The spray will probably burn plant leaves, but they will recover. In the good old days we tied newspaper on a pole, set it on fire, and fried the wasps, house and all. That was always dangerous and now it may be illegal. We have a friend who catches wasps with a butterfly net, gives the net a swirl, and steps on it. Although you do not consider it when being stung, wasps are slow fliers and easy to catch. This is the slow, effective approach and does not use insecticides.

Occasionally you can use wasps to your advantage. Years ago, when Ed had a project of testing new blackberry and grape varieties, he often had problems with people deciding to pick a few for themselves. He was not being selfish; it was just that he needed to pick parts of each plot for yield and fruit quality tests. He would then let people pick berries in specific areas. After several experiences of losing the year's results because someone wanted to harvest early, he devised a way to enlist the aid of wasps. Although he destroyed the nests in most of the plots, he would leave an occasional nest of guard wasps. When an area was ready for public harvesting he would furnish people with his wasp map. After the first year all except a few diehards learned to ask for a map before picking.

Yellow jackets and certain types of bumblebees build underground nests in loose soil. Sometimes they move into your compost pile. Do not try to catch them with a butterfly net: they are mean, aggressive creatures. It takes a while to do them in. The principle is to spray the entrance every day or two with something that they will carry down into the nest. There are several slow-acting insecticides that are effective. The one-shot sprays are not effective because they kill only a few and make the others mad.

Fairly Safe Insecticides

Many traditional insect control methods are very effective—if you understand the principles and use some common sense. Soapy water and alcohol are two good examples. Most soft-bodied insects survive by having a waxy or oily coating that keeps body tissue from desiccating. Soapy water will remove many oils; alcohol will remove most oils and some waxes. Unfortunately, they can do the same thing to plant leaves. The trick is to have a concentration that will kill the insects but will not affect the plant very badly.

We would like to give some suggestions about safe concentrations, but it is a complex problem, particularly for soap. In our section on calibration of sprayers we point out that both concentration and rate are important. On hot, dry days the water may evaporate rapidly, resulting in a higher concentration of soap. The Safer Company markets a line of fatty acid soaps that are formulated for use as insecticides. Some other companies do the same thing, but *Safer soap* has become the generic term for insecticidal soap. In theory, any true soap and many detergents should be effective if you work out the safe concentrations. You should first read the label on an insecticidal soap; we know from experience that having the right concentration, but applying too much, will burn plant leaves.

Back to the common sense angle. Regardless of what you may want to believe, soap is a synthetic insecticide. Earlier in the chapter we discussed the importance of identifying the insect and determining its life cycle to develop an effective spray schedule. This is equally true when you are using soap: spray through several life cycles to kill the small, newly hatched insects.

Another (almost) home remedy is dormant oil spray. This is simply a light petroleum product that is deadly to scale insects, such as those that damage camellia leaves. Because it will damage tender, growing leaves, it is applied during the fall or winter—dormant season. If you apply this uniformly to the plant, all scale insects that are covered will be suffocated. We understand that some heavier oils are now being developed that can be used safely on other plants for scale insect control. They cannot be used during warm weather because they will damage plant leaves.

Here is another home remedy that has potential. Earlier we mentioned the commercial preparation called BT, but you can sometimes do a better job with a homegrown disease. Almost every time a high population of caterpillars builds up you will see an occasional one that is sickly or almost dead. If you do not, spray the caterpillars with the BT mixture. Then select the first ones that are sick or dying. The principle is to select for the most virulent strain for those caterpillars and to propagate it. You want to start an epidemic; the proper term is epizootic, but epidemic sounds better. Catch all of the sick ones you can find, add enough milk to cover them well. Then squish (squishing differs from squashing in the degree of squishing) and stir the squishate well. Let the mixture age for a day at room temperature, then add 50 percent water and give it another day to work. After that you can store it in the refrigerator, with a note asking that it not be used on cereal. Mix a little of this with water and spray it over the plants. Store the rest in the refrigerator for later use. Remember that, as with all insecticides, you must understand the life cycle of the insect and spray at the proper intervals.

Leon: Ed, that is a sick, sick way to garden—using the term sick with both meanings.

Ed: It's a jungle out there. You aren't adding anything new to the garden. The disease was there but wasn't being spread well enough to control all of the insects.

We got this from a leaflet prepared by the Cooperative Extension Service. It was a new approach for us and will probably be improved. You may want to ask your county agent or garden center for current information.

We were serious about the above suggestion; now allow us a facetious paragraph. There is a natural plant product that is readily available and extremely effective as an insecticide. We realize that you quit smoking years ago, but ask your neighbor to save cigarette butts for you. Put them in a cloth bag and steep them in a quart of water. As with sun tea, it is more effective to leave the jar in the sun on a hot day. The result will be a mixture of various water-soluble forms of nicotine, which is a very potent treatment for any soft-bodied or sucking insects. It is not quite ready to use because tobacco leaves are notorious for having virus particles that will infect tomatoes, peppers, and potatoes. If you heat the solution to a boil, it will smell up your kitchen, but the virus will be killed. We should also tell you that this is a messy and unnecessary method, because you can still buy nicotine sulfate at the garden center, standardized as to strength and with instructions for use. The trade name, long ago, was Black Leaf 40. It seems significant to us that, although nicotine sulfate still has an Environmental Protection Agency label, the Cooperative Extension Service does not recommend it for any use at all. Do you remember why you stopped smoking?

We were using the cigarette tea tale to introduce another insecticide. Pyrethrin is a natural plant extract that makes an excellent and very safe insecticide. The term *pyrethrin* is not as exotic as it seems. The root word is *Pyrethrum*, the old botanical name for what is now the genus *Chrysanthemum*. It is from a Greek word meaning, roughly, "Don't eat the root because it burns like fire." The insecticide is a mixture of several complex acids (actually the esters of acids), extracted from flowers of the pyrethrum daisy, grown in the highland tropics. You could probably make a fairly good insecticide with an extract from your backyard mums, possibly by using rubbing alcohol as an extractant. The problem with a backyard extract is that you would have a mixture of unknown strength and would have to work out the treatments.

Several years ago some British chemists developed a method for synthesizing these various compounds in pyrethrin. They were then able to conduct standardized tests on insects and in animal feeding trials. Also, the compounds could be modified to make them more effective. Because these are not really plant extracts they are called pyrethroids: similar to pyrethrins but synthetic. The current ones being sold are very good, both in the garden and around the house. No pesticide can be called absolutely safe, but these are safer than most. As you might expect, people are already becoming sloppy with overdosing, and insects are beginning to develop resistance.

We have covered insect control with sanitation, soap, alcohol, oil, and the use of synthetic insecticides. We have avoided using trade names because they keep changing. Check with your garden center, which will have several safe insecticides.

Diseases

"Under the spreading chestnut tree the village smithy stands." Not anymore; his grandson has an auto parts store there, and the chestnut tree died from a fungal disease. It even wiped out the southern, "po'folks," chestnut: chinquapin. The chinquapin is beginning to make a comeback, but there seems to be little hope for the chestnut. The fungus began in New York and probably came in with some plants imported from the Orient. It slowly spread through the range of the American chestnut. An occasional tree remains here and there but only because it has still escaped infection. There seems to be no resistance. The European chestnut is just as susceptible, but the disease got there later and trees are still dying.

Dutch elm disease came to America on a shipment of lumber from Holland. These plant diseases have no direct effects on humans; Thurber's uncle did not really die of the Dutch elm disease, his aunt just thought that was the cause. It has spread throughout the Midwest, killing many beautiful old trees. In the Deep South we have lost most of our mimosa trees to another fungal disease, a fusarium. Our point is that diseases are difficult to control and almost impossible to eradicate. With a few minor exceptions, once a disease reaches your area you will have to live with it.

We do not like to classify organisms, because they do not fit well into groups. But control measures differ with the organism, so we must at least build categories.

Viruses, as you who have had flu know, are very small, tough, and can cause enormous problems. You finally overcame the flu as your body built up a resistance. We do not know of any plants able to do that; they get sick and die. Symptoms are extremely variable; distortions, spots, streaks, rings, stunting, and nothing. Some plants can carry viruses without showing any visible symptoms, but they infect other plants. Infection can be spread through seeds, by grafting, water, or insects. Tobacco smokers sometimes spread the tobacco mosaic virus to their tomato plants while picking or pruning. The virus was in the tobacco of their cigarette.

Bacteria are larger than viruses, but are still too small to see. They can cause wilts, rots, leaf spots, and galls. They are spread in the same ways as viruses.

Leon's Tale about Chestnut Trees

In 1994 I went back to French Brittany to visit the place where I helped to win the war while Ed was doing it in Normandy. I remembered a large chestnut tree where we harvested chestnuts and roasted them on an open fire. The tree is still there, but is dying from the American chestnut blight; French farmers think the disease was brought in by American soldiers.

Most of the diseases in your garden are caused by fungi. They bring about serious problems everywhere, but our warm humid climate is especially favorable for many of them. They cause wilts, rots of roots and stems, cankers, leaf and flower spots, mildews, and damping-off of seedlings.

And there are the nematodes, which are tiny threadlike worms. *Nema* means threadlike. Most plant nematodes are so small that they are only barely visible; for practical purposes, they are microscopic. They can cause galls or knots, and provide entry points for diseases. Plants with nematode-infested root systems may be badly stunted.

Those are the categories, but we would like to mention a few of the more common diseases. Fire blight is a bacterial disease of plants in the rose family, such as pears, apples, pyracantha, photinia, and others. The name is very descriptive because the young shoots turn black, as if they were burned. A wide variety of viruses affect the solanaceous vegetables, such as tomatoes, eggplants, and peppers. Black spot of roses and flower blight of azaleas and camellias are caused by fungi. Turfgrasses are susceptible to several fungi, including fairy rings (see chapter 11), which are interesting.

Control of diseases depends on the same principle as insect control. Sanitation is important. Examine all plant material you buy or that someone gives you. It is much easier to treat one plant than to treat your entire yard. This is not completely effective because some diseases are brought into your garden by air currents and some by flying insects; even greenhouse operators must watch for signs of disease on their crops.

Use of resistant plants is the best approach with some diseases. If you like to grow tomatoes, you may have noticed symbols in seed catalogs that indicate the resistance of tomato varieties to several kinds of diseases. As an example, the variety listed as "Better Boy VFN" is described as being tolerant of verticillium (V), a fungus; fusarium (F), another fungus; and nematodes (N). The variety listed as "Champion VFNT" has tolerance to those problems plus tolerance to tobacco mosaic (T), a virus. If you have seen virus problems in your garden, start using virus-tolerant or virus-resistant plant varieties.

Viruses

As with the flu, there are no medications for plant viruses, and the affected plants will die. To some degree, you can keep viruses out through sanitation, but many are spread by flying insects. Even if you keep an insecticide layer on the leaves, sucking insects can land and inoculate the virus before being killed by the insecticide. But because many insects feed randomly, and they may not have the virus until they hit your garden, sanitation will help. If individual tomato or pepper plants show signs of a virus disease, pull those plants out before more insects feed on them and spread the disease. Then wash your hands well so that you will not spread the disease. Planting resistant varieties is a good approach, if they exist. But this is a never-ending problem because new virus lines (races) develop that are resistant to the resistance, if that makes any sense. The same thing happens with the flu; when you develop resistance to one, a new kind appears.

Much of what we said about the control of viruses is applicable to bacterial diseases. There are few bactericidal treatments for living plants, but some of the copper-containing spray materials appear to help prevent infection. Sanitation, inspection, and removal of affected plants are important control measures. Resistant varieties present the only practical approach.

Before we get to the fungi we should tell a tale for you northern folk. "Why can't we grow the good old Bartlett pear that does so well everywhere else?" Fire blight bacteria are present in Iowa, Michigan, and Oregon, as here in the South; what really keeps us from growing Bartletts in the Deep South is our high humidity at blossom time. The nectar in our pear and apple flowers is more dilute than it is in Iowa—more water for the same amount of sugar. The fire blight bacteria cannot reproduce in the more concentrated nectar; the reason is unknown. It may merely be the high osmotic concentration. This is where you expect us to say that the busy little honey bees spread the disease from tree to tree as they gather the pear nectar, to which we ask, "Did you ever smell a pear blossom?" Flies love the odor of pear blossoms and help bees in spreading fire blight. That is essentially the story; raindrops help to spread fire blight, but the main problems it faces in the South are humidity and weak nectar.

Resistance to fire blight in most of the pears grown in the Lower South comes from crosses with an oriental species, usually *Pyrus pyrifolia*. The old Kieffer or sand pear is probably a hybrid between Bartlett and an oriental pear. Kieffer is not really a southern pear; it was discovered in an orchard near Philadelphia. There are a few resistant varieties of the Bartlett-type pear *(Pyrus communis)*. "Old Home" has strong resistance; the fruit tastes awful, but this variety is used as a resistant rootstock and probably has potential in the breeding of resistant varieties. But this brings us back to the question of why a variety is resistant and whether resistance is related to the poor fruit flavor. Resistance in "Old Home" may be due to the presence of a chemical that inhibits the fire blight organism, or "Old Home" may be lacking a chemical the bacterium needs. Of the two possibilities, we would prefer that it be from the absence of something rather than the presence of an unknown chemical.

FUNGAL DISEASES

Now for the fungal diseases. There are many good fungicides, and the wide array of packages offered at garden centers can be confusing. Do you really need to buy that many? Probably not, but the situation is complex. Some of the new fungicides are effective against several common garden diseases, but a truly "wide spectrum" chemical has not been developed. High humidity gives us more fungal disease problems than in the northern states. Fungi produce spores instead of seeds, but the terms are analogous. Many fungi require moisture before spores are released. They also may be carried by the wind (and occasionally insects) to other leaves and flowers, but a film of water is needed there before they will germinate. Our climate seems almost perfect for fungi.

So, how do we control fungal diseases? Sanitation is fundamental. Remove diseased leaves and fruit so they will not produce more spores. Try to select varieties with some resistance—but only in conjunction with sanitation. Massive doses of spores will overcome almost any resistance. You can hope for low humidity, but will not get it. Do not look on fungicides as the cure-all, but consider them your third line of defense. The weakness with fungicide use is that most of them are chemicals that will keep spores from germinating (more precisely, they begin to germinate and die) on the leaves or flowers. Fungicides do not work well in rainy weather; you spray in the morning, the afternoon rain washes it off, so you spray again. This is a slight exaggeration because some fungicides remain on the plant rather well, but the principle is that rainfall is the enemy of using fungicides or insecticides for pest control. Gardening in a desert with consistent irrigation makes pest control much easier.

This is a good place to emphasize disease problems of azaleas and camellias. In chapter 9 we noted that these popular shrubs were not rated high in landscape plantings. Part of the reason was that they bloom for only a short time each year and are not very attractive shrubs for the rest of the year. We omitted another important objection: flower blight. Back in the 1940s and 1950s these plants were considered key parts of any good home landscape. As with most widespread plantings, this popularity came at a cost. Azalea flowers, which normally lasted for several weeks, would begin to get "the blight" and fall off after the first rain. This was a fungal disease easily spread by rain—the same rain that washes off the protective fungicide. Extensive studies have shown that the only reasonable control method is sanitation; pick up every diseased flower that falls off and put it in the trash bin. Large azalea bushes produce hundreds of flowers, and some homes had ten or twenty such plants. Unfortunately, this kind of sanitation must be a neighborhood project; the spores will be blown by moist wind. As of now, there is no good solution, so learn to enjoy azalea flowers until the first rain. Flower blight of camellias is caused by a different fungus and is not nearly so widespread as that of azaleas, but it is equally serious, and again the only good control method is sanitation. We enjoy both azaleas and camellias, but must agree that they cannot be given a high rating.

Necessary Evils

Now we will get down to the facts of life in southern gardening. You are going to have to use fungicides on at least some of the plants. Equipment used to apply control materials is about the same for diseases as for insects, and in many cases insecticides and disease control materials may be combined. It is very important to make sure that such combinations are compatible, because some combinations can damage plants. Charts showing acceptable and unacceptable combinations are published by many extension organizations. Where lawns are attacked by diseases it may be possible to apply control materials through sprinkler equipment, but uniformity of coverage needs to be considered. Sprinklers do not make uniform patterns.

Seedlings present serious disease problems for gardeners. Young plants lack many of the protective structures, such as waxy coatings or hairs, that help adult plants stave off infections. Sanitation and use of clean planting media are vital for success with seedlings. In some cases treating the seeds themselves is important, although major seed companies usually do this routinely. If you save your own seeds, it may be important to treat them before planting. Media for seedling growth must be disease-free; do not assume that peat moss is disease-free, or sand, even though it may look clean. (See chapter 6 for a heat treatment to use on soil before using it for planting annuals.)

Household bleach is a good weapon for home gardeners in the fight against plant diseases. Diluted with nine parts of water it can be used to disinfect tools, pots, flats, hoses, and seeds. Zinnias used to be easy to grow and were a mainstay in the summer garden, but in recent years they have not been doing well in our area. This is due to several seed-borne diseases, one of which is a bacterial leaf spot and another a fungus. The seedlings are also subject to fungal damping-off. In the case of zinnias, one part bleach to four parts water is used to soak the seeds for thirty minutes, after which they should be air-dried and planted. If you are having trouble with zinnias, give this a try; it is a simple treatment that you also might use on other plants that are difficult to start.

You may wonder about the safety of adding plants that show disease symptoms to the compost pile. If the pile is well constructed and maintained, the heat of decomposition in the early stages should inactivate most disease organisms, but it is probably a good idea to dispose of virus-infested plants in the garbage.

Chapter 13

A PLAGUE ON THE LAND? CHEMICAL PESTICIDES

This chapter could be called "Yes, But." We want to show both sides of the problem of pesticides. We should add that this is a compromise chapter. We agree on the problem, but we disagree on the amount of detail that we need to discuss here. Ed wants it brief and to the point. Leon wants it brief, to the point, and comprehensive. The compromise is that we will give one good example from each side of the problem, follow that with some ideas, and summarize that it is impossible to grow plants without some degree of pest control. The hazard of using synthetic compounds is that it is difficult to prevent misuse. Dual problems of natural pesticides (produced within the plant itself) are that we know too little about toxicity and that new compounds cannot be introduced to address immediate problems. We suggest a combination approach: strict sanitation and natural resistance supplemented by the use of synthetic compounds.

Synthetic Pesticides

DDT (dichlorodiphenyltrichloroethane) is the obvious choice for the "plague on the land" side of the problem. Part of the dilemma that biologists had when working with DDT was the fact that it was saving hundreds of thousands of lives. During World War II, overseas soldiers dusted themselves and their sleeping bags weekly with DDT, which controlled typhus-carrying lice. One of the greatest threats to weak, starving, concentration camp inmates was outbreaks of typhus. When the camps were liberated, everyone was dusted with DDT and the epidemic stopped immediately. After the war DDT was used to control malaria, which was nearly endemic in the rural South: Kill the mosquitoes and the disease disappears. In entomology classes we learned that the horrible bubonic plagues of Europe would never have happened—if only DDT had been available. It seemed that DDT was the miracle chemical that would eventually eradicate such insects as flies, mosquitoes, and fleas. In cotton production, DDT was the ultimate answer to insect problems; it killed both boll weevils and boll worms. Careful tests conducted with mice indicated that it was absolutely safe for use around all mammals.

The bad news started coming in very slowly. Back in 1954 a young entomologist at LSU noticed that progressively more DDT was being needed for control of cotton insects. He found that the insects were developing degrees of resistance to DDT. He presented a paper at a national meeting—and hardly anyone believed him. They went home, conducted more tests, and found that virtually all insects were beginning to develop resistance. In the early sixties Rachel Carson published *Silent Spring,* which was about possible consequences of indiscriminate pesticide use. The scientific community looked on it with a little hesitation. Her basic information was sound, although the possibility of a genuine "silent spring" (no birds left to sing) was far-fetched and rather emotional, but almost everyone agreed that too little was known about the long-term effects of pesticide use.

It was in this atmosphere that the Environmental Protection Agency (EPA) was formed, with a mandate to provide regulations and guidelines to protect the environment and the public from the hazards of pollution, including pesticides. Research funded by the EPA and other organizations showed that chemicals that did not degrade rapidly would accumulate in the food chain and could cause serious damage to wildlife. It also proved that most plants and insects gradually develop some form of genetic resistance to any chemical being used. The complicated mechanisms for this are interesting. Essentially, if one pesticide is used consistently, a few insects develop a system to partially detoxify the chemical. Those insects survive and their offspring improve on the system, so that eventually we have a population completely unaffected by the chemical. This is what happened with DDT. It is still effective on mosquitoes in isolated tropical areas, but our fleas, lice, flies, and cotton insects are completely immune to DDT. Looking further into the problem, the scientists found that if you alternate the kinds of pesticides being used to control an insect, the development of resistance is greatly delayed. However, the insects, disease organisms, or weeds will develop resistance, even if you alternate usage.

Remember, DDT is only an example. With slight modifications, we could (and Leon would like to) say the same about most manufactured pesticides. Used carefully, most of them are safe and effective. Used carelessly, they cause environmental hazards and the pests develop resistance to them. Scientists should have moved more cautiously and we, the American people, should have been more concerned over stewardship of the land. The pioneer spirit of this country often leads us to forget that we do not actually own the land, but are holding it in trust for the use of later generations. Stream pollution, extensive soil erosion, pesticide-resistant insects, and the litter left on campus after weekend tailgate parties are symptoms of the same fundamental problem. We care too little about land stewardship.

Natural Pesticides

For our discussion, a pesticide is any compound that kills or in some way discourages a pest from feeding on a crop. This definition provides more leeway than some concepts because it allows us to include natural pesticides and repellants. *Toxic* means that it hurts a human in some way. In our discussion this will include allergies regardless of whether there is evidence that the material would eventually cause death. We will avoid using the term *poison* because it is so vague as to be meaningless: poison to what organisms, at what concentrations, and how much can be tolerated?

Breeding for resistance in plants can be tricky; insects have survived for much longer than we have, so if something kills them we should be cautious in using it. There is a marginal level of resistance at which the insect is not killed but is repelled by the plant taste or odor. That type of resistance might be safer but is not as reliable; if insects get hungry they will eat almost anything. The practice of breeding for insect resistance is sound, and good plant breeders test their results as if they had discovered a new insecticide, which is often what has happened. Our point is that we must be patient; natural insecticides are potentially as dangerous as synthetic ones.

So we have examples from both sides of the situation: we do not and cannot live in a hazard-free world. But maybe we should take the edge off with a discussion of *nonpreference*. That is the closet where entomologists hide all sorts of plant resistance to insects. *Preferred feeding* means that the insect loves to eat the plant; *nonpreferred* is everything else. It may mean that they cannot or will not eat the plant even at a starvation point. It may mean that those insects get sick or die after eating it. There also is a large gray zone of plants that insects simply do not like the taste of.

Aphids present a good illustration of this. They are excellent vectors (carriers) of virus for many plants. An aphid feeds by sticking its stylet (a long, rigid, piercing mouthpart) into a plant leaf and sucking out a little sap. If that plant is infected with a virus, a few of the viral particles remain on the aphid's stylet when it goes to feed on the next plant. Now for the nonpreference point: aphids spread a virus much more rapidly in nonpreferred crops than in those that they prefer to feed on. This is because they move from plant to plant looking for one that tastes better. When they find one they like, movement stops. Something, probably a chemical, in the nonpreferred plant makes the aphid move on after one taste—would the chemical be toxic in larger quantities? Would it be toxic to sensitive humans? The answer to both questions is probably not.

Here, then, is the question: should we fear the known hazards of synthetic pesticides over the unknown ones of natural origin? Plant pathologists say that any plant (vegetable or ornamental) that is growing successfully has genetic resistance to possibly 95 percent of the pests (diseases and insects) in our area, otherwise it could not survive. Disease and insect control programs are not directed at controlling all pests in the garden, only the remaining 5 percent that are hurting your crop.

Sorry folks, we do not have a good answer. The EPA is doing a pretty good job at warning growers about the hazards of pesticide misuse. The problem of monitoring residues on all fruits and vegetables is massive and growing more complex as we import increasing amounts of such edibles. Some countries monitor pesticide use as well or better than our EPA does—others are extremely lax.

Now we should return to the problem in your garden and your yard. The idea of growing a "without-pesticide" crop has a serious flaw. "Without pesticides" means only that the plants are grown without synthetic pesticides; they are not without naturally occurring pesticides. This is not an argument against breeding for resistance, but rather a statement that living in a world without pesticide hazards is not possible.

We advocate judicious insecticide use because we do not know of a safer approach. Sanitation is essential but that alone is not enough. It seems that ultimately we should rely on breeding for insect and disease resistance, but that must be done with caution. Consider this point. If a company develops a new insecticide for tomatoes, that chemical must be submitted to a wide range of tests before the EPA will allow it to be labeled as safe for either commercial or home use. (It should be noted that the EPA never says that anything is absolutely safe.) What comes out of that is information on the active compound, toxicity of its breakdown products, and long-term effects of extremely high dosage rates on several generations of rats.

The system really is not good enough for absolute safety because pesticides cannot be tested for every harmful effect they might have on a few highly sensitive humans. The current system is the best that can be done with the available technology. But compare that to the information we would be able to get on a new insect-resistant tomato: several people taste it, like it, and do not have an allergic reaction.

One of the popular nonchemical methods for controlling certain nematodes is to plant marigolds either before or with the crop. The practice is extremely effective, almost astonishing, and nematodes are difficult to kill. We would like to know what marigold chemical kills them, how long it stays in the soil, and what effect it has on humans. Entomologists question whether the marigold chemical kills or repels. The evidence indicates that it does kill nematodes but, if it only repels them, a very effective unidentified chemical is being released into the soil. If you want to work from the premise that naturally produced chemicals are safe, consider making an herbal tea with poison ivy. That may seem farfetched, but we recently read about two infants, aged eight weeks and six months old, who had been given mint tea made from pennyroyal. Using this kind of tea was an old family tradition for treating minor illnesses. The younger child died four days later. The older child lived, but with severe liver problems.

Do not panic; natural toxins are not terrible. We have coexisted with most of them since before written history. You know of people who are allergic to certain foods. They discovered it by getting sick, but they did not die. Doctors have a fairly complete understanding of materials that are sometimes toxic to a few people. They know the symptoms, the type of compound involved, and usually have a treatment that will alleviate the symptoms.

Actually there is very little reason to worry about the chemicals in new resistant varieties. Plant breeders are not idiots. If they transfer a new gene into a plant, they know pretty well how it works and what genes might go along with it. If the gene uses a new principle of resistance, there will be a detailed study of possible effects. Obviously, somebody, out of the millions who will eat that variety, will have a reaction to it. They will go to a doctor who will

Ed's Tale of Winter Hardiness, Sick Cows, and King Henry

This is a long but important tale, so pour yourself some coffee. One of the required courses when we were undergraduates was called Production of Forage Crops, which was not particularly exciting for someone who wanted to grow fruit and flowers. We learned that if you kept cattle on a fescue grass pasture too long they might get *fescue sickness*. When the cattle got sluggish and lay in the shade a lot it was time to move them to a pasture without fescue. If you left cattle on fescue too long they would get lame, the hooves would rot, their hair would start falling out, and they might die. Fescue sickness seemed to be caused by something in the specific pasture, because some fescue fields did not cause it; the textbook for the course said that maybe there was an interaction with something in the soil.

As plant breeding technology improved, better fescue varieties were developed. Kentucky 31 was outstanding; it was apparently a mutation that someone had found growing in a field. It had nematode resistance, insect resistance, would go through a drought easily, and was winter hardy. Kentucky 31 often was used in a pasture mixed with clover, but even then you had to watch the cattle carefully and move them if fescue sickness started.

Plant breeders developed low-growing varieties of Kentucky 31 for golf courses and highway embankments. Some of these had excellent insect resistance, retained a green color throughout the summer, and would survive hard freezes. This breeding success attracted the attention of some mycologists (people who study fungi), who noticed a strange pattern in the inheritance of resistance. With a bit of study they showed that the resistance was not genetic; the so-called varieties were infected with an endophytic fungus. *Endophyte* means that it grows inside of the plant with no exterior evidence of the infection. This endophyte produced a toxic alkaloid that killed nematodes and insects feeding on the plant. The drought resistance was a result of the toxin producing complete nematode control: the plant had a better root system. Winter hardiness was due to the stronger plant that had been protected from nematode and insect attacks. This fungus did not infect a plant easily, but the infection was passed on through the seeds. This is why some fescue pastures had caused the sickness and others had not. It is also why Kentucky 31 was such a success. After breeders learned to identify plants with the fungus, they could select fungus-free plants for pasture use and infected ones for turf and highway use.

An interesting sideline of this tale is that darnel grass, a weed of wheat, can become infected with a similar endophyte, producing an alkaloid in the seeds that can cause serious illness in humans. In chapter 14 we discuss the Biblical parable of the tares, in which an enemy sowed darnel in wheat. In Shakespeare's time, darnel was still a prevalent weed, but people had learned that flour made from darnel-infested wheat seeds could make you sick.

> —Want ye corn for bread?
> I think the Duke of Burgundy will fast
> Before he'll buy again at such a rate
> 'Twas full of darnel; Did you like the taste?
> (*Henry VI,* Part 1, act 3)

report that the variety should be used with caution. This happened with a new Irish potato that had strong disease resistance. It was removed from the market.

New methods of gene transfer, using what is now called genetic engineering, make the situation a little more complicated. In 1988 the Food and Drug Administration, EPA, and Department of Agriculture sponsored a conference that brought together a group of authorities to discuss the interlocked scientific issues associated with the use of transgenic plants. Broadly, their ideas are about what we described for the new varieties produced by traditional methods. Obviously, laboratory gene transfer methods allow for the use of genes from a wider range of biological material than do those of traditional plant breeding methods. But, as one authority pointed out, the laboratory technique focuses on the transfer of a selected gene that already has been studied in some depth. Realistically, traditional plant breeding is a form of genetic engineering, but it is more nearly hit-or-miss. With the time-tested system of cross-pollination, it is very difficult to transfer a single desirable gene while leaving other closely associated ones behind. This is sound criticism if we assume that the laboratory breeder is equally as cautious as the traditional plant breeder, which seems a reasonable assumption. Do we instinctively have more trust in the plant breeder who is fundamentally a plant-grower than in the laboratory whiz kid who could not grow a tomato plant in good soil? Actually, we (Ed and Leon) do feel that way but we try to overcome the prejudice.

Another problem that experts discussed at the conference was that of a compound that cannot be synthesized for toxicology studies by being introduced into the whole food. A new synthetic insecticide must be tested in animal feeding trials at levels of 100 times what an average human would eat. The procedure is simple; add 100 times the amount to the normal diet that a mouse would eat and continue the feeding program through several generations. But if the compound is already in the food, how do you feed a mouse 100 times what it would eat? Occasionally you can come close by feeding the mouse only that one food, but then you run the risk of strange results from feeding the animals an unbalanced diet.

Although it seems very likely that something more than 90 percent of the pesticides (insect, disease, and weed inhibitors or killers) that we eat with our fruits and vegetables have not been even identified, much less tested for human hazards, we still think breeding resistance into plants is a better approach than indiscriminate pesticide use. We do not like to use insecticides but we do not like to have insects destroying an entire crop. We do not like to describe any insecticide as "safe"; it is only as safe as the user wants it to be. The glaring flaw with insecticide usage is the Pogo Dilemma: "We have met the enemy and he is us." A small but consistent percentage of home gardeners, commercial farmers, professional pesticide applicators, and overzealous pesticide salesmen do not understand or care about judicious usage and stewardship of the land. Label restrictions are only as sound as the public support for them.

A strong argument for using insect resistant varieties is that the safe level of pesticide is already in them; Pogo cannot put too much out or pour the excess into a stream. But breeding for resistance is a slow and expensive process, particularly if the breeder is going to study the compounds giving resistance.

Chapter 14

This chapter is more about the why of weed control than the how. Telling how is simple. The keys to weed control in gardens or lawns are: (1) sanitation, (2) sanitation, and (3) sanitation. In this chapter we explain why weeds are difficult to control and that, occasionally, you must decide to use an herbicide to eliminate the more serious weeds.

One thing to remember: new weeds come from weed seeds, which came from large weeds that you ignored. If you hoe all weed seedlings once a week, the total amount of work time will be less than if you hoe every two or three weeks—when the weeds are large and hard to kill.

Why We Have Weeds

"And the earth brought forth grass, and herb yielding seed after his kind—: and God saw that it was good." Gen. 1:12.

"But while men slept, his enemy came and sowed tares among the wheat, and went his way." Matt. 13:25.

Tares was the name for darnel grass (*Lolium temulentum*), which was at that time a serious weed in wheat. We do not want to become involved with theology, but something happened between the time that God said all plants were good and His Son said some were bad weeds. The difference was that when man began to grow wheat the survival of his family depended on the crop producing well, and anything threatening his crop was bad. In nature there are no weeds, only strong competitors and weak competitors. Man decides what is a weed. Darnel (tares) grows to a height of only about twelve inches. That was enough to provide competition to the wheat of Jesus' time. But our better varieties, high level of moisture, and higher fertility produce such large plants that tares are no longer serious weeds in wheat.

Taking a more current example: your lawn is a crop. It provides aesthetic and practical yields, enhancing the beauty of your home and giving you a place to walk without getting muddy or tramping through briars. The grass is a mixture of what grew and could survive under poor management. Your neighbor has a beautiful lawn of centipede grass, with a scattering of St. Augustine and some Bermuda grass, both of which grew over from your yard. Because he likes the uniform texture and color of centipede, he spends a lot of time digging out the St. Augustine and Bermuda grass, occasionally suggesting that you should improve your lawn. But you are not much impressed with color and texture if the grass is green, does not grow too fast, and keeps your feet from getting muddy. Your neighbor has weeds in his lawn—weeds being the types of grass he does not want to grow—but you do not.

So, to discuss weeds we must have a common definition. If it competes with your crop, or has that potential, it is a weed. Weeds also are difficult to eliminate; the ones that were not are gone. Stated in a shorter form: a weed is both harmful and well-adapted to survive despite your efforts to get rid of it.

We need to make one more classification before getting down to practical facts. Most weeds are annuals and come from seeds, but perennial weeds are plants that survive the winter by dying back to roots, tubers, or rhizomes. We discuss seeds first and talk about three of the perennial weeds later.

Annual Weeds

The survival strategy of most weeds is the shotgun effect: produce thousands of small seeds that will germinate under several different conditions. Because small seeds have limited stored food reserves, if a seedling from them were to germinate at a four-inch depth in the soil, it would run out of food before the leaves could hit sunlight and start functioning. Ecologically, this is why small seeds have a light requirement; the ones that germinated at four inches died and did not produce any offspring. As a rule of thumb, small seeds will not germinate unless they are within one-quarter inch of the surface.

Besides that, some seeds have a cold requirement for germination. If seeds produced in the fall were to germinate immediately, the winter cold would kill them. They germinate in the spring only if there has been a cold period. Other seeds have what is called a hard seed coat, which only means that it is impermeable to water. They germinate if the coat has been repeatedly scratched by soil particles. Usually this happens through tillage, but with blackberries (for example) it means a bird ate the fruit and the seed was scratched in its gizzard. There are other conditions and modifications than we have described, but we only want to show that weed seeds have several devices to assure that they germinate at different times.

Using that background we can look at a typical weed to illustrate the control problems. Goosegrass *(Eleusine indica)* is a big, coarse, clumping type of grass that grows in your garden and often comes up in your lawn where the turf cover is not very thick. It does not look bad at first, but the established clump is difficult to pull up and the lawn mower cannot cut through it easily. People studying a weed love to show how many seeds a single plant can produce in a growing season (although this really depends on growing conditions and length of growing season) but the reported record for goosegrass is 135,000 seeds from one plant. Even in your yard a single plant can produce several thousand seeds.

About ten years ago Leon studied the longevity of goosegrass seeds in vegetable garden plots. The results turned out to be more complicated than he had expected, but the following figures are from that study. Within a single group of goosegrass seeds, taken from one plant and at the same time, there was a wide diversity of dormancy. A few seeds germinated easily after they had been drying for about a month. All had a light requirement. Most of them stayed dormant until the outer seed coat (a paperlike material) was removed or had decomposed in the soil. Many had a cold requirement, and some had hard-seed-coat dormancy. Put bluntly, this is a very adaptable weed; nothing could make all of the seed germinate at once and, except for the light requirement, a few would germinate under almost any conditions. Goosegrass seeds are very difficult to eradicate.

Remembering that goosegrass seed dormancy means many things, consider an example of weed seed longevity. Again, goosegrass is the example. Start with the soil in a weedy garden; because it was hot and humid in July and August and because the vegetables had played out, you just let the weeds produce seeds. In September you rented a power tiller and tilled it nicely to a depth of eight inches; the weeds rotted, and in November you took two soil samples: one at the zero-to-two-inch depth and another at the four-to-six-inch depth. You then made a water slurry of each sample, washed it through a sieve to save all the weed seeds, let them dry, and counted the viable goosegrass seeds.

Because the tiller had mixed the soil well, there are the same numbers of seeds in each sample: 750 seeds per square foot, per two-inch depth. This is the number we will start out with in late May when the goosegrass seeds begin to germinate. The number does not mean exactly what we would like, because this is from a two-inch sample though only those in the upper quarter-inch will germinate and become new weeds. We cannot take a one-quarter inch deep sample but, dividing by eight, 750 represents 93 seeds per square foot to a depth of one-quarter inch. If those 93 seeds were to remain exposed to good germination conditions throughout June and July, approximately 80 to 90 percent would germinate. But it is not that simple. Because we grow crops on raised beds, every rain washes that one-quarter inch off into the water furrow and exposes another layer. Progressive rains will probably expose all of the seeds to a depth of one inch and maybe the entire two inches. After the fall crop is harvested, the beds are prepared for a winter crop by your scooping up the topsoil that has washed into the water furrow and putting it back on the bed. Now most of the original upper two inches is back on the bed, except for a little clay that washed out of the garden. A new soil sample will show that the original 750 seeds per square foot has declined by about 50 to 80 percent, so there remain approximately 150 to 375 seeds in the upper two inches, or 18 to 45 seeds per square foot in the upper one-quarter inch. The sample from the four-to-six-inch depth still has 750 seeds.

The point of this illustration is that the population of weed seed in the top-soil will decline by about 50 percent each year, assuming there are no other weeds producing seed. This varies somewhat by species; we selected goosegrass as a medium longevity example. Although the problem will not disappear, with persistence you can reduce it to a minimum. Deep tillage brings up fresh seeds to be fought. With raised beds, and no mulch cover, the seed population of the upper two inches declines rather quickly. It will not decline as quickly if a mulch (leaf or plastic) provides the weed control; this is because the mulch cover reduces germination and because it does not allow soil erosion that progressively exposes more seed for germination. *Soil erosion* is not a bad term here, because most of the soil that washed from the bed was caught in the water furrow. Remember that back in chapter 1 we recommended a gentle slope of one-half percent.

Worst Weeds of the South

Annual weeds (coming from seeds) will usually be the most numerous in your garden, but the worst are perennial weeds. We describe three that give gardeners the most trouble.

Nutsedge

Purple nutsedge *(Cyperus rotundus)* has many common names; two of the older ones are nut grass or coco. The plant makes chains of hairy underground tubers that look somewhat like small coconuts. The name coconut grass became shortened to nut grass in some regions and coco grass in others. Although the leaves look a little like those of a grass, they are more angular, very smooth, and have sharply pointed tips. You should have no problem telling a sedge from a grass, but another characteristic to look for is that the floral stalk is triangular instead of round. Despite its name, there is nothing purple about the plant. The flowers are a deep brown color and sometimes make a good floral arrangement in a hot dry August when nothing else is blooming.

The other species of perennial sedges that can be a serious garden weed is yellow nutsedge, which has a yellow rather than a brown flower and a different kind of tuber. The tubers are edible and have a rather pleasant almond taste. They are grown as a minor crop in North Africa, where the tubers are eaten as a food. The juice of the tubers is used in the preparation of ice cream and a type of cider.

Yellow nutsedge *(Cyperus esculentus)* is occasionally promoted in this country as *chufa*. But leave it out of your garden unless it is the only crop you plan to grow. Back in the old days people used to plant a patch of chufas as bait for wild turkeys, which love to scratch around and dig the tubers. It is also a good plant to attract deer.

You should try to call this a sedge rather than grass, primarily to remind yourself that it cannot be controlled as if it were a grass. Several species of annual sedges have leaves and flowers very much like those of yellow nutsedge, but these do not produce tubers. We will lump them under the heading of annual sedges. For the following discussion we refer to purple nutsedge, but control methods are basically the same for the yellow kind, and both are horribly successful weeds.

Although nutsedge plants produce many seeds, most of them are not viable, and the few that are remain dormant for years. The real problem is that the plants produce underground tubers. Some are directly below the surface, some a little deeper, and a few form at depths of twelve to fourteen inches. Those deeper tubers were not put there by tillage but instead formed when the parent plant sent out what are called *dropper rhizomes,* going straight down and producing a deep chain of dormant tubers. (The terminology of tubers and rhizomes being used for sedges is wrong, as you can see by our discussion in chapter 5, but we are not on a crusade to right anatomical errors.)

Dormancy was a tricky word with seeds but is worse with tubers. Each tuber has five to ten buds with different degrees, and probably different kinds, of dormancy. This means that a tuber can be lying at six inches and one bud will break dormancy. It sends up a rhizome (the last rhizome we mentioned went straight down) until the tip reaches sunlight (at about one-quarter inch from the surface), where it makes a small plant with lateral roots and a shoot growing out of the ground. If you hoe, dig, or pull that plant, the rhizome that produced it will die. Then the next bud on the tuber will sprout and do the same thing. If you keep hoeing and digging until all buds have sprouted (sequentially), that tuber will die; but it is unlikely that all of the buds will sprout in one year. On the other hand, if you ignore the new nutsedge plant, it will begin producing new tubers in two or three weeks. The number of tubers one new plant will produce in a growing season is as meaningless as the number of goosegrass seeds in the previous example, but ten to fifteen is a good range. Studies to find out how bad this could get were done in Georgia. Researchers planted purple nutsedge tubers two feet apart. Their plots were small but calculations were made on a per-acre basis. In twenty weeks the plants had produced 1.3 million tubers; 1,438 miles of rhizomes; and a total plant weight of 45 tons per acre. In your twenty-by-twenty foot garden that would mean 130,000 tubers and 14 miles of rhizomes. This kind of information is only coffee talk, of course; the work was accurate, but growing conditions also were excellent.

This is where we should say "now for the good side." But there is no good side. Nutsedge is a bad weed and will get worse unless you fight it continuously. Otherwise, with high fertility, loose soil, and water, nutsedge will eventually drive you out of the garden. In addition, besides competing for light, moisture, and nutrients, nutsedge produces a toxic chemical that stunts growth of your crop plants.

With persistence, a moderate infestation of nutsedge can be eradicated from a garden through hoeing and pulling. If the infestation is heavy and the weed has been there for many years, you may have to use an herbicide. Several broad-spectrum herbicides are very good at killing the parent plant and all attached dormant tubers. However, they will not kill dormant tubers that are no longer attached to a growing plant.

Dormant nutsedge tubers dry out and die if exposed to the sun for a few hot dry days (you will remember that we suggested July and August as good times to start a new garden). But August weather is unpredictable. If repeated tillage exposes dormant tubers to light, high oxygen levels, and warm moist soil, many of them will sprout. Suddenly, your garden, which had looked pretty much weed-free before you followed our advice about summer tillage, has become a green mat of nutsedge plants. Please try to remember that spontaneous generation does not occur in nutsedge. Those tubers were there when you started and they were not going to die of old age. Tillage only showed you how many and where they were. You can now pray for dry weather, dig each tuber up and put it in a bucket (do not put those things in your compost pile), or spray with an herbicide. Within a month you should have the population down to a few plants coming up occasionally. Dig them up or spot-spray with an herbicide. For the next few years you will find an occasional shoot coming up in the garden. It might be interesting to dig up one of those latecomers even if you are spotting with an herbicide. The rhizome it came from probably will look dead but, using a trowel, you can trace it down through the hard-packed subsoil to twelve or fourteen inches. There you will find a nice plump tuber with ten more buds ready to sprout next year, or the next. You might wonder when that deep tuber began developing, how long it remained dormant before something made one bud sprout, and what broke the dormancy. We have wondered that, too.

Do not try to shade out nutsedge with black plastic or thick roofing. Have you ever noticed grass growing in the asphalt of a parking lot, not through the cracks but right through the asphalt? That "grass" is nutsedge; the continuous pressure of those pointed leaves penetrates anything short of armor plate.

Periodically people ask if there is not some insect that would kill the tubers. There is a kind of weevil called a billbug that lays its eggs on the leaves. The larvae crawl down through the shoot to one of the tubers. During the winter the larvae eat away at the tuber, leaving only a hollow shell. In a year when the weather is right this weevil may kill as many as 75 percent of the tubers and in bad years it gets about 20 percent of them. Unfortunately, although this billbug is very common in our area, entomologists say there seems to be no good way to increase the numbers enough for nutsedge eradication. Also, you should remember that some dormant tubers are not connected to a living plant. The only real significance to this information is that if you use too much of a strong soil insecticide, you may also control the billbugs and find that nutsedge spreads even faster in your garden.

One final comment on nutsedge: you may be wondering how nutsedge gets started and why we assume that it is already in your yard. Both the purple and yellow nutsedge are disturbed-soil weeds. Purple nutsedge is more common in high rainfall areas with less well-drained soils; the yellow species is usually a weed of lighter soils, but you may have both of them. If your subdivision was once planted to field crops (cotton, corn, or soybeans), nutsedge was almost certainly one of the weeds. It was spread from field to field on tillage equipment. Forty years ago the farmer retired and planted his fields to pine trees. As the trees grew, the nutsedge got weaker and finally quit producing new shoots. The tubers were dormant but not dead. A developer bought the land, cut the trees, pulled the stumps, leveled the land, and built your house; surprise, you have nutsedge.

But you may live in a subdivision where the land was never in cultivation and there is no nutsedge anywhere. In this case watch very closely when you buy well-rotted manure or pine bark, or a load of good topsoil. If a friend offers you a start from a new plant, wash it to bare roots. Even nursery plants are carriers: nurserymen use rotted pine bark, too.

Bermuda Grass

The name brings to mind images of a soft lawn in the tropics. Some selections of Bermuda grass do make a good lawn, but they are usually hybrids with another species. Farmers used to have several names for common Bermuda grass: devilgrass, hellgrass, and wireweed. It is a true grass and looks like one. Although it does make viable seeds it spreads primarily by stolons and rhizomes. *Rhizome* means a rootlike structure; it is an underground stem that usually grows within about a half-inch of the soil surface and sends up shoots from some nodes. There is a shoot bud at each node, but most of them are dormant. Anatomically, the rhizome and stolon are stems and both grow hor-

izontally. The difference between them seems small—a rhizome grows just beneath the soil surface and a stolon grows on the surface. Now you can see that
those things on the nutsedge are not really rhizomes: some grow straight down
and others grow upward. Plant anatomists have a wonderful time arguing over
terminology for sedges.

A big problem with Bermuda grass is that the bud at each node is potentially a new plant and can draw food material from the rest of the rhizome. If
you pull up a rhizome and leave it on the ground to die, one or more nodes
will sprout and form a new plant. If you work the ground with a tiller, it will
break one rhizome into ten or more parts and each one with a node will make
a new plant. Here you see the same pattern that makes nutsedge a successful
weed. Bermuda grass is not quite that bad, but it is a close second. Control
methods are identical to those for nutsedge; do everything you can to eradicate it before you start growing a crop. Tillage during hot dry weather is effective, herbicides are effective, and digging always works.

By now you may wonder how cotton, soybean, and corn farmers handle
nutsedge and Bermuda grass. Except for very early in the crop season these are
only nuisance weeds for them. After the crop gets large enough to shade the
ground both weeds become weaker and the shoots often die. When the crop is
very young, tillage or one of several postemergence herbicides will keep them
under reasonable control.

POISON IVY

This is the third of our worst weeds. Poison ivy *(Rhus toxicodendron)* is not a
weed of vegetable gardens, but it is a dandy in shrubs and in shady areas. Poison ivy looks something like ivy but is part of the sumac family. The Latin
name indicates that it has a toxin in the leaves; the literal meaning is "toxic
tree." The toxin in poison ivy, 10-pentadecatachol amine, is an oily substance
that can usually be removed by washing immediately with a strong laundry
soap. Gentle hand soap will not do the job—something like the GI soap from
the good old days is best. The myth about using rubbing alcohol is not true—
alcohol makes the toxin stick tighter.

People have different degrees of allergy to the toxin, but everyone should
avoid contact with it. Repeated exposure to the toxin will eventually cause you
to become allergic. Also, smoke from burning poison ivy contains the toxin.

If you are wondering about poison oak, be advised that there is no poison

Leon's Tale about Allelopathy

Back in 1961, before I learned to appreciate the finer things of life, I was in the botany department, fresh from graduate school with training in biotechnology. Back then they called it tissue culture, and it was of value only as a tool for studying plant growth regulators. The departmental ecologist had observed that johnsongrass (another bad weed, but not one of home gardens) rhizomes produced a toxic chemical that kept other plants from competing with it. Being young and brilliant, I thought he was wrong, but he took me out in several fields and gave me some very convincing arguments.

The ecologist had a new graduate student who wanted to study this chemical, but neither he nor the ecologist had the laboratory experience for that kind of research. Because I had no students, no research funds, and a large ego, I agreed to help.

The ecologist thought the substance would be an auxin (the popular growth regulator of the day). I disagreed, and this time I was right; it was some other strange chemical that inhibited seedling growth at very low concentrations. I played all the little tricks I had learned in biochemistry. I made a fairly good extraction but couldn't purify it and had no idea what the chemical might be.

That was disappointing. Meanwhile the student had done excellent work in proving that one competitive weapon of johnsongrass was this inhibitory substance. He submitted that as his research for his master of science degree and went to Oklahoma State for a Ph.D., deciding it should be in biochemistry rather than botany. Within a few years he had isolated the pure chemical from johnsongrass and published the first paper on the identification of what is now called an allelopathic substance. *Allelopathic* means that it harms similar plants.

My ecologist friend was not the first person to notice allelopathy. There was a study back in the 1920s showing that black walnut leaves produce a substance that is harmful to many plants. The leaves are safe when composted because the chemical breaks down rather quickly.

A research group from Michigan State did some interesting work on the use of allelopathic substances from sorghum mulch for weed control in vegetables. They grew the sorghum to a height of about a foot, cut it off, and spread it as a mulch around bean plants. The allelopathic chemicals were slowly released as the mulch decomposed, killing or inhibiting a wide range of emerging weed seedlings—with no obvious damage to the crop plant. They compiled a list of vegetable plants that are not seriously affected by the chemicals from the mulch and another showing which weeds the chemicals will control. I say "chemicals," plural, because this is a group of related substances rather than only one. This kind of work raises the question of how much weed control from mulches is due to shading the ground and how much from allelopathic chemicals. The group in Michigan devised an experiment showing that, with the thin mulch layer they used, about 80 percent of the weed control was from the chemicals.

Allelopathy is a popular research topic. People are finding that many plants produce large amounts of such chemicals. The substances have wide differences in structure and in the range of seedlings they control. Frequently, but not always, the chemicals are produced from decaying plant parts (microbial decay pathways probably add complications) and break down to ineffective substances in a few days. This continual release of the chemicals at low concentrations is the key to their value for weed control. It seems likely that all vegetative mulches control weeds partly through allelopathy, but the relative importance probably varies with species and conditions. Now for the kicker: studies are showing that most successful weeds produce allelopathic substances. Nutsedge and Bermuda grass are very good at it.

oak. It is only a variant of poison ivy with strange looking leaves. Botanically it is called *var. quercifolia,* meaning that the leaves look like oak leaves. (Some taxonomists disagree and think it is a separate species, but taxonomists always disagree.) There is also a poison sumac, *Rhus vernix,* which grows in very wet areas. The only other plant that looks much like poison ivy is the Virginia creeper, which is in the grape family. *Parthenocissus quinquefolia,* the species name, means "five-leaved." This is the key point: Virginia creeper has five leaves and poison ivy has three. Actually, these are leaflets but they look like leaves. Both are vining plants and both have beautiful fall foliage.

This brings us back to the definition of a weed. A landscape architecture friend of ours has a tale of seeing poison ivy used as a ground cover under the trees surrounding a large estate. Poison ivy is a good, low-maintenance ground cover. You might have to weed occasionally and you should keep the vines from climbing into the trees. The poison ivy ground cover was used as a barrier in place of a large fence. It was very effective, keeping most intruders out, giving nice fall color, and attracting many fruit-eating birds. Was poison ivy a weed here? What did the neighbors think of this natural fence?

Now for suggestions on control. Birds love to eat poison ivy fruit, then take a rest stop in your azalea bush and leave the seeds—complete with a shot of starter fertilizer. Bird droppings also fall in the lawn, but poison ivy seedlings cannot compete with turfgrass. If you see a young poison ivy plant under a tree or shrub, slip on some rubber gloves and pull it up. Wash the gloves with soap before taking them off. The more common problem is that you will find an established vine growing in the shrub or up a tree trunk. Old vines can be as large as an inch in diameter. Put rubber gloves on (the vine sap is toxic), and cut the vine close to the ground. Paint the freshly cut stump with a systemic herbicide. There are probably other chemicals that will work, so see what your garden center suggests. (This approach is good for almost any vine.) One application will usually kill the complete plant, but if it does not—try again. The safest way to deal with a dead vine is to let it decay. The toxin breaks down in dead plants.

Weed Control Methods

This is the section that could include herbicides but we are going to say that they are usually not practical for use in a home garden. You can manage your small garden much more carefully than can a farmer with a thousand acres of soybeans. Remember that the very best weed control tool is sanitation. Kill the perennial weeds and never let any weed produce seeds. This does not mean that you will be able to eradicate weed seeds; you are only trying to reduce the problem. Weeds, like the poor, will always be with us. They blow in, wash in, birds bring them, and you usually add a few with composted material.

The companion tool to sanitation is the hoe: cold steel, the crookneck herbicide. When students take the introductory horticulture course in the fall, their first laboratory period usually includes a lecture on the care and use of a hoe. Students who have gardened all their lives still may not know how to use a hoe effectively. A hoe is a sharp knife on the end of a wooden handle. This means that you should slice with a hoe, not chop as if you were using a meat cleaver. Your goal is to slice just beneath the soil surface, cutting the plant roots. The shoot will die if its roots are gone. Even when you are hoeing to break a soil crust and let air to the crop roots, there is no need to exhaust yourself by chopping. When you get to a large weed, use the sharp corner. *Sharp* is the key word for easy hoeing. Good gardeners often carry a file with them when hoeing. They hoe for a while and stop to put a good edge on the hoe. (If you watch closely you may notice that they renew the edge more frequently on hot days.) When you finish hoeing, wash the hoe, touch up the edge with a file, and put a light coat of oil on it.

MULCHES

Mulch made of plant materials is an excellent weed control tool in the garden—but. Most of the weed control effect is probably from allelopathic (meaning harmful to similar plants) chemicals released as breakdown products from the mulch. It seems likely that any mulch is at least slightly toxic to the crop it protects. Another problem is that the decaying organic matter provides food and protection for plant-eating insects.

We conducted a small test comparing a black plastic (polyethylene) mulch with the pine straw mulch that was popular for strawberry production until the late 1950s. Early research reported that the berry plants grew faster with the plastic mulch because it warmed the soil during late winter and early spring. We were considering pine straw with the idea that it might keep the soil cooler in late spring to early summer, which could extend the harvest season.

We had a mild winter during the year of our study, but the plants with black plastic grew much more rapidly anyway. By scratching around in the pine straw we found that mole crickets and slugs were living in the mulch and nibbling on the berry plants. The plants mulched with black plastic produced about twice as many berries as did those with straw. The difference was partly due to insect damage, but allelopathic chemicals from the pine straw might also have been involved. There may have been a slight effect of decomposing pine straw using nitrogen, but the plots were fertilized well and the plants did not seem to be suffering from nitrogen deficiency.

This was an extreme case that we selected to make the point. Mulches from plant materials provide weed control, keep the soil from crusting, and produce organic matter. But there are still many unknowns about weeds and weed control from mulches. There is some reason for concern because we know that decomposing plant material releases chemicals toxic enough to kill or stunt small seedlings. But we do not know what these chemicals are or how they might affect humans. On the other hand, the concentrations are very low and we have no evidence that these natural substances are harmful.

As an alternative, black plastic is good (nutsedge shoots will grow right through it, but no kind of mulch will control nutsedge). Do not try using clear plastic as a mulch, especially in the spring. It warms the soil up enough to make weeds germinate faster but not enough to kill them. In midsummer a clear plastic mulch will kill weed seeds to a depth of about two inches. However, the heat also will kill active young roots of your crop plant.

Speaking of temperature, here is a point you need to remember about mulches. In early spring, vegetation mulches blanket the cold soil so that it does not warm up well during the day. They also reduce the amount of heat the soil releases on a cold night. We have seen mulched plots in which the crop plants were badly frost-damaged, whereas those in the unmulched row beside them escaped injury. This is just a marginal difference but it is something to remember.

We recently read in a gardening book that newspapers make a good mulch for weed control. Do not try that in the humid South; the first rain will pack the paper on the soil surface and reduce air exchange to almost nil.

Garden centers now offer a black plastic mulch that is a woven fabric. It is not polyethylene and will last for several years.

HERBICIDES

Now for a very short discussion about herbicides. After many trials and many errors we have concluded that herbicides are not a practical tool for home gardening. Using a broad-spectrum herbicide for control of perennial weeds may be the only exception.

Used correctly, herbicides do not poison the soil or contaminate the crops you want to eat. Also, if used correctly, herbicides are an excellent labor-saving tool for large gardens. "Used correctly" is the key statement here. To be safe and effective, herbicides must be applied at precise rates and under exacting conditions. Often (usually?) you will spend more time adjusting the equipment for application than you would spend hoeing the weeds. If you decide to just spray and hope it works, it will not. Either the weeds will not be killed or they will—together with your crop plants.

The best weed control program is sanitation and a sharp hoe.

Chapter 15

THE NUTS AND BOLTS OF PLANTS AND SOILS

There is a story about a young boy who wanted to write a report on penguins. When he asked for help, the librarian gave him a big book with complete details of all that was known about penguins. He looked through it for a minute before handing it back. "No ma'am," he said, "that's not what I am looking for."

She was a little surprised. "You wanted to learn about penguins?"

"Yes ma'am, but not that much."

This is a long chapter that contains background information on how your garden grows, which will help you to understand the close interrelationships of plants, the environment, and the soil. We believe our explanations are essentially correct but, based on long experience with students and gardeners, we are sure that they are functional: these explanations work.

This material is not difficult to understand: we have gone over it about a hundred times and have not lost a student yet. On the other hand, we never offered it all at one sitting until now. Do not try to read this entire chapter in one evening. If you start feeling overwhelmed, take a break.

The Soil-Plant-Atmosphere Continuum

In the first lecture of a soils course the instructor says that soil is not dirt, but rather a living, dynamic ecosystem. The students carefully write this down to memorize it for a test question. It never appears on any test because that statement is the entire soils course; students do not realize this until years later. Now we will make our effort at saying the same thing.

Soil is more than the sum of its parts, it is more than bits of rock, organic matter, soil microorganisms, water, and nutrients. Plant feeder roots are so bound to soil particles that they cannot be separated. These roots are part of both the plant and the soil, but the plant itself has a great influence on the nature of the soil. Soil has a network of air pockets that are connected to the atmosphere. It is difficult to tell where the soil ends and atmosphere begins; this soil-atmosphere connection is essential if the microorganisms and feeder roots are to function properly. Also, the soil is strongly affected by the climate: sun (both as light and heat), temperature, and rain.

So, soil is not dirt; it is an ecosystem that includes the plant and the climate. At one time writers tried to establish the term "SPAC," or soil-plant-atmosphere continuum. We like the term but know that it will not sell. Having said that, we will talk about "soil" from now on. Each part is interlocked with and dependent on the other parts. This is why we should study the continuum as a whole but will not because it is too complex. Instead, we will study the individual pieces and gradually put them together. This is much like fitting together a jigsaw puzzle. You begin by studying the details of a small portion, then you find some pieces that seem to fit there. You leave that for a while and fit another portion together. Finally, you fit all of the segments into an entire picture but, in this case, a few pieces are missing and some parts do not seem to fit anywhere. This is unimportant because you can see what those missing pieces probably look like.

The Root of the Problem: Respiration

We start the puzzle by looking at a simplified plant (see figure 16). This is a plant stripped down to its working parts. The leaf makes sugar through photosynthesis and the sugar moves to the rest of the plant, where it is used as energy sources. With this energy the root takes up nutrients and water, which go up to the leaf. Within that setting we need to look briefly at photosynthesis, the production side of the energy cycle (see figure 17). The leaf takes energy from sunlight and stores it as sugar. Because sugar is water soluble it can be moved in a water solution to any other part of the plant. Individual cells break the sugar down, releasing energy that is used in many ways. Some of it goes into the building of structural units such as proteins and cellulose, and some is used to move nutrients into the cell. The excess is stored as starch, oil, or fat; these forms hold much more energy in a small volume. Those of you who are computer hotshots know how to store large documents by compressing them; in plants, energy is compressed as starch or oils and later reconverted to water-soluble sugar.

Basically, that is the photosynthesis-respiration cycle. Photosynthesis collects energy and respiration releases it. Photosynthesis uses carbon dioxide

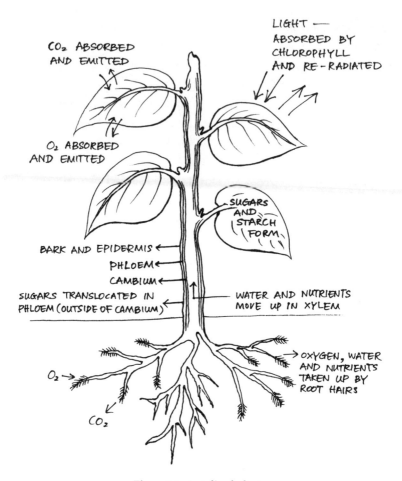

CO₂ ABSORBED AND EMITTED

LIGHT — ABSORBED BY CHLOROPHYLL AND RE-RADIATED

O₂ ABSORBED AND EMITTED

SUGARS AND STARCH FORM

BARK AND EPIDERMIS
PHLOEM
CAMBIUM
SUGARS TRANSLOCATED IN PHLOEM (OUTSIDE OF CAMBIUM)

WATER AND NUTRIENTS MOVE UP IN XYLEM

O₂

OXYGEN, WATER AND NUTRIENTS TAKEN UP BY ROOT HAIRS

CO₂

Figure 16. A stylized plant.

(CO_2) and water, giving off oxygen as a byproduct. Because respiration is the exact reverse, it uses oxygen and gives off CO_2. Photosynthesis is a fascinating topic; it is ridiculously complex and very inefficient. To put it simply, roots use a lot of sugar and oxygen; sugar comes from the leaves but oxygen comes only from air pockets in the soil. Roots use oxygen and give off CO_2, which you must flush out of the soil or potting mix.

Roots need a lot of oxygen because they do a lot of work. We will see later that they take mineral salts out of the soil using a process that draws water in and forces the water/salt solution up into the plant. The energy required for the roots to move those salts comes from respiration, and the oxygen comes

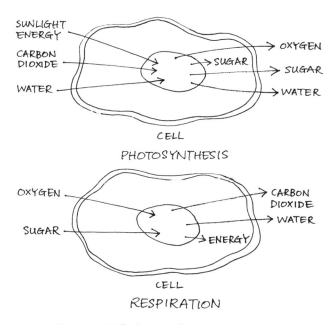

Figure 17. Cell photosynthesis and respiration.

from air pockets in the soil (except for the oxygen that is suspended in rainwater). In addition to plants, many other organisms in the soil depend on the same oxygen supply, the most aggressive of which are the microorganisms (fungi and bacteria). You may remember from our discussion of organic matter that microorganisms are very aggressive in taking nitrogen that a plant may need. They also take oxygen before plants can get to it.

Now, one more point: at higher soil temperatures most of the organisms are more active and require more oxygen. You goldfish lovers may have noted another point: at higher temperatures the water will hold less oxygen. Now that you can see where we are going with the idea of respiration and oxygen, put that piece of the puzzle aside so that we can use it later.

Root-Soil Interactions

When a seed germinates, it produces a primary taproot that grows downward regardless of the position in which the seed was placed. There is a growth inhibitor near the root tip; if the tip hits an obstruction and becomes angled to one side, this inhibitor concentrates on the lower side. The upper side continues to grow but the lower side does not, which forces the tip downward again.

Hard layers of the soil can stop the taproot and make it grow laterally. Low oxygen levels also can stop the taproot by killing the growing tip.

Biologists, who love to classify plants into categories even though nature does not work that way, divide plants into those with taproot systems and those with fibrous root systems. These are vague terms, but there clearly are wide differences among types of plant root systems. All plants have a tap (primary) root, but in some species it does not amount to much. The taproot of a corn plant does not go very deep before it develops many lateral roots that serve for support and the uptake of water and nutrients. Lateral roots are only slightly affected by the inhibitor system, which keeps taproots growing downward; some of the lateral roots grow almost horizontally. In general, plants that have large lateral root systems survive better in wet soil because lack of oxygen becomes critical at the lower depths where a taproot would be.

Some plant species have fibrous systems, some have taproot systems, and most are somewhere in between. For any single species the root system seems to become more fibrous in sandy soil and to form longer roots in heavier soil. This may mean that oxygen levels affect the type of root system. But we just said that fibrous root systems survive better in wet soils; that is not a contradiction. We are talking about different problems. Species that genetically produce more shallow roots will have a better chance of survival in wet soil. The oak tree is a taproot species but in soil that is frequently very wet the taproot dies at a depth of three or four feet, so the lateral roots develop to a greater extent. This is rather common in the humid South; a tree has enough lateral roots to survive wet conditions but is easy to blow over in a hurricane. In well-drained soil, oak trees have deeper taproots.

That discussion may have been too much for the simple point we need to make, which is that there are gradations of root patterns that are affected by the species and soil conditions.

Now we should look at the functions of a root. It anchors the plant and supplies nutrients and water. We will discuss the difference between nutrients and food later, but for now we are only referring to the minerals that plants use. Look at our crude cross-section of a root in figure 18. The center core has four strips of xylem and four of phloem; these are the tubes that transport solutions to various parts of the plant. Phloem brings sugar solutions down to the root tip, and xylem carries salt solutions away. Now look at figure 19, our

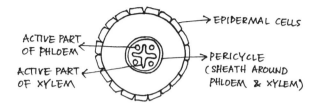

Figure 18. Cross section of a young dicotyledon root.

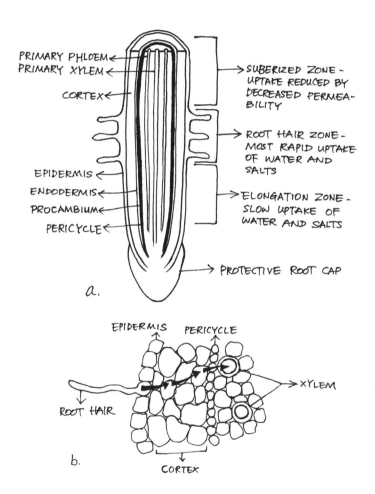

Figure 19. (a) Parts of a young root tip; (b) cross section of a root-hair zone.

root tip sketches. The extreme tip has a protective cap that sloughs off but is constantly replenished as the root pushes through the soil. Behind that is an area of cell division, followed by cell elongation. Then we reach the root hair zone, which is important for water and nutrient uptake. Beyond it, the root is encased in a fairly water-resistant material called suberin, which can take up a little water but not much. The zone of active water uptake varies in length both with the plant species and with soil conditions, but it usually starts about an inch from the tip and is about an inch long.

Calculations on total water movement show that such a small area of the root system cannot account for everything that moves upward through the xylem. A substantial amount of the water is taken up by the active root hair region.

Those root hairs in our sketches are not roots, they are simply extensions of epidermal cells on the root. These should not be confused with the fine, hairlike roots that gardening books caution you against losing when you transplant. Those are true roots, with phloem and xylem, and are very important because they represent the most active part of the root system. We are not trying to change garden book terminology here but are defining our own usage. We call the hairlike roots *feeder roots,* rather than root hairs (although this is not a very good term either because it implies the uptake of plant food rather than mineral nutrients).

When you include feeder roots (but not root hairs), the size of a root system is almost unbelievable. Back when botanists did not have to spend their time publishing large numbers of short research papers, they did very good basic work and did not publish it until they were finished. H. J. Dittmer measured the roots from one large winter rye plant that he grew in 1.9 cubic feet of soil. He carefully washed the soil away and measured all the roots; 13,815,672 roots with a total length of 2,044,256 feet—380 miles! Actually, he did not measure every root; he divided it into sections and made some calculations. But his work was good, and later studies tend to agree with his. The total surface area of those roots was 2,554 square feet, a little over half an acre. With that much root system in only 1.9 cubic feet of soil, it might seem that the root was using most of the available surface, but that amount of a loam soil has a total area of 1,164,000 square feet: almost 28 acres. The root system was using only a small fraction of it. One more point before you get tired of large figures:

although the surface area of the roots was more than 2,000 square feet, the surface area of the leaves was only 50 square feet.

To be honest, Dittmer selected the rye plant because it was an extreme example and we selected his work to get your attention. The bean plant growing in your garden will not even approach that kind of root system, and any root system will vary with soil drainage. Remember that Dittmer's figures represent just under two cubic feet: equal to a row one foot wide, two feet long, and a foot deep. And we want you to keep in mind that, measured by surface area, more than half of a plant is underground. On a total dry weight basis the aboveground portion is larger, but not much.

Nutrient and Transport System

The active, energy-requiring part of the system is that which takes up mineral nutrients as salts. Mineral salts are composed of ions that have positive or negative electrical charges. These ions are held to soil particles by the charges and are slowly released into the soil water, or roots in close contact with a soil particle might take them up directly. After the salt ions are brought into the cell, some of the soil water moves passively into it through the cell membrane. Back in high school science you studied the process of osmosis; water can pass through the membrane but salts cannot. They called this a *differentially permeable membrane,* meaning that it was permeable to water but not to sugar or salts. The salt uptake process pulls salt ions through the differentially permeable membrane but will not let them out.

Now we have blown it. We define a differentially permeable membrane as one that will not let salts through and then we refer to a system that pulls salts through it. There is no real need for you to understand exactly how this "salt pump" works, but we can give a pretty good analogy by discussing Christmas tree lights. Last Christmas you bought a set of sequential lights. The first bulb would flash on and then go off when the second one flashed. It appeared that an electrical charge was running along the line, in one direction. Envision that sort of system running through the membrane, actually through the entire cell wall. A charged ion is picked up at the outside of the cell and dragged by sequential charges to the inside, where it is released. These negatively charged ions (anions) accumulate on the inside, which creates an electrical imbalance. The positively charged ions (cations) then move in to restore the balance.

As an illustration, potassium chloride exists in the soil solution as the ions K^+ and Cl^-. The electron chain pulls the Cl^- ion in with sequential charges, and the K^+ ion follows it to restore the balance. Over time this results in a higher concentration of salts within the cell than outside.

Just to stay honest, we need to say that water coming into the root through osmosis cannot account for the large amount of water a plant actually uses. We are trying to explain only how plant uptake of nutrients requires energy. The total water uptake system is more complicated.

The only point you need to keep in mind is that pulling salt ions across the membrane, and keeping them there, requires energy. This energy comes from sugar, which requires the use of oxygen from the soil. As the supply of oxygen decreases in the small area around that particular root, the rate of salt uptake slows. As the salt uptake slows, the water uptake also is reduced. This is partly for the obvious reason that the salt concentration is what draws water in, but there is another aspect. Remember that respiration involves the uptake of oxygen and the release of carbon dioxide. Under normal soil conditions the plant membranes allow water to pass through readily, but when there are low oxygen and high carbon dioxide levels, the membranes become less permeable to water.

Now we can put the water-nutrient uptake system in a summary form. Only the active root hair regions of feeder roots contribute very much to nutrient uptake. They continuously extract nutrients and water from the soil solution. Because they also grow continuously, the tips move on to new feeding grounds when an area is badly exhausted. One of the key points to this is the presence of oxygen in the soil air pockets. If those pockets do not have a continuous connection with the atmosphere, the oxygen will be used up and replaced with carbon dioxide. This will stop the uptake of water and nutrients; if it persists the root tips—and ultimately, the entire root system—will die.

We finally have enough information to give a practical illustration. Consider that you have a good garden with good drainage and raised beds. It has rained every afternoon for two weeks; the daily temperatures have been in the high 80°s and low 90°s. Then it stops raining for two or three days and your bean plants begin to wilt. Water those poor plants: They are in a drought stress because most of the feeder roots have died in the hot, wet soil. New feeder roots will form in a few days. Also, check to see whether the soil surface has crusted; that will seriously reduce oxygen flow. Old-time gardeners will say that you need to stir the soil so the roots can get a little air. They are exactly right, but you also may need to add more water until a new root system develops. A tip: While watering wet soil, be careful to do it gently; otherwise you will recrust the surface.

CAMBIUM COMES FIRST

The term *cambium* is derived from a Latin word meaning "to change," which is a rather good description. Cambial cells are the basic undifferentiated cell units of the plant.

Cambium exists as a sheath of cells beneath the bark and outside of the wood, extending up to the end of each shoot where there is a little dome called the meristem (a Greek word for "dividing cells"). These cambium cells divide, producing new cells both on the inside and outside of the sheath. That is where the changes begin. The influence of several growth hormones causes those cells on the inner portion of the sheath to become *xylem vessels,* which are long tubes that transport water and minerals upward from the roots. The cells outside of the layer produce similar (not identical) tubes. Those are called *phloem;* they carry solutions of sugar and other substances from the leaves. Some of this material gets to the roots but most of it is taken up by various other growing tissues in the plant—flowers and fruits are two obvious beneficiaries.

This is a continuous process. So, what happens to all of that xylem and phloem? The xylem tubes continue to function for months or years, until they slowly clog up with a resin and become wood. *Xylo* is a Greek term meaning wood; *xylophone* comes from that word. In the preceding paragraph we said that cambium cells differentiate into xylem. Part of this differentiation is the formation of thicker cell walls.

Now we are going to tiptoe on the edge of a dirty word in botany. *Teleology* refers to the concept that plant structures are formed in response to a need. Carrying this idea very far leads to serious questions that we cannot answer. Sap, which is a large amount of water carrying mineral nutrients and sugars to support the growth of new leaves, rises in the spring. It seems logical that a successful plant would form xylem units with large internal diameters during that period. This is the tiptoe area: we cannot quite say that the plant produces larger xylem tubes in the spring for the purpose of handling more water. Regardless of why, wood formed in the spring has larger pores than those in summer wood. These layers of xylem cells with larger holes, alternating with cells that have thick walls and small holes, are the annual rings of a tree. The variations in ring thickness reflect differences in spring and summer growing conditions from year to year. Counting the rings gives a good estimate of how old the tree is, but if you study the stump of a tree very closely you will find some *false rings:* portions of rings that developed when there was a short growth flush or the trunk grew faster on one side. This is why counting growth rings is only a rough guess about the age of the tree.

The fate of old phloem is different. Growth of cambium and xylem crushes phloem tissue against the outer bark. The word *phloem* means bark, which is not quite accurate because most of the bark is made up of cork cells. To see what we are describing, look at our sketch of the xylem, phloem, and cambium of a woody stem (figure 20).

Now, where are we going with this? In chapter 17 we discuss how the fate of a damaged azalea plant may depend on whether little patches of surviving cambium can regenerate a vascular (xylem and phloem) system: the azalea may send out new shoots and leaves but die in June. This is because there was not quite enough living cambium to keep the plumbing system going. In chapter 8 we suggested (hesitantly) that a slight blockage of sugar movement in the phloem might stimulate a plant to flower and set fruit. Now you know what we were talking about—not whether it is true, but why we said it.

Soil, Oxygen, and Water

We are still looking at the water uptake process but are shifting our emphasis to the soil. Remember that the soil must furnish both oxygen and water. Dur-

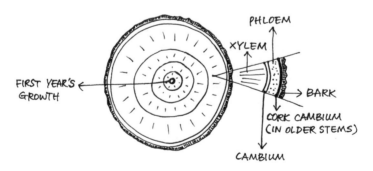

Figure 20. Cross section of a woody stem.

ing a heavy rain, air pockets become filled with water, but rainwater contains a large amount of oxygen. After a rain the excess water usually drains downward from the force of gravity, drawing a fresh supply of oxygen into the air pockets. You may remember that we said the same thing in discussing how you should water potted plants.

Do not confuse the excess water in air pockets with what is called soil moisture. The water that a plant uses is sticking to soil particles, or in small spaces, after gravity has removed the excess. The degree to which water sticks to particles varies considerably. Although it depends somewhat on the chemical nature of the soil particle, it also is largely a matter of thickness of the water layer. The first single-molecule-thick layer is held tightly by a water-to-particle bond. Each layer after that is progressively less affected by the water-to-particle force and more by the weaker water-to-water force. You learned all of this in high school chemistry. When you drew water up into a pipette, it sagged a bit in the middle and seemed to climb up the glass side. The instructor called this the meniscus (from a Greek word meaning "crescent") and said it was formed because the water-to-glass force was stronger than that of water-to-water. Plants use the same principle. Ultimately, the water layers on soil particles are so thick that the outer portion cannot withstand the pull of gravity. This is the excess water that drains out. The soil solution containing nutrients stays there as a film on the soil particle (see figure 21).

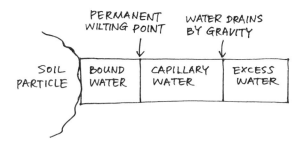

Figure 21. Water layers on a soil particle.

Using this principle of water films we can consider some soil terms. First, we need to realize that, on a comparative weight basis, sand will hold much less water than will fine clay. This is partly because the particles are chemically different but also because clay has much more surface area on which layers can form. Now for the terms. *Field capacity* means the amount of water (expressed as a percentage of the soil's dry weight) that the soil can hold against the force of gravity. This is the old excess-water principle we discussed earlier, and it varies with the amount of sand, silt, clay, and organic matter in the soil. Plant roots can easily draw water from soil at field capacity. But as they extract water, that which remains becomes progressively harder to remove from the particles. Ultimately, the moisture level reaches the wilting point. This means that the roots can remove some water but not enough to keep the leaves from wilting on a hot day. As this point is approached you will see the plants wilt every afternoon but they look good in the morning. During cool nights the roots can remove enough water from the soil to revive the leaves. Finally, a point is reached at which the roots can extract no more water, and the plant dies. This is called the permanent wilting point (PWP). There is still some water on the soil particles but it is so tightly bound that the plant cannot take it up. From our earlier discussion you can see that wilting point and PWP are more nearly concepts than actual levels of soil moisture. The PWP is supposed to be a characteristic of the particular soil (sand, silt, and clay content), but some plants can survive dry conditions longer than others; temperature and humidity are factors, and oxygen supply in the soil is important.

A soil with some clay in it takes up and holds much more water than a very sandy soil. Plants can draw water from it for a much longer time and will recover from wilting in hot weather more readily than if they are in sand. But we must always remember the oxygen problem; excess water drains out of a sandy soil more readily, so the possibility of killing roots during rainy weather is less. In general, a sandy soil is easier for water management in an area of frequent rains and a heavier soil is easier in drier areas. In describing this situation we are referring to a heavier soil as being one containing clay rather than a soil composed entirely of clay. Soil with a large amount of clay is often difficult to manage even in dry weather because the water may be so tightly bound that the roots cannot take it up.

We have fitted several pieces of the puzzle together, so we need to look at that before tackling a new area. We have seen that actively growing plant roots are easily killed if the soil oxygen is low. The amount of available oxygen needed varies with the activity of the roots. Rapidly growing plants are more sensitive to wet (low-oxygen) soil than are slower growing ones. Soils that drain readily are less affected than those that hold water longer. Soils that form a crust cause the same problems as those that are too wet. Roots located far below the soil surface are more seriously affected than are shallow roots because oxygen from the air must travel farther.

The Physical and Chemical Nature of Soil

Here is a quick soil texture test that will illustrate some points. Take a soil sample, about a cupful, and spread it out in a pan to dry for a few days. When it is fairly dry, break the clods, remove the debris, and measure out one-half cup, shaken down but not necessarily packed. Put this half cup of soil in a quart jar, add about a teaspoon of baking soda, and fill with water. Let that sit for about ten minutes, stirring it occasionally. Now put a lid on the jar and shake it vigorously for about a minute. Let the mixture settle for exactly one minute before decanting the water-soil mixture into another jar. There should be a residue of sand in the bottom of the first jar; leave it open to dry for about a day. Shake the second jar well and let that mixture stand for eighty minutes. Carefully decant the remaining water-soil mix into a third jar and let it stand for eight hours, minus the eighty minutes, or about six hours and forty minutes. Decant again, discarding the water. The experiment is over when everything has dried enough to pour back into the measuring cup.

The material that settled out in one minute was sand, which is roughly everything above 0.05 mm in size. The eighty-minute settling was what might be called coarse silt, material above 0.005 mm in size. But the material that settled out in eight hours was also silt, above 0.002 mm in size. The clay was still suspended in the water after eight hours, and some of it might never settle out.

One other point, which reiterates something we mentioned in chapter 4, is that the soda (sodium bicarbonate) was used to separate particles that had stuck together. All of the exchange sites were saturated with sodium. In chapter 4 we cautioned that if you do not flush the potting mix from potted plants regularly, the soil will become saturated with salts and the only remedy is to repot the plant and replace the soil. That is largely due to sodium, which destroys the soil structure by separating the particles.

Looking back over the test you will see that sand is primarily one particle size range and that it settles out rather quickly; silt is a group of smaller particles; and clay particles are even smaller. The results of this test explain how soils are deposited on the flood plain of streams. The soil closer to the stream is sandier than that at the extreme limit of where it floods. But the size of a spring flood varies every year, so soil that is mostly silt and clay may have a sandy strip representing a big flood that occurred long ago. Also, a stream will eventually wander out of its old streambed and form a new one. This makes the patterns of soil textures even more complex. Many of our soils are from stream deposits and most of the others were deposited as streams carried soil material into the ocean shoreline. If your yard was once in the floodplain of a stream, it is possible, but not likely, that the soil texture may vary both across the yard and as you dig downward to work up a garden.

You do not need run this test unless you want to see what your soil is like; just remember that soil particle sizes vary and the terms loam, silty clay, and so forth are necessarily broad. See figure 22 for the classification scheme.

We will add that this is a very old method for determining soil texture. In soils laboratories a hygrometer is used instead of drying samples, but our method illustrates the principle. Also, most gardeners get the same information by the time-honored test of taking a bit of soil between the thumb and

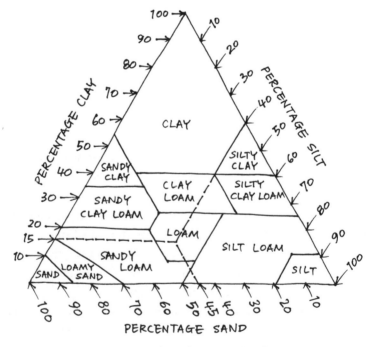

Figure 22. The soil-texture triangle.

From *Soil: The 1957 Yearbook of Agriculture.* Washington, D.C.: GPO, 1957.

A Tale about Wet Sand

Ed: A long-time friend and field worker would occasionally drive sand and gravel trucks on weekends. Sand was sold by the cubic yard, but weight was also important because of highway weight limits. He was puzzled that a truckload of wet sand was lighter than the same volume of dry sand. He didn't realize that sand is heavier than water and the water film on sand takes up space. I occasionally used his question on tests, and found that most students looked on it as a puzzlement.

Leon: I think he was working from sound logic. If the sand is only slightly wet, the particles will have films of water but none in the air spaces. As you add more water, it will replace air between the particles—making wet sand heavier than dry sand. Well, if the truck bed has leaks in it, the excess water will drain from those air pockets. All truck beds leak, so Ed is probably right.

forefinger, spitting on it, and rubbing the fingers together. The sandy fraction feels, well, sandy. The silt feels like talcum powder, and the clay is sticky; fine clay particles are very sticky. With a little practice you can make a very good estimate of the soil texture this way.

Although clay particles are defined as being everything below a certain size, it is misleading to think of clay as only small particles. Most clay particles are small because they are chemically different from sand. Most sand is composed of quartz, which is a hard, resistant material. It contains some particles of other minerals, such as feldspars and hornblende, called primary silicate minerals. *Primary* means that they will break down to secondary silicate minerals, which become the silicate clays that we will discuss in following paragraphs. The only point we need to make now is that clay is defined in terms of particle size but it is also chemically different from sand. We will not discuss silt, but it lies between sand and clay—both in size of particles and chemically. Figure 23 is a simplified illustration of the composition of sand, silt, and clay.

Physically, the amount of sand in the soil is very important because sandy soil drains faster and has more and larger air pockets. Chemically, neither sand nor silt is very important because neither is very reactive and neither has much

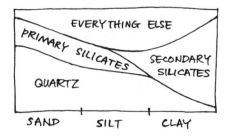

Figure 23. Composition of sand, silt, and clay.

surface area. Clay and humus are chemically the most important constituents (we discuss humus in chapter 16). Clay minerals are divided into two groups: the silicate clays that are found primarily in the temperate zones, and the iron and aluminum hydrous oxide clays of the humid tropics. In the humid subtropics we have a little of both, but understanding the silicate clays will serve our purposes, and they are easier to explain.

The silicate clays break down into three minerals: illite, montmorillonite, and kaolinite. These are related groups rather than specific chemicals, and you only need to know that they represent different stages of weathering. Illite is the least-decomposed stage, which is why our soils in the humid South have almost none of it. Our better soils have some montmorillonite, which is the next stage. Our less-productive soils have progressively larger amounts of kaolinite, the most highly weathered form.

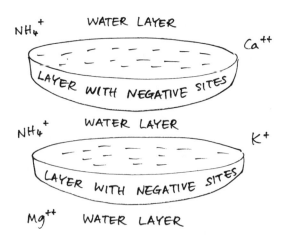

Figure 24. Layers of clay particles surrounded by thin layers of water.

The significance of clay being in various forms of related chemicals is that clay particles are made up of crystalline plates, usually stacked much like pancakes. These plates (chemists call them *micelles,* from a Latin word meaning "tiny crumbs") have many negatively charged (anionic) sites. Because of these negative sites, the plates are surrounded by positively charged cations. Look at figure 24 and notice that the plates are separated by thin films of water. In rich soil cations are plant nutrients; ammonium, calcium, potassium, iron, copper, and so forth are all cations. (The phosphorus ions are negatively charged anions, and that causes problems we address later.) The active feeder roots, often attached directly to the clay particles, take up nutrients and replace them with hydrogen (H^+) ions. (This is exactly like the ion-exchange water softeners used to remove calcium from water, except that softeners use sodium to replace the calcium.) The process is called cation exchange, meaning that the plant root exchanges one cation for another. Notice that if a root is attached to the particle, the ion does not go into a water solution, it just moves from the soil directly into the plant root. The quantity of nutrients a clay particle can hold is called its *cation exchange capacity,* or sometimes simply *exchange capacity.* This is a common term for expressing the potential fertility of a soil.

Of the different kinds of clay, illite, the kind we do not have down South, has the highest exchange capacity. On the basis of ability to hold and give off plant nutrients, our soils are not very good; but luckily, that is not the whole story.

pH, Buffers, Redox, and Latin Prescriptions

Here we will clear up some mysteries about liming of soil and why city (or well) water in some areas is so bad for your potted plants. Our discussion is fairly straightforward, and we try to give only a broad understanding of the problems.

In high school you memorized the definition of pH and the oxidation-reduction equations, but only for long enough to pass the test. The proper definition of pH is: the log of the reciprocal of the hydrogen ion concentration per liter of solution. We cannot quite see why it was foisted off on farmers and gardeners, but suspect the real reason is related to why prescriptions are written in Latin (we think doctors like to keep their patients confused about what is being prescribed). Soils management is often more of an art than a science.

The pH concept is simple: acid solutions have progressively more free hydrogen ions (H^+) and alkaline solutions more hydroxyl ions (OH^-). At pH 7 they are balanced, with the same numbers of each. At pH 6 there are more H^+ ions and pH 8 has more OH^- ions.

The concept is simple, but chemists have added a complication by putting it on a logarithmic scale (log of the reciprocal). The difference in acidity (H^+ ions) from pH 6 to pH 5 is ten times greater than that from pH 7 to pH 6. Most of our soils are between pH 6 and pH 5, with those at 6 being hardly acid at all and at 5 having serious fertilizer problems. In general, you should try to keep soil in the range of pH 5.6 to 6.0, but remember that the drop from 5.6 to 5.4 is about ten times greater than that from 5.8 to 5.6.

Why not work out a simple straight-line scale, using zero as neutral and either acid or alkaline units rising uniformly from that? We did a little daydreaming and came up with a sketch to illustrate this idea (figure 25). But it gets worse; we have to talk about buffers. You will remember that we mentioned buffers, very carefully, in talking about pH problems when you water potted plants.

When you used the pH meter in high school, the teacher first calibrated it against a buffer. He or she might have added a small amount of pH 4.5 buffer to distilled water; if the meter did not read exactly 4.5 it was readjusted because the buffer assured that the solution pH was correct. In that case the buffer was a compound that would bind extra H^+ or OH^- ions so the total in solution remained constant. Remember that the pH definition said "per liter of solution." In soil the clay and organic matter particles act as buffers. Assume

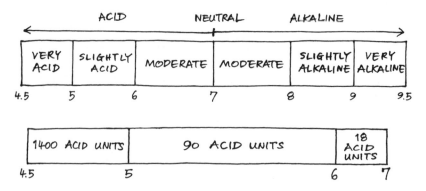

Figure 25. A simple straight-line scale for pH ranges.

that the garden center actually does sell a quick soil test kit to show the pH of a sample from your garden. If you find that your soil has a pH of 5.0, and you want 6.0, how much lime should you add? Knowing the pH is not enough, because the lime requirement depends on the degree to which clay and organic matter are acting as buffers. This means that if your soil is sandy, with low organic matter, a pound of lime would be enough for the garden, but if it has more clay and organic matter you might need ten pounds for the same area. Adding too much lime can cause problems as serious as those caused by too little. The only reliable way to find the answer is to ask the county agent to have a lime requirement test run. But that may not be necessary; you probably know someone with soil much like yours. Most gardeners simply guess on what they hope is the low side and keep adding a little lime each year until it hits the point they want. You should probably have a soils test run every four or five years, but a lot of good gardeners never do it.

We drifted a bit from the topic because buffering has other meanings, too. When we discussed watering of potted plants we used New Orleans water as an illustration. Tap water in New Orleans frequently has a pH of 11.0, which sounds like a serious problem if you want the pH of your pot mix to stay at about 5.7. Actually, it hardly matters at all because New Orleans water is so lightly buffered. It will quickly adjust to the pot pH. Tap water in other areas may have a pH of 8.0 and be so highly buffered that it causes problems.

The third illustration of a buffer may not sit well with a good chemist, but it is a common term with gardeners. If your soil is low in potassium but you made a mistake and added ten times what you should have, the clay and organic matter will probably buffer it. In this case buffering means that the excess will be taken onto cation exchange sites.

REDOX

Oxidation-reduction equations would be difficult even if the labels were not backwards, which they are. When Faraday recognized that electricity represents a flow of electrons, he believed that electrons flowed from what he called positive electrodes to the negative ones. When someone discovered that they went from negative to positive it was too late to change the terminology; this is only a problem if you have trouble thinking backward.

The above statement contributes nothing to this discussion beyond saying that the reactions are difficult to grasp. In high school you learned that, for one substance to be reduced, another must be oxidized. Putting this another way; when a substance gains electrons it is being reduced, and the substance that lost them was oxidized. *Reduced* means that electrons were gained; *oxidized* may mean that something lost electrons to oxygen, but electrons can go to substances other than oxygen. For our purposes, it does not matter which way the electrons go, only that they move. Microorganisms get energy from respiration by oxidizing sugars or similar compounds. Most of the time oxidizing will mean that the respiration process uses oxygen but, if there is no oxygen, microorganisms will use other substances; iron and manganese are good examples. Remember that when one substance is oxidized another must be reduced. When there is no oxygen present, microorganisms can oxidize sugar by reducing iron or manganese (or other substances).

In chapter 16, when we discuss troubleshooting nutritional problems, we consider how some soils have a lot of manganese but the oxidized form is not very water-soluble. If those soils are wet during warm weather (high microbial activity, low oxygen), the manganese will be converted to its reduced (more soluble) form. This leads to temporary manganese toxicity in young plants, not exactly because there is too much manganese but because it is temporarily too soluble. When the soil dries up a little and oxygen becomes adequate, the manganese will go back to the oxidized form.

The Development of Soils in the Humid South

There are many kinds of soils, differing largely by the climates in which they developed, but we are concerned only with the humid South. For convenience, soil is thought of as having three depth horizons or zones. The A horizon is commonly called topsoil or the surface soil. Over many years most of the clay has washed out of the topsoil and into the subsoil, which is the B horizon. The A horizon is mostly sand and silt, plus different amounts of organic matter. The subsoil has more clay and less organic matter. Below that is the C horizon, the original material from which the soil developed, which we can ignore here (see figure 26).

Topsoil is supposed to mean the A horizon, but only if it has not been disturbed at all. The topsoil of any good garden is a mixture of the A and B horizons. If the soil has been badly eroded, the original A horizon has been washed away and you are gardening the subsoil (B horizon). Most good soils books say that, if the topsoil has been washed away, it will take around fifty years to rebuild it. Our best guess is that those books are quoting a study conducted in Ohio, long ago. Welcome to the humid South, where farmers routinely rebuild a functional topsoil in three to five years. In the process of sloping the land (giving it a 0.5 percent slope) they frequently have to cut as much as a foot from parts of the field. They then build raised beds and grow soybeans or corn on the field for a few years. The spots that were cut down into the B, or maybe the C, horizons do not produce very well at first, but frequent rains wash the clay out and organic matter builds up; they have new topsoil, or something that does just as well. This is the basis for our statement in chapter 1 that, no matter how bad your soil is, it will improve in a well-managed garden.

The ways in which our soils developed depended largely on the degree of internal drainage, or water movement through the three horizons. That was influenced both by the amount of rainfall and by the amount of sand. If there was a substantial amount of sand, particularly in the B and C horizons, the water drained through readily and took more silt and clay from the topsoil. Also, this meant that the subsoil area, where most of the nutrients were lo-

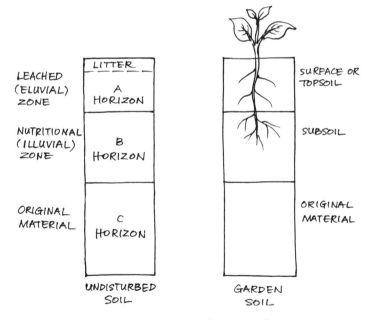

Figure 26. Virgin and garden soils.

cated, usually had air pockets and an abundant supply of oxygen. This determined the kinds of plants that grew in the soil, which also had some effects on the soil. Where there was usually enough oxygen for active root growth, the iron compounds became oxidized, leaving the soil with a bright red coloration. Soil that was less well-drained is more yellow, and poorly drained is white. Why is it white? Essentially, the clay particles are saturated with H+ ions. All of the nutrients are gone and the clay is an aluminum oxide plus H+ ions. The point we want to leave you with is that, in the humid South, the color of the subsoil is a good indicator of its potential for supporting a good garden. A bright red color indicates good internal drainage. If the soil has only a little iron, a golden brown indicates good drainage. This does not mean that a gray or white subsoil indicates your soil is hopeless; it can be very productive if you manage it properly. It needs lime, and the drainage will depend almost entirely on the raised beds and sloping water furrows.

The reasons for poor drainage vary. Sometimes there is very little sand in the soil profile; in other situations clay and silt have collected in a layer that restricts water movement. This layer is called a hardpan or fragipan, and it is easy to find in a soil profile. It usually has a mottled white and yellow coloration. The layer is very hard and nearly impermeable to water. If this pan is only a few inches thick, it can be broken by a process called subsoiling. Sometimes it is several feet thick and your management program must simply accept its existence. Another type of hardpan that restricts drainage is called a *plowsole* or *traffic pan*. This is a compacted layer just below the plowed zone, formed by the weight of tractors, horses, or human feet. Remember that you should not walk on soil while the subsoil is still wet, even if the topsoil is dry. On the other hand, some soils are poorly drained simply because too much water runs through the profile. A good well-drained soil in Iowa would probably be poorly drained given the rainfall patterns of the humid South, and our well-drained soil would be excessively drained in Iowa.

Soil Compaction

Most of the virgin pine forests in the Deep South were cut in the late nineteenth and early twentieth centuries. Loggers felled the trees, cut the branches, and used ox-teams to drag the trees to a logging road. Then an ox-drawn logging wagon carried them out to a marshaling lot. After the logs were gone the entire area was burned; the process was called "clear-cut and burn." Pine seedlings then germinated as a thick carpet and gradually the faster growing trees crowded the others out. This operation was repeated on twenty- to forty-year cycles, depending on the rate of tree growth.

It is refreshing to walk slowly along the old logging roads shaded by twenty- to forty-year-old trees and see how completely the land recovers after logging. Think now, of what we just said. The logging roads are still there, forty or perhaps even eighty years later. The old ruts are no more than two or three inches deep, but there are no trees or even undergrowth brush growing in them. An occasional tree may be growing in the middle area, but it is likely to be loblolly pine, the kind that will continue root growth in wet soil. The land recovered from the logging but not from the compaction of wagon wheels running over wet soil.

Over the past twenty years, soils people have made interesting studies of soil compaction, with results that make practical sense. Any heavy weight on the soil, a wheel or your foot, spreads the force downward at a 45° angle. The greatest force per square inch is at the surface, and the depth to which it affects structure depends on the soil type and amount of moisture. The simple weight of very wet soil has some effect on structure, and the added impact of a foot or wheel makes it worse; wet clay is slippery and packs easily. Soil is always compacted more tightly close to the surface and progressively less at greater depths. Farmers and gardeners want to believe that, because the compaction is greatest at the surface, they can eliminate the problem by *disking* or running a tiller over the upper five or six inches. A tractor wheel running over wet soil only once causes a measurable amount of compaction down to a depth of three feet. The key problem here is that you can loosen the compacted topsoil with tillage, but getting to the compacted subsoil is more difficult. There is a tractor tool called a *subsoiler* that can go as much as two feet deep, loosening the soil to some degree. It is a slow process requiring a large tractor, but sub-soiling a few rows of a cotton or soybean field makes a striking demonstration if there is a dry period during the summer. Cotton plants on the subsoiled row may be a foot taller than the rest; in a wet year there will be no difference.

This little discourse has several points that you can take to your garden and lawn. Before building the seedbed it would be good to loosen the subsoil; plants will grow well with less irrigation in dry weather and it will not matter in wet weather. Another point is that you should never stand on a prepared seedbed; the soil may seem dry on the surface but the subsoil could still be wet. Do not drive your car over the lawn at any time, and try not to walk on the grass if the soil is very wet. The effects of soil compaction will show up only in dry weather, meaning that you will have to water the lawn more frequently.

Chapter 16

FERTILIZER: WHAT IT IS, IS NOT, AND MIGHT BE

Fertilizer is not plant food. *Fertilizer* is not a very good term either, but we will use it for lack of a better one. It makes soil fertile only if all of the other soil conditions are right. In this chapter we discuss the different kinds or aspects of fertilizers. We also have a go at explaining just what organic gardening is and why the terminology is so mixed up; the fault lies with scientists, not with organic gardeners. In addition, we explain just how the concepts of organic matter and organic gardening came to be.

Organic Matter: Nature's Fertilizer

As you saw in chapter 3, we believe strongly in organic matter, for improvement of both the soil fertility and soil structure. We believe you can get more pleasure out of gardening if you understand why rather than just how. So in this chapter we explain why so many gardening books say you should have a soil organic matter level of 12 percent. The organic matter level in your garden actually depends on an ecological equilibrium. With our climate, a level of around 3 percent is very good. Managed properly, your 3 percent soil will outproduce the 12 percent soil—year after year.

There is a very old fundamental concept called the vital theory, which was based on a deep reverence for life, an emotion we share with most biologists. Life is so complex and delicately balanced that we are not even close to understanding it. This is the fascination of biology; we learn small facts that often point to greater complications and greater challenges. An awkward part of the original vital theory was the idea that living organisms produced compounds containing an essence of life that could not be duplicated in the laboratory. Complete acceptance of this essence-of-life concept made research difficult; how is it possible to study a system that cannot be duplicated? This part of the vital theory was broken by a fortunate accident. In 1828 a German chemist, Friedrich Wohler, was using a reaction that should have produced ammonium cyanate and found that he had made urea instead. His error (heating the compound too much) was the foundation of organic chemistry. Man had produced an organism-derived compound in the laboratory.

The story of a German chemist accidentally making urea is, or used to be, part of the standard introductory lecture for organic chemistry. It had no more impact on students than their being told the textbook author's name. This dull statement is a key point in the arguments about organic compounds, organic matter, and organic gardening. Chemists now define an organic compound as one containing carbon, but the vital theory had already described an organic compound as one that was organically derived. Why did chemists redefine a perfectly good term? Realistically, what we now call organic chemistry is better described as carbon chemistry. Why should anyone scoff at people who continue to use organic with its original meaning?

By the chemists' definition, black plastic film that you use as a mulch in the garden is organic: it contains carbon, as do most commercially produced insecticides. Soil organic matter is defined in textbooks as that portion of the soil derived from living organisms. For our discussion, organic matter will follow the soil definition: it is organically derived and most of its compounds contain carbon, but many do not.

Having developed a working definition of organic matter, we must now look at some subdivisions. For our purposes we will describe the original material as *plant residue:* dead bits of leaves, stems, roots, and maybe some animal parts. *Organic matter* will refer to all stages of decomposition from plant residue down to where only carbon dioxide, water, and a few minerals remain. Organic matter can also be divided into humus and prehumus, but not here; for us, humus and organic matter will be essentially interchangeable terms.

Organic matter is hundreds of thousands of compounds, changing every few minutes. The directions of the changes depend on many factors that you already understand.

You may remember that we gave the C/N (carbon-to-nitrogen) ratio a lick and a promise back in chapter 3; we need to reiterate and build on that. Microorganisms break down plant residues to obtain energy and nutrients for their body tissues. Although there is some variation according to species, microbial body tissue contains about 1.8 percent nitrogen on a dry weight basis. If the plant residue contains about that much nitrogen, it is suitable for fairly rapid microbial breakdown. Because microorganisms get most of their energy from the decomposition of carbohydrates (sugars, starches, and cellulose), the amount of this material is also important. This is the meaning of the C/N ratio, which should be the carbohydrate/nitrogen ratio, but it is easier to analyze for carbon. The point we are developing is that the C/N ratio is a fairly good estimate of a material's suitability for microbial decomposition. The standard critical level for C/N is ten or twenty parts of carbon to one of nitrogen. The ratio of most grasses is higher than this (too much carbon); they will decompose slowly unless extra nitrogen is added. Gardeners will tell you that if you work hay into the soil it will tie up the nitrogen for awhile. Microorganisms are so active and aggressive that plant roots simply cannot compete for the limited amount of nitrogen. The hay you worked into the soil will decompose eventually, the organisms that digested it will die, and their body tissue will have a good C/N ratio.

Now let's get away from hay and follow the decomposition of some balanced C/N ratio material. This is hypothetical and could be bean vines from the garden, grass clippings from a well-fertilized lawn, or even the dead squirrel that had been eating your tomatoes. We only need a situation in which nitrogen is not limiting; the soil is moist, well-aerated, and warm. Because the actual names of microbial species are difficult, and almost meaningless, we will have microbial groups—A, B, C, down to Z—to represent actual species (or groups of species).

Group A_1 is those organisms that decompose only the easy materials such as sugars and starches. Their population builds up until all of that material is gone. They die, and group A_2 begins to decompose the body materials of A_1. This may release a little excess ammonia and maybe some potassium, but most of the nutrients will go toward building healthy A_2 bodies. Then the A_2 food supply gives out and group A_3 builds up to work on dead bodies of A_2. This sounds like a grisly concept, but Mother Nature is not always nice. If you follow this path to group A_{10}, at each step some nutrients are released until finally nothing is left but nutrients, CO_2, and a little water.

Meanwhile, back at the ranch, group B_1 organisms have been building up to work on the cellulose, but only the portion that is fairly easy to decompose. If you follow the path of group B organisms, it may run out at B_7 or it may go to B_{15}. At the same time, group C organisms will begin working on more resistant cellulose and that pathway will stop when only nutrients, CO_2, and water remain. When you get down to possibly Z_{34}, you will find a few slow, stubborn organisms trying to decompose plant lignins. They may be at it for years.

This illustration is oversimplified; for example, the A_4 organisms probably have resistant materials that only B_{13} can use. We want you to see organic matter as a group of interlocked decomposition processes that are affected by the original plant material, soil nutrients, moisture, oxygen, and temperature. If you were to take a sample of soil organic matter and could analyze for all its compounds in thirty minutes, you would only know what the soil had been like thirty minutes ago. This is a fundamental point, but we must leave it temporarily for a broader view.

Your old gardening book may define humus as the remains of plant residues that microorganisms could not decompose easily. That explanation is pretty good, but it ignores the idea of microbial remains. In fact, resistant plant residues make up only a tiny fraction of humus. A single dead microbe is very small, but there are billions of them. So, for our purposes, humus or organic matter is all stages of decomposition (including the decomposition of microbial remains), with the nutrients being gradually released.

But we also have been saying that organic matter is much more than just a slow-release fertilizer: it improves soil structure. This is because most microorganisms secrete materials known as microbial gums. The materials coat soil particles and become the binding agent that stabilizes soil aggregates. It does not precisely make the aggregates form, but after the particles are pushed together by plant roots, tillage, worms, and the like, it will hold them in place. Unfortunately, these gums are water soluble and do not hold up long in very wet soil.

Now we have the idea of organic matter adding plant nutrients to the soil and improving soil structure. In chapter 15 we said that organic matter increases the soil exchange capacity, meaning that it will hold more applied fertilizer. This is because the large complex molecules have many side chains that can hold cations and anions. This will make more sense after you read the fertilizer portion of this chapter.

We are still using *humus* and *organic matter* interchangeably because it is convenient. There is an old (1927) description of humus that is about as good as any. Humus, it says, "involves no static condition, but is a dynamic equilibrium constantly shifting with the supply of raw material, alternation of biological population of the soil, and alternation of the physical and chemical conditions imposed by cultural methods or fertilizer applications." Maybe that is what we have been trying to say.

So, with this background in mind, look at the gardening books that say a good garden soil should have 12 percent organic matter. Down South, 12 percent is an impossible dream. That writer lives in a cooler climate, but he or she is also ignoring a fundamental of ecology. To explain this we must begin with the ecological concept of climax, which refers to the highest or final level for the environmental conditions. The kind of tree that ultimately takes over an area is called the climax forest. This takes into account the soil type, rainfall, temperature fluctuations, whether the Indians burned it regularly, and other aspects.

Figure 27 illustrates the concept of a soil organic matter climax in a hypothetical soil in the humid South. The reference point (4 percent) represents the soil organic matter level of an old climax forest. We are assuming that it has been in forest for about one hundred years and has just been cleared for cultivation. (Obviously, it is not possible to clear a real forest without disturbing the topsoil, but we can do it in a hypothetical forest.) During the first few years of cultivation the organic matter decomposes rapidly; because the tree cover is gone, the soil is much warmer and cultivation puts more oxygen in the soil. All of this promotes microbial activity, which breaks down organic matter, releasing nutrients in excess of what even rapidly growing plants could use. The excess nutrients leach out and run into a creek, but the crop looks wonderful.

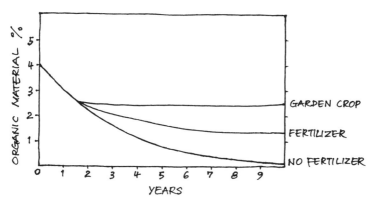

Figure 27. Soil–organic matter climax.

Leon's Tale about Tabasco™

Several years ago I helped develop a weed control program at Avery Island for Tabasco peppers, the kind the McIlhenny Company uses to make Tabasco sauce. Avery Island is a salt dome rising out of the marsh near New Iberia. It is a wonderful place for a short visit. You get a guided tour of the Tabasco factory, and for a modest admission you can wander through the Jungle Gardens, which have acres of camellias, azaleas, exotic bamboos, snowy egrets, alligators, and the original wild jungle fowl.

A retired county agent from Texas approached the field production manager at Avery Island about the possibility of testing a new kind of organic additive. The former county agent felt the additive had great potential, but experiment stations had refused to test it. Asked if I would help design a test in the pepper fields there, I agreed to help.

The material was commonly known as coal humate or oxidized lignite. It was somewhat water soluble but looked like a brownish coal dust. Obviously, coal is a plant-derived organic matter, but time, heat, and pressure have removed virtually all of the nitrogenous materials and carbohydrates. I wondered about the carbohydrate and nitrogen sources that microorganisms would use to break it down. It appeared that the problem was more than one of a carbohydrate/nitrogen ratio: both were in short supply. I went back to LSU, read some, visited with my soils microbiologist, and made some calculations. The humate company was recommending rates of forty to eighty pounds per acre. My plots were 120 square feet in size, meaning that the forty-pound rate was only fifty grams. I didn't know how to spread such a small amount uniformly, or what should be used as a standard to test it against: should it be with no additives or with an organic fertilizer? The company's literature said that the forty-pound rate would wash down and loosen the soil to a depth of twelve inches, but the Avery Island soil had a structural hardpan, a fragipan, at eight to ten inches. I decided we should ask for a meeting with the humate representative.

He was a pleasant, intelligent man, acting as salesman for the humate company, but we spoke the same language. He understood what I meant when I asked where the microorganisms would get nitrogen and carbohydrates. He didn't know the answer but assumed they would be from the soil. Nitrogen balance is critical for Tabasco peppers; the field foreman was following a precise fertilizer program. And we did not know how much more nitrogen would be required for the humate. We used the old C/N ratio and calculated an amount of extra nitrogen—if the humate were entirely carbon that would be converted (somehow) to organic matter. We went into the field with a soil auger, and I dug down and showed the humate salesman the fragipan. He understood my questions and felt sure his humate would shatter the pan. I promised to borrow a penetrometer from the soil physics people to measure soil looseness. We decided to mix the humate with sand to get uniform spreading. We would use the regular fertilizer program over the entire test and have two standards for comparison: one with no additive and another with eighty pounds (per acre) of organic fertilizer.

We met two weeks later and set out a well-designed and replicated test. The humate salesman would look at the results a week later, but I would not be back for two weeks. Well, when I returned there was nothing to see, and no humate salesman. He had been there the week before and said it was looking fine, that he would be back later with photographers. The field foreman and I looked around and saw nothing but normal field variation. I used the penetrometer to test the soil for looseness and there were no differences; the fragipan was still there.

On my next trip I found the foreman laughing. "You would have enjoyed watching the humate photographer trying to get good pictures of the test," he said. The photographer picked large plants in the treated plots, put a treatment sign in front, and took a picture. For the untreated plots he chose small plants. He even had larger plants for the eighty-pound humate rate than for the forty-pound plots.

We have not heard any more from the humate salesman, but somewhere he has photographs of a well-designed test conducted by an LSU scientist on the trial fields of the world-renowned Tabasco sauce company showing that coal humate is a wonderful additive for hot pepper production.

After the crop is harvested, the residue is plowed back into the ground. Annually, this is probably more organic matter than the original climax forest had been adding, but the soil organic matter level decreases rapidly because the entire ecology has changed.

In our illustration the organic matter level dropped to 3 percent in the first year and 2.5 percent in the second. At that point we would have to choose among three management practices. If we continue to farm the land without adding any fertilizer, the organic matter level will slowly drop to about 0.5 percent. After six or seven years the land will not produce crops well enough to justify the effort, so we would clear some more land and abandon that field. Unless serious erosion sets in, the original field will gradually revert to the climax forest. This was essentially the farming practice of the Indians and early European immigrant farmers; they had no fertilizer except for a little produced by their cows and horses.

The next management practice, started after the second year, is what we call cropping with fertilizer. Assume the farmer is raising corn or soybeans, perhaps rotating them, but he also uses commercial fertilizer to maintain a good crop yield. Even with enough fertilizer to make near-maximum crop yields, the organic matter level will continue to drop until it hits about 1.5 percent. This will be the organic matter climax level for continuous cropping of corn and soybeans with good management practices. It will fluctuate a little with weather variations, which will affect crop production and thus the amount of organic matter returned to the soil. Our point here is that although cropping adds more organic matter to the soil than a climax forest does, the organic matter level is less than half that of the forest soil because higher temperatures and tillage favor rapid breakdown. Maybe we should add that the crop yield during year one was no better than the average yields during years six and seven because excess nutrients of year one washed out of the field.

Now we come to a third management practice called garden crops: what you do in the backyard garden. Notice that it levels out at about 2.5 percent and remains rather constant. This is partly because you raise several crops per year, but also because you add compost and leaves to provide weed control. Compared with the production of corn and soybeans, this could be called an artificial organic matter climax. You are adding much more organic matter than the soil could produce. Even under that management plan you cannot approach the organic matter levels of a climax forest; in full sunlight, with good aeration and moisture, the microbial activity is much greater than it was in the cool, shaded forest.

The important idea here is that the soil organic matter level is an ecological climax reflecting management, climate, crops being grown, and the nature of the soil. If you change management practices, the level rises or falls. In general, it falls faster than it rises, but there are no average figures. That is about all we can say about managing organic matter levels. (See chapter 1 for a discussion of raising the soil organic matter levels.) Remember that our illustration here is for a hypothetical soil. Soil organic matter levels of climax forests in the humid subtropics range from about 2 to 6 percent. (Farther north the climax is much higher, up to 20 percent.) Good row-crop farmers try to stay at about 30 to 50 percent of the original, but their success varies with the crop grown. Corn will give a higher cultivation climax than will cotton, regardless of management.

But you are not planning to raise corn and cotton in your backyard, and you want to raise the organic matter level by adding leaves or grass clippings. Assume your garden plot is an area where the contractor scraped down to subsoil. It has an organic matter level of 0.2 percent, and you think its cultivation climax under intensive vegetable production should be 2 percent. Your objective here is to improve soil structure; the nutrients will come in a bag of fertilizer from the garden center. A good general figure in the humid South is that it takes about ten pounds of plant residue (dry weight) to produce one pound of organic matter (gums and humus). Assume a 50- by 20-foot garden, because this is 1,000 square feet or about one-fortieth of an acre. The upper 6 inches of your garden soil weighs about 46,000 pounds. To raise the organic matter level by 1 percent (from 0.2 to 1.2 percent) will require 460 pounds of humus, meaning 4,600 pounds of crop residues. Four cubic feet (roughly a garbage bag) of dry oak leaves weighs about 10 pounds; you will need 460 bags, which would make a pile about 2 feet deep over the whole garden. Hauling in a truckload of decayed manure would cause serious problems with excess nitrogen and possibly microbial competition for oxygen. A good cover crop would produce about 5 tons per acre or 230 pounds in your garden; but you cannot grow a good cover crop yet because it requires good soil.

The above figures are very rough, but our point is that you cannot quickly raise the organic matter level of soil. As we have said, gardening requires patience.

Farming in the Good Old Days

Because we are Scotch-Irish, both culturally and genetically, we still resent the condescending attitudes of the old Anglo-Saxons toward our dirt-poor Irish forefathers. When the English landlords took possession of Ireland, they wrote about the barbarians who kept the large manure piles near the house, raising flies and creating an awful odor. That was the Irish farmers' only source of fertilizer, and the survival of their children depended on reliable crop production. The manure pile was probably close to the house, which was on high ground—the manure liquids drained along a ditch to the garden.

In 1944 each of us won an all-expense-paid trip to Europe as a result of our proficiency with the M-1 rifle. Ed arrived first, where he studied the manure piles of Normandy with respect to their use as protection from shrapnel and small arms fire. Leon conducted a parallel study in Brittany, including a detailed examination of the local soil profiles. By that time the Normans and Bretons had improved composting techniques through the addition of a cement floor, raised sides, and a trough leading to a tank for storing liquid waste. The piles were still located near the house because the barn was usually part of the house; cows helped to keep the house warm. The houses were still on high ground; the well for drinking water was downhill and contained high counts of coliform bacteria.

Every few days the farmer cleaned the barn of straw that had absorbed urine and manure, stacking it neatly on top of the pile. The liquids, plus rainwater, washed downward and into the tank. Once a week the farmer pumped the liquid into his honey wagon and spread that on the grain fields. The composted straw/manure was his fertilizer source in the garden.

This was a balanced ecosystem, accepting the reality of life during the 1930s. They lost some nitrogen to the air as ammonia, and the phosphorus level was probably low. Commercial fertilizer would have increased production by possibly 50 percent, but they could not afford it. If we American soldiers had been drinking their well water, our casualties from disease would have rivaled combat losses. The civilians probably were not completely immune to those diseases, but they had strong resistance. In the 1960s Leon was talking about this composting system with a Wisconsin graduate student who had been the assistant to a county agent in southern Germany. He said that farmers in the poorer areas of his district still kept five or six cows, primarily for the manure. They milked the cows, used the butter, and fed milk to the pigs; but that was secondary to the need for garden fertilizer. This was not from ignorance or from great faith in manure; economics prevented them from buying commercial fertilizer.

Organic Gardening

A chapter devoted to fertilizer requires some thoughts about organic gardening. We know that some people will not entirely agree, but we look on organic gardening as more nearly a philosophy than a definitive program of using certain materials for soil improvement and avoiding others. We agree that all garden produce should be safe and healthy food. We cannot agree with the implication that all synthetically produced substances will produce flawed vegetables.

We look on organic gardening as an affirmation of thrift and stewardship of the land. We admire the beauty of nature and the dignity of physical labor. We do not like the concept of waste disposal—hauling leaves and grass clippings to a landfill instead of recycling them into your own land. We are concerned over the waste of nonrenewable phosphates, regardless of how large the deposits are; how long do we expect humans to live here?

We believe this book can be a guide for you to practice organic gardening according to your individual beliefs. We hope you will realize that there is no practice that can be described as purely synthetic gardening. Please remember that we are discussing home gardens and not the problems of commercial vegetable production. If the welfare of your family depends on the profits from vegetables or from Christmas poinsettias, you cannot afford to be patient and hope insects do not eat the crop.

We addressed the problems of indiscriminate pesticide use in chapter 13. Our judgments on medical questions, such as toxic residues and carcinogens, are based on the same news reports you are reading. Broadly, our approach is to use pesticides sparingly. With minor exceptions, we feel that herbicides are unnecessary in a home garden. The matters of insect and disease control are made difficult by our long growing season and high humidity. There are other options for pest control, and you must decide which to use.

Supplying Additional Fertilizer

Garden books and gardening gurus advise us to "have our soil tested" to determine the need for fertilizer and how to supply those needs. It would be nice if we could get such information for our gardens, and, indeed, soil tests will be run on samples submitted through county agents anywhere in the country. The results will be close estimates of the amounts of nutrients in the sample tested. Unfortunately, the sample may not begin to represent the variations in soil encountered even on a city lot, and recommendations for alleviating any lack, excess, or imbalance of nutrients are largely based on research with a few large-scale agronomic crops rather than the vast array of plant material found in home gardens.

City lots present a real challenge because prior use probably has been so variable. Low areas are often filled as cities develop, and landfills can contain almost anything. Soil lab recommendations are based on knowledge of crop needs and general nutritional status of recognized soil types.

However, soil tests can help to detect glaring problems such as high or low pH levels, obvious excesses of salts or certain elements, or deficiencies. They can be of great help to gardeners starting on recently cleared land, for example, or gardening anew in areas where they have no experience. Most gardeners are aware that supplements of nutrients are needed from time to time and want to do something about it. Unfortunately, our experience leads us to conclude that people use too much fertilizer on potted plants and vegetable gardens and not enough on landscape plants and lawns.

Fertilizer Formulations

Nutrients may be applied as solids, liquids, or gas (usually ammonia gas used on large-scale agronomic crops like sugarcane). They may be derived from organic materials such as crop residues, manures, or by-products of animal or fish slaughter such as tankage; blood meal, bone meal, or fish emulsion; synthetic chemicals; or from naturally occurring minerals. The essential elements are the same regardless of the source. Ease of handling or shipping and application, cost, rate of release of nutrients, and effects on soil can influence the choice of formulation.

Complete Dry Fertilizers

These contain the elements most often needed—N, P, and K (nitrogen, phosphorus, and potassium). Some may contain micronutrients, and they vary in the materials supplying nutrients as well as fillers or materials added to prevent caking. Labels note the content of the nutrients and may tell from what they are derived.

Many dry fertilizers are pelletized, or produced in small granules to ease application by spreaders (or by hand). The nutrients they contain are usually from water-soluble salts and are "readily available."

Dry organic fertilizers can be dried manures or blood, bone, or fish meal. These are much more expensive sources of nutrients than dry chemical fertilizers (which may be of minor importance to small gardeners) and release their nutrients slowly (which can be important).

Where only one nutrient is wanted, chemical salts are the usual source. Nitrogen, for example, can be supplied as sodium or calcium nitrates or as ammonium nitrate, which contains nitrogen in both the ammonium and nitrate forms. Phosphorus can be obtained from mono- or dipotassium phosphates, and potassium from potassium chloride or sulfate. All these salts are deliquescent (take up water) and some may be formulated as wax-covered pellets.

Several types of dry inorganic fertilizers are in slow-release formulations; such as pellets coated with a type of resin that allows water to enter at a controlled rate to release the nutrients from the salts inside. You may have bought container plants that appeared to have little spheres resembling fish eggs in the potting mix. Originally those were pellets of fertilizer, but by now they may be empty shells.

Other dry inorganic fertilizers release nutrients slowly through microbial action. Among these is urea-formaldehyde.

An interesting situation arises concerning the classification of some materials as organic or inorganic. This can have important consequences when attempts are made to define the status of materials used in producing organic produce. Natural Chilean nitrate of soda, derived from guano (the droppings of sea birds), is certainly not synthetic, but is it organic? It is a salt. On the other hand, urea-formaldehyde is a synthetic organic material supplying nitrogen. Perhaps we try to classify things too absolutely.

Leon recalls another memory of our early days in and around the fertilizer industry. The Chilean nitrate of soda we just mentioned was sold in the United States under the brand name Bulldog Nitrate of Soda. It was a fairly cheap and readily available source of nitrogen and was widely used in growing cotton— so widely that "bulldog sody," as it was called in many southern states, became synonymous with nitrogen fertilizer. With the coming of World War II, large plants were built to produce ammonia from natural gas to be used in munitions. When the war ended, the plants went into producing ammonium nitrate, with 33 percent nitrogen compared with sodium nitrate's 16 percent. Farmers learned that only half as much of this new sody was needed, or the cotton would *go to stalk* and produce fewer bolls. Ammonium nitrate became known as "double dog sody."

Fully soluble fertilizers are formulated to be dissolved and applied in irrigation water. These usually have a dye so one can tell by the color of the water that it contains fertilizer. These can be obtained in a wide range of analyses, most of which are used by commercial greenhouse growers. The average home gardener probably needs only something like a 20-20-20 analysis unless there is evidence to support using a different analysis.

Early on in this discussion we commented on our experience on over- or underuse of fertilizers. Can we give some generalizations on how much to use and how often? We can always generalize. Here goes.

For trees, use one to two pounds of a complete dry mix per inch of trunk diameter near ground level, four times a year—early spring, late spring, late summer, late fall. Spread this out beyond the drip line because roots go much further than that. If trees are in lawn areas, placing at least some of the fertilizer in holes eight to ten inches deep around the drip line will ensure that the tree gets some.

Shrubs can get one-eighth to one-quarter pound per plant in each of four applications. Flower beds can be given one-half to one pound per 100 square feet in early spring and probably will benefit from a couple of applications of nitrogen during the summer. This can be from ammonium nitrate at a rate of two level teaspoons per gallon of water or sodium nitrate at a rate of two tablespoons per gallon of water.

Vegetable plants that require side dressing with nitrogen can use the same solutions of ammonium or sodium nitrate as given in the previous paragraph, or light applications of urea-formaldehyde.

Err on the side of too little rather than too much with potted house-plants—maybe a little soluble fertilizer once or twice a year. Plants in pots out-doors, however, with the frequent irrigations they require, can use more fre-quent applications. Consider using a slow-release coated fertilizer on these at manufacturers' recommended rates.

A helpful gadget for applying soluble fertilizer can be obtained that siphons concentrated fertilizer solution into a water stream from a hose. This can be applied through a sprinkler where desired.

Fertilizer that Plants Really Need: Essential Elements

Maybe we can begin this with an old county agent's tale. He was assigned a new assistant who had just gotten a bachelor's degree from LSU. The boy spent his first few days driving around the parish to meet the farmers. He walked out in the field where an old farmer was plowing. The farmer stopped, shook, and howdied. Then the boy said, "I'm here to teach you how to farm better."

The old man thought for a minute, looking for a tactful answer. "Mais cher. Me, I already know how to farm better than I do."

Most of you already know more about fertilizer than you need to. This is just a short discussion, which begins with some principles.

Until early in the nineteenth century most scientists believed what was called the humus theory; that plants used some "essential earthy substance" from the soil that could not be duplicated chemically. (Yes, this was part of the vital theory that we discussed earlier.) In 1804 de Saussure published a paper in which he showed that plants would grow well in distilled water to which he had added mineral ashes plus nitrate. Because this idea was so different from the old concepts he was nearly laughed out of the scientists club. As other sci-entists confirmed his work, a search was begun to discover which minerals were needed and in what amounts. By 1930 the effort was largely complete. There are sixteen elements known to be needed by plants. Because carbon, hy-drogen, and oxygen are abundant they can be disregarded, which leaves thir-teen mineral elements. Back when we took plant physiology we remembered the primary essential elements as C. HOPKINS CAFE, Mn., Mighty Good. The *Mn* stood for manager (and manganese); *Mighty Good* stood for Mg, or mag-nesium. Then you only had to add Cu, Cl, Mo, and Zn. Well, maybe it was not such a good system, but it did help you to get started when an obnoxious faculty member asked the question on an oral examination.

As you might expect, there are many types of nutrient solutions proposed by different individuals as the best for certain plants or for general use. Although there are slight differences in the requirements of various plant species, the most important need is for a proper balance of nutrients. Of the sixteen essential elements, ten are needed in such small amounts that they are not usually critical. There are some exceptions, which we will mention occasionally. Calcium and sulfur usually are disregarded as rather abundant. Maybe we should say that there are probably other essential elements, needed in such small amounts that it is difficult to prove they are essential. Also, there are some elements that stimulate growth of some plants but do not seem to be essential for growth. So, for most plants in most soils, the really important nutrients are the standard N, P, and K that you can buy at any garden center.

NITROGEN

Nitrogen is the nutrient most often deficient in soils of the humid subtropics. In warm humid conditions nitrogen is released from organic matter too rapidly for the plants to use efficiently, so the excess leaches out or is converted to nitrogen gas. In nature virtually all of the nitrogen available to plants comes from nitrogen fixation by microorganisms. Decomposition of the primary and secondary soil minerals does not furnish any nitrogen.

The air has about 78 percent nitrogen gas, but plants can only use fixed nitrogen. *Fixed* has several meanings in discussing gardening, but for our purposes here it means nitrogen as the ammonium ion (NH_4^+) or as the nitrate (NO_3^-) ion. This is rather important because, although most plants can use either form, large amounts of the ammonium ion are toxic to some plants, and even very small amounts of ammonia (NH_3^+) are usually bad. Without going into the chemistry, nitrate is often converted to gaseous forms of nitrogen in wet soil (low oxygen). If the soil is wet for very long, all of the nitrogen is converted to nitrous oxide or nitrogen gas, which is lost to the air. Microorganisms reduce the NO_3^- in several steps (as we discussed earlier).

PHOSPHORUS

Although a plant needs relatively little phosphorus, it is the second most deficient element in humid soils. The reasons for this deficiency are different from those for nitrogen. Phosphorus is only taken up by plants as the phosphate ion, which has three forms:

$$H_2PO_4^- \qquad HPO_4^= \qquad PO_4^=$$
Acid soil   pH 5.5 to 7.0   Alkaline soil

The whole story is not quite that simple, but this is not a soils chemistry class.

The phosphorus deficiency problem is that both the $H_2PO_4^-$ and $HPO_4^=$ ions react with iron or aluminum to form nearly insoluble compounds. (Remember that organic matter and clay are not very efficient at holding anions.) Because these reactions happen much more rapidly in acid soils, liming is done primarily to conserve phosphorus. But even with the best management practices, approximately 90 percent of the phosphorus is lost for plant use through (nearly) insoluble compounds. At an agricultural level this may be a serious long-term problem because virtually all of our phosphate fertilizers come from nonrenewable rock phosphate mines. For your garden it is less of a problem than it seems; we will discuss that later.

POTASSIUM

The chemical symbol for potassium is K from the Latin *kalium.* In Europe they still call it *kalium;* our term has an interesting origin. Early farmers used the ashes left from burning firewood as a fertilizer and to make soap. *Potash* refers to the ashes from around the pot. It is the common term for KCl, which is the chief commercial fertilizer source. The use of potassium is much simpler than that of nitrogen and phosphorus. It is taken up by the plant as the cation K^+, which can be held on soil exchange sites. Except in very sandy soils it does not leach badly.

MICRONUTRIENTS

Many essential elements are needed in small amounts; they were once called minor elements, but people argued that if one of these is missing the plant will not grow. An element that is essential can hardly be called minor. The popular terms then became trace elements or micronutrients. In one sense *minor element* was a good term, because the elements are needed in such small amounts that they seldom present a fertilizer problem. There are sometimes micronutrient deficiencies in sandy soils, and occasionally, where large amounts of organic matter are used, the microorganisms use up most of the copper or zinc. The more common hazard with micronutrients is that someone adds too much or that the soil has a pH problem or poor drainage.

Nutrient Balance

There are so many facets to balance; many of them seem to be more nearly art than science. In general, the total amount of nutrients available to a plant is not so critical as is their balance. If the nutrient balance is badly upset, the plant will not grow normally. However, there are two kinds of buffers against this. Within limits, plant roots have a selective uptake mechanism, taking the nutrients in roughly the needed proportions. Also, clay and organic matter particles tend to buffer such problems. For example, if the soil has enough nutrients to support normal plant growth and a gardener adds more nitrogen and phosphorus, the plants might develop potassium deficiency. On the other hand, if that soil has a high exchange capacity, the imbalance will not matter because the roots can take more potassium from the soil particles.

Nutrient balance problems usually involve pairs of elements. In the example in the preceding paragraph, adding excess magnesium would have created a greater hazard of potassium deficiency than adding phosphorus and nitrogen. Iron and manganese balance are closely related. Phosphorus and calcium are related nutrients. These are not important matters for gardeners if the soil has a good exchange capacity, which is tied to the clay and organic matter content.

Nitrogen balance is important in relation to almost any other nutrient. Excess nitrogen causes rapid plant growth, which causes the plant to take up more of everything else. If the supply of some nutrient is already low, the addition of nitrogen could cause a deficiency. If there is a good supply of other nutrients, the excess nitrogen will produce a large, healthy-looking plant that will make only a few flowers and hardly any fruit. This is fairly common when someone adds a lot of manure to the garden: "I had wonderful, dark green, healthy tomato plants," they will say. But do not ask whether they got large healthy tomatoes.

Those N, P, K Terms

Here is an arcane topic you can bring up sometime when the garden club meeting gets dull. Soil scientists are the offspring of geologists and have inherited many of their ways. Long before computer printouts, geologists analyzed the phosphorus content of minerals by converting it all to the pentoxide, P_2O_5, which they could weigh. The potassium in minerals was measured as K_2O. They were not really concerned with the nitrogen content of rocks, but the procedure was to convert it all to ammonia, which was bubbled as a gas into a standard acid solution. The amount of used-up acid could then be related to the ammonia that had been produced.

Now look at the label on the fertilizer bag. That 8-8-8 does not really refer to the percentages of N, P, and K. The label gives the correct total amount of N; usually it also shows how much is from ammonia and how much from nitrate, which is important for use with some plants. The label may give sources of phosphorus, the form of which is probably as some kind of calcium phosphate. But the 8 does not represent the actual amount of phosphorus, it is the percentage calculated as P_2O_5: guess why! The potassium in your fertilizer nearly always comes from KCl, but the number refers to the percentage of K_2O.

You can make rough calculations that the second 8 means something like 4 percent phosphorus and the third number is about 7 percent potassium; this means that 8-8-8 is really 8-4-7. Periodically, some group starts pushing for accuracy in labeling, but the old ideas are too deeply planted. Besides, the accurate ratio would still have little meaning about the actual amounts of nutrients a plant would get from the fertilizer because there are too many other variables such as soil moisture, oxygen, the rate of phosphorus becoming insoluble, and others. So, should you get the 8-8-8, the 13-13-13, or maybe the grass fertilizer 20-8-8? It does not matter much for most situations; fertilization is an art, but not much of a science. Later we will give a few exceptions and comment on factors you should consider. But do not let the garden center dazzle you with the massive selection of special fertilizers. Buy whatever they have on sale.

Fertilizer Placement in Row Crops

The key point to fertilization methods in our soils is the loss of available phosphorus to insoluble iron and aluminum complexes. In row crops we can reduce this problem by applying a thick band of fertilizer a few inches below and to the side of where the seed will be planted. Although phosphorus on the outer edge of the band reacts with iron and aluminum, the inner part remains water-soluble. Because the plant does not need a large amount of phosphorus, only a few roots supply enough for it. Water and other nutrients are taken up by the entire root system, but phosphorus is mainlined through the one or two roots that hit the phosphorus band. An encouraging aspect of this method is that phosphorus becomes part of the organic matter in the entire plant. After the crop is mature and the roots die, the phosphorus is slowly released by the decomposing roots; this forms part of the phosphorus supply for the following crop. After three or four years of good management a soils test will show that there is no need for added phosphorus, but if you never add more the supply decreases with each crop. So, even after phosphorus becomes built up you should continue to add a little.

Ed: Wait a minute, Leon. We said earlier that the soil testing lab at LSU has found over the years that about three-quarters of home garden soil samples contained so much phosphorus that the level ran off the scale of their equipment. Now you are saying that they should keep adding more and that you should keep applying the fertilizer as a band.

Leon: Well, maybe. I know you're thinking that too much phosphorus can tie up the iron and possibly some other trace elements. But that happens only when you have way too much. Adding a little extra every year won't hurt. Well, ethically, it does hurt, because the rock phosphate we use now is a nonrenewable resource.

You will remember that in chapter 1 we said you should apply all the fertilizer to row crops as a band. Maybe this is old-fashioned, but it does work and is easier than working the fertilizer into the soil uniformly. After the crop comes up you can side-dress with a little nitrogen. *Side-dress* is an old term meaning that you sprinkle a little fertilizer on the soil surface close to the growing plant. This works well with nitrogen and makes more sense than applying it as a band because much of the banded nitrogen leaches out of the soil before a plant uses it. Side-dressing places it very close to the active roots.

Liming

Earlier we said that liming is done primarily to save phosphates; this is true, but you also should look briefly at the information on our pH chart (see figure 28). Although there is no "best" pH for all nutrients, we use pH 6 as a good compromise for availability of all nutrients. The liming process also adds calcium, which is a plant nutrient and is useful for improvement of soil structure. In chapter 1 we suggested that you have the soil tested and add enough lime to bring the pH up to around 6.0. The garden center will probably have only one kind of agricultural lime (avoid slaked lime), but you may have a choice. Dolomitic lime has some magnesium as well as calcium. That is usually no real

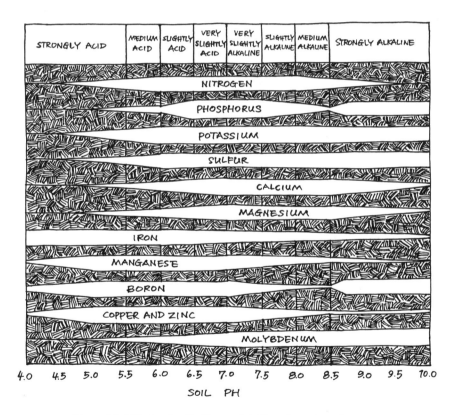

Figure 28. Effects of soil pH on solubility of nutrient elements.
From *Research Circular 268.* Wooster: Ohio Agricultural Research and Development Center, Jan. 1982.

improvement over calcium lime if you do not need magnesium; it also could throw the potassium out of balance, but probably will not because the magnesium is very slowly available. Another option may be finely ground oyster shells. They are good, and usually react with the soil a little faster. Do not expect any lime to react very quickly; it usually takes several months for the pH to adjust properly. Good gardening requires patience.

Practical Advice on Fertilizer

When you consider the fertilizer needs of the wide range of horticultural crops grown in home gardens or landscapes, soil type generalizations do not hold up very well. One of the reasons is that some of the material used for landfills can hardly be called soil. In the low elevations of New Orleans, people have filled building sites with a staggering array of materials. One typical fill is plaster, removed from old houses in modernizing efforts. This makes the pH of the soil too high for many plants, and in some cases almost nothing will grow. Easily available muck soils from surrounding marshes have been used extensively, often in combination with what contractors sometimes call river silt—but they may call it good topsoil. River silt is mostly silt-sized particles of quartz that was deposited by the Mississippi River after a flood. (Remember that in chapter 15 we explained that *sand* is defined only by particle size.) These soils can range from good to very poor. In some cases the mucks have high salt levels from sea water intrusion; the river silt can have damaging levels of heavy metals, and usually has very poor structure.

The assortment of potting mixes used for container-grown plants is even more variable than New Orleans fill dirt. With some potting mixes you can only guess about the fertilizer needs. The standard answer to fertilizer questions is "have the soil tested." Sure, but the soils recommendations are based on fertilizer needs of field crops in real soils. Regardless of the pompous assurances, nobody knows much about how soil test results can be related to potting mixes, which often rely heavily on pine bark.

In the following paragraphs are some generalizations based on our long and frequently embarrassing experiences. Let us repeat: people use too much fertilizer on potted plants, too much in vegetable gardens, and not enough on the landscape plantings, especially if the grass clippings and leaves are being bagged and sent off as trash.

Troubleshooting Nutrient Problems

You cannot garden without having occasional strange nutritional problems. After many years of being called to help find the difficulties, we have developed a mental check list to follow. Sometimes it works and sometimes it leads nowhere, but this kind of troubleshooting should help you to solve at least some of the problems.

Gardens: Vegetable and Ornamentals

Is only one crop affected? Some crops are notorious for specific problems; with azaleas and similar plants it is probably a pH-related problem.

What is the pattern of injury in the garden? If it follows a straight line of one or more rows, it probably indicates an error in fertilizer or pesticide applications. Circular patterns usually indicate a disease, but in lawns it could be chinch bugs or, in cold weather, brown patch disease. Another problem in lawns could be that fertilizer was applied carelessly. Check to see whether the circular spots represent a handful of fertilizer. If random isolated plants are affected, the culprit is probably an insect, perhaps one that spreads a virus disease. If it is worse on one side of the garden with the damage decreasing in the other direction, it could be drift injury from something your neighbor sprayed; sneak a look into his yard.

Potted Plants

Do you see evidence of insect or disease damage? This is unlikely but an easy point to eliminate. Light and temperature conditions are the first problems you should suspect. Plants might survive, with no growth, under low light intensity and in cold spots, but they will never look good.

Another problem for houseplants is overwatering. You will remember from our earlier discussion that this covers several aspects of poor watering practices. The problem may involve roots killed by staying wet for too long or an accumulation of salts caused by not flushing the excess out.

As a final possibility, your houseplant might actually need a bit of fertilizer. If the plant is in a well-drained mix, has good lighting, high temperature, and high humidity, it might need a little shot of fertilizer. Realistically, most houseplants do not grow well enough to need much fertilizer.

Nutrient Deficiencies

The most likely problem in new gardens is some sort of nutrient imbalance; too much or too little of something in relation to other nutrients. Our description of symptoms is fairly standard. First we need to give some warnings. Back in the late 1940s and 1950s mineral nutrition was growing from an art to(ward) a science, hydroponics was an exciting laboratory exercise, and books with color photographs of deficient plants were popular. Ed was sent a copy of a new book titled *If They Could Speak.* He mused over the thought; if you could simply ask a plant what was wrong it would probably say, "Well, I don't know. I just feel sort of yellow. The last time I felt this way a little shot of nitrogen seemed to help. But it had been raining a lot then, maybe I got better when my roots recovered."

Nutrient deficiencies can be so complex that the cause is very much a guess. Sometimes a soil test helps, but that takes time and the plants might be dead before the results get back. Also, the term *deficiency symptoms* is a bit misleading. *Starvation* may be better, because if the leaves are showing symptoms, the nutrient (or nutrient combination) has been deficient for a long time. Try not to let the situation become bad enough for leaf symptoms to appear. This is the same argument your doctor advocates: you should follow a wellness program rather than waiting until you are sick. The wonderful difference between treating plants and people is that if you make a mistake with plants it is easy to pull them up and start over.

Some books build a key to follow in diagnosing deficiency symptoms. Our objection to such an approach is that it gives the impression of an exact science. Nutrient troubleshooting is an art.

There are two points to consider when looking at deficiency problems.

(1) Are the symptoms developing on new or old leaves? Certain nutrients are mobile in the plant; they can be drawn from less active areas to the growing points. If the first evidence of deficiency is seen in the older leaves, the nutrient was drawn from them and moved to the newer growth. Conversely, if the new leaves are affected first, that nutrient is not mobile in the plant. As a general, but not absolute, rule the nutrients used in larger amounts (nitrogen, phosphorus, potassium, magnesium, and sulfur) are mobile, with the micronutrients being nonmobile. *Mobile* is a variable term because some nutrients are extremely mobile and others much less so.

(2) What is the pattern of injury? This should cover the range from leaf chlorosis (yellowing) to necrosis (dead areas). Injury patterns are generally characteristic of the nutrient problem, but (there is always a "but" when diagnosing nutrition problems) injury patterns for the same nutrient occasionally vary according to the crop.

Nitrogen

Because nitrogen is a very mobile nutrient, symptoms of deficiency appear first on the lower leaves and quickly spread over the entire plant. The characteristic sign is a light green coloration moving upward over all of the leaves, followed by a distinct and uniform yellowing.

An exception to this occurs in azaleas and blueberries. This group of plants can use a little nitrate as a nitrogen source but most of it should be in the ammonium form. With these plants, ammonium deficiency shows up in the younger leaves and looks very much like iron deficiency. We mentioned this earlier and will revisit it a little later in this chapter when discussing iron.

Excess nitrogen is also a problem with crops. Tomatoes are particularly sensitive to this. Plants with excess nitrogen have very large dark green leaves. The common description is that it has *gone to bush*. The plants seem to be in excellent condition except that they have only a very few flowers and will produce hardly any fruit. Monster tomato plants are of little value in the garden if they produce no tomatoes.

Phosphorus

Phosphorus is less mobile than nitrogen, but the symptoms of deficiency usually appear on the lower leaves. The first symptom is one of reduced growth and a slightly darker green color, but you probably will not notice a problem until the lower leaves begin to turn purple. This is usually as purple streaks along the margin or on the underside of the leaves and petioles. Under severe conditions the entire plant may have a reddish purple color. By that time the plant will have stopped all growth and it will be very difficult to correct the problem.

Potassium

The main characteristic of potassium deficiency is necrotic (dead) spots scattered near the leaf tips and along the edges. A mottled coloration is also char-

Ed's Tale of Blackjack Oak Land

Back in the days nearly beyond recall I worked for the U.S. Department of Agriculture on a project to develop methods for growing tung trees in cut-over, worn-out pine land. Tung nuts were the source of an oil needed for the manufacture of varnish. Tung nut oil originally came from China, but wartime problems made the supply unreliable. My co-worker and I were assigned to study tung nut production in an area of deep sands in western Florida, north of Panama City. This sand had supported a fairly good pine forest. After the trees had been cut, the land produced a few crops of cotton, corn, and peanuts before it was abandoned "to let the trees grow back." But pine trees couldn't survive in the almost pure sand, with very little organic matter. The result was hundreds, maybe thousands, of acres of scrubby blackjack land. Blackjack oak *(Quercus marilandica)* will grow, although not very well, on the poorest kind of soil. People who tried growing tung on it said that the trees barely survived during the first five years but, after the roots grew down to a rich layer of clay, there was pretty good growth. Listening to the story over a cup of coffee, we thought this account made sense. Then we dug around the trees to find just where the clay layer was. There was no clay layer—just sand and more sand. We noticed that the active tree roots were clustered in the upper inch of sandy soil, which meant that the key lay with the accumulation of organic matter from leaves and other debris that had gradually accumulated under the small trees. After five years of accumulation this narrow layer became capable of holding nutrients of the fertilizer that was applied every year.

Now that we understood the problem, the solution seemed simple: farmers should mulch around the trees with a source of organic matter. The farmers, not wanting to waste anything, decided to use tung hulls left over after the nuts had been removed. This idea turned out to be disastrous. They didn't realize that the hulls contained very high levels of potassium. As the potassium leached into the sandy soil it displaced the small amount of magnesium that was being held on the small amount of organic matter. The magnesium was washed away and the trees developed magnesium deficiency symptoms. Back to the drawing board.

Then we realized that the tung farmers had another by-product that could serve as an organic matter source. Tung meal, the material remaining after oil had been extracted from the nuts, was a good source of slowly released nitrogen, besides the carbohydrates needed for development of organic matter. We tried using tung meal and *voila!* The young trees grew beautifully and farmers could produce a good crop on blackjack land.

acteristic in many plants. The symptoms appear first on the older leaves. The plant is not as badly stunted as with phosphorus deficiency and the leaves have a light green color.

Magnesium

Because the balance of magnesium and potassium is important, magnesium deficiency often means that too much potassium was applied, sometimes in a hurried attempt to correct potassium deficiency. The symptoms will appear along the newly matured lower leaves as a yellowing in between the veins of the leaves. This condition will spread upward but rather slowly. In time, the leaves will curl or pucker and the spots between the veins will die.

Iron

Iron is a nonmobile nutrient, with symptoms of deficiency first appearing in the new growth. The young leaves develop a light green color between the veins but quickly become completely yellow and then almost white.

As the table on nutrient solubility (figure 28) shows, iron is most soluble under acid conditions. Iron deficiency is typical of overlimed soil; for most plants it indicates a pH well above 7.0. However, azaleas and blueberries are different. If the pH is above about 5.5, you can expect azaleas (blueberries, camellias) to show symptoms that are at least partly due to iron deficiency. This does not mean that azaleas use more iron than other plants, but that they are less efficient in taking up iron, or moving it in the plant.

A complication is the one we mentioned under the nitrogen discussion. In azaleas, ammonium deficiency looks exactly like iron deficiency and can be corrected by adding iron, particularly the less-oxidized forms. As the iron is oxidized, some nitrogen forms are reduced back to ammonium, which is taken up by the plant. Lo, it must have been iron deficiency because the addition of iron corrected it! Well, if you say so; we are not going back over all that for the sake of an argument.

Iron deficiency is a common problem in azaleas when they are used as foundation plantings around a new house with a poured slab. The first year they look great, but after that they decline slowly, with yellowing of the new growth. "But it can't be a pH problem, I added sulfur to make it acidic," the homeowner complains. But the chunks of mortar left in the soil were not removed. Making the soil acid is only a temporary solution if mortar keeps raising the pH. This does not mean that azaleas cannot be planted around a new house; just be sure to remove all the mortar and acidify the soil first. And do not plant azaleas in a spot where the contractor washed out the cement truck.

Manganese

Manganese deficiency is rare but is occasionally seen in very sandy soil, over-limed soil, or where you tried to correct iron deficiency by dumping a large amount of iron. This is a nonmobile nutrient, so symptoms appear in the new growth. The symptoms of the deficient leaves resemble magnesium deficiency except that they first appear in new leaves rather than the older ones.

The more common manganese problem is that of toxicity. For a rather strange reason many of the soils from Memphis down to Baton Rouge have high levels of manganese. This is usually in the silt and silt loam soils along the east bank of the Mississippi. The key point is that the reduced form (called *manganous*) is much more soluble than is the oxidized (manganic) one. In acid soil conditions the element tends to become reduced, progressively more so as the soil is more acid. This is not a big problem because you should have limed the soil if it was below pH 5.5.

A more complicated problem is that of temporary manganese toxicity during rainy weather combined with high temperature and soil with a high organic matter content. This relates to our earlier discussion of oxidation-reduction. With high temperatures and high organic matter content, microbial activity will place a heavy demand on soil oxygen. If the soil is very wet, mi-

Ed Tells a Tabasco™ Tale

Back many years ago the CEO of the McIlhenny Company was a retired Marine Corps general who had been a battalion commander during the bitter fighting for Guadalcanal. He was also a smart, broadly educated man. Our head of the Horticulture Department was a pretty good scientist but very much dedicated to giving an answer to every question—regardless of what he knew about it. One spring after a heavy rain, the Tabasco company CEO noticed that some of his newly transplanted pepper plants were wilting in a pattern of circles. By the next week those plants had developed what looked like a virus disease. He telephoned the Horticulture Department head, explaining the situation and asking that someone come over to see what was wrong. The reply was, "Well, I don't think you need to worry. Those plants have just got a touch of wet feet." The general was not at all happy with such an explanation, particularly with the vague term *wet feet*. He demanded that an experienced man be sent over immediately. The next day Ed was ushered into the general's office. They talked a bit, and Ed noticed a surveyor's level standing in the corner, apparently used for checking the slope of the terraces. They went to the field and saw circles of Tabasco plants with classic symptoms of manganese toxicity. The general was reluctant to accept the diagnosis because he had checked the pH of the field: 5.7. Ed said, "General, the answer to your problem is standing in the corner of your office. Run the levels on those circles and you will find that they are slightly lower than the rest of the field." He had recognized that the circles of sick plants marked the spots where puddles had stood after the rain. Ed explained the relationship between wet soil, high organic matter, microbial activity, and reduced manganese. The general thought for a minute and said, "I believe you are right."

Actually, the Horticulture Department head had been essentially right, but he had not explained it properly. The production fields at Avery Island are kept in excellent condition, with good terraces, fairly uniform slopes, and a rotation program that maintains a good organic matter level. This was just an unusual situation of too much rain, puddles of standing water, high temperature, and Tabasco plants at a very sensitive growth stage.

croorganisms will use all of the oxygen and begin reducing manganese as an oxidation source. Plant roots will take up large amounts of the more soluble manganese (manganous). After the water drains away, the manganese will re-oxidize quickly and the original problem will be gone, but the excess manganese already will have gotten into the plant. Young seedlings (especially beans) are very sensitive to this; the new leaves develop chlorosis, primarily between the veins. Then symptoms spread quickly over the entire plant, producing cupped and crinkled older leaves. Severe manganese toxicity symptoms are frightening; some of the seedlings may die and others will be stunted for several weeks. It is usually best to replant those affected areas. The high level of soluble manganese probably lasted for only a few days and may have been gone before the symptoms appeared. The only permanent solution is to improve drainage, but you may decide not to bother with that. The toxicity appears only during very rainy periods with high temperatures.

Zinc and Copper

Zinc and copper deficiencies occur only in very sandy or overlimed soils. It is possible, but not likely, to see them in soils with high organic matter. Zinc deficiency causes very small new leaves with chlorotic mottling. Leaves then become yellow and develop necrotic areas or die. This differs from iron deficiency in that the condition does not spread to older leaves. Zinc deficiency is occasionally a problem with pecan trees growing in sandy soil and is called little leaf disease. Old-timers used to swear that it was iron deficiency because they could relieve it by driving a few rusty nails into the tree. But the nails had originally been galvanized and still contained some slightly soluble zinc. Another old-time treatment was to simply beat the tree into submission: take a rusty chain and whip the trunk so hard that you knock part of the bark off. Like the nails, the chain had originally been galvanized; it takes very little zinc to cure a sick tree. Maybe we should hedge a bit—the explanation is oversimplified. This is also an oxidation-reduction pattern in which iron is oxidized and the insoluble forms of zinc are reduced, making them more soluble.

Copper deficiency symptoms vary somewhat with the crop. The symptoms develop first in the young leaves. The leaves become yellow and die. This differs from zinc deficiency in that it spreads over the entire plant and differs from iron deficiency in that the shoots die. Copper deficiency is rare.

Excesses and Toxicities

These problems sometimes happen in the garden but are more common in potted plants.

Excessive Salts. The first symptoms of excessive salt (too much fertilizer or watering in a dry atmosphere with high salt water, common in coastal areas where salt intrusion is progressing) looks much like nitrogen deficiency. However, later a foliar burn develops. This is often at the leaf margins because some leaves have vascular elements that extend to there. You may remember in high school they told you about guttation (oozing) of water from leaf margins. This is guttation, but the salt concentration is high enough to cause a burn.

Here is a trick you might try if your plant seems to have excessive fertilizer salts: sugar. Chrysanthemums grown for cut flowers require high fertility levels. After the production period is over, the nurseryman may want to grow plants like snapdragons that cannot tolerate such high salt levels. A fast way to rid the bed of the excess salts is to spray it with a sugar solution. This high-energy treatment will stimulate microbial activity; the microorganisms will use up the excessive salts, die, and leave the salts bound up in organic matter. The snapdragons will grow well and make use of the salts that are slowly released from the organic matter. Rather than repotting a sickly plant, try watering it with a sugar solution; maybe a tablespoon of sugar to a quart of water. Sometimes, but not always, this will revive a plant that was suffering from too much salts.

Several years ago a story was making the rounds about using birth-control pills to revive a houseplant. We were skeptical but heard several reports that adding a glass of water containing one dissolved birth-control pill would reinvigorate the plant. We do not know what the pill was made of or how someone came up with the idea to try it on plants, but it seems likely that the pill would supply an energy source just as sugar does.

Chlorine Toxicity. This is also more common in coastal areas where salt water is intruding into the aquifers. This is not chlorine gas but chloride ion. Some plants are more sensitive than others. You can easily test for chloride by crushing the leaves and adding a little distilled water, then add a drop or two of silver nitrate solution. A white precipitate (silver chloride) says you have too much chloride in your irrigation water.

Fluoride Toxicity. We mentioned this when discussing water problems in chapter 4 but should note it here. Fluoridated "city water" is safe for most plants, but some will be injured, including chlorophytum (airplane plant), maranta, and potted lilies. Affected plants show scorched leaf edges.

Boron Toxicity. This is also an irrigation water problem. The symptoms are difficult but there is leaf scorching in the later stages. This is another reason for getting a water chemistry report.

COMPLEXES AND ANTAGONISMS

There are other possible nutrient deficiencies, such as calcium, boron, and molybdenum, but the symptoms are difficult to detect. Often the problem is not one of an absolute deficiency but of the nutrient balance that we mentioned earlier. This condition is described as *antagonism.*

That is about all we need to say about nutritional problems. Most gardens require only the NPK fertilizers unless the pH is badly off or a problem was overcorrected by the addition of too much fertilizer. Keeping a fairly high organic matter level usually buffers against serious nutritional problems. The trace element problems are more likely to occur in greenhouse plants where the well-drained pot mixes do not have a good buffer capacity and are watered frequently.

Maybe we should mention that some nutrients can be applied as foliar sprays. This is sometimes used by commercial fruit growers. If apple growers notice that the spring shoot growth is not quite what it should be, they apply nitrogen as a foliar spray and get improved growth in a few days. They want the high nitrogen level to be temporary because excess nitrogen at ripening time can reduce the formation of a good skin color. Cotton farmers use airplanes to apply midseason nitrogen for a similar reason. They want to promote midseason growth but to have a slight nitrogen deficiency at harvest, so that the leaves will fall easily. Applying nitrogen as a foliar spray is a short-lasting treatment.

Chapter 17

THREE-DOG NIGHTS

It gets cold down here, the bitter wet kind with a strong wind biting into you. Every time a cold front starts toward us, the rumor spreads that it is snowing just twenty miles north of where we live. The children get excited; but if it does snow, the flakes melt when they hit the ground. Then the front moves through, the cloud cover is gone, and the weatherman predicts a hard freeze. Everyone begins to move plants into a shelter, covering sensitive ones that cannot be moved, and wondering how they should have prepared for the freeze. As you know from our earlier discussion, the weather in the coastal South varies considerably. In an average winter where we live, Baton Rouge, we can expect one three-dog night (temperatures around 20°), and New Orleans will get one about every two or three years. Real old-fashioned four-dog nights with temperatures around 12° will hit Baton Rouge, Houston, Mobile, and Tallahassee about every ten to fifteen years. (The formula for estimating the number of dogs required per bed as a function of outside temperatures is complex and beyond the scope of this elementary book.) This chapter is a collection of our thoughts on the topic. More honestly, it contains Ed's thoughts; Leon believes in "root-hog or die"—do not plant things that will freeze. When it gets cold, build a huge fire, toast your toes, and enjoy remembering how miserable you were during the cold winter of the Great War.

Our winters seem to be getting colder in this part of the world. We can only speculate about what significance this might have relative to the greenhouse effect. Maybe the higher CO_2 is keeping winters from getting even colder. Short-range trends are deceptive. Our coldest recorded trend was back in the 1890s. It was bitterly cold and got down to 3° in Baton Rouge. Then a warm spell set in—for about sixty years. When Ed and Leon moved to Baton Rouge people were growing citrus—satsumas, oranges, and grapefruit—in their yards. Some streets were lined with massive camphor trees. Then came the winter of 1961–62. The citrus was killed to the rootstock and the camphor trees down to the bases of their thick trunks. We had a series of cold winters until about 1975, when it started getting warmer, until the bitter cold pre-Christmas freeze of 1988. Just forget about trends. Our main interest is in the freezing weather that the weatherman says will be coming tonight or tomorrow, and the plants that will die if we do not go out and cover them.

Water, Weather, and Cold Hardiness

Some plants come right through the freezes and keep on growing and blooming. Ed uses pansies outside the kitchen window as an indicator of how low the temperature dropped during the night. If they are rolled up into hard balls, it got below about 28°F—they do not change much below that; when temperature rises they will go right on blooming. Other plants, such as impatiens and coleus, are killed by the first light frost that comes if they are out in the open, but may survive if they are under trees. The more tropical plants are injured by temperatures above freezing—even the low 40°s. Sansevierias and pineapples develop sunken, whitish areas on the leaves after exposure to such temperatures, and the leaves on crossandras turn black and drop.

Why are some plants cold hardy and others not? We need to explain some points that the weatherman brings up nearly every time a freeze or frost is expected. It will get much colder on a clear, windless night. If the wind is blowing, it will keep moving warmer air close to the ground, so the plants will not be hurt as badly. If clouds move in, it will not get quite as cold. Cover sensitive plants on cold nights. Occasionally, somebody will say that you should water your plants well before a freeze, which is probably useless advice. You might hear that leaving a sprinkler on the plants will protect them; it probably will not. We explain this later in the chapter.

Water is a strange chemical. Like any other liquid, water contracts as it cools down, but the minimum volume is reached at about 40°F. Below that point it expands with lower temperature, which is not so bad while the water is liquid. However, when it freezes and continues to expand, your water pipes burst. The colder it gets, the more the ice expands. The temperature at which the ice quits expanding is even lower than a cold night in Siberia. The same thing can happen in the "pipes" of plants (or the *vascular bundles,* which really means "pipes, or tubes"). Sugars and salts in the sap of plants decrease the temperature at which sap will freeze but, if it gets cold enough, the sap freezes and the vascular bundles burst. It is sometimes more complex than this, but the principle is correct.

The effects of a freeze on leaves and buds are essentially the same as those on stems; they are killed when ice crystals form within the cells and rupture cell walls. When there is only a light frost on your plants, the temperature may not be low enough to cause crystal formation in the cells because the sugars and other soluble materials in the cell sap lower the freezing point below that of pure water.

On cold still nights there is another condition that takes place—*supercooling*. This refers to a situation in which the temperature of a solution may be slightly lower than its freezing point but the crystals have not formed because they need a *nucleus* to start them. If the cell is physically disturbed, the crystals form and rupture the cells. On a frosty morning you throw on a light robe and thin slippers and rush out to get the paper. You could follow the sidewalk but you are cold, and walking across the grass is faster. That afternoon you will be able to see your footprints in the dead grass. This may not matter much because a hard freeze will kill the rest of the grass next week. As a general rule, stay off of cold-damaged grass and do not shake the leaves of frosted shrubs. This also applies to satsuma fruits that were almost ripe but have frozen; do not even touch them. They contain a lot of sugar, and if the temperature goes up slowly, they will thaw uniformly and be perfectly good. If you shake the fruit, crystals will form and the fruit will rot.

Water takes up a lot more heat when it evaporates than it gives off when it freezes. A pound of evaporating water, at 32°F, takes up 1,036 units of heat, but if the pound freezes it only gives off 144 units. On a cold windy night a plant loses about seven times as much heat from evaporating water as it would gain by freezing. Thereby hangs a dilemma for you and the citrus growers when they want to protect plants from a severe freeze. We will illustrate this later.

You may notice that we refer to heat being retained rather than the plant simply getting cold. We are saying that heat is a form of energy and cold is a form of nothing; cold is just the absence of heat.

The growth habits of some plants help them escape damage from freezing. Because bulbs are underground, they are not exposed to freezing unless the cold snap lasts long enough for groundwater to freeze. In colder areas, low-growing plants are protected from hard freezes by the insulation of snow.

Annual plants overwinter as seeds. Other plants can actually freeze without damage. Some things that improve cold resistance are obvious—the accumulations of sugars and salts that we mentioned previously lower the freezing point of cell sap, working like the antifreeze in a car radiator. As the days get shorter, plant growth slows, leaves fall, and sugars accumulate in the sap. High temperatures and soil moisture in the fall delay this, and young plants do not adapt as readily as older ones. In general, if the fall has been dry with frequent cold snaps, most plants have developed some cold resistance.

Earlier in the book we mentioned hardening off of seedlings before they are moved from the greenhouse and transplanted into the garden. Gradual exposure to lower temperatures hardens the seedlings so they can survive cold (but nonfreezing) exposures that would probably kill them if they were moved directly from the warmth. This means that sugars and starches accumulate, lowering the freezing point of the sap. Gardeners use several devices to protect young transplants from the exposure, but first we should explain the principles.

FROSTS AND FREEZES

To explain the weatherman's predictions about cloud protection we need to bring up two more terms from chemistry: heat transfer by *conduction* and *radiation*. Radiation heat travels like a beam and does not heat until it hits a solid object. Radiation from the sun travels through bitterly cold space and does not heat anything until it hits our plants and the soil around them; the plant warms up during the day. At night, the plants get cold, mostly from conduction of the heat. Cooler air in direct contact with the plant takes some of the heat, which then rises and is replaced by more cool air. This produces convection currents; warm air rises, cools off, and drops to ground level, where it is warmed again. Notice that it is at the expense of the poor little plant, which is continuously giving up heat and getting colder. This frequently produces a situation in which colder air is near the ground and warmer air above it. The weatherman calls it a *temperature inversion*. What it really means is that your plants are going to get very cold.

But the plants and soil are also losing heat by radiation. Some of the heat radiated out of plants growing under trees is absorbed by the trees and radiated downward. Compared with plants in the open, those under a tree will remain warmer. This is why a mild frost may kill impatiens or coleus in the open, but not those under trees.

Frost is a tricky word, with several meanings. For us gardeners it usually refers to a *radiation frost*: plants are damaged because of radiant heat loss and from the convection currents we have described. These are the frosts that we get on calm, clear nights. If there is even a light breeze, the heat being lost from the plants is replaced by more air that is being warmed by the soil.

Now for another aspect of frost. The most sensitive parts of a plant are thin tissues such as flower petals; there is almost no stored heat to replace that lost by radiation. On a still night thin tissues can be killed by frost when the air only a short distance away is above freezing. On some mornings your thermometer may say there was no freeze but you can see frost on the grass. This means that a thermometer holds more heat because it is much thicker than a grass blade; of course, the thermometer is also close to your warm house and located higher than the grass. If the night is cloudy instead of clear, the clouds may act as a large cover to hold radiated heat near the ground, which means that you will have no frost on the grass.

Having said that a breeze will keep warm air moving by your plants, we need to talk about the bitter arctic blasts that come roaring in from the north. *Wind freeze* means that the wind is blowing too hard and removing heat from the plants faster than the soil can replace it. If you do not rig up some sort of lateral protection, those plants will freeze to the ground. Permanent windbreaks such as trees, hedges, and buildings help to reduce heat loss. Or you might build temporary barriers with plastic film, blankets, or newspapers. If the barrier is not touching the plant parts, a little warm air will insulate against heat loss; you have created a microclimate. Where the barrier touches the plant, there will be heat loss through conduction. Remember that conduction is much more efficient in heat loss than is radiation. Covering your plants with plastic or blankets works pretty well for an overnight cold snap because the plant receives heat from the warm soil. During long cold spells, however, you need a heat source plus the wind barrier to protect the plant—perhaps a light bulb in mild cases, or a kerosene lantern or heater for larger plants or more severe exposures.

Leon personally recommends using something with a thermostat. He notes that if you forget to turn a lantern or light bulb off early the next morning, the tent created by the barrier could warm up enough to kill your plant.

Plants with a thick, shrubby growth provide some windbreak protection; the outer branches might be killed but the main stem could survive. This is partly from the wind protection, but large main stems have more stored heat than thinner or smaller ones.

We have a few thoughts on the question of how badly a freeze hurts your plants. The differences between severe cold damage, moderate damage, and minor frost damage depend on what you expect from the plant. Remember when we mentioned that thin tissues may be killed by a mild frost? The thin, threadlike styles of peach flowers have very little stored heat. A frost, even when the air temperature is above freezing only a short distance away, can kill most of the styles in flowers on a peach tree, resulting in complete crop loss. The thin, delicate flower petals may look fine the next day, but if the styles were killed you will have no peaches. That is a case of severe cold damage but, if the frost had come a week earlier or later, you would have had minor frost damage. Dormant flower buds are cold hardy but they become increasingly frost susceptible as they progress to open bloom. This is why late-blooming varieties can survive cold snaps that would kill the flowers on early-blooming ones. Peach varieties with showy flowers (having large petals) come through better than those with small flowers; the large petals can radiate heat to the thin styles. A later frost is less damaging because the small fruits that appear after flowering have more bulk and hold more heat.

Location is also important. Peach trees planted on the north side of a slope sometimes survive better than those on the warmer, south side: the colder, north slope has kept the buds from blooming too early. On the other hand, if there is a hard-blowing wind freeze, nothing will protect the flowers, and the trees on a south slope would have better protection from actual killing of the shoots or trunks.

Saved by the Sprinklers?

Now, what about using water sprinklers to protect your plants? Well, maybe, sometimes. On a windless night this helps in several ways. The water brings stored heat into the planting, which warms the plants and the surrounding air. When the water freezes, it releases more heat and this warms the plant. After freezing, there is a layer of ice that gives a little insulation from lower air temperatures. Sometimes cold injury to thin tissues is partly due to desiccation: an ice layer will prevent that.

But consider the situation if sprinklers are used and a cold, dry wind is blowing. Remember when we said that evaporating water takes up about seven times as much heat as freezing water gives off? Do not use sprinklers on a cold windy night.

Another problem that you should consider when using sprinklers, even on a still night, is that the extra weight from ice can break some limbs. You can avoid this by bracing the limbs with poles. Ice forms along them and makes a temporary pillar. The next morning you have an interesting ice sculpture, which may be protecting the plant. Remember that a layer of ice provides a little insulation. Another tricky point is that when the sculpture starts melting, you should turn the sprinkler on again. This is because you want the ice to melt from the top down. If the ice in contact with the soil melts first, you will lose the bracing effect and the remaining ice will break tree limbs.

So, does sprinkling work? Commercial strawberry producers rely on it for frost protection when the plants have sensitive blossoms. Saving the early blooms means being able to get the early season prices for berries. Lightweight row-cover fabrics have now largely replaced sprinklers as frost protection. Sometimes sprinkling works for citrus, but you need to have the limbs braced or they will break. It might help you in protecting yard plants, but remember that our cold fronts are usually accompanied by wind. If the wind is dry, you may be doing more harm than good. Another thing to remember is that when a freeze is coming the weatherman warns you not to leave faucets dripping because it might reduce water pressure, which could be very important if someone's house catches on fire. Running a sprinkler uses a lot more water than does the dripping faucet.

We have not yet addressed the matter of watering plants just before a freeze. If the soil is dry and a cold dry wind is coming through, it could help. This is not a common situation down South. Our soil is usually wet in the winter, and cold fronts are frequently accompanied by rain. Occasionally, you will hear the suggestion that watering frozen plants will help them survive. This may be, but keep in mind that any physical movement of frozen plants is injurious. If you water the plants very gently, you might help them; but a more common situation is that melting ice falls off and jostles the still-frozen stems. It is usually safer to let the plants thaw slowly and try not to jostle them.

Leon's "root-hog or die" philosophy is pretty good advice if you are planning for long-term trees or shrubs. It is easy to get weather records showing the probability of various exposures, and you can count on a slightly warmer environment if the plants are close to the house or a lake, or have good wind-breaks. Generally, we think you should plan on growing trees and shrubs that will not need protection beyond the first few years. Give them some TLC for a few years, but you should not burden yourself with having to cover or heat shrubs and trees. It is just not worth the effort.

Freezes That Kill the Cambium

After a particularly hard freeze the gardening articles in your newspaper will warn you not to prune the dead branches until spring. We agree that dead branches look bad, but there is no way to determine how far down the damage went. Back in chapter 15 we said that cambium tissue is the living sheath around the trunk, with phloem tissue on the outside and xylem inside. A strong north wind slowly kills the phloem and then the cambium. Ultimately, it kills the xylem, but for the following illustration we assume the xylem remains functional. After a freeze your citrus tree dropped all its leaves and the fruit rotted. But with the coming of spring it put out new leaves, flowered, and even set fruit. You breathed a sigh of relief; it survived! Maybe. In a few weeks the leaves may wilt and the entire tree may die. This is a common situation. Apparently, the phloem and cambium were killed. In the spring the sap began to rise through the xylem, which provided enough food material (sugars, etc.) for new leaves and flowers. But with no living cambium there was no new xylem or phloem being formed.

You will find the same situation with the large type (Formosa) azaleas. They will produce new leaves, flower, and look great. In May or June the bark will split on the main trunk and the plant is suddenly dead. With many other plants you know whether they are dead or have survived within a few weeks. Camellia varieties show large differences in their cold tolerances. The first sign of severe damage is that all the leaves fall off. If, when you scratch the bark, the cambium is a dull green, the plant is dead. Actually that green layer is cork cambium rather than the kind we were describing, but it should be a bright green.

Here is a survival trick that old-timers promote. Occasionally, the cambium may be dead except for a few isolated "islands" that were somehow protected. If you spray the trunk about once a week with a dilute soluble fertilizer solution (one tablespoon per gallon), it might support that cambium long enough for it to spread and rebuild a vascular tissue–root connection. We know of no research supporting this, but sometimes it seems to work.

While we are on the subject of trunk survival, remember that your citrus (and most other fruit trees) were grafted onto different rootstocks. Nurserymen use trifoliata orange for citrus because the rootstock goes dormant in the fall and limits growth of the upper portions, which gives the branches a little cold resistance. If buds come out below the graft junction but not above it, dig that thing up. It is possible, but very difficult, to regraft one of the shoots.

SURVIVAL OF POTTED PLANTS

Now, what happened to the potted plants that you could not bring in? Nurserymen usually crowd the containers close together and wrap plastic around the outside as something of a wind barrier. A new approach being used by nurserymen is called pot-in-pot. Empty pots are sunk into the ground up to the rims and potted plants are set into them. This protects roots from freezing and keeps the plants from blowing over. You might want to consider this as a precaution for your favorite plants. Nurserymen may also put pine straw or newspapers over the top, but the critical point is that they must protect the roots from freezing. Shoots may grow back if the roots are still good. After a freeze, check your plants by tapping the outside of the pot (to loosen the roots) and pulling the entire plant out. If the young roots growing around the outside are white (or a healthy light-brown), you made it. If they are not, you are probably in trouble. You could cut the dead roots away, down to living ones in the center. This often helps with plants that are less susceptible to root-rot diseases. The disease organisms are always there and the cut roots offer easy points of entry.

Reliable nurserymen shut down all sales for a month or longer after a hard freeze. They inspect the root systems, throw out the damaged plants, and check for living cambium on the stems. Some plants are clearly dead but there are always some that are marginal; they might make it with good care, and if root-rot does not set in. These should be thrown out, but what if the family needs shoes and the kids need braces for their teeth? Maybe the nurseryman can salvage a little of his loss by finding a retailer somewhere who will put on a really cut-rate plant sale. How can you decide whether it is a good price? In the same way you checked your plants at home: inspect the roots and scratch a stem to look for living cambium. Ask the garden center whether they have a policy of replacing freeze-damaged plants that die.

Our primary problem with cold damage in the Deep South is that we try to grow marginally tolerant tropical plants. The extent of cold damage depends on several points: whether earlier weather has hardened the plants, the kind of cold (dry, clear, windy nights, or a little cloud cover), how cold it gets, and how long it lasts. This can be modified by selecting more tolerant plants and providing temporary protection.

So You Think You Want a Greenhouse

Hobby gardeners can have a number of reasons for wanting greenhouses, and the reasons, or goals, may change over time. With a little advance planning you can have a greenhouse versatile enough for changing interests or abilities. If you are primarily interested in vegetable gardening, the greenhouse will be a place where seeds are planted early and young transplants are kept until the weather warms up. In northern areas with late springs, this can give a jump on the season after the long winters. Our situation down here is similar, but with an additional need. Some of the plants must be put in the garden early to avoid late spring and summer heat, which may stop fruit set or kill the plants. Another function is that of producing out-of-season vegetables, which can be grown to maturity during the winter in the greenhouse. With our modern systems of transport providing a wide assortment of produce in the markets year-round, having fresh vegetables in winter is not so unusual as it was back in olden times, but having vine-ripened tomatoes that actually taste like tomatoes in winter is a pleasure that requires greenhouses—either your own or somebody else's.

These are the main topics you should consider in deciding on a greenhouse: (1) What kind of structure best fits your needs? (2) What sort of covering material will you use? (3) How will it be cooled and heated? (4) What kind of benches will you need? Some of these questions are more complicated than the others, but all are important.

Beginning with structural questions, first you should check with local authorities to see what permits are required or if restrictions prevent building a greenhouse. It is a good idea to consult with your insurer to see how a planned greenhouse will affect your insurance.

You may ask, "Can I build it myself?" This will depend on how handy you are, and sometimes on the law. Most communities require that wiring be done by licensed electricians, and inspected. This is a good idea, because the moisture in most greenhouses provides excellent grounding if you contact a live wire. You may be permitted to do some plumbing. If gas heat is planned, there are safety precautions that licensing agencies usually require—proper separation of combustion and recirculating air, proper venting of flue gases, and proper treatment of gas pipes between the source and heater. Many greenhouses need a footing to support the structural members. This may not be needed in utilitarian plastic houses, but for others it is very important. This is often best left to a mason, especially if you are building a glass-covered house. Glass comes in rigid panels and does not stretch or compress. It must fit the framing, and the spacing between glazing bars must be such that the glass can be bedded onto the shoulders of the bars, allowing some space for a small amount of expansion and contraction of those bars. The framing must be more precise than would be needed if you were planning a greenhouse covered by plastic film. This precision starts with the footing.

A home greenhouse.

Deciding on the Size of a Greenhouse

In planning a greenhouse do not think too small. As your plants and interests grow you will find yourself overcrowding plants or being hampered in other activities. How big your greenhouse should be depends largely on your planned use for it and the space available in your yard. In addition to being plant environments, some greenhouses serve as winter living rooms, which requires more space. Some greenhouse manufacturers provide modules for extending the space as your needs grow, and this might be important in the selection process.

Here is a critical point: small greenhouses are affected by outside weather changes more quickly than are larger ones. Having a small greenhouse can present serious challenges in heating and humidity control. In a sense, the same is true for summer weather but, if you decide to install air conditioning, the cost of cooling a large greenhouse would be horrendous.

Allow for a work and storage area attached to, but separate from, the greenhouse. Do not sacrifice growing space for storage, and remember that, although working in the greenhouse may be pleasant in the winter, it also is very important to have a cool shady place to work in midsummer.

Basic Designs

When you start looking at designs and costs, you will find a wide selection to choose from; greenhouse kits are becoming very popular. There are advantages to having the greenhouse attached to your house; for example, you will not have to bundle up in the winter or run through the rain in summer. In some cases, the home heating system can be extended to warm an attached greenhouse at night. During most winter days the greenhouse can act as a solar accumulator. Some energy-efficient houses could include a greenhouse as part of the design for winter heating. You should look on this with some skepticism; remember that the greenhouse will be there throughout the summer and, in the Deep South, summer is much longer than winter. Plan either to find some way to close it off from the rest of the house, or to have a large air conditioning bill.

There are several variations for attached greenhouses. The simplest is a lean-to, using the house as one of the walls. If the greenhouse is to be attached at an end of the house, the sides may be straight or sloped, and the eaves may be curved or not. There probably will be a masonry or wooden wall below the glass. The option of "glass to ground" allows more light to enter but is seldom worth the extra cost. Using curved glass makes an attractive greenhouse but, again, you should consider the cost. This is especially important in a baseball neighborhood. The use of sloped sides is more than an attractive feature; the design allows more of the sun's rays to enter when the sun is low on the horizon in winter.

The pitch of a greenhouse roof is designed primarily to allow for shedding snow. The roof should be strong enough to withstand ten pounds of snow per square foot. That is equivalent to an eighteen-inch snowfall. You may think we are going to say that the standard roof is overdesigned for use in the humid South. We are not, for two reasons: (1) the Deep South gets some very powerful windstorms and (2) you probably will use the support beams for hanging baskets. Wind pressure, especially the lifting force of wind, also is critical for greenhouses covered with light plastic film. Poorly anchored plastic houses will simply blow away.

Glass-Covered Greenhouses

Do not try to skimp on greenhouse glass; it should always be double strength. Broken glass can fall on the people inside.

Most glass-covered greenhouses today use aluminum for the members on which the glass panes and puttylike bedding material are bedded. These are called glazing bars or sash bars. In a sense, they are also rafters that transfer the weight of the roof to side posts and footing. In very large greenhouses there may be steel structural members under the aluminum glazing bars. Steel and aluminum must not be allowed to touch, or electrolytic corrosion occurs. Gaskets of rubber or plastic are used to separate these metals. All bolts or screws used must be of the same metal, or separated by rubber or plastic washers.

Redwood or cypress glazing bars are more attractive but also more expensive. Another expense is that wooden portions must be painted about every two years on exteriors and five years on the inside. Aluminum does not need painting, but it transmits more heat than does wood: wood-framed greenhouses are easier to heat than are aluminum ones. On the other hand, aluminum bars can be spaced farther apart and allow you to have larger panes of glass. This is another marginal advantage for us, but important farther north where winter light intensity is much lower.

If you decide to use wooden glazing bars, the glass panes will be bedded on a puttylike matrix placed on the shoulders of the bars and secured by small nails or glazing points—triangular pieces of flat galvanized steel driven into the wood. At the bottom of each pane, brads are driven into the bars to prevent the pane from slipping down. This leaves a gap between the edge of the glass and the bar, which is filled with the puttylike material, which tends to dry out and crack unless it is painted regularly. Aluminum bars make the installation of glass much easier. Bar caps of thin aluminum are placed over the upper glazing material and fastened to the bars with aluminum screws. These bars keep the panes from slipping down, exert a springlike pressure that ensures a good seal, and keep glazing material protected from weathering.

Wooden components used in greenhouse or benching materials should be treated to prevent rapid decay. Most treated wood has been impregnated with safe material, usually copper or chromium salts. You should check this out because, not very long ago, the conventional treating materials were creosote or pentachlorophenol. When the greenhouse became hot, the wood gave off vapors that killed or damaged plants. You should also be careful about any paint you use in the greenhouse. It is better to get safe paint from a greenhouse supplier than to trust the judgment of the local paint store.

While we are thinking about toxic vapors, we should caution you never to use a mercury thermometer in a greenhouse. Eventually it will fall and break, mercury will spread over the concrete or soil, and you will have a big problem. Mercury vapors are toxic to plants and are not good for your health either.

Plastic-Covered Greenhouses

Now we come to the less expensive, and less permanent, plastic film-covered houses. These, too, come in kits. The framework consists of arched supports that are fastened to longitudinal members called *purlins*, which are essential for stability. Because films can be obtained in very wide pieces, many greenhouses are covered with single panels fastened at the bottom on both sides. This film must be fastened down against wind lift; a good storm can blow your greenhouse over into the neighbor's yard. You will find a variety of devices that allow the plastic to be fastened without puncturing it; a small puncture, in a strong wind, will cause rips.

Some greenhouses use a double-layer film to provide better insulation. Small blowers provide just enough air pressure to keep the layers separated but not enough to stress the film sealing. Beyond this insulating effect, double plastic cushions the outer layer from abrasion against structural parts. A disadvantage is that the doubled layer reduces light transmission. This matters less here than it would farther north, where winter light intensity is lower.

Now we move into the topic of rigid plastic, substituted for plastic film, or as panels substituting for glass. These are becoming popular, especially in areas where hailstorms are frequent. The trend began back when fiberglass-reinforced panels were more popular than they are now. Fiberglass is available in various colors, but clear is much better for the greenhouse. Ed was once contacted by a lady who operated a small retail greenhouse, complaining that her plants had a sickly looking yellowish color. When he got to her greenhouse the problem was obvious. In full sun the plants had a healthy green color. They looked sickly in the greenhouse because the fiberglass was yellow. Plants grow pretty well in yellow light, but this was a retail operation: customers will not buy yellowish plants. Green panels might have made the plants look better, but the plants would not have grown very well. Plants are green because they reflect green light—meaning that it cannot be used in photosynthesis. Use clear plastic in your greenhouse.

The matter of rigid plastic panels being used to replace glass looks very promising but that is about all we can say for certain. The new panels are made from a polycarbonate and have built-in dead air spaces for better insulation. These provide some heat savings and are less likely to break than glass. The installation process is tricky; make a mistake and humid air will creep in, providing an excellent place for algal growth. We are still waiting to see just how long the panels will endure our long summers, with high ultraviolet (UV) light intensity. We know that fiberglass panels weather after a while, and become "fuzzy"; this traps dirt and reduces light penetration. The change is so gradual that it may go unnoticed until plant growth rate is affected. It is possible to refinish fiberglass, but that is expensive and may not be worth the effort.

Having mentioned UV light, we can return to the problems of plastic film greenhouses. The plastic films currently being used are degraded by UV light. New barriers to UV light are constantly being evaluated and advertised by manufacturers, but remember that in the Gulf South the summer sun is very intense. For the present, it is safe to assume that most films will make it through a winter and, maybe, the next summer, but you should not trust them for a second winter. Even if the plastic looks pretty good, re-cover the greenhouse in the fall. The most common time for film to fail is when north winds accompany cold fronts in winter. You have not experienced real excitement until you have seen broken plastic flapping in the cold wind, knowing that you are going to have to replace it before dark (before the freeze sets in).

Summer Heat Protection

Then there is the matter of shading the greenhouse in summer. There are shade fabrics available to cover the greenhouse, offering a range of shade, or compounds may be sprayed or painted on the glass (coating plastic is more difficult). If using a shade compound, be careful to let each thin coat (if needed) dry thoroughly before adding more, or the compound will bead up and run off. A shade compound should stick well, but not too well. If you are lucky, the summer rains will have washed most of it off by the time cool weather comes.

Shade fabrics are distinguished according to the percentage of shading they produce. Because the material is made of polypropylene, check whether a flame retardant has been added. Shade fabrics usually are placed outside the greenhouse for maximum reduction of both light and the accompanying heat. You may occasionally want to use a supplemental shade on the inside to protect sensitive plants; cloth or paper may serve as well as additional shade fabric.

HEATING A GREENHOUSE

At this point you have decided on the greenhouse design and the type of covering. Now is the time for a hard-nosed look at heating needs. How much heat will you need, and what will it cost? Back when Ed taught a greenhouse management class he began this topic by saying that greenhouses were devised to protect plants from low temperatures in areas where winters are long and severe. You will need some greenhouse heating in Louisiana, but remember that heat is not the only reason for having a greenhouse. The control of water on plants is a benefit. But let's get back to heat.

Bear with us while we talk a bit about the infamous greenhouse effect, which influences the earth's temperature. No, we do not know whether the earth is going to heat up and destroy life as we know it. But we need to discuss the principles involved to explain how greenhouses are heated and cooled.

Consider a greenhouse with no artificial source of heat. A greenhouse will be warmed by sunlight even though it has traveled across very cold space, in the shorter wavelengths. If the greenhouse is glass-covered, most incoming light from the sun can pass through the glass. Inside the greenhouse it will strike some object and be absorbed or reflected as heat. The key point is that this heat is in longer, warmer wavelengths that do not pass easily through the glass, but are again reflected inside the greenhouse, heating the interior even more. A greenhouse in the sunlight (even reflected sunlight) will warm up if it is tightly closed. This is largely due to radiation, plus subsequent storing of the heat. You will notice that we said "if the greenhouse is glass-covered." The long wavelengths, which do not pass through glass very easily, are not held as well by a polyethylene film, but film-covered greenhouses still warm up. Plastic greenhouses accumulate heat by preventing warmed air from escaping. Warm air rises because it is lighter than cool air. At the plastic (or glass) surface, it cools slightly and moves downward along the wall; then warmed air from the center of the house moves upward, creating a circulating convection current. Warmed air in a greenhouse that is closed or partially closed actually becomes somewhat pressurized, enough to press against the covering. In glass greenhouses the lap spaces between panes of glass may allow warm air to leak out; in cold weather, water vapor forms in the spaces and freezes, blocking the leaks.

During the night, with no more incoming radiation, the greenhouse becomes a heat exchanger—the characteristics that allowed it to heat during the day promote heat loss at night. Heat from the warmer air is lost to colder structural members and coverings, and this cooler air is held against the roof and walls by the pressure of the warmer air. Instead of falling directly, the cool air flows downward along the roof, down the wall, and pools on the floor, just as a liquid would. The coldest place in a winter greenhouse is usually the junction between the wall and floor. This is the spot where plants are most likely to be damaged. (Many commercial greenhouses have heating elements located there, so that the cold air will not spread across the floor. You may want to consider this system.) On a cold night, with the wind blowing, heat is steadily moved away from the greenhouse. The greater the difference in temperature between the outer air and the greenhouse, the more heat is transmitted. Wind blows this heat away, increasing the rate of loss.

How large a heater you will need (heaters are rated in BTUs, British thermal units) depends partly on what kinds of plants you will be growing and how cold you think it might get in a very cold winter. All of these are essentially guesses. Your library has local climatology records to improve your estimate. The manufacturer of your greenhouse kit probably has suggestions about heating.

Using a heat-loss calculation formula, you can plug in the size and shape of your greenhouse, type of covering, and the desired inside temperature for a range of outside temperatures and come up with the approximate number of BTUs your greenhouse needs to have added per hour to replace the heat lost. This will tell you how large a heating unit you need. The same thing is done to determine your home heating needs. Also, you can tell approximately the cost of heating for a winter in your locality.

How sophisticated your heating system needs to be depends on your objectives. If you are simply trying to get your plants through the cold spell, large fluctuations will matter less than they would for commercial producers. The standard textbook for commercial flower production says that the temperature should not vary by more than one degree centigrade. Some growers actually achieve that, but you do not need such precision. Make your heating system as dependable as possible, but be prepared to accept fluctuations. If frequent power failures are a fact of life in your area, you should have a standby heat source that does not depend on electric controls: having a small kerosene heater for backup will help you to sleep on cold nights. Speaking of cold nights, you might consider installing an alarm that will sound in your bedroom if the power goes off during the night. Lying in the warm bed, you may wonder just how much you value the plants—then you will get up and solve the problem.

VENTILATION

Although you may think of air movement primarily as a method for maintaining temperature, it is also useful for disease control. When the sun goes down, the air in a greenhouse cools quickly, which means that it holds less moisture. Because the air is already humid, the excess water condenses on leaf surfaces. Fungal spores, which are everywhere, germinate on that film and cause disease problems. Yes, keeping the leaves covered with a fungicide will help, except that growing leaves grow. As they grow, new, untreated surfaces are exposed. A rule of successful greenhouse operators is to bring up the heat before the sun goes down. Even with that, it is a good idea to keep greenhouse air circulating. The current trend is called horizontal airflow: two small fans are placed in opposite diagonal corners in the greenhouse, with one blowing to the front and one to the rear. For most hobby-size houses, fans about twelve inches in diameter with perhaps 1/32 hp motors will keep air moving effectively.

Besides the inside air movements, greenhouses need ventilation: replacing carbon dioxide, providing more oxygen for the heater fuel, and readjusting humidity. How much do you need and when? Not long ago a landscape architect asked Ed to look at his plans for an elaborate "greenhouseoid" building that resembled the old orangeries used by the French monarchs in their glory days. Because the structure had what was essentially an airtight glass roof, the architect wanted some guidelines for ventilation. Most greenhouses have vents near the roof ridge and similar ones near the floor; warm air goes out the top and is replaced by cooler air at the bottom. With this kind of system, the open vent area should be around 15 to 30 percent of the total floor area. Because greenhouses covered with plastic film do not have this convective air system, they need forced air, provided by fans. This is the kind of problem the architect was facing; the roof had no vents and would need a forced air system. Guidelines vary with the climate. In the Gulf South, with high humidity and light intensity, the best estimate is that you need around sixty air exchanges per hour.

Do you really need to calculate ventilation requirements for your little greenhouse? Probably not, but this is a goal if you want to check on it. Commercial growers, whose greenhouse space may cover acres, must make the calculations—or go broke.

Now, for cooling; greenhouses get very hot in the summer. Mechanical air conditioning is the best option—except that it costs an arm and a leg. You might want to consider an evaporative cooling system, consisting of a fibrous pad that can be continually wetted and fans that will pull outside air through the wet pad. This fan-and-pad approach is not nearly so good in our humid conditions as it would be in the arid Southwest, but it is pretty good and fairly economical. A common problem with this system is the growth of algae on the wet surface, which can ruin the pads in a very short time. The best solution is to use an algal control material such as those used in swimming pools. The pads are kept wet by water pumped from a holding tank. The water drips down the pad, into a trough, and flows back into the tank. The chemical used for algal control will come with instructions on the amount to be used per gallon of water in the tank. It does not tell you how often to add the chemical because that depends on evaporation rate. Generally, you should add more chemical when the algae start building up on the pad.

Although this is an evaporation system that removes water vapor and leaves the salts, salt buildup should not be a serious problem. The tank has a float valve (as in a toilet) that replaces evaporated water. Assuming your water supply does not have a high salt content, salts in the tank will not increase very much during the entire summer. You will need to drain the system every winter anyway to keep it from freezing.

Planting Beds and Displays

What about benches or beds in the greenhouse? Consider beginning with beds, especially if you are interested in vegetables or in cut flowers. Do not pour money into wonderful permanent beds that you may want to change later. Beds in a greenhouse should be built like outdoor beds. Raised beds are a good general principle even though they will not be subjected to flooding rains. Eventually, you will want to grow potted plants and will decide to build some benches; otherwise you will be continually stooping or bending. And you might consider having raised benches over the original ground-level beds. Most benches are made of something like welded wire fabric or a treated-wood lath. Ed's greenhouse has welded wire fabric, one-by-two inch mesh size, fastened to wooden frames made of two-by-four wood and supported by two lightweight concrete blocks, stacked end to end. This height is convenient for Ed and he likes being able to rearrange the benches as his interests change. Because nothing is nailed down, he can store extra benches for times when pot space becomes more critical.

Often some kind of staging, perhaps a stair-step arrangement of narrow shelves, is useful for plant display. In some cases this provides more space than conventional benches—you will need to do some calculations on this. The same kind of things may be involved in deciding on wall shelves, or placing hanging baskets overhead; remember that they all affect the light getting to other plants, and the dripping might damage plants below them. These are the things that make greenhouses interesting. But do not look on them as problems; your hobby should have interesting challenges.

Chapter 18

LAGNIAPPE

Lagniappe is said to be a combination of Spanish and French words, meaning "more of the same." In French Louisiana it means "a little extra." Back in the old days, if you complained to the oyster man that his oysters were just a bit small he would say, "*Mais couillon,* I give you two for lagniappe yea!" Those two were even smaller.

The following topics are all lagniappe—idle points that we like to talk about. There is no extra charge; but then, the ideas may not be worth much either.

Things That Go Bump in the Night: The Dark Period, Sleeping, and Resting

THE DARK PERIOD

Gardeners have known for a very long time that plant flowering was associated with seasons, and they probably suspected that differences in day length also were involved. In about 1918 Garner and Allard, with the U.S. Department of Agriculture, were trying to determine why the tobacco variety Maryland Mammoth did not flower; it was called *mammoth* because it just kept growing. With a very simple experiment they showed that the plants would flower if they made the days shorter by putting them in a dark chamber every afternoon. They called this response *photoperiodism* and showed that other plants would flower only when the days were long. This set off a flurry of studies to classify all plants by their photoperiodic requirements: short day, long day, and day neutral. Eventually they developed two main points. First, *short day* does not refer to any specific day length; it means that the plant will flower after periods of exposure in which the day is shorter than a certain critical time. For an extreme example, a plant might flower only if the day length were shorter than 16 hours. Obviously, 16 hours is a rather long day; but this would still be a short-day plant because it would flower if exposed to daylight for any time period less than that. Conversely, a long-day plant flowers at periods longer than its critical time. Now we come to the second point, which scientific terminology wisely decided to ignore. This comes from the simple fact that all days are 24 hours long; thus, a short-day plant is also a long-night plant. And the length of the dark period is what really counts, except for the other fact that, without a reasonable daylight period, the plant cannot carry on photosynthesis. There was a short halfhearted drive to change the terminology from *photoperiod* to *skotoperiod* but it died mercifully.

The next great leap forward was a discovery that some plants seemed to require a few long-day exposures followed by short days. There were even shorthand formulas to describe flowering requirements: LD, LD, SD, LD. This meant that the plant needed two long-day exposures (LD) followed by one short day (SD) and another long day. It was a terrible time to be a graduate student, but eventually the mess cleared out. One other complication: The length of the critical photoperiod is also affected by temperature, and the people who worked out the complex formulas had failed to hold temperature constant.

Now there are only three categories: long day, short day, and day neutral. The critical time periods for a species or variety may vary with temperature. But you should keep in mind that *long day* should refer to a *short night,* and that conditions that prevent floral initiation will maintain vegetative growth. Floral crop producers manipulate both exposures to tailor-make plants of specific sizes and forms that will bloom at desired dates. More than one inductive exposure (the one day or night of the timing needed to start, or induce, the flowering process) is needed for most plants to flower. However, some ultrasensitive plants respond to a single exposure and will continue the flowering process if placed back in noninductive conditions.

The major photoperiodic flower crops are short-day plants: chrysanthemums and poinsettias. Poinsettias are forced almost exclusively for the Thanksgiving-Christmas sales period, but by manipulation of day length they can be produced at any time of the year, providing temperatures are controlled. Chrysanthemums, which bloom naturally in the late fall or early winter, are now flowered year-round. When days are long (and nights short) mums are black-clothed—given artificially long nights by covering them with black cloth or plastic covers every night for about six weeks. In winter, when days are short and nights long, the plants are lighted for several hours each night for a week or more after planting. This makes for long days (shorter nights), which keeps them vegetative. After the plants have produced enough stem growth, the night exposures are stopped. With longer nights the plants start making flowers at the ends of shoots. Chrysanthemums are produced for two kinds of markets: cut mums and potted mums. Because cut mums require longer stems, they are exposed to the lights-at-night regimen for about three weeks more than those intended for sale as potted plants.

Cinerarias and calceolarias are examples of commercial crops that flower naturally during the long days of summer. However, they also are *cool weather* crops. If the night temperature is above 50 to 55°F, they remain vegetative, re-gardless of day length. Notice that the critical temperature comes at night; *long day* is a misnomer. Down here we can flower these in the winter when night temperatures can be controlled by lowering the thermostat.

There is one more point about photoperiod that is interesting. The mech-anism that responds to photoperiod is a kind of timing device. Not only does it trigger the flowering process, but also leaf fall and dormancy in deciduous trees. The switch that turns the mechanism on or off is a compound called phytochrome. One wavelength of red light turns the timer on and another (also in the red spectrum) turns it off. This makes sense because the last light in the afternoon is red and so is the first light of dawn.

DORMANCY

Now we need to talk a little about dormancy. The term was devised long ago to describe plants or plant parts that were not growing; it literally means they are sleeping, which was a poor word choice but we are stuck with it. Then sci-entists began to realize that there were several kinds of dormancy. Horticul-ture developed the term *rest period* to describe the condition in which buds will not grow until they have been exposed to a certain number of hours with temperatures between 32° and 45°F (time below freezing has no effect). You will remember that we talked about rest periods and cold requirements in dis-cussions of fruit trees. Obviously, the buds are not really resting, but the dor-mant buds are not sleeping either. In horticulture, dormant buds are buds that are not growing because weather conditions do not allow it. This is a useful distinction because you can speak of buds that are dormant after the rest pe-riod has been completed; they have been exposed to enough cold but are not growing because the weather is still too cold.

Meanwhile, back at the ranch, plant physiologists decided that *rest* was not a good term. They subdivided dormancy into three groups: induced dormancy, innate dormancy, and enforced dormancy. Using that terminology, rest is called induced dormancy, and what horticulturists mean by dormancy is enforced dormancy. There are also several other classifications but we have made our point: Buds with a cold requirement are resting; anything else that is not growing (buds or seeds) is dormant.

Mycorrhiza

Myco refers to fungus and *rhizo* to roots. This is a root-fungus association. The situation is parallel to that of *Rhizobium,* a bacterium living symbiotically (meaning for mutual benefit) on legume roots, except *mycorrhiza* refers to a fungus. In a sense the roots are infected with a fungus and the root structure is modified, but in a way that is beneficial to the plant. We need to get some terminology straight before we can discuss the importance of this.

These fungi are not of a single genus and are commonly described by the type of infection. The ecto group forms a sheath over the outer tissues of the root and extends threadlike structures called mycelia into the root cortex (a Latin word meaning "outer shell"). The endo group has a loose network of mycelia in the soil but is also connected to a fairly extensive network in the cortex. Essentially, both groups have mycelia in contact with the soil and are connected to the root through growth into the cortex. The primary difference is that the endo group has mycelia that extend into the soil.

The endo group probably has the most potential importance for vegetable production, but it is the one that we know the least about. This group seems to be entirely obligate parasites, meaning that they can grow only in a relationship with living roots.

The ecto group has been studied because it can be cultured on artificial media. It is composed mostly of basidiomycetes (the mushroom group), and they are found in relation with pine, oak, and beech trees. The outstanding point about this is that pine trees will grow well in acid, low phosphorus soil, if that soil contains the proper mycorrhiza. If it does not, the trees will grow slowly and show phosphorus deficiency. Putting this another way: acid, low-fertility land will support good pine growth only if pines have already been growing on it or if you inoculate the area with soil from pine land. Studies of this show that the mycelia of mycorrhiza take phosphorus from soil much more efficiently than do the roots of pines.

Another interesting point is that most, and possibly all, crop plants have the potential for this kind of root-fungus relationship, but because the fungi involved are primarily of the endo group they are very hard to study. There is reason to hope that methods can be worked out to add selected strains of these fungi to soil in which there is little soluble phosphorus and avoid the need for adding phosphorus fertilizer. We see mycorrhiza as having potential for a breakthrough in solving soil fertility problems. Unfortunately, at this time it is only a bit of interesting information, mainly because mycorrhiza do not grow well in fertile soil.

So at present we have a system that could at least double a plant's ability to use soil phosphorus, but it works only when the plant is under nutritional stress. That is not the kind of system we need for high levels of vegetable production. It is unlikely that we will accidentally find a fungal strain without this problem, but it seems possible that a selection process might develop one. This would make it possible to improve the ability of plants to take up phosphorus. You may remember that although there are large amounts of rock phosphorus in mines around the world, it is fundamentally as nonrenewable as petroleum products.

Ripe Watermelons

You may have read that a dead tendril on the stem of a melon means that the melon is ripe; actually it just means that the tendril is dead. With some varieties, the yellow or white spot on the bottom shows that the melon is ripe, but this does not apply to all melons. Field harvesters can do a pretty good job of visual selection, but only if they know the variety well. When a watermelon is ripe, the skin undergoes a subtle color change, usually becoming just a bit lighter. This is a reliable method in the field because selectors have unripe melons to compare against; selection by color in the supermarket is a wild guess. Ultimately, you must fall back on the old tried and true. We realize that thumping a melon creates about the same impression as thumping the tires on a used car, but it does work. The sound of a ripe melon is music to the ears of a gourmet. The key is resonance; a ripe melon resonates and a green one sounds flat. If you form your lips into an oval and thump your cheek, that is the sound of a ripe melon. Thump your forehead, and that will give you the sound of a green melon. Now close your mouth and puff out your cheeks; thump them and that is the sound when the melon is overripe.

The thumping test is absolutely reliable, but as a caution we must add a few words regarding postharvest physiology. Ripe watermelons are supposed to be sweet and flavorful, but some are not. Immediately after a watermelon is picked, it begins to use up sugars through respiration; at high temperatures the sugars are used up rapidly. Now, consider a south Florida (early season) producer who carefully picks only the ripe melons and places them carefully in a wagon. Then he pulls the wagon to the edge of the field, unloads the melons in the sun, and goes back for another load. The next day the melons are loaded into an open truck and hauled for two days to a large shed, which is also hot. The supermarket picks up a load of ripe melons and chills them. The next day you thump the melons, pick one that is ripe and ice cold—and it is almost tasteless. Your friends will say that those Florida melons are no good, the locally grown melons are much sweeter. This is not quite true. Freshly harvested Florida melons are sweet and, if they are handled properly, week-old melons are nearly as sweet. The problem is that handling them properly is expensive and most customers do not want to pay the difference in price.

Photosynthesis: Bureaucracy in Action

In civics class we all learned that our federal government system is actually efficient because, with the interlocking maze of redundancy plus checks and balances, it can adjust to almost any situation. Those of you who believed that would love to study photosynthesis. Fundamentally, it is a very simple reaction:

$$6CO_2 + 12\,H_2O = C_6H_{12}O_6 + 6H_2O + O_2$$

The energy comes from sunlight and breaks the water into hydrogen and oxygen, which combine with carbon dioxide to produce sugar, water, and some leftover oxygen. In fact, the total number of interlocked reactions and alternate pathways is probably close to a thousand. Some wag said that photosynthesis makes you believe in polytheism because the system must have been built by a committee of gods. Why is photosynthesis so complex? Because plants love complications. Philosophically, it probably represents adaptations through millions of years to widely varying conditions. Plants survive because they can adapt to new situations.

Having said that, we can get on to some more interesting points. The rate of photosynthesis is affected by three aspects of light, the amount of carbon dioxide in the air, temperature, and the availability of water. The last two are so obvious that we will not discuss them, but the others are fun.

Regarding light use, the plant is a little less efficient than our government is with taxes. Given excellent gardening conditions the more efficient plants will use about 3 percent of the solar energy for conversion to sugars, but 1 to 2 percent is more common. Part of this is because photosynthesis is most effective in the red and blue color spectra, but the other end of the spectrum contains more energy. Some pigments will absorb other colors and convert them to photosynthetic wavelengths.

The second aspect of light that affects photosynthesis is light intensity. We mentioned this in chapter 4, saying that in dim light the plant reaches a compensation point at which it can produce only enough sugars for its own respiration needs. The other end of this is the *light saturation* point, at which further increase of light intensity will not produce more photosynthesis. Obviously, this point will vary with plant species; but this gets more complicated when we talk about carbon dioxide.

Light duration is another point we mentioned in discussing potted plants. If the light is too dim during the day, you can improve growth by exposing your plants to artificial light for a while every night. With some exceptions, longer exposure to even dim light will increase the total amount of sugars made through photosynthesis.

Carbon dioxide is the main reason we wrote this discussion on photosynthesis. Normal outside air contains about 0.03 percent carbon dioxide, 21 percent oxygen, and most of the rest is nitrogen. Because 0.03 percent is normal, you would expect that to be the optimum level for efficient photosynthesis. In fact, the optimum rate is reached only after the carbon dioxide level is five times normal. We have to hedge some here and point out that this assumes an abundance of light. If your plant is already suffering from the dim light of your house, increasing the carbon dioxide level does little good because what it needs is light.

In full sunlight more carbon dioxide will be a big help and make plants grow faster. This may be a part of why compost and high soil organic matter improve plant growth. As microorganisms break the material down, carbon dioxide is released.

This high carbon dioxide observation does have applied value. For example, Colorado has strong sunlight and few cloudy days. Artificially increasing the carbon dioxide level in Colorado greenhouses is of some importance, especially at high altitudes where the carbon dioxide levels are low. Also, there have been suggestions that commercial greenhouses might be constructed near the shafts of abandoned coal mines in Appalachia. Air drawn from the mines would be relatively warm in the winter, cool in the summer, and would contain high levels of carbon dioxide. Unfortunately, the mine atmosphere also contains carbon monoxide.

Does the plant requirement for carbon dioxide have any significance in relation to the greenhouse effect of higher atmospheric carbon dioxide levels throughout the world? Our climatologist says there is no question about carbon dioxide levels increasing, but no one knows enough about temperature trends to say that it is affecting the average temperature. If world atmospheric carbon dioxide content were to increase by a factor of five, what would happen? We suppose most plants would grow faster, if the world did not get too hot for them to survive. Our Deep South would disappear into the Gulf.

"Gibbing" Camellias

Gibberellic acid is a plant growth regulator with an interesting history. A rice disorder called bakanae had been long known in Japan and was characterized by causing giant plants that did not fruit well or did not fruit at all. Early in this century a Japanese plant pathologist noticed the presence of fungal mycelia in affected rice plants and speculated on a relationship between the disease symptoms and the fungus. One of his assistants proceeded to investigate this and published a classic paper (1926) in which he attributed the problem to secretions of a fungus. Another fungus, known as *Gibberella fujikoroi*, was later shown to be involved in the responses of affected plants, and the substance responsible was named gibberellin, from the botanical name of the fungus. A crystalline form of this growth promoter was isolated in 1938.

The Japanese work was little known outside of that country, largely because of the language difficulties involved but also because of the attitude prevailing against outside cultures in Japan. Following World War II the western world became aware of the work, which caused a rash of activity involving gibberellic acid, or GA, as it was commonly called, during the early 1950s.

Among plant responses noted was that of camellia flowers, which were accelerated in development, frequently became much larger, and produced more vivid color after applications of GA. Exhibitors at flower shows in those early years were shot down by a few canny individuals who had learned the secret. Along with the kind of acrimony peculiar to flower competitors, this led to setting up separate competitive categories for *gibbed* camellias, as they came to be known.

Even today, the camellia competitors suspect that any flower that beats theirs might have been gibbed or grown in a greenhouse, or both.

GA-treated or gibbed camellias may bloom early enough to escape much of the flower blight infestation that can devastate blooms in many seasons, and that reason alone can make it a good practice. GA is not difficult to obtain (if you have trouble, call your friendly county agent). One percent in water is used for camellias. Adding a few drops of ammonia will help dissolve the crystals before you add water. The most common means of application is to place a drop of the solution in the cuplike structure left after removing the vegetative bud near a well-developed flower bud. Treating too early is not good, and there is room for experimentation to find the best time to treat your particular cultivars.

You Say "Ca-mell-i-a" and I Say "Ca-meel-i-a"

Along with genteel competition at flower shows, we find people who pronounce "camellia" with a short *e* and others who pronounce it with a long *e*. Who is right? Well, the plant was named for one George Joseph Kamel, known also as Camellus, a Moravian Jesuit who traveled in Asia during the seventeenth century. We feel that he preferred the short *e* sound in his name but, in our part of the country, a short *e* marks you as trying to be more uptown than the good old boys and girls who use the long *e*. Remember about doing as the Romans do. That is, if the long *e* Romans happen to be in the majority, use the long *e*; unless, of course, the flower show judges are pronouncing it the other way and you think you might improve your chances by following them.

Tulip Bulbs

When planting tulips in pots, place the flat or concave side of the bulb to the outside of the pot. The first large leaf emerges on this side, and proper placement makes a much more attractive pot than one in which the leaves are crowded up in the center. Bulbs need at least two inches of potting medium under them to allow good root growth, so choose containers with this in mind.

The tunics (tan covering) on tulip bulbs appear to have some antibiotic activity. The standard practice is to leave them on when planting, but it helps to remove tight, heavy tunics from the base of the bulb where the roots will emerge because they can interfere with proper root development. This is especially important for potted bulbs when the water supply may at times become limited between irrigations. The tunics can cause a condition called tulip finger in some people who handle a great many of them, such as in packing them for sale. This appears to be an allergy; your skin may crack and become painful. Most of us need not worry about it, with the price of tulips being what it is (unless we get a job packing bulbs).

Spanish Moss

Spanish moss usually grows in association with trees and is very much a part of the southern landscape. From a how-to-do-it viewpoint, we only need to say that you can hang some moss on a tree and, if conditions are right, it will grow. If it dies, you need not bother trying again; there is probably too much sun or too little humidity.

We know some interesting trivia about Spanish moss, much more than the old cliché about it being a relative of the pineapple. In the United States there are at least three plants called Spanish moss. In California, Spanish moss is a lichen *(Ramalina menziesii)* that looks very much like ours in the humid South and grows in a climate similar to parts of Spain. It seems likely that this was the original Spanish moss. Or maybe the Spanish explorers down here thought ours was like what they knew at home. In the northern states another lichen *(Usnea,* of which there are several species) is called Spanish moss; it also is sometimes called "old man's beard."

Our Spanish moss is not a lichen, but a bromeliad. Bromeliads are true flowering plants, as contrasted with the lichens, which are much simpler. Most bromeliads are often called *air plants,* meaning that they obtain water from rain and the air, and mineral nutrients from dust particles. The tree is only a support and partial protection from intense, drying sunlight. If you look closely at Spanish moss, you will see that the gray color comes from the rough surface that catches dust particles. Beneath that, it is a normal green plant. Yes, pineapple is also a bromeliad, but it takes up moisture and nutrients from roots.

The botanical name of our Spanish moss is *Tillandsia usneoides,* which has several interesting tales. Elias Tillands was a Swedish professor who was acquainted with Linnaeus. The name means "by land," and there is a story that he adopted the name after becoming seasick and swearing to always go by land. (As you know by now, we do occasionally embellish a story, but this one is directly from the taxonomist's classic reference: *Gray's Manual.*) Linnaeus named the genus after Tillands because of an erroneous belief that the plant would not grow in wet places.

The specific appellation *usneoides* means that it looks like *Usnea,* the lichen that is called Spanish moss in the northern states. Another species of this lichen *(Usnea trichodea)* grows on trees in swampy areas, and the taxonomic description says that it is sometimes confused with Spanish moss—which brings us back to the point that our Spanish moss is named *T. usneoides.* Taxonomy is an interesting game if you do not take it too seriously.

We have another species called ball moss *(Tillandsia recurvata).* It grows as a ball, clasping around the limbs of trees. You may see large amounts of it growing on a crape myrtle tree, with a nearby one being completely free of it. We do not know what meaning that may have but, because it grows well on power lines, we know that it is not parasitic. The moss-free crape myrtle may be producing a substance that keeps moss off, or possibly no seeds have germinated on it. Ball moss has been a topic of some concern because of its rapid spread. Ten or fifteen years ago someone published a paper in a state horticultural journal reporting that ball moss had recently spread to Louisiana from Florida. The writer had not bothered to read the much older literature saying that it was once very common over much of south Louisiana. Some people ask whether ball moss hurts the tree. Well, that depends. It is not a parasite; but you planted the crape myrtle for its appearance. If you do not like ball moss, it is a weed. Pull it off.

There is still a small industry of gathering moss, allowing the soft outer part to decompose, then drying and milling it to leave the tough, wiry central portion of the stems. At one time it was used as stuffing for furniture, and some old timers remember when it was the poor folks' mattress. They say it would lump up badly and was noisy when you turned over. We do not know what the moss is used for now, but hear that the industry is still alive.

About fifteen years ago it appeared that our Spanish moss was dying out. This was around the time when we began to realize that leaded gasoline was releasing a lot of lead into the air. One study relating to this used Spanish moss as the indicator plant, not because the moss was dying but because its rough surface collected particles from the air. The test results showed that the lead content on moss near heavy traffic was extremely high, decreasing with distance from the highway. Parallel with the increased use of unleaded gasoline, the growth of Spanish moss has luxuriated until it is now almost as abundant as back in the old days.

We phrased the above paragraph carefully to make a point. We do not know whether leaded gasoline played any part in the moss decline problem. Circumstantial evidence suggests that, at most, it was only contributory. Throughout the moss decline period Ed was a frequent fisherman in the marshes. Moss was dying far away from highways at about the same rate as near them. It did not completely die out even very close to highways, which is why it was used as the indicator plant in that lead study. There is a fusarium fungus disease that affects Spanish moss. Plant pathologists showed that at least some of the decline was due to disease. Another plausible reason is that the Spanish moss was getting old. Some plants live for a few years and others for a few hundred years. Like everything else, Spanish moss gets old and dies. We know nothing about its life span, but many plant populations grow in flushes. If most of our Spanish moss started growing at about the same time, eventually there would be a flush of dying. This answer does not exclude disease and lead poisoning. As our friends get older, they die of heart problems and cancer. But they are also getting older.

Puckery Persimmons

We told you earlier about green persimmons containing a tannin that puckers your mouth. *Tannin* is a group of chemicals that coagulate proteins, which is why the oak tannin was once used extensively for tanning leather. In Japan, the kaki-tannin was used to make rice paper more durable. Japanese folk artists still use it in paintings. Green persimmon fruits are crushed to extract the juice, which is then stored in bottles for at least a year; it becomes a reddish-black when ready for use. Kaki-tannin also is used in Japan as a folk remedy for high blood pressure.

Persimmon tannin puckers up your mouth by coagulating proteins on the surface of the tongue; it is a matter of dehydration. During the ripening process tannins react with some fruit proteins, inactivating them. As you might expect, the nonastringent cultivars contain only minimum amounts of tannin.

There are several methods for artificial inactivation of persimmon tannin. The Japanese growers used to store nearly ripe persimmons in old sake barrels; the astringency disappeared in about ten days. The standard practice now is to pack the persimmons in cardboard boxes and spray them with a 35 to 40 percent ethyl alcohol solution. Leon ripens kaki persimmons by putting them in a plastic storage box, covering them with a paper towel, and pouring a little vodka over it. He puts the lid on the box, and the fruit ripens in four or five days. The establishment of fairly large populations of people from southeast Asia following the Vietnam War has opened market opportunities for oriental persimmons. The preferred varieties are nonastringent and semisweet when as firm or firmer than a hard apple and are often used in cooking.

We personally prefer the sweet, soft, gelatinous ripe fruit. This ripening process is identical to that of any other fruit: the starches are converted to sugars and the pectins break the fleshy part into a gelatinous, juicy mass. We like to freeze the ripe fruit and slice it, partly thawed. Then you can eat it like sherbet.

Ripening Figs Early

If you have a fig tree or know somebody who does, here is a little-known practice that you can use to demonstrate the art of horticulture. Oil (usually olive oil) applied carefully to the eye of a fig at the proper time can make it ripen in a really dramatic fashion, often as much as thirty days before untreated figs of the same age growing on the same branch. This practice is referred to as oleification, a fancy word for oiling, and, according to experts on the history of figs, was noted by Theophrastus as being practiced in Greece as early as the third century B.C. The practice probably started when people with olive oil on their hands accidentally got it on the figs at the right time and in the right place. Because treating figs one at a time is not labor efficient, this is an old-timers' trick that most fig growers have forgotten. Our historian also says that early Minorcan residents of St. Augustine, Florida, used it to produce ripe figs for the early market. This topic was hotly debated by the Horticulture Society of Charleston, South Carolina, and a paper on the issue was presented before that learned group in 1831, later published in the *Southern Agriculturist* (vol. 4, 1831). The paper's conclusion: this works, but we do not know why.

For the oil treatment to work, the figs should be about half their ripe size, but the center must be hollow, with perhaps a hint of pink in the otherwise white pulp. Figs with solid insides are too mature and those too small for the treatment will fall off. Usually the figs in our area are right for treatment in early June (ripening naturally in late June or early July). All you need to do is apply a drop of olive or mineral oil to the eye of the fig. If things were timed right, the treated figs will be ripe in a few days, sometimes as few as three or four, whereas the untreated figs will remain green for weeks longer.

If you are still curious about why this works, here is the secret: oil seals the hole and causes a buildup of ethylene gas in the fruit. The only real problem with this technique is that birds just love early figs, and if your tree is the only one with ripe figs it will be popular with your feathered friends. Your only evidence of horticultural genius may be the stems they leave you. Try covering the tree with bird netting, which usually will protect the fruit.

Coffee

French statesman Charles-Maurice de Talleyrand-Périgord said:

> A cup of coffee lightly tempered with good milk detracts nothing from your intellect, your stomach is freed by it and no longer distresses the brain; it will not hamper your mind with troubles but give freedom to its working. Suave molecules of Mocha stir up your blood, without causing excessive heat: the organ of thought receives from it a feeling of sympathy; work becomes easier and you will sit down without distress to your principal repast, all of which will restore your body and afford a calm delicious night.

Considering all of our references to coffee, it seems that we should mention its production. Together, we know a surprising amount about coffee. Ed, growing up in New Orleans, roasted and ground coffee at the neighborhood grocery where he worked. When he was about four years old, he and his mother would have late breakfasts of French bread crusts dipped in café au lait. In south Mississippi, however, coffee would stunt your growth. Leon was not allowed to drink coffee until he was sixteen. Apparently, the south Mississippians were right, because early drinking did stunt Ed's growth—he is about four inches shorter than Leon. In Malaysia, Leon taught the coffee course, "Production of Beverage Crops." Coffee, tea, and cocoa have no horticultural relationships to one another, but are always studied together in colleges of tropical agriculture. The logic is that you cannot justify teaching an entire course on each crop.

We will begin with the obvious question: can you grow coffee down South? Coffee is an attractive shrub with rather pretty flowers that give off a pleasant aroma. Because the plant needs protection from temperatures above 85 to 90°F and below 45°F, you should grow it as a large potted plant. Also, coffee requires a well-drained soil, and flowering (breaking dormancy of flower buds) is caused by a dry period instead of the cold requirement of temperate-zone plants. Because coffee is a shade plant, it would do rather well indoors. Sure, you could grow coffee—but it is not worth the trouble.

Coffee has been in the Near East forever. There are several references in the Old Testament to what possibly is coffee. Parched corn and parched beans seem to be rather generic terms for seeds. Abigail gave David five measures of parched corn. The parched corn Boaz gave to Ruth may have been coffee or roasted barley, used as a coffee substitute (coffee was an expensive luxury). Another "maybe" is that the red lentil pottage for which Esau sold his birthright was coffee. The key word here is that the Bible refers to "red" pottage and the ritual use of coffee was in a red clay vessel. In that context, coffee makes more sense than pottage; on a cold Monday morning in January reasonable people would sell their birthright for a good cup of coffee. All of this makes interesting coffee talk if you are willing to ignore the problem that, as of now, our earliest written mention of coffee is by a man named Rhazes (A.D. 850–922), long after the Old Testament was written.

The wild plant *Coffea arabica* is found in Ethiopia and may have originated there, but there is evidence that it might have been brought there from highland areas of Arabia. The early intensive cultivation was on terraces in the mountains of Yemen, irrigated by spring water. Coffee in the Near East is closely intertwined with Islamic culture; the word comes from the Arabic *quahweh,* which obliquely refers to wine, except that Muslims do not drink wine. In a sense, coffee is the wine of Islam.

There are many myths concerning the origins of coffee drinking and Arabic regulation of the market. It is difficult to separate fact from folklore, but they are good coffee stories. The primary port for coffee shipments was Mocha, in Yemen, which is why the word *mocha* often refers to coffee. To protect the monopoly, the Arabs required that all exported beans be heated long enough to destroy viability. Well, maybe. Coffee seeds are included in a group of tropical seeds called *recalcitrant,* meaning it is almost impossible to keep them viable for very long. If they dry out, get too cold, too hot, or just decide to die—they do. The more plausible story is that people who tried to smuggle coffee seeds could not get them to germinate. Anyhow, a Dutch merchant stole a small tree in 1616 and took it to the Amsterdam Botanical Gardens. Seeds from it were the origin of many tropical plantations. The seeds used to start Java plantations came from Malabar, India, but the original plants were from Yemen. The Dutch had the first large commercial plantings, grown in rich well-drained soils of lowland Java and Sumatra. Hardly any coffee is now grown in Java, and the key word is *lowlands*—there are disease problems. The French began growing coffee in the West Indies and the British in Ceylon and India.

After that, coffee became the social drink throughout Europe. In 1715 there were more than 2,000 coffee houses in London. There have been many religious prohibitions against coffee drinking. In Mecca it was used as part of religious rites; coffee was kept in large red vessels from which the worshipers would dip a cupful while chanting their prayers. When it began to be served in coffeehouses while the men were listening to music and watching dancing girls, religious leaders tried to have coffee banned for all but religious purposes. Italian priests tried to have Pope Clement (1592–1605) forbid coffee drinking by Christians because the Muslims used it to replace wine in their rituals. (It seems likely that they were also trying to protect the wine and beer industry.) Frederick the Great was opposed to the rise of coffeehouses in Germany, especially the practice of soldiers drinking coffee: real soldiers drink beer. In 1674 English women complained to King Charles II that, in times of crisis, their husbands would stop off at the coffeehouse rather than rushing home to share news with their wives. A more critical problem was the women's account that coffee made their husbands as "unfruitful as the deserts where that unhappy berry is said to be bought." In 1675 the king issued a Proclamation for the Suppression of Coffee Houses. The order was issued on Dec. 23, with all houses to be closed by Jan. 10, but the proclamation was rescinded on Jan. 8 because of "Princely consideration and royal compassion."

Voltaire drank great quantities of coffee—one report says 72 cups a day. When told that coffee was slowly poisoning his body, Voltaire said: "I think it must be, I've been drinking it for eighty-five years and am not dead yet." That is a pretty slow poison. Beethoven drank less coffee, but it was strong; he used eighty beans per cup.

An old Bourbon proverb says: "To an old man a cup of coffee is like the door post of an old house—it sustains and strengthens him."

Now, why did the British go from coffee drinking to tea sipping? Because of coffee leaf rust *(Hemileia vastatrix),* which wiped out large plantations of coffee growing in the lowland tropics. The whole story is more complicated, but that statement is an old standby for the introductory lecture of plant pathology courses. More realistically, *C. arabica* is grown primarily in the highlands because the fungus does not grow well in a cool climate; *C. liberica* flourishes in the lowlands.

Cultural practices for coffee production are rather dull. The plant is usually propagated by seeds, but there is an interesting aspect of rooted cuttings. Coffee has orthotropic and plagiotropic shoots. If you cut shoots that were growing upright (orthotropic), the rooted plant will grow upright. Do not root cuttings from lateral branches—you will get a low, spreading shrub. *Plagiotropic* means that it will not grow upright, and no one seems to know why. The fruit of the coffee plant is called a berry and the seed is called a bean, even though the berry is actually a drupe and the seed is not a bean. The pulp of coffee berry is pleasant tasting, rather sweet. A group of monkeys can eat a lot of coffee in a day, and the beans go right through them. In some areas "monkey coffee beans" are a delicacy; collect the droppings, wash the beans, and roast them. Harvesting by humans is more sanitary but very labor-intensive. Some varieties under the proper climatic conditions ripen rather uniformly but others must be harvested every other day.

Although there are about fifty species of coffee, for practical purposes coffee is *C. arabica.* The varieties *C. liberica* and *C. robusta* (a variant of *C. liberica*) are sometimes added in blends but the flavor is not very good. There are hundreds of *C. arabica* varieties (cultivars). Over the centuries selections have been made for variants that will grow well in a particular climate and have certain flavor characteristics. Besides that, small variations in climate affect the bean flavor for each variety. This is the primary reason for blends. For example, Community (the south Louisiana word for coffee) coffee was originally blended to give a certain characteristic flavor and taste. It is very important that the company maintain uniformity of flavor even though the varieties used for it vary with weather conditions during the particular crop year. So, with each new shipment the blender tastes a sample and devises slight variations in the blend to keep a standard "Community" taste.

Without going into great detail, there are three general types of coffee: mocha is the small, strong-flavored bean used for arabic coffee. Santos is the standard coffee of Brazil; the man who introduced large-scale coffee production into Brazil named the selection Santos because that was his wife's maiden

A Tale of Prospecting for Gold

We try to believe that all plant processes have a purpose, or possibly had some purpose in the distant past. We try, but are not very successful. Don't get excited over this coffee tale; it belongs to the theater of the absurd, botanical section.

There is a desert plant, *Phacelia sericea,* which accumulates gold in its leaves. It is one of 200 species of *Phacelia,* some of which are used as ornamentals in areas where the climate is cool and not too wet. *P. sericea* releases free cyanide from its roots, which reacts with gold in the soil, producing a soluble gold-cyanide compound. This is taken up selectively by the roots and translocated to the leaves. Gold, in its ionic form, is extremely toxic to plant tissue but it is stored in the leaves as an inactive gold-cyanide complex.

This is not the commercial source for gold leaf. We can see no reason why such a mechanism would give this plant a competitive advantage, and accept the possibility that it has no meaning at all. But it is worth a cup of coffee.

name (maybe he was using her money). Java is the line selected by the Dutch, but it is now grown in many highland areas.

We are walking on thin ice to tell you about coffee making but will do it anyhow. Starting with the way it was made in the old country, arabic coffee is made by pounding the freshly roasted beans to a powder and pouring boiling water over the powder. The English method is to take finely ground coffee, add it to boiling water, and let it boil for a while. The old U.S. Army method was a slight variant: boil a garbage can full of water (with just a twist of iodine added for flavor), dump in a few scoops of coffee, and let the grounds settle out. An old army ditty said: "The coffee that they give you, they say is mighty fine, it's good for cuts and bruises, and tastes like iodine!" The old Dutch method (it probably is not used anymore because it takes so much coffee) was to pack ground coffee in what is now called a drip coffee pot and let cold water drip through it very slowly. After dripping, the coffee was heated to the right temperature.

Then there is the right way to make coffee: French drip. Ground coffee is placed in the upper part of a drip coffee pot and boiling water is added over the coffee one tablespoonful at a time. It takes forever but you end up with a good cup of coffee. *The Southern Agriculturist* is a journal that used to engage readers in a wide range of topics. Back a long time ago, maybe in 1830, there was an article about the proper way to make French drip coffee. One authority said that you should moisten fresh grounds and leave them in a cool place overnight. The next morning you should slowly drip boiling water over the grounds. You should save the old grounds and, the next morning, add them to the water that will be boiled for dripping over new grounds. The French got every last bit of flavor from coffee.

The current electric coffee makers are a poor imitation of the real thing. Boiling water is poured over the grounds, but much too fast. That could be corrected by letting the hot water drip over the grounds rather than gushing. If you hunt around, you can find a maker on which the flow of water can be adjusted, but they cost more. The going-out-of-style pump percolators are not quite French drip because the weak coffee that runs through the grounds first is boiled and run back over.

Back in the days beyond recall, New Orleans grocery stores roasted coffee beans every day. This was partly for convenience and partly because the aroma attracted a lot of customers. Home roasting is an art, but freshly roasted and freshly ground coffee tastes wonderful. You can do a fair job with a heavy, covered frying pan, shaking it occasionally for even heating. Try to keep the temperature at around 400°F. and roast to a medium-brown color. A well-roasted bean cracks easily.

You probably will not roast your own coffee very often, but a small coffee grinder helps in making a good cup of coffee. You may have to hunt a bit to find one but they are not expensive, much cheaper than an electric coffee maker. Although large grinders have adjustments for the type of grind, these small ones are regulated by the length of grinding time. Guessing at the fineness is an art, but it is also a matter of preference. You can buy excellent coffee bean blends and keep them frozen, taking out just enough to grind for one good pot of coffee.

Will used coffee grounds make the soil acid? Probably not, but they should make a good mulch or addition to the compost. The brewing process extracts very little protein, and grounds contain around 11 percent protein. Leon's lecture notes said that people on the Ile de Groix (off the coast of French Brittany) use roasted coffee beans as a food. Leon asked a friend who lives near the island to get some details on it. Unfortunately, nobody on the island had heard of that. Then Leon asked his food technology friend about the nutritional value of coffee beans: almost nil. The roasting process makes the proteins indigestible. Well, it made a good story.

This may surprise you, but we have run out of ideas. The hour is late and the coffee pot is empty.

Appendix A

CALENDAR

Things to Look Forward To and a Few to Dread

This is our approach to the calendar that every gardening book must have. We began by writing up a checklist of things to do each month; it was boring and looked like a list of chores. Gardening should not be a chore; it is a hobby. The calendar should be a list of things you can do, and some you ought to postpone until next month. It may take a little imagination to convert chores into opportunities, but gardening builds character. Sometimes we repeat points that we made throughout the book; in that sense, maybe this calender is a reminder list.

The better gardening columns in magazines often feature a "pest of the month" in which the writer describes a pest (weed, disease, or insect) in great detail and gives some control measures. We feature a "hassle of the month," which may or may not be a pest.

We favor sanitation over chemical control, partly because the list of labeled chemicals seems to be declining each year. This does not mean that we will not suggest some chemicals; when sanitation fails, do what you must.

This is a pretty good summary of what you can expect to happen in the yard. The timing of these gardening opportunities varies from extremely southerly to more northerly areas, but not enough to lessen usefulness. We suggest that you begin each month by reading our ideas of things to do and to watch for. Then make a list of what you really want to do and a few chores that should be done if you feel like it. Stick that list on the refrigerator door so you will feel guilty every time you look in for a snack.

January

January and February are cold, dreary months, and it is sometimes difficult to find fun jobs. Statistically, you can expect a short (ten-day) dry spell in January. You can hope, but do not depend on it. If the ground is fairly dry, this is a good time for transplanting; if it is wet, you can do some pruning. Some seeds can be planted in the ground and others can be started in protected places for later transplanting. Days are short and many are cloudy, so make an effort to give seedlings as much light as possible to keep them from getting spindly. Annual ornamental seeds that may be planted now include achillea; alyssum; begonia; calendula; dahlia; dianthus; geranium; hibiscus; impatiens; lisianthus; lobelia; marigold; nicotiana; nierembergia; ornamental pepper; petunia; phlox; salvia; torenia; and verbena. Keep them in areas protected from cold and rain until transplanting time. Some annuals are in bloom from plantings you made last year: pansy, calendula, dianthus, alyssum, and ornamental cabbage and kale (the colored leaves on these make an ornamental display). This is a good time to trim some perennials for better appearance or size control: liriope or monkey grass and Asian jasmine, for example. Consider giving your daylilies a granular systemic insecticide application for control of aphids that are hiding down in the unfolded leaves. You cannot see them now but as the new leaves emerge, the newly shed skins will show that aphids are getting bigger and happier at the expense of plant vigor.

Tulip and hyacinth bulbs that have been chilled for at least eight weeks near 40°F can be planted into prepared areas. This depends partly on the ground temperature. If it is much above 40°F for very long, the chilling effect will be nullified and the flowers either abort or bloom on very short stems down in the leaves.

A few shrubs are in bloom, though occasional freezes may keep them nipped back. Camellias, flowering quince, and sweet olive may flower. Some people used gibberellic acid on camellias in November to encourage earlier bloom that escapes freezes and much of the petal blight that attacks camellias later in the season.

Watch your lawn for signs of brown patch or dollar spot diseases, which should be treated with a good fungicide.

Vegetable gardeners might plant seeds of broccoli, cabbage, cauliflower, Chinese cabbage, lettuce, and tomato in protected places for later transplanting. This is a good time to plant Irish potato seed pieces if the weather allows it—and if the soil is not too wet. If you get that January dry spell, plant seeds of beet; carrot; radish; turnip; mustard; collards; kale; spinach; and English peas. Consider trying the edible pod peas; if we have a cool spring they may make enough pods to justify the effort. Some vegetables from plantings in the fall may be ready to harvest now, such as cabbage, collards, carrot, mustard, turnips, spinach, parsley, and brussels sprouts—the no-nonsense winter vegetables.

Most fruit trees are dormant, but these can benefit from pruning and fertilizer applications later in the month. If you notice scale insects, this is a good time to use dormant oil sprays.

Taiwan cherries may bloom this month in response to warm spells, and the earliest azaleas sometimes make a show. Oriental magnolias often bloom, freeze, and bloom again. It is encouraging to see such springtime optimism in a plant.

JANUARY HASSLES

Main hassle: day after day of cold drizzles with the ground too wet to work. Look for aphids on new shoots of calendulas, sweet pea, and daylily and for scale insects on camellia, holly, plums, peaches, and magnolia. In the cold wet soil look for damping-off of new seedlings. Damping-off is a generic term: several fungi can cause it but a single fungicide treatment will help.

February

Winter is beginning to break a little and you can take on the pruning, transplanting, and planting jobs that you postponed from last month. Because the weather will set your schedule there is no rigid calendar for many of the jobs. Some are keyed to the stage of growth of the plants, which is also partly dictated by weather. This is a good month to apply fertilizer to most trees and shrubs, but it is too early for lawns. Planting times are much more flexible today than in the old days when we used bare-rooted plants. Just keep in mind that with container-grown plants any disturbance of the root system causes a lessening of water uptake for a while. Reducing the top growth and taking care to lessen water loss from the plant is important until new roots form.

Alyssum, pansy, pinks, and calendula are beginning to look good. The ornamental cabbage and kale can be very pretty if the weather stays cold. If it warms up, they will turn green again. As last month, annual seeds can be planted in protected locations for transplanting later. They include about the same kinds: ageratum, abelmoschus, alyssum, coleus, cosmos, begonia, hibiscus, impatiens, larkspur (which reseed themselves in most gardens), lisianthus, marigold, nicotiana, pepper, petunia, phlox, rudbeckia, salvia, vinca, torenia, and zinnia. Nasturtiums should be direct-seeded in the ground.

Perennials such as gerbera daisy and violets will start blooming. Sometime this month you can start planting gladiolus corms at weekly intervals to get an extended blooming period in the spring. A good rule of thumb is to watch for the first signs of growth in native trees (maple or cypress)—that is the beginning of glad-planting time. Tulip and hyacinth bulbs that were precooled can be planted now and should bloom before the weather gets too warm. Some narcissus and daffodils are blooming, along with galanthus, leucojum, anemones, and ranunculus. Lily bulbs that were left in the ground may show new shoots emerging.

Most varieties of camellias are still blooming, and azaleas come in strongly. If January was very cold, there may be late Taiwan cherries blooming, and forsythia in cooler areas will be popping out. Roses should be planted now, and those in the beds need pruning. Fertilize shrubs if you did not get the job done last month.

Oriental magnolias continue to bloom, and redbuds start along with flowering quince. The Carolina jessamine vines bloom golden yellow.

If the lawn has many broad-leaf weeds, you may want to apply the proper herbicide for control. Be sure to follow instructions to avoid injury to other plants.

Vegetable gardeners can still plant, in protected places, seed of basil, broccoli, cauliflower, dill, eggplant, lettuce, and tomato. In the ground they can plant bush snap beans, carrots, sweet corn (at two-week intervals, but to ensure pollination do so in blocks of several rows rather than long single rows), lettuce, mustard, parsley, radish, shallots, spinach, and Irish potato (if January was too wet). Transplants of broccoli, lettuce, shallots, and English peas can give a jump on the season. Harvests can be made of anise, cabbage, carrot, collard, endive, leek, mustard, parsley, shallots, and spinach, all from last year's plantings.

If you postponed pruning of fruit plants last month, that and fertilization have become "gottas." Late in the month mayhaws may bloom. If a large bloom results in very few fruits for you and the birds and squirrels, the problem is either frost damage (which can occur when the air temperature is well above freezing), or a lack of pollination, or both. Some fruit trees require cross pollination or simply do not produce enough pollen. Here is a trick that sometimes helps. Arrange to get a bouquet of blooms from another tree (that does set fruit) and place these in a container of water tied up in your tree when it is in bloom. If fruits set near the bouquet, you can tell that your tree needs another nearby for pollination. Try grafting a few branches of the other kind into the same tree if space is a problem.

February Hassles

Bad news for February sometimes involves petal blight on azaleas and camellias (from different organisms, but with the same dismal results). Spectacular displays of azaleas can, in a single day, look like they have been scalded with hot water, and camellias may become blotched with ugly brown spots. This is a difficult problem for individual gardeners to combat, and really takes the efforts of whole neighborhoods, because the spores that infest the flowers are airborne and travel from overwintering locations to other plants. The resting stages of the fungi overwinter on the old flowers under the plants; if possible, rake up and remove the old flowers. You may decide to cover them with fresh mulch. There are some materials that may be applied to the ground and others to the opening flowers but, without a community effort, they may not have much effect.

In the vegetables look for downy mildew on cabbage and related plants. Mole crickets can be a nuisance.

March

This is a busy and fun month in the garden. More competitive vegetable gardeners will be planting tomatoes outdoors (prepared to protect them from cold weather, of course). If the weather allows transplanting of vegetable and ornamental plants into the ground, they will need some side-dressing of fertilizer within three or four weeks, assuming they were watered in with a little starter fertilizer solution at transplanting. If the soil is light-textured, and you get a lot of rain, more frequent applications of fertilizer are in order than will be the case with heavier soils or less rain. In general, a light application every three to six weeks during the season should be adequate.

Annual beds should be pretty now with alyssum, centaurea, calendula, pinks, myosotis, bellis, geranium, viola, lobelia, nasturtium, pansy, petunia, phlox, poppy, snapdragon, sweetpea, Sweet William, and verbena giving you a wide choice. Take advantage of this because the hot summer cometh, when only a few heat-resistant standbys will survive. It is time to seed those hot summer plants: abelmoschus, ageratum, amaranth, celosia, cosmos, gomphrena, hibiscus, marigold, thunbergia, vinca, and zinnia. (Be sure to treat your zinnia seed with dilute bleach solution, one part in four parts of water for thirty minutes, air-dry, and plant—this will greatly lessen two important seed-borne diseases.)

Perennials now blooming include coreopsis, gaillardia, gerbera, Louisiana phlox, stokesia, and verbena. Some begonias will have overwintered in an "average" winter and will bloom this early.

You may want to continue weekly gladiolus plantings through March. Blooms will be spectacular on amaryllis, and the St. Joseph's lily *(amaryllis x Johnsonii)* will make its regular show in mid-March. Anemones and ranunculus will bloom until it gets warm, and tulips, hyacinths, narcissus, daffodils, bulbous iris, and some German iris bloom this month. The big *Iris pseudacorus* makes its yellow blooms this month. It is so well adapted that many people think this is a native plant rather than introduced; others are beginning to think it is a weed of iris plantings.

Azaleas can peak this month, whereas most camellias are finished. Forsythia, raphiolepis, spiraea, banana shrub, philadelphus, and the "Summer Snow" rose are beautiful. Climbing roses should be pruned after the first big bloom is over. All spring-flowering shrubs need pruning as soon as possible after bloom so the new growth will have a chance to store up food resources for initiating next season's bloom.

Live oak trees have dropped many older leaves and are shining light green with the new leaves. Redbud, dogwood, and some oriental magnolias bloom, and many shade trees as well—to the dismay of allergy sufferers. Some of these trees also present a problem with staining of automobile finishes and almost anything else they touch, especially in the frequent March rains. At their peak, the oak blossoms may actually stop up storm drains.

Carolina jessamine covers many rural mailboxes and fences with golden flowers. If the winter was cold enough, the primrose jasmine will be beautiful with its golden blooms. Wisteria flowers appear in many trees where the vines have climbed, and the Lady Banks roses can take your breath away for the brief time they bloom. Honeysuckle may get your attention with its fragrance as you drive along before you even see it. Stop for a minute, turn off the engine, and listen to the bees humming.

Restrain yourself: it is still too early to "green up" the lawn with fertilizer. If you must read the garden center ads telling what good bargains they are offering, buy the fertilizer and store it. Continue to watch for brown patch or dollar spot.

Vegetable gardeners, it is not too late to seed (in protected spots) basil, cantaloupe, corn, cucumbers, lettuce, okra (transplanting okra is tricky, though), real peas, pepper (bell and hot), pumpkin, squash, and watermelon. Irish potatoes could still be planted before mid-March, but that is stretching it a little. Earlier seeded plants of cantaloupe, cucumber, and tomato can be set out. Toward the end of the month you may decide to put out eggplant and pepper plants, but not if it is cool.

Harvest can continue from the plants seeded last year of carrot, collard, leek, lettuce, onions, mustard, parsley, English peas, radish, shallots, spinach, and turnip.

Peaches and plums may begin to bloom. At petal fall and "shuck" fall, apply sprays for control of curculio (various types of weevils) to avoid wormy fruit. Pecans will begin shoot growth, and if phylloxera is to be controlled, sprays must begin when the shoots are only about half an inch long. The best approach is to hope phylloxera will not be very bad this year. Strawberries will be giving good harvests now, and weekly applications of dilute fertilizer to the foliage will help if they seem to lack vigor.

March Hassles

Keep watching for scale insects. Mole crickets and cutworms get bad on vegetable transplants. Start your annual fight against black spot on roses. Watch for fire blight on pear flowers—not that you can do anything about it except watch. If you have a resistant variety, the blight will affect only the flowers.

April

Spring is here and the sound of lawn mowers is heard throughout the land. The weather is still a bit cool for grass growth but mowing will keep winter weeds from producing seeds. Annuals are still showy, but many shrubs begin to bloom as well.

Annual beds will have blooming ageratum, amaranth, begonia, celosia, columbine, cosmos, pinks, digitalis, geranium, hollyhock, impatiens, larkspur, lisianthus, marigold, nicotiana, pentas, vinca, phlox, salvia, snapdragon, helichrysum, sweet pea, and zinnia. Poppies may have reseeded to make a good show. You can still seed or transplant abelmoschus, amaranth, balsam (it is good at reseeding), celosia, cleome, cosmos, four o'clock, gomphrena, mallow, vinca, and zinnia. Collect seeds of Taiwan cherry as they fall to the ground. Seed them in flats immediately and a few will germinate. The others will require cold treatment, but that is not necessary if you only want a few plants. Perennials in bloom include echinacea, hosta, Louisiana phlox, blue salvia, stokesia, gerbera, gaillardia, daisy, and verbena.

Blooming bulbous, or bulblike, plants include amaryllis, anemone, gladiolus, early zephyranthes, ornithogallum, triteleia uniflora (this is pretty as a border and will send seedlings blooming out into the spring lawn), bulbous iris, Louisiana iris, lilies, crinum, and daylily.

Caladium tubers may be planted now. They should have shoots emerging.

Shrubs blooming are azalea, bottlebrush, clethra, pineapple and strawberry guava, elaeagnus, hawthorn, raphiolepis, philadelphus, pomegranate, pyracantha, and roses. Tropical plants may be moved out with care. Do not expose them to bright sun. Spraying for black spot on roses needs to be done regularly, and you should watch for whitefly on gardenia and ligustrum. Spray if necessary.

Silver-bell trees and other natives, such as fringe tree and smoke tree are in bloom, and early magnolia grandiflora blooms appear.

Blooms begin on Confederate jasmine vines and clematis, and honeysuckle continues to bloom.

At last you can fertilize the lawn, if you really want to. A well-fertilized lawn is beautiful and requires more frequent mowing throughout the hot summer, but you will probably decide to do it. A fertilizer higher in nitrogen than in phosphorus or potassium is best; there are many "lawn fertilizers" marketed but the standard 8-8-8 will do. On St. Augustine grass, apply about a pound of nitrogen per 1,000 square feet every two or three weeks, aiming at a total of about three to six pounds in all. Do the same with centipede but cut the total to about two and a half pounds per 1,000 square feet. You should make another application late in summer. When starting to mow, do not remove more than about one-third of the grass blades and mow often enough so that this will result from the height setting chosen. It is not necessary to remove clippings. Your neighbors will argue that the clippings are unsightly and cause serious thatch problems: They are; but no, they do not.

Vegetable gardeners do not have to stop planting yet—they can still seed butter beans, pole beans, cantaloupe, cucumber, okra, real peas, peppers, pumpkins, and watermelons. Transplant sweet potato slips. Harvesting of broccoli, carrot, lettuce, parsley, English peas, potatoes, shallots, and spinach is possible if planting was done on time.

Strawberry harvest continues; the berries will be smaller and sweeter. Longer days and hot weather will make the plants start to produce runners later on. Continue to spray peaches and plums for curculio control and pears for control of leaf spot. Figs should be sprayed with a fixed copper material (which you can purchase at the garden center) for control of rust.

Mayhaws will be ripening in southerly areas in May farther north. Many fruits may be misshapen due to cedar rust, and squirrels compete strongly with your efforts to harvest enough fruit for jelly. Wild plantings still exist in some areas, and in some the spring high water floods the trees, allowing floating fruit to be scooped up with nets, which is a lot easier than picking. Early blackberries ripen starting this month, and the mockingbirds believe all blackberries belong to them. They can help by driving off other birds, a small price to pay for the fruits they eat.

April Hassles

The primary hassle is not a pest, but the rain. When the ground is about dry enough to plant, the TV weather forecaster says a real "frog strangler" is coming in. If you plant the beans and a heavy rain packs the surface, the seeds will rot—no oxygen. If you wait, it will be at least a week before the ground dries again.

You eager-beaver gardeners who wanted to have the earliest tomatoes may have beautiful plants with healthy, dark green leaves and thick stems. But did you read the fertilizer chapter about the effects of too much nitrogen? If you skipped that chapter, quit adding fertilizer or that nice rich compost and the plants eventually will bloom.

The pest problems are about like those of March: mole crickets, cutworms, and black spot. Cabbage loopers may be a bother. Watch for brown patch on lawns.

May

Summer is beginning and we will probably have a few dry spells. Water the plants well, especially if April was a wet month. Remember our discussion about soil oxygen and active roots. Hot weather will begin to take a toll on the cool-season flowering plants, and pansies will have to make room for things that can stand the heat. Larkspurs will be dropping seed for next year's crop, along with poppies. Lots of blooms will be seen on ageratum, balsam, celosia, cosmos, gomphrena, impatiens, marigold, nicotiana, pentas, purslane, salvia, portulaca, verbena, and zinnia. Heat tolerant perennials include coreopsis, daylily, echinacea, gaillardia, hibiscus, lantana, summer phlox, rudbeckia, blue salvia, stokesia, and verbena. Gerbera may oversummer, but hot weather will stop most of them from flowering. Daylilies continue to flower, along with agapanthus, habranthus, brodiaea, and zephyranthes. Foliage will be dying back on many of the narcissus and daffodils, and it is important to leave the foliage on until it is brown so that food is stored in the bulb for next year's growth.

Some late azaleas, such as Gumpos, will bloom. Gardenias, hydrangeas, oleander, plumbago, and roses make a good show. Confederate jasmine blooms if it has been allowed to climb. Some clematis can be spectacular in May, others earlier and later. Magnolia trees may have some flowers opening, but they will soon start to drop older leaves. These are quite leathery and durable. This is a natural process, but your new neighbor will wonder if the trees are dying. Tell him to quit worrying.

Lawns will need to be watered in dry spells, and this means letting sprinklers run for at least one hour at one location—shallower wetting means shallower roots and later grief.

Vegetable gardeners can still seed lima beans, pole snap beans, cantaloupe, okra, peas, pumpkin, and watermelon, but the list is getting much smaller. Eggplants may be transplanted now along with pepper plants and sweet potato slips. Harvests can continue from beans, carrot, corn, cucumber, garlic, onion, potato, shallots, and squash. Those intrepid souls who protected their early plants may have ripe tomatoes.

Blackberries continue to ripen, the trailing types first, followed by the more erect kinds. As soon as all fruit is gone, remove the canes (branches) that bore fruit—these grow one year, fruit the next, then die. When the new shoots reach about five feet in height, pinch out the tips to encourage branching. Next winter prune these laterals back to about twelve inches—this makes them much easier to handle and harvest later on.

Blueberries start later in the month, and a covering with bird netting has remarkable effects on the volume of fruit left for us. Let the berries get fully ripe on the plant, as they do not increase in sweetness when picked. Fig trees need to be watered in dry spells, and deep mulches help. The dry weather in late May and early June causes figs to drop off in late June and early July, but by then it is rainy and we forget that we had dry weather only a few weeks earlier. Native black cherry trees ripen fruit this month. The fruit can be shaken off onto sheets or plastic for making cherry bounce or jelly.

In the upper United States (anywhere north of Memphis) fruit trees have a "June drop." We use the same term here even though it may occur in some areas in April. This is nature's way of thinning the crop, but sometimes Mother Nature is less than effective. You may want to do even more thinning for good size and quality on many fruits, especially peaches. Work toward having the immature fruit at least eight inches apart.

May Hassles

Everything begins to go wrong. The big, ugly caterpillars come out on the trees. Watch for chinch bugs in St. Augustine grass during dry spells, and you might want to spread some insecticide granules. There is a sooty mold on pine needles. You could spray if the tree is not too large. The pine tip moth kills back growing shoots (spruce pine seems to be resistant); you could spray but the tree will recover anyhow. Watch for powdery mildew on roses and chrysanthemum leaf spot; spray for these. You might get algal spot on camellia, magnolia, and osmanthus. Cabbage loopers are all over the vegetable garden. Colaspis beetles may start killing pine needles. The trees will be weakened but probably will not die. Fire ants began swarming last month and you will see new mounds in the flower beds and lawn. They are rather easy to control with insecticide granules, if you decide to do it. Corn ear worm is in the sweet corn and leaf miners are on tomatoes and cucumbers. Have a nice day!

June

This is usually a rather dry month, but you should not count on it. High temperatures are a certainty. Many cool weather annuals are finished now, and the summer standbys become important. Color also comes from caladiums, coleus, crotons, and other tropical plants that were overwintered or you purchased only for summer enjoyment. Some annuals may be seeded this late, including amaranth, cosmos, marigolds, and zinnias. Impatiens and begonias should be outstanding in open shade or locations with morning sun. Hibiscus, Mexican heather, ixora, copper plants, and jacobinia are among perennials that are excellent summer performers. Bulbous plants fill in some garden areas nicely in the summer heat, including the caladiums, agapanthus, calla, canna, dahlia, hymenocallis, Philippine lily, montbretia, gladiolus, habranthus, zephyranthes, and crinums.

Crape myrtles are near their peak; altheas, hydrangeas, oleanders, vitex, and brunfelsia all are blooming. Magnolias continue to shine, and our few surviving mimosas will be flowering. Vines make a show, including allamanda, honeysuckle, mandevilla, passionflower, morning glory, and thunbergias of several kinds. The lawn will need regular mowing, of course, and when dry will need those regular soakings on a five- or seven-day schedule.

Fall tomatoes may be seeded in June or July, preferably July. The spring tomatoes begin to play out in June because heat prevents the flowers from setting fruit. Breeders keep working for heat-resistant varieties, and they are making progress. Maybe you will soon be able to keep those vine-ripe tomatoes coming all summer. Sweet potato slips may still be transplanted, and you can expect harvests from butter beans until the temperature gets up in the 90's regularly; then the flowers will drop from all beans. Until then you can pick snap beans, cantaloupe, corn, cucumber, eggplants, peas, okra, peppers, watermelons, and squash, and you can harvest some of the spring-planted potatoes.

Blueberries peak this month, peaches and plums ripen, and figs begin late this month or early next. Unless you use netting, birds and squirrels will get most of them. Keep all of the fruit watered.

June Hassles

These are about the same as May. It is raining a bit more and summer is setting in. The stinging caterpillars are almost gone.

July

Back in Iowa you began to get cabin fever in January, wondering why you chose to live in such a cold place. July and August are the months of our discontent. Why did you ever decide to take up gardening as a hobby? Work early in the morning or in late afternoons. The hazards of heat stroke are real.

You will be surprised at the array of annuals that continue blooming if you took care of them: abelmoschus, ageratum, amaranth, balsam, begonia, celosia, cleome, coleus, cosmos, geranium, gomphrena, hibiscus, impatiens, marigold, pentas, peppers, periwinkle (vinca), purslane, salvia, torenia, and zinnia. A lot of perennials bloom in midsummer, including datura, coreopsis, echinacea, gaillardia, hibiscus, jacobinia, lantana, lisianthus, phlox, rudbeckia, verbena, stokesia, Confederate rose, and duranta. Also blooming now is a newcomer in the past year or two, evolvulus, called Blue Daze, a greyish green, small-leaved shrub with one-inch sky blue flowers. It is rather cold tender but can be overwintered.

Habranthus and zephyranthes continue to bloom, and gingers of several kinds begin to make a spectacular show—some are strongly perfumed. Hymenocallis, crinum, agapanthus, gladiolus, montbretia, achimenes, and canna add to the bulb list.

Altheas, crape myrtles, oleander, and abelia are blooming shrubs for hot summer. Vines come on strong, including allamanda, bougainvillea, cypress vine, Mexican flame vine, Rangoon creeper, butterfly vine, rose of Montana, honeysuckle, moonflower vine, morning glory, passionflower, and gloriosa lily.

Chinch bug attacks are worse on drought-stressed grass, so keep the lawn watered. You may want to make a second application of fertilizer in late July, with no more than half a pound of nitrogen in mixed fertilizer per 1,000 square feet on St. Augustine and centipede grasses. In the more northerly areas, it might be better to omit the nitrogen and apply only potassium, one to two pounds per 1,000 square feet; use potassium chloride. Nitrogen might promote active growth in early winter.

Now is the time to prepare your fall vegetable garden. Turn under old plant materials for decomposing and make plans to rotate crops to different beds from those they occupied in spring. Tomato seeds may be planted in early July, in the ground or in peat pots for transplanting in late July or early August. Most vegetables for the fall garden will be direct-seeded in the ground. Okra,

English peas, and collards might be seeded in early July. Later on, from mid- to late July, seed broccoli, brussels sprouts, cauliflower, Chinese cabbage, and bell peppers. Eggplants may be left from the spring plantings. If the plants still look good, they will begin to set fruit as the weather begins to cool. You may still be able to harvest butter beans, pole beans, cantaloupes, corn, cucumbers, peas, okra, peppers, eggplants, squash, and watermelons.

Figs reach peak yields near July 4; if rains start, the fruits split and turn sour. You can avoid this a bit by watering the trees during dry spells. Peaches and plums need spraying for control of borers, and the figs trees can benefit from spraying trunks and branches for control of borers that might attack them. Some varieties of blueberries continue to ripen through July.

July Hassles

Sod webworm can be bad in the turf. As you walk over the grass, small light-colored moths will fly up. You can apply a granular insecticide. Look for borers on tree trunks. Sooty mold from crape myrtle will fall on anything you leave under the tree. Pecan aphids cause the same problem. Stink bugs may invade the vegetable garden, producing misshapen beans, peas, and okra pods. Squash vine borer will cause vines to collapse.

August

Hang in there, the nights will start cooling off in September. Watering becomes critical in this hot weather because the effects of a good rain last only a few days. Mulching helps reduce the number of times you need to water. You probably dream about how nice it would be to have some kind of irrigation system in the garden, and even in the lawn as well. People usually forget about irrigation systems when September rains start. You can obtain information and assistance from the dependable extension service—the county agent's office.

Gardeners who grew up in this area, or who have been here for a few years, know what to expect in the late summer garden. There are old standbys that have provided good reliable color every year—vinca is probably the most popular hot weather annual, based on sales at nursery outlets, but advances in impatiens breeding in recent years have resulted in long-lasting kinds with the toughness needed to persist through our summers. Zinnias used to be more common than in recent years, and this is largely due to the presence of seed-borne diseases. The treatment of seed before planting can largely eliminate these diseases and allow you to grow good zinnias again. Salvia can be really outstanding in the heat. There are a number of kinds in different sizes and colors, including white, pink, and purple as well as blue among the annual kinds. There are also perennial salvias with blue flowers. A recent introduction to our hot weather spectrum is abelmoschus, called silk flower—the same genus as okra and related to hibiscus. It makes lots of mostly red or pink flowers on plants that get about two feet tall. The plants are not the most attractive things, but any dependable bloomers are welcome in the late summer. The same can be said for many of the heat-tolerant perennials, such as the echinaceas and rudbeckias that stay with us through the summer. Some of the cool-season ornamentals should be seeded in August, including pansies, alyssum, flowering cabbage and kale, calendula, dianthus, hollyhock, lobelia, petunia, and verbena. Keep the seed flats or pots where they will get good light without direct sunlight, as this will produce stocky seedlings.

This month is a good time to divide and transplant Louisiana iris, daylilies, and bulbs on which the foliage has died back. Caladiums may be getting tired now, and if the leaves are starting to die back it is a good time to dig up the tubers. Let the leaves dry completely in the shade, then clean off the old leaves and adhering roots and soil. Place the tubers in a dry, fairly cool place. They must be kept warm in winter; do not forget about them when the temperatures drop below 50°F—this is critical. Lycoris bulbs (red spider or hurricane lilies) may start to send up flower buds in response to late August rains. Thrips sometimes attack lycoris, causing the flowers to appear misshapen and streaked with white. If you see any evidence of thrips, carefully drench the clumps of bulbs with an insecticide.

Some shrubs continue to flower sporadically, such as crape myrtles, altheas, Confederate rose, and datura. Roses should be pruned in late August or early September. Remove old or weak shoots and prune the remaining shoots to twenty-four to thirty inches in length. An application of a soluble nitrogen fertilizer, such as sodium nitrate at the rate of one or two ounces per plant is a good idea. Continue spray programs for black spot control, and irrigate when needed. The summer-blooming vines continue to flower, and lawns continue to need mowing. Will fall never come?

This is a good month for vegetable gardeners to plant a wide range of crops. Tomatoes and bell peppers that were seeded earlier may be transplanted into the ground in early August, and among direct-seeded crops are broccoli, brussels sprouts, cauliflower, collards, Chinese cabbage, mustard, turnips, squash, cucumbers, lima beans, shallots, and English peas. In late August or early September you may want to seed carrots, beets, snap beans, and lettuce. Irish potatoes may be planted in late August. Use small whole potatoes instead of the cut seed pieces used in early spring; this reduces disease problems. Insect problems may be more severe on some crops than in the spring due to a buildup of populations over summer. Be alert for squash vine borers, and loopers on all the cabbage-related crops. Bean beetles may be bad enough to justify spraying beans and peas. Various kinds of stink bugs seem to be a regular summer occurrence. Consult your insect control guide information for methods of control. Do not forget to rotate crops as much as possible to avoid planting into the same areas where spring crops were grown. This holds down insect and pathogen populations.

Muscadine grapes begin to ripen this month and continue into October. A few pears may ripen enough to be removed from the trees and allowed to continue ripening in cooler places—ideally around 65°F. This greatly increases the quality and reduces the amount of grit cells in the fruit. When pears are full size, and the green "ground color" begins to fade to yellow-green, it is the time to start to harvest them. Others may be left on the tree for later harvest.

August Hassles

The long hot summer syndrome: it is so hot that little piddling things get to you. There are lace bugs on the azaleas and white fly on citrus, ligustrum, and gardenia. They probably are not bad enough to hurt much but it will help to spray. There are English ivy blight, cabbage loopers, and onion thrips. Make a pitcher of lemonade.

September

We should get at least a hint of cooler weather this month, but it is accompanied by the possibility of hurricanes. With the cooler air (if it comes) the annual beds seem to revive and take on better color; marigolds will look much better. If you have carried over chrysanthemum plants through the summer, the earlier ones will start to flower. Lycoris flowers pop up, sometimes in unexpected places.

If you have not seeded the cool weather annuals in August, get with it. They should be planted out in October for bloom all winter. Our same heat-resistant flowering plants continue to bloom and, like the marigolds, will become prettier with cooler weather. The day length shortens, affecting some plants, whereas others are not sensitive to it. You may notice reseeded celosia plants blooming when they are only a couple of inches tall; this is because of the shorter days. If your chrysanthemum plants are located where security lights shine on them at night, they will be much taller and later to bloom than those that get long, uninterrupted nights.

Bulb catalogs should have arrived along with seed catalogs, and it is a good time to order spring-flowering bulbs. If you plan to bed out tulips or hyacinths, ask for delivery in November so you can chill them near 40°F until planting in mid-January.

Some early *Camellia sasanqua* will start to bloom, and you may want to try a few *Camellia japonica* flowers with gibberellic acid treatments this year; now is the time to do it. Golden rain trees, if they survived last year's freezes, will bloom. The vines continue to flower, and butterfly vine starts to make the seed pods that look like tan butterflies.

Avoid applying nitrogen to lawns, because you want the grass to be lean and mean for early cold weather. Continue to watch for and treat any areas with chinch bug or brown patch. If you want to overseed with annual ryegrass for a green winter lawn, this is a good month to do it. Be very sure that you want to mow grass year-round.

Vegetable gardeners who were on vacation during August still have time to get in some crops for the remaining cool weather of fall and some that will overwinter. It is not too late for transplants of broccoli, brussels sprouts, cabbage, cauliflower, Chinese cabbage, collards, tomato and direct-seeded beets, carrot, endive, English peas, garlic, kohlrabi, lettuce, mustard, onions, parsley, radish, rutabaga, shallot, spinach, swiss chard, turnip, and kale. Harvests can be expected from butter beans once the heat stops making the blooms drop off. You can be harvesting snap beans, eggplant, okra, peas, peppers, and sweet potatoes.

Muscadines are at peak production this month, as are many fire blight-resistant pears. Where apples can be grown, they will be ripening. (This may be a little late. Ed sometimes forgets that he isn't at Cornell.) Continue with sprays for borer control on the stone fruit trunks and branches as well as on fig trees.

September Hassles

These are about the same as August, but a little worse. There are leaf miners, loopers, and brown patch on the lawn. Look for fairy rings in the lawn and tell your children that fairies did it. The fungus does not hurt much but you may want to cut the mushrooms and throw them away (do not try eating them). Exorcism might drive the fairies away. There are squash bugs and stink bugs. The roses have mites, and a new kind of caterpillar is in the trees. Nothing very bad is happening except that it may be raining a lot.

October

The cool dry weather is almost as welcome as an early spring. Some gardeners go through a summer dormancy—they have not worked in the yard since June. The tough ones who hung in through the heat can actually enjoy the work rather than only pretending that they do. Because it is often dry, watering is important, and once in a while we get early freezing weather; plants that are well-watered survive much better. The prominent plants in landscapes are probably chrysanthemums, which come in such a variety of forms and colors as well as sizes that it is sometimes difficult to recognize that they really are mums. Roses are usually very pretty this month. Cagey rose enthusiasts often try to influence their garden clubs to have flower competitions in October.

The fall annuals continue to bloom with no notable new appearances. Some spring-flowering annuals might be seeded now, such as larkspur, poppy, and snapdragon. The pansy plants that were seeded in late July or August should be set into beds now for all-winter bloom. Pinks are good companion plants that can be relied on for winter bloom, and calendulas, although subject to damage from early freezes, may be worth planting now.

Among the perennials, some of the cold-tender types that need to be taken in before freezing weather will be at their finest just before the really cold weather comes. You might consider just leaving them out to die and buy more next year: hibiscus, copper plants, crotons, and lantana are examples. *Camel-*

lia sasanqua is at a peak of bloom now. Buds on *Camellia japonica* may be thinned. Some varieties are bad about making clusters of buds near shoot tips, and these should be thinned to only one bud if you want good quality blooms. Watch for scale insects on the camellias and take control measures. Remember the caution on oil sprays about avoiding their use with predicted temperatures above 85°F or below freezing.

Vegetable gardeners may direct-seed carrot, garlic, lettuce, mustard, parsley, radish, shallot (bulbs), spinach, and turnips. Place special emphasis on getting beets, collards, Chinese cabbage, and celery (a challenge) planted early in the month. Some of these crops will not be ready to harvest until next year, but among those that will be ready before the year's end are lettuce, mustard, spinach, turnips, beets, endive, Swiss chard, shallot, and radish. It is time to prepare beds for strawberry transplants.

Harvests from earlier plantings can be made on pumpkins (Halloween pumpkins, planted in the early part of July), winter squash, snap bean, butter bean, cauliflower, cabbage, Chinese cabbage, collards, eggplant, mustard, peppers, radish, shallot, tomato, and turnips.

Muscadine grapes continue to ripen, and strawberry plants may be set. Keep up those borer control sprays on peaches and plums.

October Hassles

Things are not so bad. The rains may have stopped and the weather is a lot better. Tent caterpillars look bad in the trees, but they will not hurt much. Enjoy the weather. We may even begin getting some fall color.

November

This is another cool dry month that makes gardening a pleasure. Some areas in the South can expect frost, whereas others seldom get it before the month's end or later. *Camellia sasanquas* continue to be showy, a few *Camellia japonica,* especially those treated with gibberellic acid, bloom this month. Tender annuals last up until the first frost of the season, which you can expect soon. Annuals that can take the cold weather include pansy, viola, snapdragon, dianthus, flowering cabbage and kale; and in all but hard freezes, calendulas, petunias, and alyssum should do well.

Gerberas begin to bloom after the heat subsides, and mums can bloom through the entire month until hard freezes. Sweet peas may be planted.

Many spring-flowering bulbs may be planted this month. If dahlias are to be saved, they should be cut back to six or eight inches, dug, dried for a day or two in the shade, then stored in a cool dry place, but protected from freezing.

If some of the tender plants that were placed out of doors during the warm weather have become too large, consider taking cuttings or making air layers to provide smaller plants for overwintering. Most of the tropicals root easily if the leaves are kept under plastic so they do not lose too much water while the new roots are forming.

Loquat trees begin to bloom but do not expect to get fruit; low temperatures probably will do them in. In the city they sometimes get enough protection to allow ripening, and their tart-sweet combination is enjoyable.

Lawns may show the first signs of brown patch disease, and you should watch for it as the weather turns cooler. Vegetable gardeners can continue to pick tomatoes up to frost. If a freeze is predicted, the just-breaking tomatoes should be picked and taken inside and allowed to ripen. They will be at least as good as the "store-bought" ones, but not up to vine-ripe. Broccoli can be cut when the individual floral buds are as big as a match head, but have not turned yellow. Most varieties then make side shoots that are small but good, so do not be hasty about pulling those plants up. Cauliflower, on the other hand, does not have this ability, so when the heads are cut dump the plants in the compost pile. If a frost kills Irish potato plants, remove the dead parts but you can leave the tubers in the ground for quite a while. If you decide to dig them up, store them at near 40°F, out of the sunlight. If sweet potatoes are still growing, they should be dug before freezing weather hits them. Remember to cure them at near 85°F and 85–90 percent relative humidity for four to seven days. Potatoes treated this way are sweeter and keep better, and skinned areas heal over in the curing process. After the curing period, store sweet potatoes at about 60°F with high humidity. Cabbage plants should be cut when they are big enough and firm. If left too long they tend to split, but if you have too many to harvest all at the ideal size, twist the plants to break off a few roots— this reduces the water uptake and the tendency to split. Cabbage looper caterpillars continue to be a problem with all the plants in the cabbage family, but you now have control materials based on *Bacillus thuringiensis.*

If you are fortunate enough to be where satsuma orange trees can survive, look for the first ripe fruit this month. It may still have green skin but will be ripe enough to eat.

November Hassles

Worry about an early freeze. Slugs and snails love newly transplanted petunias and pansies. A saucer of stale beer actually does help to control them. Squirrels are a year-round hassle. They eat tomatoes, plums, peaches, broccoli; if you grow it, squirrels like it. Do not leave an opened can of beer unguarded when you go in to answer the phone. Every time you transplant something into a pot or in the beds a thousand eyes are watching you. Later they will check it out—dig it up. We have no answer except netting. Birds are almost as bad but we have fun watching blue jays tease mockingbirds.

December

Winter is almost here, but if there was no frost in November you may still be mowing the lawn when you would rather be Christmas shopping. The annual beds still have color from the winter-hardy annuals, pansy, viola, pinks, Drummond phlox, alyssum, snapdragons, and flowering cabbage and kale. Gerberas and begonias bloom in protected places. You can be seeding centaurea and sweet peas in the ground and transplanting alyssum, pinks, myosotis, hollyhock, Sweet William, viola, pansy, lobelia, larkspur, poppy, snapdragon, and statice. You also can seed impatiens and petunias in protected places. Some narcissus bloom in the cold, and *Camellia japonica* and sweet olive bloom. Abutilon blooms are becoming popular again.

Harvest of some vegetables can continue this month, including broccoli, cabbage, Chinese cabbage, carrot, collard, lettuce, mustard, English pea, radish, shallot, spinach, and turnip. You can direct-seed carrot, English pea, radish, shallot, turnip, and spinach and transplant pencil-size onion plants. Get beds ready to plant Irish potatoes next month. Cabbage seed can be planted in protected places for transplant next year.

This is often a good month for pruning (not the spring bloomers, remember), planting, and transplanting. Rose beds should be prepared if new plantings are planned for next year.

Enjoy the various plants grown with skill and care for sale during the Christmas season. If you do not have a greenhouse, think how nice it would be if you could grow those yourself in the cold, often dismal days of winter.

December Hassles

If we did not get a freeze in November, it will come this month. Moles have been around all year but we tend to notice them more when there are fewer other problems. Leaves are covering the lawn. Sometime you will have to get them up and put them in the compost. Maybe that will wait until after Christmas.

Appendix B

HOW TO MAKE POTTING MIXES

The purposes of the potting medium for a container-grown plant are to provide enough support for the roots to hold the plant up, enough water to replace that lost to transpiration and evaporation, enough pore space to allow the exchange of carbon dioxide and oxygen by the active roots, and to supply some nutrients. Any decent soil will fill those roles in the garden, but it might fail badly if you confine that soil in a container. The movement of water and gases through soil or a potting mix is controlled by an equilibrium between the pull of gravity and the suction force that holds water in the smaller pores. In deep soils (or pots) the water in pores is connected by something like a chain of water film to the water below. This exerts a downward pull on the water in those pores. If the soil is in a shallow pot, the water chain is shorter and this downward force is reduced.

You can prove this by filling a shallow pan (with drainage holes) with soil or a potting mix, adding water, and allowing it to drain in a horizontal position. When no more water drains out, lower one end a few inches and more water will drain from the pan. This is in response to the increased gravitational pull on the longer water chain.

So the problem with using soil as a potting mix is that the pot is too small for adequate drainage. Some kind of aggregate must be added to improve the porosity. The problem with having no soil in a potting mix is that plant nutrients are held on the clay fraction of soil. Soilless potting mixes have been developed that drain well and provide air spaces but the nutrients must be supplied by frequent applications of soluble fertilizer in the irrigation water.

Soil Mixes for Containers

In the following mixes, the amount of soil is adjusted to the texture of the soil, with less of heavy soils and more of lighter soils. Measurements are by volume.

For heavy soils, such as clays or clay loams:

> • 1 part of clay loam
> • 2 parts organic matter, such as bark, peat, rice hulls
> • 2 parts coarse aggregate (sand, perlite, vermiculite)

For medium soils, silt loams, or sandy clay loams:

> • 1 part of soil
> • 1 part organic matter
> • 1 part coarse aggregate

For light soils, such as sandy loams:

> • 1 part soil
> • 1 part organic matter

To each five gallons of the above mixtures, add four ounces ground lime-stone (dolomitic limestone is best; for azaleas and tropical foliage plants, use gypsum instead of limestone) and four to six ounces 20 percent super phosphate.

Potting Mixes without Soil

A wide range of media consisting of mixtures of peat or ground pine bark and coarse aggregate in about equal parts are satisfactory. The aggregate may be perlite, vermiculite, calcined clay, or sand. Sand is used less often because it is variable and heavy, whereas the others can be obtained in more consistent forms. Some pine bark is quite acidic, whereas that from other regions may be less so or even slightly alkaline. If possible, determine the pH of the bark, and if it is acidic, say below pH 5, add one ounce hydrated lime to five gallons of mix in addition to the ground limestone. The final pH of the mix should be approximately 6.5 for a wide range of crops, lower for some.

Suggested Reading

We like a few classic horticultural references that you may find in a used-book store at good prices; some of the books are rather old, but we are too. Many of the books listed will be available in more than one edition, and we do not believe that you must consult the latest one. Plants have not changed much, and the principals of good gardening remain the same.

The first name to know is Liberty Hyde Bailey, whose excellent books range from simple how-to-do-it guides to standard references on all cultivated plants. They have been issued in several editions; the older ones cost less and are still very good. Our favorites are *Manual of Gardening* (New York: Macmillan, 1910); *The Nursery-Manual: A Complete Guide to the Multiplication of Plants* (New York: Macmillan, 1954); *The Standard Cyclopedia of Horticulture* (New York: Macmillan, 1947), which tells everything you might want to know about cultivated plants; and *Hortus III* (New York: Macmillan, 1976), a dictionary-type version of the *Cyclopedia* revised by Bailey's daughter, Ethel Z. Bailey.

Other fundamental books include *Plant Science: Growth, Development, and Utilization of Cultivated Plants*, 3rd ed., by Margaret McMahon, Anton M. Kofranek, and Vincent E. Rubatzky (Upper Saddle River, N.J.: Prentice Hall, 2002); *The Nature and Properties of Soils*, 8th ed., by Harry O. Buckman and Nyle C. Brady (New York: Macmillan, 1974); *Soil Conditions and Plant Growth*, 10th ed., by E. Walter Russell (London: Longmans, Green, 1973); *Soil Organic Matter and Its Role in Crop Production* by Franklin E. Allison (Amsterdam, N.Y.: Elsevier Scientific, 1973); *Plant Anatomy*, 2nd ed., by Katherine Esau (New York: Wiley, 1965); *Plant Physiology*, 4th ed., by Frank B. Salisbury and Cleon W. Ross (Belmont, Calif.: Wadsworth, 1992); and *Plant and Soil Water Relationships: A Modern Synthesis* by Paul J. Kramer (New York: McGraw-Hill, 1969).

Louisiana State University and some land-grant universities in other states house Agricultural Experiment Stations for research and Cooperative Extension Services for dissemination of information. Some of their bulletins, directed to the general public, are extremely good, but others are not. The U.S. Department of Agriculture also puts out some worthwhile handbooks. The Chevron Chemical Company publishes a series of gardening guides called Ortho Books that covers a wide range of topics. The books are generally quite good. Because they are written for the entire country, however, they tend to ignore the specific problems that occur in the humid South. We make use of many USDA and Cooperative Extension Service publications as well as some of the Ortho Books. The following list includes some, but not all, of the sources we used for this book. Much information also came from old-time gardeners like ourselves.

Bear, Firman E. *Soils and Fertilizers.* 4th ed. New York: Wiley, 1953.

Blake, Claire L. *Greenhouse Gardening for Fun.* New York: M. Barrows, 1967.

Caillet, Marie, and Joseph K. Mertzweiller, eds. *The Louisiana Iris: The History and Culture of Five Native American Species and Their Hybrids.* Waco: Texas Gardener Press, 1988.

Chandler, William H. *Deciduous Orchards.* 3rd ed. Philadelphia: Lea and Febiger, 1957.

————. *Evergreen Orchards.* 2nd ed. Philadelphia: Lea and Febiger, 1958.

Childers, Norman F., ed. *Fruit Nutrition.* New Brunswick, N.J.: Horticultural Publications, Rutgers University, 1954.

Conserving Energy in Ohio Greenhouses. Series of pamphlets. Wooster: Ohio State University Cooperative Extension Service, 1978–.

DeHertogh, August E., ed. *Holland Bulb Forcer's Guide.* Hillegom, Netherlands: International Flower-Bulb Center, 1996.

Demers, John. *The Community Kitchens Complete Guide to Gourmet Coffee.* New York: Simon and Schuster, 1986.

Ebling, Walter. *Subtropical Fruit Pests.* Berkeley: University of California, Division of Agricultural Sciences, 1959.

Giles, F. A., Rebecca Keith, and Donald Saupe. *Herbaceous Perennials.* Reston, Va.: Reston Publishing Company, 1980.

Girling, C. A., P. J. Peterson, and H. V. Warren. "Plants as Indicators of Gold Mineralization." *Economic Geology* 74 (1979): 902–7.

Graf, Alfred B. *Exotica, Series 3: Pictorial Cyclopedia of Exotic Plants from Tropical and Near-Tropic Regions.* East Rutherford, N.J.: Roehrs, 1976.

————. *Tropica: Color Cyclopedia of Exotic Plants and Trees from the Tropics and Subtropics.* East Rutherford, N.J.: Roehrs, 1978.

Hauser, Ellis. "Establishment of Nutsedge from Space-Planted Tubers." *Weeds* 10 (1962): 209–12.

Heat Requirements of Greenhouses. Plan no. Ky 11.811-4. Lexington: University of Kentucky Department of Agricultural Engineering, 1965. Revised edition, 1971.

Holcomb, E. Jay, and Pennsylvania Flower Growers. *Bedding Plants IV: A Manual on the Culture of Bedding Plants as a Greenhouse Crop.* Batavia, Ill.: Ball, 1994.

Howie, Virginia. *Let's Grow Lilies: An Illustrated Handbook of Lily Culture by the North American Lily Society.* Lexington, Mass.: North American Lily Society, 1984.

Joiner, Jasper N., ed. *Foliage Plant Production.* Englewood Cliffs, N.J.: Prentice-Hall, 1981.

Maynard, Donald N., and George J. Hochmuth. *Knott's Handbook for Vegetable Growers.* 4th ed. New York: John Wiley and Sons, 1999.

McDonald, Elvin. *Handbook for Greenhouse Gardeners.* Irvington-on-Hudson, N.Y.: Lord and Burnham, 1971.

Nelson, Paul V. *Greenhouse Operation and Management.* 5th ed. Upper Saddle River, N.J.: Prentice Hall, 1998.

Odenwald, Neil G., Charles F. Freyling Jr., and Thomas E. Pope. *Plants for American Landscapes.* Baton Rouge: Louisiana State University Press, 1996.

O'Rourke, Edmund N. Jr. "Diagnosing Nutritional Problems, Part I." *Vegetable Grower* (Dec. 1979): 20–1, 321–4.

———. "Diagnosing Nutritional Problems, Part II." *Vegetable Grower* (Jan. 1980): 22–6.

Professional Guide to Green Plants. Southfield, Mich.: Florists Transworld Delivery Association, 1976.

Rees, Allen R. *The Growth of Bulbs: Applied Aspects of the Physiology of Ornamental Bulbous Crop Plants.* New York and London: Academic Press, 1972.

Rice, Elroy L. *Allelopathy.* 2nd ed. Orlando, Fla.: Academic Press, 1984.

Richards, Bryant N. *Introduction to the Soil Ecosystem.* New York: Longman, 1974.

Sprague, Howard B., Stanley Arthur Barber, and the American Society of Agronomy. *Hunger Signs in Crops: A Symposium.* New York: McKay, 1964.

Standifer, Leon C. "A Technique for Estimating Weed Seed Populations in Cultivated Soil." *Weed Science* 28, no. 2 (1980): 134–9.

Streets, R. B. *The Diagnosis of Plant Diseases.* Tucson: University of Arizona Press, 1972.

Truog, Emil. *Mineral Nutrition of Plants: A Symposium.* Madison: University of Wisconsin Press, 1951.

Turgeon, Alfred J. *Turfgrass Management.* 3rd ed. Englewood Cliffs, N.J.: Prentice Hall, 1991.

Wallace, T. *The Diagnosis of Mineral Deficiencies in Plants by Visual Symptoms.* New York: Chemical Publishing Company, 1953; London, Her Majesty's Stationery Office, 1961.

Westwood, Melvin N. *Temperate Zone Pomology: Pysiology and Culture.* Portland, Oreg.: Timber Press, 1993.

Index

Note: page numbers for illustrations are in boldface type